The Cambridge Companion

Choral music is now undoubtedly the foremost genre of participatory music making, with more people singing in choirs than ever before. Written by a team of leading international practitioners and scholars, this *Companion* addresses the history of choral music, its emergence and growth worldwide, and its professional practice. The volume sets out a historical survey of the genre, and follows with a kaleidoscopic bird's-eye view of choral music from all over the world. Chapters vividly portray the emergence and growth of choral music from its Quranic antecedents in West and Central Asia to the baroque churches of Latin America, representing its global diversity. Uniquely, the book includes a pedagogical section where several leading choral musicians write about the voice and the inner workings of a choir, and provide their professional insights into choral practice. The *Companion* will appeal to choral scholars, directors, and performers alike.

ANDRÉ DE QUADROS, as a conductor, scholar, music educator, and human rights activist, has conducted and undertaken research in over forty countries. He is a professor of music at Boston University, where he also holds positions in African studies, Asian studies, and Muslim studies. He is the conductor of the Manado State University Choir (Indonesia) and artistic director of Aswatuna, Arab Choral Initiative, editor of *Music of Asia and the Pacific* and *Salamu Aleikum: Choral Music of the Muslim World*, and general editor of the Carmina Mundi series.

The Cambridge Companion to

CHORAL
MUSIC

....

EDITED BY
André de Quadros
Boston University

CAMBRIDGE
UNIVERSITY PRESS

CAMBRIDGE
UNIVERSITY PRESS

University Printing House, Cambridge CB2 8BS, United Kingdom

Cambridge University Press is part of the University of Cambridge.

It furthers the University's mission by disseminating knowledge in the pursuit of education, learning and research at the highest international levels of excellence.

www.cambridge.org
Information on this title: www.cambridge.org/9780521128957

© Cambridge University Press 2012

First published 2012
Reprinted 2014
Printed in the United Kingdom by Clays, St Ives plc.

A catalogue record for this publication is available from the British Library

Library of Congress Cataloguing in Publication data
The Cambridge companion to choral music / edited by André de Quadros.
      p.   cm.
Includes bibliographical references and index.
ISBN 978-0-521-12895-7
1. Choral music.   I. De Quadros, André.
ML1500.C36   2012
782.5–dc23

                                                                                                    2012013422

ISBN 978-0-521-11173-7 Hardback
ISBN 978-0-521-12895-7 Paperback

Contents

Illustrations

Contributors

Patricia Abbott is Artistic Director of CAMMAC (Canadian Amateur Musicians/ Musiciens amateurs du Canada) and a lecturer in choral conducting at McGill University in Montreal, where she has worked as a conductor, singer, music educator and arts administrator for thirty years. For sixteen years, she served as Executive Director of the Association of Canadian Choral Communities (ACCC). Ms. Abbott has shared her passion for Canadian choral music, notably that of French Canada, in workshops, festivals, and conferences across Canada and the United States, as well as in Belgium, France, and Argentina.

Chester L. Alwes has an established reputation as a choral conductor, composer, editor, teacher, and author of *A History of Western Choral Music*. Dr. Alwes conducted choirs and taught graduate choral literature at the University of Illinois for nearly thirty years.

Mike Brewer OBE has a worldwide reputation as choral director and workshop clinician. Director of the National Youth Choirs of Great Britain since 1983, he is equally known as the author of a series of books for choral directors, including *Kickstart Your Choir*, *Fine Tune Your Choir*, and *Warmups*. His publications include arrangements for choirs (notably "Hamba Lulu" and "Banuwa") and four volumes of *Mike Brewer's World Tour*.

Simon Carrington, professor emeritus of choral conducting at Yale University, has enjoyed a long and distinguished career in music, performing as singer, double bass player, and conductor. He was the co-founder and creative force for twenty-five years with the internationally acclaimed British vocal ensemble The King's Singers. Carrington served as the director of choral activities at the University of Kansas and New England Conservatory in Boston before being appointed to Yale where he founded Yale Schola Cantorum and brought it to international prominence. He now maintains a busy schedule as a freelance conductor and choral clinician, leading workshops and masterclasses internationally.

Gene J. Cho is a professor of music at the University of North Texas and received his PhD from Northwestern University. His publications include *The Replica of the Ark of the Covenant in Japan: The Mystery of Mi-fune-Shiro* (2008), *The Discovery of Musical Equal Temperament in China and Europe in the Sixteenth Century* (2003), monographs, pedagogical manuals, and journal articles. His compositions and arrangements have been published and performed in the United States and overseas. He has been awarded honorary professorship appointments by Xinghai Conservatory, Yunnan Conservatory, Shandong Arts College, and Huanan University of Technology.

Rudolf de Beer is a South African conductor whose research is focused on choral music in sub-Saharan Africa. In addition to pursuing a career in conducting, he also arranges and composes choral music. He often receives international invitations to do presentations on African choral music. He received a master's degree from the University of Oslo, and completed a doctorate in choral conducting via a combined study at the Nelson Mandela Metropolitan University and the Norwegian State Academy of Music in Oslo.

André de Quadros, as a conductor, scholar, music educator, and human rights activist, has conducted and undertaken research in over forty countries. He is a professor of music at Boston University, where he also holds positions in African studies, Asian studies, and Muslim studies. He is the conductor of the Manado State University Choir (Indonesia) and artistic director of Aswatuna, Arab Choral Initiative, editor of *Music of Asia and the Pacific and Salamu Aleikum: Music of the Muslim World*, and general editor of the Carmina Mundi series. www.andredequadros.com

Cornelia Fales is an ethnomusicologist who specializes in vocal and instrumental timbre, both acoustic and synthetic, in traditional and popular music. Her work has been published in most of the major ethnomusicology journals and she has taught at the University of California, Santa Barbara and Indiana University. In addition to ongoing research on the traditional music of Rwanda and Burundi, she is working on a book comparing concepts of timbre as they developed in the seventeenth and eighteenth centuries with notions of "sound color" as used in twentieth-century electronic dance music.

Liz Garnett is a musicologist, choral clinician, and close-harmony arranger. Her research focuses on music and social values, and her publications include two books, *The British Barbershopper: A Study in Socio-Musical Values* (2005) and *Choral Conducting and the Construction of Meaning: Gesture, Voice, Identity* (2009). She was Head of Postgraduate Studies at the Birmingham Conservatoire until 2009 and now works as a performance coach with choirs, conductors, and vocal ensembles internationally.

Mary Goetze's professional activities are centered around multiculturalism and children's singing. She contributed to the children's choir movement in the United States as a clinician, author, composer, and conductor. While on faculty at Indiana University, Dr. Goetze founded the International Vocal Ensemble with whom she explored singing styles from around the globe. Now retired, she continues to develop *Global Voices* DVDs for teaching music from diverse cultures using multimedia. She is the co-author of *Educating Young Singers: A Choral Resource for Teacher-Conductors, Share the Music* and *Spotlight on Music*, and the author of numerous published compositions and arrangements.

Karen Grylls ONZM is Artistic Director of Choirs Aotearoa, New Zealand and Musical Director of the New Zealand Youth Choir and Voices New Zealand Chamber Choir. With these choirs, she has established her reputation as an advocate of the many traditions of New Zealand choral music in which they specialize. The disc *Spirit of the Land* (2006) won the award for best classical disc in the New Zealand Music Awards. Karen Grylls is currently an associate professor of music and head of choral studies at the University of Auckland, and she is much in demand as a clinician, adjudicator, and teacher of choral conducting.

María Guinand is a choral conductor and professor whose work is focused on Latin American contemporary choral music. She has released several recordings of this repertoire with the Schola Cantorum de Venezuela and the Cantoría Alberto

Grau. Guinand is frequently invited to guest-conduct many prestigious choirs and to lecture at universities and international symposia. She is head of the graduate program in choral conducting at the Simón Bolívar University in Caracas, advisor of the choral program of "El Sistema," and editor of the Música de Latinoamérica series of choral music.

Paul Hillier is an English conductor and founding director of the Hilliard Ensemble. He has taught at the University of California (Davis and Santa Cruz) and served as director of the Early Music Institute at Indiana University. Hillier has published books on Arvo Pärt and Steve Reich. In 2006, he was awarded an OBE for his contributions to choral music. The following year he received the Order of the White Star of Estonia and received a Grammy for Best Choral Recording. Hillier currently directs choirs in Copenhagen, Porto, and Dublin, and his own group, Theatre of Voices.

Aida Huseynova is an associate professor at Baku Music Academy (Azerbaijan) and a visiting faculty member at Indiana University Jacobs School of Music. Dr. Huseynova's work in musicology focuses on East–West synthesis in music. Her books, articles, and multimedia projects have been published in Azerbaijan, Europe, and the United States. Dr. Huseynova has taught music from Azerbaijan to the Indiana University International Vocal Ensemble and has prepared recordings of choral performances from Azerbaijan for the Global Voices in Song DVD series (2005). Since 2007, she has served as a research advisor and interpreter for the Silk Road Project under the artistic direction of Yo-Yo Ma.

Ann Howard Jones is a professor of music and director of choral activities at Boston University where she is responsible for a highly regarded graduate program in choral conducting. Widely recognized for her conducting, leadership, and teaching, she received the Robert Shaw Choral Award from the American Choral Directors Association (2011) for distinguished professional achievement and service, and the Metcalf Award from Boston University for exemplary teaching. Dr. Jones has written on score preparation, rehearsing, and healthy singing in the choral rehearsal. For many years, she worked alongside the late Robert Shaw with the Atlanta Symphony Choruses and the Robert Shaw Institute.

Jing Ling-Tam is a professor of music at the University of Texas at Arlington, where she served as director of choral studies from 1999 to 2009.

Matthew Mehaffey is an associate professor of music at the University of Minnesota, where he conducts several choirs and teaches classes in conducting and choral repertoire. He also serves as artistic director and conductor of the Oratorio Society of Minnesota and has taught at the George Washington University and Macalester College. He has published extensively on the topics of choral repertoire and music education and frequently presents his research at national and international venues. www.matthewmehaffey.com

Victoria Meredith is a professor of music and associate dean at the Western University (Canada). Her research interests include Canadian choral repertoire, the adult voice, and interrelationships between physical and vocal conditioning. She has published numerous critical performing editions of Renaissance and Baroque choral compositions, over forty scholarly articles, and the award-winning book *Sing Better As You Age*. She is a frequent guest conductor, clinician, and adjudicator, and choirs under her direction have received over a dozen national awards. She has served on the editorial board of the *Choral Journal* and as president of the Association of Canadian Choral Communities.

Francisco J. Núñez, a 2011 MacArthur Fellow, is a conductor, composer, visionary, leading figure in music education, and the founder of the award-winning Young People's Chorus (YPC) of New York City, cited as a national model of artistic excellence and diversity under the Clinton, Bush, and Obama administrations. Núñez is working with the Dominican Republic to create a national choral program inspired by YPC to unite the country's children – rich and poor. Among Núñez's many honors are an ASCAP Concert Music Award, the New York Choral Society's Choral Excellence Award, and the 2009 La Sociedad Coral Latinoamericana's Man of the Year Award.

Andrew Parrott has always put choral music at the forefront of his musical activities – as a widely traveled freelance conductor, as director of his own Taverner Choir & Consort, and as an independent scholar. Alongside work in opera, orchestral, and contemporary music, a succession of pioneering choral recordings (including works by Machaut, Tallis, Gabrieli, Monteverdi, Purcell, Vivaldi, Handel, and Bach) has charted his exploration of performance practices across the ages. In addition to major articles on related matters, his publications include *The New Oxford Book of Carols* (co-editor), *The Essential Bach Choir*, and the first full reconstruction of J. S. Bach's Trauer-music for Prince Leopold.

Doreen Rao is a conductor and master teacher whose distinguished career links the standards of professional performance with the goals of music education. She has held the Cameron Baird Conductor's Chair as Music Director and Conductor of the Buffalo Philharmonic Chorus and is the Elmer Iseler Chair in Conducting (Emerita) at the University of Toronto Faculty of Music. Rao's influential work fostered the children's choir movement in America and inspired a generation of conductors and teachers to lead young choirs around the world.

Kathy Saltzman Romey is the director of choral activities at the University of Minnesota and artistic director of the Minnesota Chorale. She is also chorus master of the Oregon Bach Festival Choir and has prepared this ensemble for American and world premiere performances and recording projects. She regularly serves as chorus master for the Internationale Bachakademie Stuttgart and has prepared programs with the Westminster Symphonic Choir, Netherlands Radio Choir, Berkshire Choral Festival, Carnegie Hall Festival Chorus, and Grant Park Chorus. A strong advocate of community engagement, Romey coordinates the Junges Stuttgarter Bach Ensemble and BRIDGES, the Minnesota Chorale's nationally acclaimed outreach program.

John Rutter is a British conductor, editor, composer, arranger, and producer. His well-known choral works include *Gloria* (1974), *Requiem* (1985), *Magnificat* (1990), and *Mass of the Children* (2003), performed many times in Britain, North America, and a growing number of other countries. He co-edited four volumes in the Carols for Choirs series with Sir David Willcocks, and, more recently, edited *Opera Choruses* (1995) and *European Sacred Music* (1996).

Leo Samama is a composer and musicologist who specializes in choral music, music philosophy, music theory, and contemporary music. He has taught at Utrecht

University and the Royal Conservatory of Music in The Hague, has written books on Dutch music in the twentieth century, on British music, and on Beethoven, and contributed to the *New Grove Dictionary of Music and Musicians*. He is co-founder of the Tenso network for professional chamber choirs in Europe and gives masterclasses for young choral composers. For many years he was artistic manager of the Residentie Orkest in The Hague and general manager of the Netherlands Chamber Choir.

Wilson Shitandi is a lecturer at Kenyatta University in Nairobi where he teaches courses in ethnomusicology, African music, and choral music. Shitandi sings, conducts, composes, and arranges African indigenous and national songs, and Euro-American classical music. Among his choral compositions are ten masses for mixed chorus in Kiswahili and English. He is the director of St. Cecilia Holy Cross Choir in Nairobi, a member of Nairobi Choral Music Society, and he has also performed with several choral groups in Germany.

Wolodymyr Smishkewych has specialized in medieval song, chant, and new music since the mid 1990s, and is a member of the ensembles Sequentia and Theatre of Voices. He is a sought-after pedagogue in medieval, contemporary and world vocal music, and has lectured and performed throughout the United States, Europe, South America, Canada, and Australia. Formerly the director of Indiana University's International Vocal Ensemble, he is the course director for the Master of Arts in Ritual Chant and Song at the Irish World Academy of Music and Dance, University of Limerick.

Nick Strimple serves on the faculty at the University of Southern California's Thornton School of Music, where he teaches courses in choral literature, sacred music, and music related to the Holocaust. Author of numerous articles and two critically acclaimed books, *Choral Music in the Twentieth Century* (2002) and *Choral Music in the Nineteenth Century* (2008), he has lectured at Oxford University, Yale University, and other leading institutions, and has conducted some of the world's finest ensembles, including the London Symphony Orchestra and the Chorus and Orchestra of the Polish National Opera. www.nickstrimple.com

Foreword

JOHN RUTTER

Choral music has both a longer history and a wider global spread than almost any other musical genre. Opera was born in seventeenth-century Florence and until the nineteenth century was mainly written and performed within a thousand-mile radius of its birthplace; orchestral music appeared in eighteenth-century Europe, and the symphony orchestra did not crystallize into its present form until the nineteenth century; pop music and its electronic soundworld were products of twentieth-century technology, rooted in America and its musical and ethnic fusions before being copied and developed elsewhere.

Contrast this with a recital program I recently heard sung by an American college choir in New York's Carnegie Hall. It opened with a thousand-year-old Gregorian chant, moved on to Renaissance polyphony by Lassus and Victoria, took in some Brahms part-songs and Russian liturgical music on the way to Barber's *Agnus Dei*, crossed the Pacific for a group of Japanese folk songs and traveled back again for a finale of American spirituals. The young performers and their conductor were perfectly at ease with all this musical time- and space-travel, and I found myself marveling at the global nature of choral music today.

The appearance of *The Cambridge Companion to Choral Music* is a timely reflection and reminder of this easily overlooked miracle. People have gathered together to sing since earliest times, and in doing so they have created marvelous sounds which could not be made in any other way. They have adorned religious ritual, celebrated the landmark occasions in the life of their community, inspired and uplifted their listeners, created a unique instrument for composers, and in doing all this have expressed their innermost souls and forged a communal identity. This volume explores all these themes and more, in just the way a good companion should: informatively but not exhaustingly, pointing the way rather than dragging us down every byway; surprising us now and then with a new perspective on a familiar landscape; and offering sound practical advice for those of us starting out on the road that our guides have already traveled.

In editing what is necessarily a compact symposium, André de Quadros has been unafraid to make bold and wide-ranging choices of topic to complement the global history and survey that form the main part of the book. Despite all the differences of approach and topic, it seems to me that three overarching themes emerge at the end of it all: first, that in engaging with choral music, individuals can be at one with themselves – made whole; second, that people can be at one with each other; finally, that peoples can be at one with each other. In choral music, we can discover and express our own selves, we can form social units that are potentially a microcosm of an ideal society, and at the same time we assert that a diverse world can celebrate its diversity and yet be at one. I can think of no more powerful messages for our times.

Acknowledgements

This project has been made possible through the generous assistance of many people, only some of whom I can name individually. Ann Howard Jones's graduate conducting studio at Boston University has always had a large number of knowledgeable, intelligent, and committed professionals. With her support, and their extraordinary willingness, I received exceedingly competent editorial assistance. To all of them – David Castillo Gocher, Jamie Hillman, Emily L. Howe, Jennifer Kane, Joshua H. Nannestad, Stephen Stacks (for indexing), Lei R. Yu, Christopher M. Walters, Timothy Westerhaus, Cory D. Wikan, and Nathan Zullinger – go my heartfelt appreciation. Thanks also go to Hussein Janmohamed for feedback. Victoria Cooper, the Senior Commissioning Editor at CUP, believed in this book and, with great insight, assisted the refining of its concept and design. The authors of each chapter were wonderfully stimulating collaborators. Their work represents the very finest of our profession in scholarship, research, and perspective, and I am both humbled and honored by their faith in this enterprise. Finally, my two assistants, Miguel Felipe and Jamie Hillman, deserve my boundless appreciation. As perceptive and thoughtful friends, critics, and colleagues, they helped guide every stage of the book, Miguel Felipe in the beginning phases and Jamie Hillman towards the conclusion.

1 Introduction: choral music – a dynamic global genre

ANDRÉ DE QUADROS

Many years ago, I was fortunate to have been invited to conduct performances of Handel's *Messiah* in Indonesia. It struck me several times during this visit that at the time Handel composed this eternal masterpiece, the ancestors of these Indonesian singers were making a music that was very far removed from the European baroque, and Handel, toiling away at a rapid pace in his tiny abode in London, would only have vaguely heard of the relatively recent exploration to what was then called the East Indies.

So much has changed in choral music in the last two hundred years, as these formerly distant worlds have come together; all over the world, choirs abound and repertoire has become global. The founding of the International Federation for Choral Music in 1982 and subsequent international collaborations of all kinds – festivals, competitions, symposia – have offered unprecedented prospects for learning, partnership, and development. Therefore, as a passionate participant in choral activities, it seemed to me that the omission of a volume on choral music in the Cambridge Companion series needed to be rectified. Easy to justify, but difficult to conceptualize! The rationale for the book was clear; choral musicians claim that singing in choirs is the world's most popular form of participatory music making. In the United States alone, Chorus America's 2009 *Chorus Impact Study* suggests that around 42.6 million Americans participate in choirs.[1] Worldwide, choirs are transforming the lives of their members and their local communities. The genre that started in European communal and religious life has spread throughout the world, and wherever it has gone, conductors and singers have made it their own. Far beyond conventional choral situations in churches and educational institutions, the chorus is part of prisons, hospitals, and slums. Communities that are marginalized, whether because of sexual orientation, political status, illness, or poverty, are finding opportunities for new expression.

In order to produce a coherent volume, it was vital to define what we mean by choral music. Although group singing traditions all over the world have variously been labeled "choral," they are distinctive, in some cases unique, bearing little relationship with the Western choir. To mine the riches of indigenous group singing traditions would have been way beyond the scope of anything less than a series of books. Therefore, logically, the book should concern itself with this single genre, the Western choral ensemble, as it arose and developed worldwide. The substance of the book could have focused on choral manifestations all over the world, just informing the reader of the nature and depth of choral participation, or it could have been a historical overview of choral music. Perhaps, with conductors' endless appetite for professional development, the *Cambridge Companion to Choral Music* could have provided knowledge for achieving excellence in the choral art. None of these single objectives seemed to be desirable, particularly because almost all of these already exist in a variety of publications. The logical solution then was to design a book that accomplished many goals. First, it needed to put choral music in a historical perspective, not in an extended, encyclopedic fashion, but more in a situated, contextualized view of how and why choirs developed and how we got to where we are now, chorally speaking. Second, we needed to uncover and celebrate the wide diversity of the choral enterprise as it exists globally, to shed light on the extent and excellence of choral music in parts of the world about which we know so little. Third, to honor choral activity and contribute to its advancement, a section should be devoted to practice and pedagogy.

Fortunately, Cambridge Companions are not encyclopedias, and therefore are liberated from the mission of being comprehensive and exhaustive on any given topic. Hence, readers will find in these chapters perspective and insight combined with information and analysis. All of the authors have constructed different lenses even where the tasks may appear similar.

The beginning of choral music as we understand it is contentious, particularly in an age where just about any music from any period is sung chorally. Most choral singers believe that choral music existed in the Renaissance, while others choose to recognize its surfacing considerably later. Andrew Parrott takes us on a journey that begins towards the end of the fifteenth century, describing the emergence of the genre, with careful consideration of repertoire, civic and liturgical life, the role of instruments, and so on. With reference to a wide body of primary sources, he succeeds in resolving some controversies and in creating new ones. In a very thoughtful discussion of culture and context in the nineteenth century, Chester Alwes brings the people, the nation building, and the rise of secular choral life together. He describes some of the key trends in the development of specific compositional styles in this formative period. In like manner, Nick Strimple casts a wide net over the development of choral music in the past hundred years or so, not only in Western Europe and North America but also in a host of other countries. In particular, Strimple delves into choral music in the ugly period of World War II, looking closely at choral activity by Holocaust victims in concentration camps.

The final chapter in Part I, by Paul Hillier, takes us from antiquity to the present day in a discussion of how choruses came about and how they function within themselves internally and in their interactions with audience and community.

The second part of the book describes the world of choral music through three large chapters and six smaller ones. While at some level the authors write with similar mission – to inform the readers about choral music in their part of the world – for each of them, it manifests differently. In his chapter on Europe, Leo Samama focuses on the present circumstances of choral music – a formidable task, to squeeze into one chapter what could take many books to write. Samama, like the other authors, writes with a broad descriptive brush, looking at trends in choral activity, and differences in several European regions. By contrast, the authors of the next two chapters on North America – Canada and the United States – Patricia Abbott and Victoria Meredith, Matthew Mehaffey and Kathy Saltzman Romey respectively, take us to the early days of choral music in their countries. Both immigrant societies with different social and political systems, Canada and the USA have vibrant and diverse choral cultures captured by these four authors.

Latin American choral music is part of the standard repertoire but how little many of us know of choral life in this immense continent, and who better to write about it than María Guinand, whose name is synonymous with Latin American choralism. Her focus is on the last hundred years with some historical background. Rich in information and description, Guinand's chapter provides the reader with a rare insight into the immense variety of Latin American choral music.

The vast continents of Asia and Australasia have been divided into geographical regions – East, South and Southeast, West and Central, and Oceania. Gene Cho and Jing Ling-Tam deftly survey choirs and composers in Japan, China, Taiwan, and Korea. East Asia with a population of many more than a billion is similar in size to the area of South and Southeast Asia, but the resemblance ends there. East Asia, influenced greatly by the West, was largely not colonized as South and Southeast Asia have been. In the chapter on South and Southeast Asia, I discuss how cultural, colonial, religious, and linguistic differences have had an impact on the choral cultures of these parts of the world. Understanding this part of Asia is vital if we are to recognize the immense potential of this region to change the course of choral culture in this century. Aida Huseynova had the challenging, but rewarding task of describing the Islamic antecedents and political realities of choral music in the Arab world and the republics of Central Asia that were associated with the former Soviet Union. Western in orientation, and building choral bridges to their indigenous cultures, Australia, New Zealand and their Pacific neighbors are the subject of Karen Grylls's chapter on Oceania.

In general, the choral world knows more about choral music in South Africa than anywhere else on the African continent. Rudolf de Beer and Wilson Shitandi do their best to unveil the treasures of African choirs, their forms of organization, and their repertoire.

Finally, in the third part of the book, experienced and distinguished choral leaders share their experiences. Rather than providing recipes and simple instructions, they employ a wide range of styles, from autobiographical to scientific and philosophical, to unpack some of the issues in choral leadership, conducting, and teaching. Francisco Núñez's work with the Young People's Chorus of New York City has positioned him to discuss the transformative role that children's and youth choruses can play in their communities. Mary Goetze, Cornelia Fales, and Wolodymyr Smishkewych explode several misconceptions held by our profession about the appropriateness and vocal health of various singing styles. Furthermore, they build a bridge between research and practice, discussing laryngeal position, registers, and resonance. Doreen Rao's discussion of authenticity and its link with "engaged musicianship" utilizes personal narrative to construct a large philosophical picture of excellence in choral music making. She constructs a much-needed new paradigm for socially responsible conducting practice in the twenty-first century. The tensions between individuality and consensus have beset choral conductors through the ages. Mike Brewer and Liz Garnett take on these issues and explore conflicting concepts. The final two chapters describe rehearsing from different perspectives. Ann Howard Jones brings years of experience of working with Robert Shaw, and her own valuable expertise to present a systematic look at preparing and planning for rehearsal. Simon Carrington transfers the insights gained from being a founding member of the King's Singers to the rehearsal processes of a large choir.

There are too many experienced choral directors, musicologists, and writers, people I admire greatly, whose voices could have been heard in this book. The selected writers represent a broad cross-section of our profession, people with disparate views, with whom one could imagine long hours of stimulating conversation. If their writings provoke you to understand more about the origins of choral music, its worldwide manifestations, and professional practice, and most of all, if this book leads you to greater personal and community transformation through choral music, it has achieved its goal.

PART I

Choral music: history and context

2 A brief anatomy of choirs $c.$1470–1770

ANDREW PARROTT

Josquin des Prez, Tallis, Victoria, Monteverdi, Charpentier, Bach – the great choral composers of the past may be presumed to have understood the inner workings of their choirs comprehensively well; most had received a choir-boy's education and virtually all spent a lifetime amongst their chosen singers. But to what extent do we share their understanding? Was Dufay's body of singers little different from those that Handel knew some 300 years later? Has "the choir" somehow managed to remain essentially one and the same thing through the ages to our own time? Though much transcribed, discussed and performed, music written for choirs in earlier centuries generally reaches us through a filter of more recent choral expectations, with unfamiliar features disregarded, overlooked, or misconstrued. Thus, while close attention is routinely paid to specific works and their composers, and to compositional genres and choral institutions, the focus here will instead be on the very nature of those diverse musical bodies we call choirs.

Since for much of the period under consideration choral performance was nurtured almost single-handedly by the Church, it will suffice to define a "choir" provisionally as "An organized body of singers performing or leading in the musical parts of a church service."[1] This has the merit of making no attempt to prescribe *how* such a body is musically organized (whether for unison singing, or for music requiring just three solo voices or a multiplicity of voices intermixed with instruments), and it therefore encourages us not to concentrate unduly on familiar aspects of "choral" performance as we now understand it.

Improvised polyphony

The bedrock of the Church's music making was plainchant, much of it sung from memory,[2] and the evolutionary link between solo or unison chant and later composed choral polyphony lies in the hidden (and little explored) world of extempore chant-based singing. This could take many forms (variously named), from simple note-against-note affairs to the

The author is indebted to Hugh Griffith for his expert assistance with various texts and for invaluable advice at the final stages of preparation of this chapter.

intricate counterpoint of highly skilled singers;[3] by the mid fifteenth century English clerical singers were practicing at least three such techniques – faburden, descant and "counter."[4] Different techniques tended to attach themselves to different portions of the liturgy: at the church of Our Lady in Antwerp (1506), the Alleluia and Sequence were to be performed in *discant*, the Communion with *contrapuncte*, and the Introit "without singing upon the book."[5] Though not required in this instance, the technique of singing "upon the book" (*super librum*) is perhaps particularly relevant to the story of the choir. Its underlying principle, according to Tinctoris in 1477, was that

> when two, three, four or more people sing together upon the book, they are not subject to one another. In fact, it is enough for each of them to accord with the tenor in regard to the rule and ordering of consonances.[6]

Was something of this sort what Thomas Morley (1597) had in mind?

> As for singing uppon a plainsong, it hath byn in times past in England (as every man knoweth) and is at this day in other places, the greatest part of the usuall musicke which in any churches is sung. Which indeed causeth me to marvel how men acquainted with musicke, can delight to heare such confusion as of force must bee amongste so many singing *extempore*.[7]

We may well share Morley's scepticism (and a Neapolitan writer likened the results to "music made by cicadas"),[8] yet Banchieri (1614) assures us that "In Rome in the Chapel of Our Lord, in the Santa Casa di Loreto and in countless other chapels" such extempore singing (*contrapunto alla mente*) was "most tasteful" to hear:

> It is a general principle that, with as many as a hundred different voices singing in consonance over a bass, all are in harmony, and those wicked 5ths, octaves, oddities and clashes are all graces which create the true effect of improvised counterpoint . . .[9]

Although small numbers of skilled singers are likely to have produced more consistently "correct" results, this particular method of improvising over chant seems to have been capable of accommodating more than a mere handful of solo voices:[10] in mid eighteenth-century France there were still churches where "almost everything is sung according to *chant sur le livre* [upon the book]," perhaps by "thirty or so musicians . . . all at the same time; some according to the rules and others completely at random."[11]

Extempore traditions of one sort or another were clearly a major part of choral practice far and wide.[12] From St. Mark's, Venice, at the end of Monteverdi's tenure as *maestro di cappella*, it was reported that "ordinarily they sing from the large book, and in the *cantus firmi* they improvise counterpoint."[13] And, as a Dutch traveler observed at the basilica well over a century earlier in 1525, the elaborate liturgy of a major feast day demanded that the choir's duties were variously distributed amongst the singers present:

> Outside the sanctuary there is a beautiful round large high *stuel* [tribune/ pulpit], decoratively hung with red velvet cloth of gold, where the *discanters* stand and sing. And those who psalmodize sit on both sides of the choir, on the one side plainsong, on the other side *contrapunt* or *fabridon* (whichever name you prefer); these three [groups] each await their time to sing, up to the end of the Mass . . .[14]

This serves to alert us to two recurrent difficulties in establishing the size and nature of earlier choirs. Just as the institutional strength of a choir will not reflect any extra singers brought in on a temporary or occasional basis, so too does it fail to take account of absences, rota systems, the function or importance of an event, and – not least – such divisions of labor within a service as have just been noted. As for depictions and documentary tallies of singers, it is exceptional to be certain whether composed or improvised polyphony or even simple chant is being sung.

These questions arise with a source that may otherwise appear to be a key guide to the performance of composed choral polyphony at the Burgundian court in the time of Busnoys. New ordinances for the court chapel drawn up in 1469 specify that

> for *chant du livre* there shall be at least six high voices, three tenors, three *basses-contre* and two *moiens* ["means"] without including the four chaplains for High Mass or the *sommeliers* who, whenever they are not occupied at the altar or in some other reasonable way, will be obliged to serve with the above-mentioned.[15]

First, by proceeding to ensure "that the service be always provided with two tenors and two *contres*,"[16] the ordinances remind us that this institutional complement (or "pool") of singers will not have been expected on all occasions. Second, "*chant* du *livre*" may well be no more than a synonym for "*chant* sur le *livre*,"[17] an improvisatory technique both suited to fluid numbers of singers and requiring a good spread of voice ranges – a technique, moreover, used "when they sing each day in the chapels of princes" and notably by "those from across the Alps, especially the French."[18]

Composed polyphony

With the music of Dufay we are on slightly firmer ground. In his lengthy will drawn up at Cambrai in 1474, the composer requests that on his deathbed – "time permitting" – two pieces of music be heard; first a chant hymn sung softly (*submissa voce*)[19] by eight Cathedral men, then his own *Ave regina coelorum*[20] sung by the (four to six) "altar boys, together with their master and two companions."[21] Instead, as time did not permit, both items were apparently given in the Cathedral the day after his death, together with Dufay's own (lost) Requiem,[22] for which he had specified "12 of the more competent vicars, both great and lesser" (about half of the total).[23] Dufay's will also provides for a mass of his to be sung on a separate occasion by "the master of the boys and several of the more competent members of the choir," the allocated funds allowing for exactly nine singers.[24] It is worth noting that the precise location for this, and almost certainly for the Requiem, was not the choir of the Cathedral but one of its chapels.[25] Indeed, the (private) chapel, whether part of a church or an independent structure, arguably counted as "the most important place for music-making in the late Middle Ages," perhaps explaining why the chaplains of a princely chapel, whose duties were many and varied, frequently out-numbered the singing body of a great cathedral.[26]

Substantially larger vocal forces than those specified by Dufay were certainly heard from time to time, but only in exceptional circumstances. In 1475, for example, at a Sforza wedding mass in Pesaro two *capelle* sang "now one, now the other, and there were about 16 singers per *capella*."[27] A century later Lassus annotated the alto, tenor, and bass parts of a twelve-voice mass by Brumel with the names of thirty-three men – including himself as "Cantor"[28] – and for the Medicis' extravagant 1589 *intermedi* a madrigal *a*30 was sung in seven choirs by sixty voices with opulent instrumental support.[29] By contrast, the musical establishment at Florence Cathedral in 1478 comprised just four boys, their master and four other adult singers.[30] Ensembles of this nature were evidently something of a norm:

- Venetian ambassadors traveling through the Tyrol in 1492 enjoyed "the singing of five boys and three masters";[31]
- as "song master" at St. Donatian's in Bruges (1499–1500) Obrecht was "obliged to bring with him to each Salve, besides his children [choirboys], four companion singers from the church, and those who sing best";[32]
- Jean de Saint Gille's testament (1500) promises a *pour-boire* to six named singers and "several" of the boys at Rouen, who were "to sing the Mass for the Departed that I have composed."[33]

Some of these boys may have been the equivalents of today's eleven- or twelve-year-olds, but the more complex polyphony of the period reminds us that boys' voices were commonly not changing until sixteen or even later.[34] Northern Europe led the way in training young singers, and in France (1517–18)

> there is not a cathedral or major church where they do not have polyphony constantly and more than one mass sung every day; each one is supplied with six or eight little boy clerics who learn singing and serve in the choir, tonsured like little monks and receiving food and clothing.[35]

Figure 2.1 Arnolt Schlick, *Spiegel der Orgelmacher und Organisten* (Speyer, 1511); woodcut – straight cornett, organ and singers (three boys and two men)

Institutionally these choirboys were often independent of their adult counterparts – Cambrai's boys served as acolytes and sang at their own lectern near the high altar[36] – and the collaboration of men and boys in elaborate composed polyphony marked a significant development in the fifteenth century.[37]

Interest in this new wider choral range may in turn have driven the cultivation of another type of high voice: that of the adult falsettist (better known as today's "countertenor"). To Pietro Aaron (1516) a *cantus* part was now one to be sung by either a boy's voice or a man's "feigned" voice ("*cum puerili voce, vel ficta*").[38] In the absence of earlier hard evidence,[39] we may conjecture that the increasing value of keeping boys singing for as long as possible led to an adolescent "falsetto" technique[40] which some then retained and developed into adulthood as falsettist sopranos. (In Germany it may have been quite usual for boys to move from soprano to alto before settling into a lower range.)[41] Revealingly, non-child sopranos, many of them described as youths, were often taken on only for "as long as their voices shall last" (and sometimes "placed in the house of the choirboys"),[42] or given a one-year contract specifically "in case ... the singer should lose his voice."[43] In one instance, a soprano who signed such a contract in Florence shortly before Christmas 1481 received a "farewell gift" just eleven days later.[44]

The need for dependable high voices could, of course, be satisfied in another way – by castrati, who as a musical force seem to have emerged in Spain only a little later. At Burgos Cathedral a castrated boy "who has a good voice" was noted as early as 1506,[45] and by the 1560s Spanish castrati could be found in Italy at the court of Ferrara, in the papal chapel, and at St. Mark's, Venice.[46] (Homegrown Italian castrati eventually displaced these Spaniards in Italy.)[47]

Ranges, clefs, and vocal scoring

Only slowly did the "voice" labels of polyphonic music (*cantus, contratenor* and so on) begin to attach themselves not just to parts but to distinct vocal ranges and thence to particular categories of singer. In practice, the "key" to vocal scoring – widely assumed today to have been a distinctly casual affair – was the humble clef,[48] which mapped out an individual core range (of up to eleven notes) and fixed its relationship to others; see Example 2.1. A composer, having chosen a mode and vocal scoring, worked from a corresponding set of clefs, always aware that

> you must not suffer any part to goe without the compasse of his rules
> [=lines], except one note at the most above or below, without it be upon an
> extremity for the ditties [=words'] sake or in notes taken for *Diapasons* in the
> base. (Morley, 1597)[49]

The clef configuration $C_1C_3C_4F_4$, for example, can thus identify and broadly define the four principal vocal ranges of later Renaissance music, *cantus, altus, tenor,* and *bassus* (*CATB*). Confusingly enough, however, these very same voices could also be expressed by a different set of clefs and consequently at different written pitch levels.[50] The motet *Absalon, fili mi* (variously attributed to Josquin and Pierre de la Rue) – an extreme example perhaps – survives in "contradictory" sources, the earliest one lying exceptionally low ($C_3C_4F_4F_5$), others a surprising 9th higher ($G_1G_2C_2C_3$).[51] In fact, only the clefs and key signatures have changed; the notes themselves occupy identical positions on each stave, divergent pitch names being (as Cerone puts it in 1613) "of no

Example 2.1 The implied range of a five-line stave and the most commonly used clefs

Example 2.2a Original notation

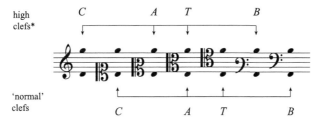

* Only the most common configuration of high clefs is given here

Example 2.2b As generally transcribed today

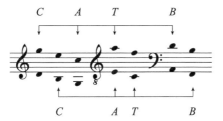

concern to the singer, who is concerned only to sound his notes correctly, observing the intervals of tones and semitones."[52] Musical notation, in other words, deals in *relative* pitches – and is frustratingly reticent about their absolute *sounding* pitch.

What may appear to be a bewildering array of clef configurations employed by Renaissance composers is perhaps best viewed as a series of purely notational permutations of a limited number of reasonably standard vocal ranges. By the end of the sixteenth century most choral music was in practice notated either in "high" clefs (later dubbed *chiavette*) or in a set that had become increasingly more "normal"; see Example 2.2. As it happens, two-thirds of Palestrina's considerable output is notated in high clefs, giving us the misleading impression that it was intended to *sound* distinctly higher than the remainder (in "normal" clefs), simply because that is how it *looks* to us – a view that would surely have amused Palestrina's singers, just as theirs may baffle us.

Apparent discrepancies of this sort naturally became real issues whenever instruments were involved, and consequently the art of transposition

Example 2.3 Relative ranges with high clefs transposed down a 4th

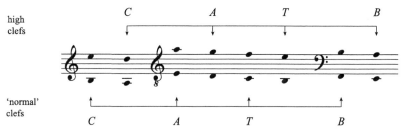

was viewed by Zarlino (1558) as "useful and highly necessary both to every skilled organist involved with choral performance and similarly to other instrumentalists."[53] Thus, while all high-clef items in a book of Palestrina motets reissued in 1608 are found transposed downwards in its newly added organ part,[54] all 37 in a similar collection by G.P. Anerio (1613) bear instructions such as "*alla quarta bassa*" ("to the 4th below").[55] The necessary procedures are set out by Praetorius in 1619 in the clearest possible terms:

> Every vocal piece in high clefs, i.e. where the bass is written in C_4 or C_3, or F_3, must be transposed when it is put into tablature or score for players of the organ, lute and all other foundation instruments, as follows: if it has a flat, down a 4th . . ., but if it has no flat, down a 5th . . .[56]

Example 2.3 compares core ranges of "normal" and transposed high clefs (down a 4th). *Primary* transposition of this sort – almost always obligatory – is not to be confused with any smaller *secondary* adjustment designed to suit specific circumstances: to deal with differing instrumental pitch standards and/or to accommodate particular voices. In both cases the abiding principle was that instruments should defer to voices, rather than the opposite. Hence,

> organists are always (or at least usually) compelled to play lower than the written key in order to accommodate the singers. This is what is done at St. Mark's in Venice . . .[57]

High- (and low-)clef notation, considered the worst "among the many abuses which are traditionally current in music,"[58] eventually died out, but as late as 1657 Schütz could still publish a work with the vocal parts in one key (using high clefs) and the organ in another (a 4th lower).[59]

Voice types

To compound the difficulties of understanding these notational conventions, known pitch standards could vary enormously, anywhere from roughly a tone below today's a' = 440Hz to a tone above (as, respectively, with many late

Table 2.1 *Sixteenth-century vocal scoring – Italy and elsewhere*

Part	Person		Today's nomenclature
cantus	boy; man (falsettist, castrato)		treble,* countertenor, castrato
altus	man – high		1st tenor
tenor	man – middle	"changed" voices	2nd tenor/baritone
bassus	man – low		bass

*Neither "treble" nor "countertenor" adequately evokes the part's intermediate "mezzo soprano" range.

Table 2.2 *Sixteenth-century vocal scoring – England*

Part	Singer
triplex/treble	boy (high)
medius/mean	boy (low)
contratenor/countertenor	1st tenor
tenor/tenor	2nd tenor/baritone
bassus/bass	bass

seventeenth-century French woodwind instruments and Buxtehude's organs in Lübeck)[60] – and from the fifteenth century and earlier there is virtually no reliable information. It is therefore critical to recognize that *cantus, altus, tenor,* and *bassus* are not necessarily direct equivalents of today's SATB classifications. A particular cause of misunderstanding is the view that "Falsetto singing has been the most common source of alto voices in all-male choirs throughout the history of Western music."[61] Wherever they are known to have been employed in the sixteenth century, falsetto (and castrato) voices were associated not with alto parts but only with soprano parts – which in turn lie significantly lower than those of later periods.[62] As for the (non-falsetto) alto voice, it corresponds to our (high) tenor and formed a pair with a slightly lower "middling" tenor, generally considered the "ordinary" voice.[63] Palestrina's voices, for example, are distributed as shown in Table 2.1.

English vocal scoring, especially in the earlier part of the sixteenth century, differs significantly from this in often employing not four but five basic ranges (Table 2.2). The lower three of these voices correspond to those of Palestrina and are "changed voices" covering the two octaves or so above a bass's lowest note, but where Palestrina has just a *cantus* above them, English music often has two distinct upper voices, "treble" and "mean."[64] Not only is there a total absence of documentary evidence for falsetto singing in sixteenth-century England (unlike Italy, for example), but English organ pitch – no higher than a semitone or so above today's $a' = 440\text{Hz}$[65] – all but rules out today's countertenor for *contratenor* parts.[66] Moreover, though the "mean" part may appear well suited to today's countertenor,[67] the associated voice was "higher than mens voyces."[68] It is only ever documented as belonging to boys: the Earl of Northumberland's "Childeryn of the chapell," for example, comprised "ij Tribills and iij Meanys" (*c.*1505),[69] while Salisbury Cathedral specified "eight choristers having good commendable voyces for trebles and meanes" (1580).[70]

Instruments

By the mid 1400s the organ had become well established as a church instrument, but only later did other instruments slowly gain admission on any regular basis. While scattered references to "trumpets" and other wind instruments often relate to the Mass (sometimes specifically to the Elevation), there is little to suggest their direct involvement with liturgical singing on any frequent or systematic basis before 1500.[71] But in that very year we read of masses being sung (at John the Steadfast's wedding in Torgau) "with the help of the organ, three trombones and a cornett, [and] likewise four crumhorns with the *positif*."[72] Did these instrumental groups merely play, for example, at the Gradual and *Ite missa est* (as the organ might otherwise have done, and as trombones evidently did at Innsbruck three years later),[73] or were they used to bolster the vocal forces in polyphonic settings of the Kyrie, Gloria, and so on? The same questions are raised by recurrent reports (1501–6) citing Augustein Schubinger, an Imperial cornettist in the retinue of Philip the Fair, playing at mass.[74] The matter is at least partly settled, however, by a woodcut of Maximilian I's *Hofkapelle*, showing a trombonist and a cornettist (almost certainly Schubinger) reading from the same choirbook as a dozen or more singers. England's court singers perhaps first encountered this type of mixed ensemble a little later, at the Field of the Cloth of Gold (1520), when their French counterparts were joined in a Credo by trombones and "*fiffres*."[75] For Erasmus (1519) these instrumental intruders contributed to the objectionably "elaborate and theatrical" nature of church music,[76] whereas Vasari's reaction to hearing "a multitude of trombones, cornetts and voices" perform a Gloria at a Florentine ceremony in 1535 was to proclaim that "the earth seemed gladdened."[77]

Instrumental participation of this kind was clearly intended to enhance the pomp and ceremony of grand occasions, but there could also be a more general practical purpose:

> Cornetts and trombones have been invented and introduced into musical ensembles more from the need for soprano and basses, or rather I should say to add body and sheer noise ... than for any good or desirable effect that they may create. (V. Galilei, 1581)[78]

More specifically,

> singers with sufficiently deep bass voices are extremely rare, which is why the
> *Basson*, sackbut and serpent are used, in the same way that the cornett is
> employed to stand in for treble voices, which are usually not good.
> (Mersenne, 1636)[79]

At the reopening of England's Chapel Royal in 1660, cornetts were
accordingly drafted in to help "supply the superiour Parts" of the music,
"there being not one Lad, for all that time, capable of Singing his Part
readily,"[80] while a full century later the bassoon was proving "in great
Request in many Country Churches . . . as most of the Bass Notes may be
played on it, in the Octave below the Bass Voices."[81] As Roger North put it
in 1676, "nothing can so well reconcile the upper parts in a Quire, as the
cornet (being well sounded) doth."[82] With their distinctly vocal colour,
range and flexibility (of tuning and volume), cornetts and trombones
integrated themselves into vocal choirs to the extent that in the late
1580s one singer at a Roman church was able on occasion to send a
trombonist to deputize for him,[83] while elsewhere the permanent membership of a courtly chapel included "two basses, one is a *trombone*."[84]

Stringed instruments were slower to find a place in church music
making – and slower in England than elsewhere: in 1636 it was noted
that "in our Chyrch-solemnities onely the Winde-instruments (whose
Notes ar constant) bee in use".[85] (The viol consorts associated with
English verse anthems of the period belong to the world of domestic
performance and are undocumented in church sources.)[86] In Rome,
however, the upstart violin had clearly made its entry by 1595, when a
maestro di cappella might be expected to present "two Vespers and a Mass
for three choirs, with voices (some from the papal chapel) combined with
instruments (namely cornetts, trombones, violins and lutes)."[87] Earlier
still in Madrid, Marguerite of Valois had attended a mass "after the
Spanish fashion, with music, *violons*, and cornetts."[88]

New directions

The gradual acceptance of instruments besides the organ led church music
in new directions. While double-choir writing of the mid sixteenth
century had in essence been entirely vocal (although instruments might
double or even replace voices), the polychoral works of Giovanni Gabrieli
and others commonly included not only a basso continuo but additional parts specifically for instruments. The various "choirs" – perhaps
separated vertically as well as horizontally – might thus be either

- purely vocal (some for single voices, others for multiple voices with or without instrumental doubling),
- purely instrumental (whether or not for a single family of instruments), or
- for a particular combination of voices and instruments.

No longer was the compass of each choir restricted to that of human voices:[89] a tenor might supply the top line of a "low" choir with trombones beneath, or the lowest line of a "high" choir headed by a cornett or violin. And in many cases the number of choirs could be varied simply by omitting or duplicating certain of them. Thus Viadana's *Salmi a quattro chori* (1612)

> may also be sung by just two choirs, namely Choirs I and II. However, if one wishes to put on a beautiful display with 4 to 8 choirs as the whole world likes to do nowadays, the intended effect will be achieved by doubling Choirs II, III and IV, without any danger of making an error; for everything depends on Choir I *a*5 being sung well.[90]

While the four-part Choir II functions here as "the *capella*, the very core and foundation of a good musical ensemble" (for which "there should not be fewer than sixteen singers"), the choir on which "everything depends" – Viadana's "favored" first choir – consists of just one singer per part:

> Choir I *a*5 stands in the main organ gallery and is the *coro favorito*; it is sung and recited by five good singers.[91]

In practice, *ripieno* or *capella* singers rarely needed to be quite as numerous as Viadana suggests: Usper (1627) speaks of "doubled and tripled voices together with proportionate instruments on each part, as is done in the most famous city of Venice."[92]

This new Italian polychoral manner was soon adopted by German composers, notably by Schütz, who explains in his *Psalmen Davids* (1619) that

> the second choir is used as a *capella* and is therefore strong [in numbers], while the first choir, which is the *coro favorito*, is by contrast slender and comprises only four singers.[93]

And in France the same underlying principles produced the French *grand motet*:

> the *grand choeur*, which is *a*5, is always filled with a number of voices; in the *petits choeurs* the voices are one to a part.[94]

(For Du Mont, sections marked "*omnes*" are "when there are two people on the same part.")[95] This distinction between an elite one-to-a-part vocal choir and a larger – though not necessarily large – body of singers is fundamental to a proper understanding of much "concerted" vocal music, whether polychoral or otherwise.[96] The chief protagonists of most seventeenth-century concerted music were these select one-to-a-part vocal ensembles (or "consorts," as they are now often called); in Praetorius's words, such "choirs" of *concertato* voices constituted "the foundation of the whole *concerto*."[97] Moreover, where there is *capella* writing, it is generally subsidiary and frequently optional;[98] even for a *grand motet* "it would suffice to have five solo voices."[99]

One-to-a-part choral singing was, of course, nothing new. A foundation at Chichester Cathedral (*c.*1530) had provided for just four adult singers of polyphony, stipulating a combined vocal range for them of 15 or 16 notes.[100] In Venice in 1553, the Cappella Ducale's seventeen members could form four separate choirs for employment outside St. Mark's,[101] while at the basilica itself in 1564, in an intriguing anticipation of later practice, they sang psalms "divided into two choirs, namely, four singers in one choir and all the rest in the other."[102]

In keeping with his earlier small-scale "ecclesiastical concertos," Viadana's *Lamentationes* (1609) are designed for "just four good voices" (though without organ), but for different reasons. These highly charged texts called for the particular expressive capability of an ensemble of expert solo voices,[103] and at the papal chapel one-to-a-part singing by select singers is documented in this and other Holy Week music (including Miserere settings such as Allegri's).[104] Different conditions demanded different treatments, and the *Responsoria* from the same publication are expressly to be sung by four or five singers per part, but with the *falso-bordone* verse taken by four solo singers.[105] Similar alternations of solo voices and "full" choir characterize Byrd's *Great Service* and are all but explicit in the red- and black-ink underlay of the Eton Choirbook (*c.*1500).[106] In many other repertoires – notably in most sixteenth-century masses – certain portions of text (Crucifixus, Benedictus etc.) may imply single voices, especially when set in a reduced number of parts.[107]

Certain idioms lent themselves equally to single and multiple voices. In the largely homophonic writing in Cavalieri's *Rappresentatione di Anima, et di Corpo* (1600), variety was evidently also welcome:

> When the choir's music is in four parts, one can, if desired, double them and have now four singing and sometimes all together, provided the platform can accommodate eight.[108]

Doubled voices, however, had at least one clear disadvantage:

> adding *coloraturae* in a choir spoils the result, for when one part is assigned to be sung by several people, it is inevitable that the *coloraturae* will be completely different, and hence both the beauty and the nature of the sound are obscured. (Finck, 1556)[109]

As a general rule, vocal writing containing wide ranges, extended runs, complex rhythms or chromatic intricacies is most likely to have been intended for single rather than multiple voices. Defining "*da Capella*" in compositional terms, Walther (1732) explains:

> if many voices and instruments are to do one and the same thing accurately together, the composition must also be designed so that this can happen properly. Accordingly one finds that good and experienced masters employ only whole-, half- and quarter-notes in an *alla breve*, but dispose them in sundry ways with such great artistry and skill . . .[110]

From Monteverdi to Bach

Single- and multiple-voiced choirs continued to coexist and to complement each other, as did new- and old-style repertory (in *stile concertato* and *stile antico*). Thus Monteverdi's famous 1610 publication opens not with the Vespers music but with a rigorously contrapuntal *Missa da capella* based on a motet already many decades old,[111] and a century later we find amongst Alessandro Scarlatti's diverse church works a *Messa breve a Palestrina*. Even right at the end of our period, Charles Burney, in Florence, could hear vespers music "all in the old coral style of the sixteenth century,"[112] and, at Milan Cathedral, music from "about 150 years ago":

> the service they were to sing [was] printed on wood in four parts, separate, cantus–altus–tenor–bassus – out of which after the tone was given by the organist . . . they *all* sung, namely 1 boy, 3 castrati, 2 tenors and 2 basses, under the direction of the Maestro di Capella, without the organ.[113]

In Germany, where the motets of Handl, Lassus, and their contemporaries formed the staple diet of Lutheran choirs well into the mid eighteenth century, a printed anthology of such works – *Florilegium Portense* (1603 and 1621) – may still have been in use in Leipzig as late as 1770.[114]

While Monteverdi's *1610 Vespers* gives not the slightest hint of requiring more singers than there are voice-parts (*solo/tutti* indications are entirely absent), the sober writing of the Mass is clearly suited to a reasonably "strong" *capella* of singers (with continuo, and therefore not *a cappella* in the sense of "without instruments," a meaning which dates from the nineteenth century). Similarly the traditional Lutheran motet could invite "wherever possible . . . a very strong contingent of singers,"[115] in clear contrast to concerted music. "How many persons are actually needed for a well-appointed musical ensemble?" asks Johann Beer in 1690:

> I say that one can make a fully satisfying harmony with eight persons,
> namely four vocalists, two violinists, one organist and the director ... For
> with six parts there is a complete body of sound, and it is not necessary to
> trouble oneself further with a larger group ...[116]

Mattheson (1728) duly countered by proposing an ensemble of at least twenty-three persons (plus director), in which Beer's two violins have turned into what we recognize as an "orchestra." Yet Mattheson seems content with just the four singers.[117] Lutheran composers were particularly keen to expand their instrumental resources (notably with the newer woodwind instruments), but the essential vocal choir of their concerted music remained in effect the solo-voiced *coro favorito* of Praetorius, Schütz *et al.*, with instruments now almost invariably outnumbering voices by at least five to two.[118] (Telemann's "pool" of singers in Hamburg seems generally to have consisted of seven, alongside twenty or so instrumentalists.)[119] As before, the four or so *concertists* – standing well forward[120] – might be doubled from time to time by an optional vocal *capella* or *ripieno* group:

> *Capella* is when a separate choir joins in at certain sections for the
> splendour and strengthening of the *Music*; it must therefore be separately
> positioned in a place apart from the concertists. With insufficient people,
> however, these *capella* sections can even be left out, because they are in any
> case already also sung by the concertists. (Fuhrmann, 1706)[121]

The sources of J. S. Bach's earliest-known large-scale cantata *Gott ist mein König*, BWV71 (Mühlhausen, 1708) illustrate these principles with exceptional clarity: the ripieno group – explicitly optional ("*se piace*") – appears in under half of the choral writing.[122] And from the other end of Bach's working life, the ripieno parts added in 1742 to *Dem Gerechten muß das Licht*, BWV195 operate in exactly the same way: concertists remain responsible not only for solo movements but for each and every chorus, with ripienists occasionally added (under certain conditions) simply to add weight.[123] The dozen or more young singers in Bach's elite First Choir at Leipzig may perhaps all have sung in the congregational chorales and traditional motets (directed by the Prefect), but his own extraordinarily "intricate" concerted music required only the very best of them to sing. Consequently Bach was able to have the second violin "mostly ... taken by pupils, and the viola, violoncello and violone always so (for want of more capable persons),"[124] in line with his earlier formal undertaking to "instruct the boys not only in vocal but also in instrumental music, so that the churches may not be put to unnecessary expense."[125]

Female voices

At the Thomasschule Bach faced specific difficulties caused by "the admission hitherto of so many unproficient and musically quite untalented boys,"[126] but dissatisfaction with boy singers was a widespread occurrence and, as we have seen, the cornett had been frequently employed "to supplement ... trebles, which are not usually good" (Mersenne, 1636). In Glarean's experience (1547), boys were "frequently unacquainted with the song,"[127] while in Banchieri's (1614) they were "universally in all cities scarcely to be found, and those with little grounding";[128] the better ones, according to Mattheson (1739), tended moreover "to think so much of themselves that their behaviour is unbearable."[129] The main problem, of course, was that "when one has taken great pains to train a boy's voice, it disappears as the voice breaks, which usually happens between the ages of fifteen or twenty" (Bacilly, 1668)[130] – or at "about thirteen" (Banchieri, 1614).[131] For his *concerti ecclesiastici*, Viadana (1602) consequently advised that "falsettists will make a better effect"[132] – though within a short time castrati had all but ousted that particular species of soprano from Italy.

For the Church the problem rested on the words of Saint Paul: "Let your women keep silence in the churches" (1 Corinthians 14:34). Rich traditions and high standards of polyphonic music making were nevertheless maintained in many all-female convents, often despite stringent restrictions imposed from outside. In musical publications dedicated to nuns, keyboard transpositions are dealt with by both G. P. Cima (1606) and Penna (1672),[133] suggesting one way of making certain vocal works accessible to female choirs. A double-choir motet by the Modenese nun Sulpitia Cesis (1606) has a different solution: the Tenor of choir I is expressly to be sung up an octave and the Bass not sung but played, as is choir II in its entirety.[134] In music with basso continuo there was an alternative way of tackling vocal bass parts: nuns "can sing the bass at the octave, which produces an alto part" (Donati, 1623).[135] This did not convince a German visitor to Venice in 1725, who "took a strong dislike" to one aspect of the "fugal and contrapuntal" psalm settings as sung by the *figlie* of the Pietà:

> the bass part was sung by a contralto, thereby creating a succession of
> very clear 5ths and octaves with the continuo bass and with the viola which
> was beneath the alto part.[136]

To a Frenchman, the Italian female contralto was simply

> not of the same kind as ours: no type of French voice could render their
> song well. They are female *bas-dessus* voices, lower than any of ours.[137]

Exactly how Vivaldi's SATB writing for the Pietà was performed nevertheless remains somewhat unclear. While several "tenors" and the occasional "bass" are documented amongst the *figlie*, a significant amount of Venetian *ospedale* music survives in SSAA format.[138] And when Burney visited in 1771 it seems that music at the *Mendicanti* was "never in more than three parts, often only in two," yet very effective.[139] Quite possibly practices varied according both to fashion and to the availability of singers with exceptionally low voices.[140] (An ingenious practice by Vienna's Ursuline nuns, when no female bass was available, was for a man to sing "through a window [which opened on] to the musicians' choir.")[141]

The outstanding quality of Venice's best *ospedale* singers repeatedly attracted the attention of the city's many visitors, causing a German courtier in 1649 to reflect wistfully: "I have often wished that the sound of such music might spread to the electoral court chapel in Dresden."[142] As the demand for elaborate concerted music grew and especially wherever castrati were not an option, one question came increasingly to the fore: "whether it be allowed to make use of female singers in music making in church." The frequent shortage of good trebles, declared a German theologian in 1721, was something "a good female singer could easily supply"; surely it would be "better if a musically intelligent woman sang devotional arias in church rather than secular and amorous ones at the opera," using "this their talent primarily for the praise of God."[143] Whilst acknowledging that this would be "a vast improvement of chorall musick," Roger North in 1728 conceded that "both text and morallity are against it."[144] A proposal in 1762 to admit women as members of the French chapel royal, "in order not to have to send for more Italians" (i.e. castrati), seems to have been rejected on everything but musical grounds.[145] (As soloists, however, female singers had long been accepted there; Lalande's two daughters are known to have taken part in *grands motets* around 1700.)[146]

Away from close ecclesiastical scrutiny, the use of "female quiristers" alongside males may have been quietly pioneered in private chapels. An English Jesuit priest gives us a tantalizing hint of clandestine worship in the 1580s at the home of a musical Catholic gentleman: not only were there "choristers, male and female, members of his household" but "Mr. Byrd, the very famous English musician and organist, was among the company."[147] A century later, various musically skilled chambermaids in the employ of Mlle. de Guise sang the upper parts in her household ensemble (with Charpentier as singer and composer in residence), for both secular and chapel music.[148] By 1717 at least one German court had followed suit: at Württemberg the ten people needed for "a complete and well-set-up" church ensemble included four female sopranos (the younger two designated as "Ripieno" singers).[149]

Introducing female singers into Germany's municipal churches may have been more of a challenge: "Initially it was required that I should at all costs position them so that nobody got to see them; but ultimately people could not hear or see them enough."[150] These early experiences of Mattheson's in Hamburg *c.*1715 evidently supported his later view that women were "absolutely indispensable" in a *Kapelle.*[151] Defining a "complete choir ... for use both in the theatre and in church and chamber," Scheibe in 1737 was equally adamant that "Of the eight principal singers the sopranos *and altos* should be women, because their voices will be more natural, and of better durability and purity."[152] Practice varied, of course, but female singers – soprano and alto, younger and older – are documented at the Würzburg court (1746),[153] at Stuttgart's Stiftkirche (from before 1720),[154] and, perhaps most remarkably, at Cologne Cathedral (from as early as 1711 and right through the century).[155]

Handel

The abiding image of 250 choral singers – just six of them female – packed together in Westminster Abbey for the 1784 "Commemoration of Handel"[156] raises the question of exactly how large Handel's own choirs may have been. Opportunities to write on the grandest scale arose predominantly in connection with royal or state events, yet the "Utrecht" Te Deum and Jubilate (1713), given in the vast spaces of St. Paul's Cathedral, involved perhaps no more than twenty singers out of an estimated fifty or so performers.[157] It was the Coronation of George II in 1727 that gave rise to the "first Grand Musical performance in the Abbey" and with it some of the most enduring large-scale ceremonial music ever written, not least Handel's setting of *Zadok the Priest.* For the event, the combined Chapel Royal and Abbey choirs reportedly comprised "40 Voices,"[158] while instruments – well over a hundred of them – again outnumbered singers. Music making on this scale, however, was exceptional.[159] The clear majority of Handel's Chapel Royal music was designed for St. James's Palace and for around twenty singers (with occasional modest orchestral accompaniment), while the musical establishment at Cannons (1717–18), where the Duke of Chandos lived "en Prince,"[160] would have reminded him of many a small German court, with its complement of three to eight voices and eight to ten instruments.

Earlier still the 21-year-old Lutheran had left Hamburg for Italy with operatic ambitions. According to a French traveler, accustomed to the lavish vocal forces of Parisian opera, "everyone knows that choruses are out of use in Italy, indeed beyond the means of the ordinary Italian opera house"; instead, any choral writing was routinely delivered by the opera's various characters, "the King, the Clown, the Queen and the Old Woman – all singing together."[161] Oratorios worked in much the same way; thus, for Handel's *La Resurrezione* (Rome, 1708), which contains two choruses, we find payments to the solo singers and to more than forty instrumentalists (headed by Corelli) but none for any additional singers.

In Italy's churches, as we have seen, "Renaissance" polyphony (with or without organ) remained current. Major feasts, however, when extra musicians could be hired,[162] routinely demanded up-to-the-minute *concertato* music – and this is exactly what Handel's three Roman psalm settings of 1707 deliver, each in its own way. The original set of parts to *Laudate pueri* makes it clear that its choral writing was designed for five *concertato* singers (including the starring soprano) with a "Secondo Coro" of (five?) ripienists, while the concluding double-choir "Gloria Patri" of *Nisi Dominus*, performed on the same occasion, implies a similar arrangement. In the case of *Dixit Dominus*, however, the consistently challenging vocal writing nowhere suggests a need for vocal reinforcement of its five virtuoso soloists (despite the single appearance of some chant-like writing marked "*cappella*").[163]

A quarter of a century later Handel was turning his attention to the English oratorio. "'Tis excessive noisy, a vast number of instruments and voices, who all perform at a time," declared an aristocratic lady on hearing *Athalia* at a London theater in 1733. Yet, although the orchestra was probably at least sixty strong, singers (including six soloists) were estimated to number no more than "about twenty-five."[164] *Messiah* (1742) began its remarkable life in relatively modest circumstances, in Dublin's New Musick Hall, "a Room of 600 Persons."[165] All indications are that the work's many choruses were taken by the various soloists (seven of them, male and female) with perhaps half a dozen or so additional singers. Records of subsequent London performances at the Foundling Hospital in the 1750s show payments to five or six vocal soloists, four or six boys and eleven to thirteen other adult male singers, together with the conventionally larger complement of instruments (thirty-three or thirty-eight plus continuo).[166] More interesting perhaps than these numbers and ratios is the "mixed" nature of the resultant choral soprano line: two female "theater" sopranos (usually Italian) and a few Chapel Royal choirboys, doubled by as many as four oboes. (It should be added that the presence of chorus music in the soloists' books bequeathed by Handel to the Foundling Hospital confirms the expectation of their choral role.)[167]

After Handel's death in 1759, annual performances of *Messiah* at the Foundling Hospital continued for many years – as did the institution's careful bookkeeping. While orchestral numbers remained much the same, what these later accounts clearly document is a sudden and sharp increase in the number of singers from 1771 onwards, when the number of boys rose to twelve and a considerable body of unpaid chorus singers was added – twenty-six or more of them.[168] This moment in the emergence of large non-ecclesiastical bodies of amateur singers, male and female in now-familiar SATB formation, is therefore a fitting place to leave the present brief survey.

From Dufay to Handel, composers of earlier choral music knew their choirs intimately – as choirmasters and directors, and frequently as singers themselves. Pitch levels, singer numbers and ratios, voice types and vocal scoring, conventions of notation and of instrumental participation – rarely do these correspond directly to current practice, yet only exceptionally would any explanation have been required by those for whom the music was carefully crafted. An appreciation of the diverse anatomies of vocal choirs from the first 300 years of modern choral history can only serve to enrich our understanding of the music those composers wrote.

3 Choral music in the culture of the nineteenth century

CHESTER L. ALWES

In his study of Romantic music, Alfred Einstein suggested that the nineteenth century was no longer "a period of great choral music."[1] He based that judgment on his belief that the large-scale choral works written in that century presented nothing new, only a continuation of genres (mass, oratorio, requiem, motet, etc.) already well established in the preceding century. He dismissed the nineteenth century's singular contribution to choral repertory – the part-song – as mere musical trifles designed to engage and entertain a new class of amateur singers. While there is an element of truth in Einstein's assessment, he failed to consider the new political, economic, and social realities to which composers of the time were responding. In this chapter, I shall (all too briefly) consider how the new cosmology of the nineteenth century transformed the nature of choirs and the music they sang.

Collision of cosmologies

While 1800 is a handy chronological marker, it is not particularly useful when defining cultural history. To understand nineteenth-century music, we must first understand the ideas of the preceding century that shaped it. The philosophical engine that fueled Europe's growth in the eighteenth century was the Enlightenment, a period dominated by scientific method and reason that postulated that, given sufficient time and information, humanity could construct a new Eden. Correlative to this philosophical stance was the emergence of the Industrial Revolution (*c.*1750) that offered the ideal laboratory for implementing the theoretical formulations of such "enlightened" thinkers as René Descartes, John Locke, Isaac Newton and Jean-Jacques Rousseau.[2] In the history of music (especially choral music), the Enlightenment found clearest expression in the ecclesiastical reforms (*c.*1780) enacted by Emperor Joseph II of Austria and his disciple Hieronymus Colloredo, who served as Archbishop of Salzburg during Mozart's time there. Many have attributed Haydn's cessation of mass composition in 1782 to these reforms, even more blaming Colloredo for Mozart's departure for life in Vienna, outside the patronage system that had been the prime mover of European art since the Renaissance. While nineteenth-century commentators saw Romantic aspects in Mozart's music and Haydn's late works, the first unabashedly Romantic composer was Ludwig van Beethoven (1770–1827).

The role enlightened thinking played in fomenting the successful revolution of the American colonies against England seemingly endorsed its idealism as the *Weltanschauung* of the future. But that promising beginning foundered on the French Revolution's descent into chaos (1789). Indeed, without the breakdown of the social fabric that accompanied the Reign of Terror, Romanticism would not likely have become the potent cultural force it was. The Romantic's response to reason run amok was to retreat into fantasy, fairy tales, and the benign pleasures of nature as antidotes for a reality that was unthinkable. For choral music, the French Revolution's destruction of the Catholic Church and the secular religion (the *Culte de l' Être suprême*)[3] that emerged from the Church's demise inspired a new kind of church music – the massive hymns of Gosssec, Méhul and, ultimately, Hector Berlioz that established choral music's new dimensions and place in society.

Even more disruptive was the emergence of Napoleon Bonaparte, who, in contrast to the dreamscape espoused by E. T. A. Hoffmann, Friedrich Schegel, Ludwig Tieck, W. H. Wackenroder and Immanuel Kant, acted politically and militarily, ultimately becoming not only the fallen hero of Beethoven's *Eroica* Symphony (1804), but also the reality behind the subtitles *in tempore belli* and *in angustiis* that Haydn applied to his late masses. The havoc Napoleon wrought on the European landscape found a musical analog in Beethoven's *Missa Solemnis* (Op. 123, 1819–23), which effectively relocated the inherited choral/orchestral mass from the church to the concert hall. Beethoven's new conceptual model of the festival mass and its imitations by Schubert, Schumann, Liszt, and Bruckner forged a new synergy between these previously distinct musical entities.

The other factor that shaped the chorus's new identity was the Industrial Revolution, which transformed the largely rural, agrarian European economy to one dominated by machines and cities. The new factories it spawned altered both European commerce and the skylines and environments of the new centers of technological innovation. This new industrialization produced fundamental changes in economic, political, religious, and cultural values that forever altered the nature of choral music. Capitalism created a new class of wealthy people whose success played out in the novelties of leisure time, disposable income, and a disposition to charitable acts prompted by the increasing gap between the nouveaux riches and those whose labor created their wealth. The activity that eased the discomfiture of the new bourgeoisie was music, in the form of domestic music making (notably involving the piano), the need for music lessons (and teachers), the acquisition of printed music and the eventual emergence of that quintessential group music-making enterprise, the choral society. This new class of musical amateurs increased the size of choirs and, their need both of music to perform and appropriate venues (both physical and cultural) in which to perform.

Choral singing in the nineteenth century: a paradigm shift

Contemporary Western notions of choral singing are a nineteenth-century invention. Documentary, iconographic, and anecdotal evidence indicates that eighteenth-century choirs were generally small and more likely to consist of "professional" singers than their nineteenth-century counterparts. Handel would have been shocked by the choir of one thousand singers that performed his music at Westminster Abbey in the 1791 concert that Haydn attended.[4] Indeed, newly discovered documentary evidence suggests that the choir that performed Haydn's late masses at Esterháza consisted of four soloists and a choir of twelve to fifteen singers, of whom probably eight were employed at court.[5] The situation in Salzburg was similar in 1757 (a year after Mozart's birth); the archbishop's *Kapelle* had the relatively grand complement of ten solo singers, fifteen boy choristers and twenty-nine adult choristers (with an orchestra of thirty players).[6] By the premiere of Haydn's *Die Schöpfung* (1798), the chorus had swelled to between sixty and eighty singers accompanied by an even larger orchestra.[7] But these numbers pale in comparison with the size of nineteenth-century choirs. Late eighteenth-century performances of Handel's oratorios, both in England and on the Continent, routinely involved choirs of several hundred singers, culminating in the huge chorus for the 1791 concerts at Westminster Abbey. The trend established by these Handel celebrations continued to play out in the performances of European choral societies.[8]

The tipping points from the old to the new notion of a chorus were Beethoven's unprecedented expectations of the chorus and the simultaneous rise of Grand Opera in France. Beethoven's impact was already evident in his Mass in C, Op. 86 (1807), commissioned by Prince Nikolas Esterházy to continue the tradition established by Haydn's last six masses. Its redefinition of "symphonic" mass was evident in the unusual use of tonalities, cyclic return of music,[9] orchestral interludes based on motivic continuity to create seamless connections between otherwise disparate movements, and the curious string of tempo words by which Beethoven tried to quantify "tempo rubato" in the mass's Kyrie.[10] But it was the *Missa Solemnis* and Symphony No. 9 in D minor, Op. 125 (1817–24) that truly raised the bar of choral expectations to unprecedented heights.

The advent of a five-act format in French grand opera initiated by the collaboration of the composer D. F. E. Auber and the librettist Eugène Scribe created an expectation of choral participation in the drama not found in the operas of Mozart, Gluck or Weber. With the operas of Rossini, Meyerbeer, Halévy, *et al.* the chorus transcended its prior restriction to providing what Victor Hugo called "couleur du temps," becoming a dramatically active, costumed and staged ensemble.[11] The visual and dramatic needs of this new format led to an assumed choral presence in the operas of Verdi and Wagner.

The beginnings of public concert life (as early as the Concert Spirituel in Paris [1725–90] and the Bach–Abel Concerts in London [1765–81]) also contributed to the increased size of both choruses and orchestras. In many locales, the popularity of choral singing led to the creation of civic orchestras to accompany them (as was the case, for example, with the Birmingham Festival). The use of concerts as philanthropic, charitable events, a precedent established by Handel's performances of *Messiah* for the Foundling Hospital and codified by the mission of the Tonkünstler Sozietät of Vienna (1771), prompted the growth of new choral festivals and societies.[12] The late eighteenth and nineteenth centuries witnessed the birth of important English concert-giving institutions such as the Three Choirs Festival (1715–present) and the Birmingham Festival (1768–1912), as well as the institutions listed in Table 3.1, many of which remain active today.

By the mid nineteenth century, symphonic concerts began to dominate public concert life; existing local choruses were typically drafted when choral works were programmed. For the remainder of the century, extant choral societies were increasingly absorbed into symphonic organizations or newly created as adjuncts to them.

Public concerts were less numerous and consistently available than performances linked to traditional institutions, for example domestic chamber music and liturgical choral music. Even such a venerable institution as the Gesellschaft der Musikfreunde limited participation in its concerts to its membership, which by 1834 totaled two hundred; the "season" typically included four large "Society Concerts" and sixteen "Abendunterhaltungen." The former were primarily symphonic concerts (with occasional choral works by Handel, Haydn, Mozart or local composers); the latter were salon concerts, smaller in scale and commensurately more professional.[13] It was not until considerably later that the organization sponsored dedicated choral and orchestral ensembles.[14] Similarly, the Birmingham Festival didn't have a professional orchestra dedicated to giving concerts of symphonic music until after 1855.[15]

Table 3.1 *Choral-orchestral societies in Europe and America*

Date	Name	Location
1781–present	Gewandhaus	Leipzig
1785–93	Professional Concerts	London
1793–present	Sing-Akademie	Berlin
1800–present	Cincinnati May Festival[a]	Cincinnati
1802–54	Singakademie	Leipzig
1813–67	Philharmonic Society	London
1814–1938	Gesellschaft der Musikfreunde	Vienna
1815–present	Handel and Haydn Society	Boston
1818–present	Frankfurter Cäcilienverein	Frankfurt
1819–48	Concerts Spirituels	Vienna
1832–33	Fétis's Concerts historiques	Paris
1832–89	Sacred Harmonic Society	London
1833–60	Orphéon	Paris
1842–48; 1860–present	Vienna Philharmonic Society	Vienna
1842–present	New York Philharmonic	New York
1852–?	New Philharmonic Society	London
1853–present	Budapest Philharmonic	Budapest
1858, 1860, 1874–1970	Leeds Triennial Festival	Leeds
1858–present	Singverein	Vienna
1861–1939	Academy of Music[b]	London
1868–present	Tonhalle Orchester	Zürich
1869–present	Orchesterverein	Vienna
1873–present	Oratorio Society of New York	New York
1874–present	Mendelssohn Club	Philadelphia
1875–present	London Bach Choir	London
1881–present	Boston Symphony Orchestra	Boston
1882–present	Berlin Philharmonic	Berlin
1888–present	Concertgebouw Orchester	Amsterdam
1893–present	Munich Philharmonic	Munich
1898–present	Bethlehem Bach Festival	Bethlehem, PA
1900–present	Philadelphia Orchestra	Philadelphia

[a] This festival began as a German *Sängerfest*, later becoming the more prototypical choral/orchestral festival.
[b] The name of this organization changed to the London Academy of Music and Dramatic Arts in 1935 (*NG* 2, vol. 15, p. 167).

Choral societies and the rise of music education

Since the membership of these new choral societies consisted largely of amateurs, the teaching of sight-reading and singing technique became virtual "cottage industries" essential to the success of the enterprise. In America, this phenomenon was embodied by the itinerant Yankee tune-smiths, most notably William Billings (1746–1800), who went from town to town, teaching singing by using his own music and methods. Later, in the early nineteenth century, similar concerns in the American South led to shape-note singing, a movement the cultural and religious bases of which could not have been more different than those of their northern predecessors. In England, the concern with pedagogy galvanized the activity of three important figures: Joseph Mainzer (1801–51), John Pyke Hullah (1812–84) and the Reverend John Curwen (1816–80).

Joseph Mainzer, a former German priest residing in Paris, went to England in 1841. Within a year, he had begun publishing materials based on his earlier sight-singing method book, *Singschule* (1831), which he developed into his landmark publication *Singing for the Million* (1842). As Percy Scholes has noted, the success of Mainzer's work must be understood within the milieu of a new social consciousness that sought to better the intellectual, moral, and religious life of the "lower classes."[16]

Mainzer's principal disciple was Guillaume-Louis Wilhelm (1781–1842), who adapted his teacher's methodology to provide music education to Parisian schoolchildren (beginning in 1819). So successful were Wilhelm's classes that a reunion of former students in 1833 led to the formation of a permanent choral ensemble, the Orphéon,[17] which was later conducted by Charles Gounod.[18]

The leading English exponents of sight-singing classes were Hullah and Curwen. Hullah, who traveled to Paris in a vain attempt to study with Mainzer, eventually learned his methodology from Wilhelm in 1839. In 1841, Hullah returned to England and began teaching sight-singing classes using Wilhelm's methods (*Wilhelm's Method of Teaching Singing Adapted to English Use*, 1841). Initially intended for schoolteachers, his popular classes were eventually opened to the general public, leading to the certification of some fifty thousand pupils by July 1842.[19]

In that pivotal year of 1841, John Curwen, a Congregational minister in Yorkshire, was commissioned to produce a method to teach young Sunday School children to sing by note. He adopted the methodology of Sarah Glover (1785–1867) of Norwich, whose unique visual aid, the "Sol-Fa Ladder," illustrated the key notes of every scale, substituting Anglicized versions of Guido d'Arezzo's solmization syllables (doh, ray, me, fah, soh, lah, te [or *si*]). Unlike Mainzer and Hullah, Curwen's system used movable doh, resulting in a new notational system (still found in the editions of the publishing house that bears his name) to visualize pitch and rhythm (Curwen's "Tonic-Sol-fa system"). Curwen's publications eventually included: *The Standard Course* (1861); *The New Standard Course* (1872); *The Teacher's Manual of the Art of Teaching in General, and especially as applied to Music* (1875) and *A Tonic Sol-fa Primer* (ed. John Stainer, published by Novello).[20]

Choral societies and their repertory

Initially, British choral societies existed to perform oratorios, specifically those of Handel; the popularity and growth of this activity created demand for new compositions that emulated Handel's style. Ironically, the most notable results came not from British composers but from Joseph Haydn (1732–1809), who had been inspired by hearing the Westminster Abbey performances of

Handel's music in 1791. Haydn's two principal oratorios – *Die Schöpfung* (1798) and *Die Jahreszeiten* (1801) – became templates for the increasingly diverse array of pieces called 'oratorio' in the nineteenth century. Haydn's *Creation* was based on an English libretto ostensibly intended for Handel, which Gottfried van Swieten translated into German. His text consisted of modules of biblical narrative, followed by poetic texts intended for use as arias and choruses. *The Seasons* was an even more radical departure from the Handelian template; Swieten adapted James Thompson's secular poetry into four separate, self-sufficient musical compositions. This oratorio's abandonment of biblical stories produced what some have described (for lack of any better terminology) as secular oratorio. The textual independence of the four "Seasons" led others to classify Haydn's composition as a "grand cantata" (especially if they were performing only a single part of it).[21] Works like *The Seasons* resembled oratorio primarily in the retention of multiple movements of varying character scored for chorus, professional soloists, and orchestra. In the concert listings of the *Allgemeine Muiskalische Zeitung* (established in Leipzig in 1798/99) one finds numerous works that fit this generic description.[22] In her dissertation on Mendelssohn's *Die Erste Walpurgisnacht*, Op. 60, Catharine Melhorn provided a representative list of secular "grand cantatas" (augmented in Table 3.2 by the present author) performed in the opening decades of the nineteenth century. Haydn's *The Seasons* heads this list, further emphasizing the increasingly blurry line between oratorio and new works for chorus, soloists and orchestra.

In their day, these compositions ably served the repertorial needs of choral societies; today, most, if not all, of these compositions have disappeared from the concert programs of choruses and orchestras. Beethoven's paradigmatic Ninth Symphony not only generated a series of choral symphonies (by Mendelssohn, Liszt, Mahler, et al.), but also made it fashionable for

Table 3.2 *Nineteenth-century "grand cantatas"*

1801	Franz Josef Haydn	*Die Jahreszeiten*
c.1809	Sigmund Romberg	*Das Lied von der Glocke*
1809	Peter von Winter	*Timotheus oder Die Macht der Töne*
c.1811	Andreas Romberg	*Die Macht des Gesänges*
c.1812	Ferdinand Ries	*Der Morgen*
1814	Ludwig van Beethoven	*Der glorreiche Augenblick*
1814–15	Ludwig van Beethoven	*Meeresstille und glückliche Fahrt*, Op. 112
1815	Carl Maria von Weber	*Kampf und Sieg*
1816	Franz Schubert	*Prometheus*, D. 451 (lost)
c.1817	Andreas Romberg	*Was bleibet und was schwindet*
1818	Carl Maria von Weber	*Jubel Cantate*
1828	Felix Mendelssohn	*Grosse Festmusik zum Dürerfest*
1830	Friedrich Schneider	*Die Seefahrt*
1832	Felix Mendelssohn	*Die erste Walpurgisnacht* , Op. 60
1840	Heinrich Marschner	*Klänge aus Osten*

composers to write choral-orchestral works that differed from the oratorio primarily by being secular, more dramatic and shorter.

European choral societies first performed oratorios and a cappella church music because such music was increasingly neglected by church choirs of the day. The new nineteenth-century symbiosis of chorus and orchestra produced choral repertory primarily conceived for the concert hall. While early symphonic concerts occasionally featured oratorios and opera excerpts (and occasionally complete concert performances), changes in contemporary taste and expectation led composers to produce music similar to what Felix Mendelssohn proposed to the directors of the Lower Rhine Festival to replace a performance of Bach's B Minor Mass during the 1842 festival; in its place, he argued that "an easier, more cheerful piece ... would seem to me, and I think to everyone else, a better choice."[23]

Mendelssohn and other mainstream German composers created a body of choral-orchestral music that defied easy classification; even the composers themselves were not sure what to call their new compositions. Consider the case of Robert Schumann, whose list of instrumentally accompanied choral works (arranged chronologically in Table 3.3 by date of composition) epitomizes the problem.

Schumann does not describe any of this diverse group of compositions for chorus, solo voices and orchestra as "oratorio," although *Das Paradies und die Peri* and *Der Rose Pilgerfahrt* closely resemble what many have called "secular oratorio." His *Manfred* and the *Scenes from Goethe's Faust*

Table 3.3 *Choral-orchestral works by Robert Schumann*

Title/Opus	Year of composition	Schumann's description
Das Paradies und die Peri, Op. 50	1843	Dichtung aus Th. Moore's *Lalla Rook*
Beim Abschied zu singen, Op. 84	1847	*Lied*
Adventslied, Op. 71	1848	
Requiem für Mignon, Op. 98b	1849	Aus Goethe's *Wilhelm Meister*
Nachtlied, Op. 108	1849	von Friedrich Hebbel
Manfred, Op. 115	1848–49	Dramatisches Gedicht
Neujahrslied, Op. 144	1849–50	von Friedrich Rückert
Der Rose Pilgerfahrt, Op. 112	1851	Märchen nach einer Dichtung von Moritz Horn
Der Königssohn, Op. 116	1851	Ballade von Ludwig Uhland
Verzweifle nicht im Schmerzensthal, Op. 93	1852	Motette
Des Sängers Fluch, Op. 139	1852	Ballade nach Ludwig Uhland
Vom Pagen und der Königstochter, Op. 140	1852	Vier Balladen von Emmanuel Geibel
Fest-Ouverture, Op. 123	1852–1853	"Rheinweinlied"
Szenen aus Goethe's Faust, WoO3	1844–53	
Das Glück von Edenhall, Op. 143	1853	Ballade nach Ludwig Uhland

Table 3.4 *Johannes Brahms: secular dramatic
choral-orchestral works*

Begräbnisgesang, Op. 13	1858
Rinaldo, Op. 50	1863–68
Alt Rhapsodie, Op. 53	1869
Schicksalslied, Op. 54	1870
Triumphlied, Op. 55	1870–71
Nänie, Op. 82	1880–81
Gesang der Parzen, Op. 89	1882

are essentially multi-movement dramatic works with an operatic bent,
whereas the *Requiem für Mignon* seemingly defies placement in any genre.
The most interesting descriptor Schumann himself used was "Ballade," a
Romantic vocal genre ranging from solo songs (Loewe, Zelter, *et al.*) to
multi-movement works that averaged a half-hour in length.[24] In works
such as Opp. 116, 139, 140, and 143 Schumann created works perfectly
suited to the burgeoning choral festival market without having to wrestle
with the formal complexity and expense required to perform either choral
symphonies or operatic scenas.

The influence of Robert Schumann extended to Johannes Brahms's
body of small dramatic choral-orchestral works, which are far more
frequently performed today than any of Schumann's works (see
Table 3.4). These pieces have remained popular not only for their intrinsic
musical beauty, but, perhaps more important, also for their ability to lend
variety to the typical orchestral concert without overextending either the
orchestra or the chorus. That Brahms composed all of these works after
Ein deutsches Requiem (Op. 45) suggests that he regarded works of such
scope as more pragmatic than works like the *Requiem*.

Three of these – the *Begräbnisgesang*, Op. 13, *Rinaldo*, Op. 50, and the
ultra-nationalistic *Triumphlied*, Op. 55 – are rarely performed today. The
other four rank among the most beloved and oft-performed choral-orchestral
works of any type, probably because, though significantly less demanding
than the *Requiem*, they do not compromise or restrict his expressive power.

Nineteenth-century choral music as microcosm

The production of choral-orchestral works constitutes only one side of the
nineteenth-century choral revival. Alfred Einstein acknowledged a totally
different type of choral music, the intimate proportions and simple style of
which more readily accommodated the explosive growth of small choral
ensembles, both mixed and gender-based. For lack of a better term, I refer
to this genre as the part-song, realizing that the term is quite generic.

This new type of choralism began with the creation of the *Liedertafeln*, small male choirs comprised of amateurs who were at least as interested in socializing as they were in making music. In his article in the *New Grove Dictionary of Music and Musicians* (2nd edn.), Ewan West reports:

> The term was coined by Zelter, at whose instigation the first group was formed in Berlin on 24 December 1808 from his celebrated larger Singakademie . . . Liedertafel sprang up through Germany: in Frankfurt an der Oder (1815), Leipzig (1815), Thüringen (1818), Magdeburg (1819), Münster (1822), Hamburg (1823)[and] Bremen (1827).[25]

From these humble beginnings, this movement grew rapidly, eventually engulfing all of Germany and Austria and necessitating the formation of a governing body, the Männerchorvereine.[26] At first, these groups disdained the participation of professionals, preferring to create their own music. But as the movement grew, professional composers became more involved as both composer and conductor (e.g. Mendelssohn, Schumann, Bruckner, Rheinberger). The music these groups sang explored predictably masculine topics – songs about drinking, hunting, love, and the joys of nature. The songs about nature, in particular, reveal the most important aspect of such organizations; political disenfranchisement and longing for nationalistic unity transformed the processes of nature into a metaphor for the negative aspects of technological innovation.

Analogous to the *Liedertafeln*, but operating within a decidedly more sophisticated level of society, were informal musical evenings like the *Abendunterhaltungen* instituted by the Gesellschaft der Musikfreunde in Vienna or the famous *Schubertiades*, musical soirées mostly dedicated to the presentation of Schubert's Lieder and piano music held in the homes of benefactors such as Josef Witticzek, Karl Ritter von Enderes, or Josef Freiherr von Spaun.[27] Such events hovered in a nether world between the aristocratic salons of celebrities such as Clemens Metternich and the informal social get-togethers of the lower middle class. Differences of class and purpose may account for the often significant variation in style, text, scoring, and difficulty found in Schubert's part-songs for male voices. Works like "Nachthelle" (D. 892), "Grab und Mond" (D. 893), "Der Gondelfahrer" (D. 809) or the famous "Ständchen" (D. 921) exhibit a virtuosity and aesthetic concept strikingly different from his several "drinking songs" (*Trinklieder*), which more closely approach the style of the *Liedertafel*.[28] His setting of Franz Seidl's poem of transfigured night, "Nachthelle," demonstrates this distance in the demands of both its piano accompaniment and the tenor solo which dialogues with the choir.

Contrast Schubert's Romantic tone-painting with the more direct, masculine topics of the six songs that comprise Mendelssohn's Op. 50 (1840):

1 "Türkisches Schenkenlied" (Turkish drinking song)
2 "Der Jäger Abschied" (The hunter's farewell)
3 "Sommerlied" (Summer song)
4 "Wasserfahrt" (Water travel)
5 "Liebe und Wein" (Love and wine)
6 "Wanderlied" (Wanderer's song)

The first and fifth songs deal with drinking, while the remaining four involve some aspect of nature. Mendelssohn even marked "Liebe und Wein" "Im betrunkenen Ton zu singen," employing his signature meter, 6/8. That "Der Jäger Abschied" is a somber hymn to the forest, sung by departing hunters, is made clear by Mendelssohn's provision of an *ad libitum* accompaniment for hunting horns and trombone and a vocal appropriation of the stereotypic "horn fifths" for "Lebe wohl!" (Farewell!)

The part-song reached new heights of expressivity and musical complexity with Robert Schumann (1810–56) and his protégé Johannes Brahms (1833–97). Whereas Schubert had focused nearly exclusively on songs for male chorus, a preference that Mendelssohn diverged from only by adding an equal number of mixed chorus songs, both Schumann and Brahms wrote a significant body of music for women's voices. Unlike Schumann, however, Brahms wrote very little music for male chorus (Op. 41, 1867). Both composers' music for women's chorus was concert music that tended towards sacred texts because the church was frequently the only concert venue available to women (this in a time when the participation of women in traditional church choirs was still the exception).

A distinguishing feature in both composers' part-songs was the integration of counterpoint (particularly canon) into a genre previously dominated by simple, homophonic settings of mostly strophic poems. While Schumann's oeuvre also contained this simpler type of music, it was his adroit yet expressive use of canon in the *Ritornelle in canonische Weisen* (Op. 65, 1849) for men's chorus, works like "Die Kapelle" (Op. 69, no. 6) and "In Meeres Mitten" (Op. 91, no. 6) for women's chorus and the *Vier doppelchörige Gesänge* (Op. 141, 1849) that presaged Brahms's elevation of the part-song to a new artistic prominence. From Schumann (Opp. 67, 69, 75, 91, 145, and 146) Brahms also borrowed the designation *Romanzen und Balladen*, used in Op. 44 (women's chorus) and Op. 93a (mixed chorus). The influence of Schumann's fascination with counterpoint is similarly apparent in Brahms's canons for women's voices (Op. 113) and in mixed chorus songs such as "Beherzigung" (Op. 93a, no. 6) and "Verlorene Jugend," Op. 104, no. 4 (not to mention motets like "Schaffe in mir Gott," Op. 29, no. 2).

Though most choral conductors would agree that the part-songs of Brahms are the crowning achievement of this genre, a host of other composers in Germany and England also made significant contributions. In Germany, the enormous output of Josef Rheinberger (1839–1901), Anton Bruckner's (1824–96) significant contribution to the *Liedertafel* repertory, the fascinating body of choral songs by Peter Cornelius (1824–74) and the daunting works of that arch-Romantic Max Reger (1873–1916) are all important. After Germany, the part-song flourished in England (largely because of Mendelssohn's lasting influence), where its cultivation was even longer in duration and more diverse in style than in Germany.

Well before the foundation of the first *Liedertafel*, part-song singing was a well-established tradition in England. Such organizations as the Noblemen and Gentleman's Catch Club (1761) and the more egalitarian Glee Club (1763) laid the foundation for the future growth of the English part-song. Given Mendelssohn's enormous influence in England (*c.*1840), English adaptations of his songs were a foregone conclusion, culminating in Joseph Novello's publication *Orpheus, A Collection of Glees by the Most Admired German Composers with English Poetry* (1836). To give equal time to English composers, Novello published an *English Part Song Book* (edited by E. G. Monk) in 1850. In that same year, the English Glee and Madrigal Union was founded to "preserve from oblivion the masterpieces of our English school."[29]

Ultimately even more important for the development of the English part-song was the founding by Henry Leslie (1822–1896) of the choir that was to establish a new standard of English choral performance, eventually winning the Paris Choral Competition in 1878. Even though Leslie disbanded his choir in 1880, its many successors led to the creation of the English choral competition as early as 1885. These competitions featured "test pieces," typically new compositions designed to provide a measurement of the quality of choirs in each competitive division. Well-known composers of such works included Robert Lucas de Pearsall (1795–1856), Charles Villiers Stanford (1852–1924), C. Hubert H. Parry (1848–1918) and Edward Elgar (1857–1934), whose part-songs are the English equivalent of Brahms's achievement in the genre.

The role of music publishing

An important distinction needs to be drawn between the physical act of printing music and the process of publication and distribution.[30] Printed music began in early sixteenth-century Venice, experiencing steady growth with little comparable technological innovation. Consequently, printed music remained the preserve of institutions or individuals who had the substantial financial means needed to acquire the relatively small quantities of printed music that were issued. The next major step forward was the advent of engraving in the eighteenth century, but this innovation was limited by the prevalent use of letterpress printing for music with simple notation, when large print runs were possible or when the material was mostly text (as in treatises). The year of Bach's death (1750) was also significant for the emergence of the music-printing house founded by J. G. I. Breitkopf in Leipzig. Not only did Breitkopf figure significantly in the development of musical typography, he was also the first publisher able to produce large enough quantities of music to satisfy the needs of the new choral societies at a reasonable price. He accomplished this feat by using two different techniques – typeset music that allowed larger press runs of acceptable quality, allowing him to undersell the competition, and music manuscript (engraved and then printed) that allowed much wider dissemination of a greater range of repertory than his rivals.[31] Breitkopf's successful marketing strategy was soon adopted by other firms, creating a number of financially viable music publishing houses in England and Europe (see Table 3.5). That these firms remain well known today underscores how significantly nineteenth-century innovations changed the world of choral music. Other pivotal events in creating quantities of affordable printed music were the advent of lithography, (*c.*1810), offset printing (1860) and Novello's invention of the octavo (1847).

Table 3.5 *Music publishers of the eighteenth to the early twentieth century*

1750	Breitkopf und Söhne	Leipzig
1770	Schott	Mainz
1793	Simrock	Bonn (Berlin)
1778–1837	Artaria	Vienna
1808	Ricordi	Milan
1811	Breitkopf und Härtel	Leipzig
1811	Novello	London
1814	C. F. Peters	Vienna
*c.*1816	Boosey	London
1838	Bote und Bock	Berlin
1839–80	Heugel et Cie.	Paris
1853	Wilhelm Hansen	Copenhagen
1861	G. Schirmer	New York
1863	Curwen	London
1864–1970	J. Fischer	Dayton/New York
1872	Carl Fischer	New York
1874	E. Eulenburg	Leipzig
1883	Theodore Presser	Philadelphia
1891	Fazer	Helsinki
1901	Universal Edition	Vienna

The rise of historical music

Prior to the nineteenth century, all choral music was contemporary save for the important exceptions of the choral music of Palestrina and Handel, which continued to be performed (in Rome and London respectively) after the composers' deaths. These were, however, the exceptions that proved the rule that the music of living composers was still preeminent. This changed completely when Felix Mendelssohn revived J. S. Bach's *St. Matthew Passion* with Zelter's Singakademie in 1829. This rediscovery of Bach's music not only invigorated the compositions of Mendelssohn but also provided (along with Beethoven and Brahms) the repertorial foundation of music conservatories established in countries that had previously lacked a substantial national musical tradition. The renewed interest in Bach also led to the founding of the Bach Gesellschaft in 1850, the creation of which led Leipzig-based Breitkopf und Härtel to issue the first complete edition of the compositions of a non-living composer. Indeed, Breitkopf und Härtel's ascendancy established Leipzig as the center for producing collected works editions of Handel (ed. Friedrich Chrysander, 1856–94), Schütz (ed. Philip Spitta, 1885–94), and Lassus (ed. Adolph Sandberger, 1894–1926). At roughly the same time, a series of musical "monuments" was initiated with the publication of the *Denkmäler deutscher Tonkunst* (1892–1931), followed by its Austrian companion, the *Denkmäler der Tonkunst in Österreich* (Graz/Vienna, 1894–1959).

The greatest choral composer of the nineteenth century, Johannes Brahms was a pioneer in the programming of historical choral music in contemporary concerts, as well as composing music that in various ways revealed his indebtedness to the past. Consider, for example, the motets of Op. 74 – "Warum ist das Licht gegeben dem Mühseligen" and "O Heiland, reiss die Himmel auf." Not only do both works depend upon such historical practices as canon, cantus firmus, polychorality, and a surprising understanding of modality, but they were also dedicated to Philipp Spitta, the author of the first definitive biography of J. S. Bach (1873–80) and editor of the original Schütz *Gesammelte Werke*.

Berlin soon attained a status equal to Leipzig's with the appearance of landmark publications such as Johannes Winterfeld's pioneering study of Giovanni Gabrieli and his contemporaries (1834), which did much to fuel the revival of interest in Schütz's music. The edition by F. A. X. Haberl and Caspar Witt of Palestrina's music (1862–1907) followed an earlier Italian edition by Alfieri (1841). The firm of Bote und Bock in Berlin produced two important anthologies of sacred music – Franz Commer's *Musica Sacra* (1834–42, 1860–87 as *Cantiones*) and a companion volume intended to serve the repertorial needs of the Königliche Berliner

Domchor (1843–1905). The conservative, largely Catholic Cecilian movement inspired historical editions by Caspar Witt and Karl Proske, whose
anthology, *Musica Divina* (1853–76), established Ratisbon (Regensburg)
as the center for the study and dissemination of the music of the
"Palestrina" school.

Indeed, the conservative tenets of the Cecilian movement provided a
viable alternative to contemporary composers for whom the mass was no
longer a viable genre of concert music. Beethoven's *Missa solemnis* had its
imitators, but for those not so bold as to challenge its lofty heights,
Romanticism's fascination with antiquity provided the necessary impetus
for modern re-creations of the a cappella style of Palestrina and his contemporaries. Among the more famous products of this movement were
Bruckner's Mass No. 2 in E minor (WAB 27, 1866) and Franz Liszt's *Missa
Choralis* (1859–65). Bruckner parodies the Sanctus of Palestrina's *Missa
Brevis* in the Sanctus of his Mass in E minor, while Liszt prominently uses a
Gregorian intonation throughout the Credo of his mass, originally intended
for a cappella performance in the Sistine Chapel.

The effects of the Cecilian movement had far greater influence on
smaller sacred works. For composers such as Mendelssohn, Schumann,
Brahms, Rheinberger, Bruckner, and Liszt, this influence manifested itself
in the composition of Latin liturgical motets for both women's choirs
(where they would, of necessity, have constituted concert repertory) and
mixed choirs. This retrospective reform, which embraced the study and
performance of early music, also championed a myth about choral performance that persists to this day, namely that "old" music (whether
chronologically or stylistically so) was, *ipso facto*, performed a cappella;
while a cappella performance was the norm for the Sistine Chapel, no
evidence suggests its widespread use elsewhere. Yet, even today, there are
choirs the very names of which perpetuate this tradition. Indeed, this
enduring myth may be one of the nineteenth century's greatest legacies
to contemporary choral performance, even as we increasingly understand
how misguided that notion was.

Conclusion

For some time, the stature of nineteenth-century choral music has been
questioned not only by Alfred Einstein but also (tacitly) by the editors of
the *Norton Anthology of Western Music*, the fourth edition of which
included only two choral excerpts in its 997-page second volume – "Wie
lieblich sind deine Wohnungnen" from Brahms's *Ein deutsches Requiem*
and Bruckner's motet *Virga Jesse floruit*.[32] What I hope I have made
abundantly clear in this chapter is that choral music, as we understand it

today, is still indelibly marked by historic and aesthetic conventions that were products of the nineteenth century – choral societies, music education, the importance of historical music, technological advances that made possible affordable scores of larger choral works and choral octavos (the choral octavo itself was a nineteenth-century invention), the "glee club" tradition, the choral competition, the amateur church choir and the ideal of a cappella singing. Not only do works like Beethoven's *Missa solemnis*, Mendelssohn's *Elijah*, Brahms's *Ein deutsches Requiem* (not to mention his motets, part-songs and choral-orchestral songs), Schubert's Mass in G and Verdi's *Requiem* remain vital parts of the canon of performed choral repertory, but there are also literally innumerable works for choruses of all types that are still regarded by choral conductors and music educators at all levels as valuable reminders of the era whose ideas spawned our own.

4 Choral music in the twentieth and early twenty-first centuries

NICK STRIMPLE

During the first two decades of the twentieth century, composers were presented with more stylistic options than at any previous time. While often associated with national schools, these options were not, in reality, confined to them. In America, Charles Ives (1874–1954), laboring in near anonymity, trusted that people who appreciated the simultaneous sounds of separate marching bands in a parade could listen the same way in a concert hall. In France, Claude Debussy (1862–1918), after hearing a Javanese gamelan orchestra, invigorated Western music by subtly blurring ideas of tonality. The Russian Igor Stravinsky (1882–1971) emancipated rhythm in previously inconceivable ways. In Austria, competing ideas emerged: on one hand Gustav Mahler (1860–1911) continued to expand the limits of traditional tonality and form,[1] while on the other Arnold Schoenberg (1874–1951), believing that his muse was the true heir of German Romanticism,[2] experimented first with expanded orchestral timbres before moving on to atonal expressionism and thus to dodecaphony. In England, Sir Edward Elgar (1857–1934) summarized all that was noble in Victorian tradition, while his younger contemporary Ralph Vaughan Williams (1872–1958), driven by impulses similar to his contemporaries Béla Bartók (1881–1945) in Hungary and Leoš Janáček (1854–1928) in Moravia, discovered what could be achieved by a complete assimilation of folk traditions. At the same time, jazz musicians were striving for respectability while Dame Ethel Smyth (1858–1944) in England and Amy Beach (1867–1944) in America were endeavoring to prove that women also could compose music of high quality. In addition, the two world wars had profound impact on choral music. All succeeding composers were thus influenced, in some way, by these people and events and, as the century progressed, they incorporated into their own music the various techniques pioneered during the first two decades of the century.

Charles Ives: polytonality, tone clusters, collage, and chance

In 1894, Charles Ives composed Psalm 67. The same year he began work on Psalm 90, a work on which he would not put the finishing touches until 1924.

In 1898 he began *Three Harvest Home Chorales*, which he would not complete until 1912. These works, at the beginning of their creation, anticipated many of the innovations that occurred in twentieth-century music: bitonality, atonal melodic lines, dissonant harmonies, whole-tone scales, chord clusters, and serialized rhythm. Works that Ives composed well within the time frame encompassed by *Psalm 90 – General William Booth Enters Heaven* (1914), *Serenity* (1919), the Symphony No. 4 (1910–16), and other pieces that include chorus – incorporate collage technique, polytonality, and exceptionally complicated rhythmic constructs.

It is difficult to ascertain Ives's influence on European composers during the twentieth century's first two decades because many of his important compositions either remained unperformed or were performed only locally. By the end of World War II, however, he was a familiar name among composers. Even those not usually associated with the avant-garde occasionally found something in Ives that could be adapted for their own purposes. For example, the "Pleni sunt coeli" section of Benjamin Britten's *War Requiem* (1961), as well as the initial choral entries in Béla Bartók's *Cantata Profana* (1931) and Steven Stucky's (b.1949) *Drop, Drop Slow Tears* (1979) are direct descendants of the outwardly expanding chord cluster in Ives's *Psalm 90*. Other composers obviously influenced by Ives include: Bernd Alois Zimmermann (1918–70), whose enormous *Requiem für einen jungen Dichter* (1967–69) masterfully utilizes collage technique; John Cage (1912–92) and all others who experimented with indeterminacy; those who experimented with *musique concrète* and other forms of electro-acoustic music; early leaders of the Scandinavian avant-garde, including the Norwegian Alfred Janson (b.1937), whose *Tema* (1966) uses wordless chorus and indeterminacy within a measured structure to create a collage effect; and the Swede Lars Edlund (b.1922), whose *Gloria* (1969) constructs chord clusters in quarter tones.

Claude Debussy and Impressionism

The Javanese gamelan music, modes, whole-tone scales, parallel chord motion, smooth edges, and visual images that informed Debussy's music cast a remarkably wide net of influence during the twentieth century. Early on, composers as dissimilar as Stravinsky and Vaughan Williams found common ground in Debussy's universe. Very few, however, followed his lead totally. Maurice Ravel (1875–1937) is often mentioned in the same breath as Debussy, but his music, including the famous *Trois chansons* (1914–15) and the ballet with wordless chorus *Daphnis et Chloe* (1909–12), is more cleanly etched than Debussy's earlier *Trois chansons de Charles d'Orléans* (1898–1908) or his *Nocturnes* (1897–99), which also uses wordless chorus.

In addition to Vaughan Williams, several English composers of the same generation fell under Debussy's spell. In the work of Gustav Holst (1874–1934), the influence is most apparent in portions of *Hymn of Jesus* (1919) and the third set of *Choral Hymns from the Rig Veda* (1910). The affinity of Herbert Howells (1892–1983) to Debussy is apparent in his lovely *Hymnus Paradisi* (1938). But the most consistently Impressionistic of the English is Frederick Delius, whose *Sea Drift* (1904), *A Song of the High Hills* (1911), and other works owe most of their inspiration to the example of Debussy.

Harmonic aspects of Debussy's style colored much of the music written in the middle of the century, as exemplified in the works of Bohuslav Martinů (1890–1959) and Frank Martin (1890–1974). Martinů managed to successfully combine elements of Moravian folk music with impressionistic harmonic progressions and textures in compositions such as *The Spectre's Bride* (1932) and *The Opening of the Wells* (1955). Martin progressed from modality, as in his impressive *Mass* (c.1922–26), to a unique dodecaphonic technique, as found in the opera-oratorio *Le Vin Herbé* (1938–41), in which tone rows were harmonized with major or minor triads.

Olivier Messiaen (1908–92) presents an outstanding example of Debussy's continued influence in France during the twentieth century. Like Debussy, Messiaen was profoundly moved by the music of the East, in his case Hindu chant. He also experimented with various modes and non-retrogradable rhythmic constructs. For him, music was color. All this can be heard in his splendid *Trois petites liturgies de la Présence Divine* (1944), and the enormous *La Transfiguration de Notre Seigneur Jésus-Christ* (1969).

More recently, Debussy's continued influence in rather undiluted form can be seen in the choral compositions of Romanian-French composer Edgar Cosma (b.1925). Other younger composers have continued to use swathes of impressionistic color to balance various avant-garde techniques, as can be observed in compositions as different as *The Path of the Just* (1968) by the Norwegian composer Knut Nystedt (b.1915), and *A Maya Prophecy* (1985) by the Israeli Meir Mindel (b.1946).

Igor Stravinsky and eclecticism

Along with Ives, Stravinsky remains the quintessential twentieth-century composer in that he fearlessly incorporated into his music – as it suited him – all of the styles and elements then known. Impressionism, neoclassicism, folk music, jazz, and dodecaphony were all, at one time or another, incorporated into his music with startlingly original results. After the appearance of *Les Noces* (1914–23), which utilized Russian folk materials, he was applauded by the Russian press as a great champion of the Russian tradition established in the previous century by Mikhail Glinka, Piotr Tchaikovsky, Nicolai Rimsky-Korsakov, and others. But as his style evolved and his musical impulses became more cosmopolitan, the official communist press turned on him with a vengeance, as did many others. *Les Noces* became an aberration, while his later works – many of them also masterpieces – were viewed as abominations. The Russian communists, in particular, could not see that *Symphony of Psalms* (1930, revised 1948) – with its initial struggle to achieve consonance, the second movement's exquisite double fugue, and the triumph of Russian Orthodox mysticism in the finale – was a veritable storehouse of tradition. Many could comprehend neither the neoclassical originality of *Oedipus Rex* (1926–27, revised 1948),[3] nor the loving admiration of Bach exhibited in *Chorale Variations on "Vom Himmel hoch"* (1956). The acerbic religious objectivity of *Mass* (1944–48) offended some, while his adaptation of Schoenbergian dodecaphony in works such as *Threni* (1957–58) and *Requiem Canticles* (1965–66) was viewed as puzzling, if not troubling. Still, more musicians reacted positively to his music than not, and long after his death he remains one of the twentieth century's most influential composers. It is therefore important to remember that Stravinsky wrote choral music through-out his career, although he was not essentially a choral composer. In this he is like the others named above, whose collective work set the course of music during the century.

Among those who counted Stravinsky as a major influence was the Bavarian Carl Orff (1895–1982), who absorbed Stravinsky's driving, often asymmetrical rhythms to create a percussive style now referred to as Primitivism. His most successful work is the ever-popular *Carmina Burana* (1937), which weds secular medieval texts (in Latin, Old German and Old French) to Bavarian dance rhythms. Typical of other choral composers impacted by Stravinsky are the French Jean Langlais (1907–91), who was attracted by Stravinsky's often austere added-note harmonies; the Russian Georgy Sviridov (1915–98), who was profoundly influenced by elements of Stravinsky's Russian style; the Italian Luciano Berio (1925–2003), whose early works, in particular, are immersed in Stravinskian neoclassicism; the Chinese Bright Sheng (b.1955), whose propulsive rhythms and harmonic textures are informed by Stravinskian processes; György Ligeti (1923–2006), the great Austrian composer of Hungarian birth, whose attractive early folksong arrangements and Hungarian-inspired part-songs give no hint of the immense polyphonic constructs in his later avant-garde masterworks, *Requiem* (1963–65) and *Lux aeterna* (1966); and Krzysztof Penderecki (b.1933), whose *St. Luke Passion* (1963–66) – an amazing amalgam of the latest avant-garde devices and loving glances back at traditional modes of expression – stands as one of the twentieth century's most significant works.

At the turn of the twenty-first century, Stravinsky's procedures were still apparent, in a more subtle way, in the music of such composers as the Americans Morten Lauridsen (b.1943) and William Bolcom (b.1938). Like Stravinsky, both absorbed the work of previous masters before launching into their respective explorations of antique or popular genres. As Stravinsky learned the classical symphony before writing one, Lauridsen learned thoroughly the Renaissance motet, Italian madrigal, French cabaret song, and the Broadway musical before composing his loving, respectful, and occasionally mystical tributes: *Madrigali: Six "Firesongs" on Italian Renaissance Poems* (1987), *Chansons des roses* (1993), *Nocturnes* (2004), and various Latin motets (most notably 1994's *O Magnum Mysterium*). Bolcom cleverly parodied various styles of jazz and popular music, mixing them freely with postmodern effects, a collective technique made obvious in his sprawling *Songs of Innocence and Experience* (1984).

Gustav Mahler and the indestructibility of tonality

Although Mahler's music had retreated to the fringes of the repertoire until Leonard Bernstein revived it in the 1960s, his influence had still continued: his three great choral symphonies, No. 2 ("Resurrection," 1894), No. 3 (1898), and No. 8 ("Symphony of a Thousand," 1906) – each one different from the others – provided many more sympathetic bridges to the original example of Beethoven than did the earlier efforts of Berlioz, Mendelssohn, and Liszt. Beginning with Vaughan Williams's *A Sea Symphony* (1905) and continuing through the twentieth century, the genre would be exploited by composers whose art represented virtually all schools of twentieth-century composition, including Igor Stravinsky, Darius Milhaud (1892–1974), Leonard Bernstein (1918–90), Peter Mennin (1923–83), Alfred Schnittke (1934–98), Dmitri Shostakovich (1906–75), Luciano Berio, and Hans Werner Henze (b.1926).

More important, Mahler's stretching – but not breaking – of tonality comforted composers who were not inclined to follow Schoenberg or the avant-garde. Richard Strauss (1864–1949), Alexander Zemlinsky (1871–1942), Eric Zeisl (1905–59), and Paul Hindemith (1895–1963) are among those who created beautiful and challenging choral works whose tonal language sprang from the harmonic rhetoric of Mahler.

Further, composers such as Leonard Bernstein, Jan Hanuš (1915–2004), and Luciano Berio adapted more personal aspects of Mahler's aesthetic. In Bernstein's problematic masterpiece the Symphony No. 3 ("Kaddish," 1962, revised 1977), various Mahlerian devices of orchestration and musical gesture are combined with elements of American musical theater, jazz, serial technique, and chance. In Hanuš's *Ecce homo* (1977–78), touches of

Mahlerian harmony are combined with aleatoric writing and pre-recorded sounds. In *Sinfonia* (1968), Berio borrowed large chunks of Mahler's Second Symphony, around which he built a collage of sounds inspired by other wildly varying sources. In the last quarter of the twentieth century, as interest in minimalism increased and in serialism waned, many younger composers were attracted to these examples and utilized all manner of avant-garde devices within a tonal framework, good examples being: *Magnificat* (1995) by the German composer Wolfram Buchenberg (b.1962), and *Leonardo Dreams of His Flying Machine* (2000) by the American composer Eric Whitacre (b.1970).

Arnold Schoenberg and dodecaphony

As the twentieth century began, Arnold Schoenberg created the immense, sprawling *Gurrelieder* (1900–1), a work remarkable for its experimental combination of late German Romanticism and impressionistic textures and tone colorings. Like Mahler, Schoenberg was intent on continuing the German Romantic tradition, but whereas Mahler focused on a simplification of harmonic language to accommodate otherwise complex contrapuntal writing, Schoenberg concentrated on an intense chromaticization of the lines themselves. By the time *Friede auf Erden*, Op. 13 (1906) was completed, Schoenberg had realized the need to develop new ways of sustaining chromatic lines. This led first to atonal expressionism and ultimately to the formulation of his dodecaphonic technique, in which all twelve notes of the chromatic scale, as equal partners, replaced the hierarchy of tonal harmonic progression.

The first work utilizing this new technique was *Four Partsongs*, Op. 27 (1925), for mixed chorus (unaccompanied except for the last, which includes the exotic instrumental ensemble of violin, clarinet, mandolin, and cello). The twelve-tone technique had a profound influence throughout the century; composers such as Anton Webern (1883–1945), Pierre Boulez (b.1925), René Leibowitz (1913–72), Luigi Nono (1924–90), and Ross Lee Finney (1906–97), liberated by adherence to the technique's discipline, wrote compelling and difficult choral music.

But Schoenberg himself was not bashful about returning to tonality when it suited him, as in his two sets of German folksong arrangements, and the brilliant *Kol Nidre*, Op. 39 (1938). Moreover, this willingness to move in and out of dodecaphony provided a more enduring influence on younger composers, beginning with his own students: Viktor Ullmann (1898–1944), who created excellent folksong arrangements in Terezín during World War II; and Ernst Krenek (1900–91), who enriched the repertoire with choral works in styles ranging from twelve-tone to neo-Renaissance. Others who created interesting and often stunning choral music – thoroughly informed by twelve-tone technique, but not limited to it – include Luigi Dallapiccola (1904–75), Hans Werner Henze, Frank Martin, Boris Blacher (1903–75), Witold Lutoslawski (1913–94), and Iannis Xenakis (1922–2001).

In the late 1960s other composers, reacting negatively to atonal serialism, began writing in a style incorporating the simplest kind of diatonic harmonies coupled with hypnotic rhythmic structures. Among the leaders of this style, known as minimalism, were Philip Glass (b.1937) and Steve Reich (b.1936), who would each produce important choral works as minimalism evolved during the century.

Edward Elgar and the continuance of national traditions

When Elgar composed *The Dream of Gerontius* (1899–1900), in a world far removed from Arnold Schoenberg's, he probably did not realize that it was the culmination of nineteenth-century British music. In addition to its harmonic richness and lyrical beauty it contains three of the most brilliant passages in the choral repertoire: the double choir incantation pleading for the prayers of Old Testament heroes, the great demonic chorus "Cast aside, thrust," and the angelic chorus "Praise to the Holiest, in the Height." Having assimilated all that British music had to offer in the nineteenth century and comfortable in his style, Elgar, like his great contemporaries Sir Charles Villiers Stanford (1852–1924) and Sir Charles Hubert Hastings Parry (1848–1918), was not inclined toward the bolder innovations of the new century's avant-garde. Still, he continued to compose and influence younger British composers until his death.

Many of the British composers who carried forward the torch of tradition excelled in the composition of choral music. While some, such as Martin Shaw (1875–1958) and John Ireland (1879–1962), achieved moderate fame outside the British Commonwealth, theirs was essentially an insular art which, like Elgar and his contemporaries, avoided the "Shock of the New."[4] Others, like John Rutter (b.1945), embraced popular aspects of traditional British music to create part-songs, anthems, and folksong arrangements that captured a broad international audience. But there were also those who were able to combine their inclination toward nationalism with an interest in a new means of expression. Outstanding examples include Benjamin Britten (1913–76), Sir William Walton (1902–83), Malcolm Singer (b.1953), and James MacMillan (b.1959). Benjamin Britten's view of British musical tradition extended far beyond nineteenth-century Romanticism. Profoundly influenced by Henry Purcell (1659–95), his music is laced with textures, dotted rhythms, ritornelli, modal inflections, and cross-relations of the French baroque, as filtered through Purcell. Many of his choral compositions are standard repertoire, including *War Requiem* (1961), one of the twentieth century's greatest works, and the charming *A Ceremony of Carols* (1942). William Walton, whose music varies from the serious and dramatic part-song "Where Does the Uttered Music Go?" (1946) to the splashy and provocative cantata *Belshazzar's Feast* (1931), invigorated his essentially Victorian musical vocabulary with jazzy rhythms and spicy harmonies built from seventh and ninth chords. Malcolm Singer's choral works, both secular and sacred, are subtly informed by the Jewish modes; MacMillan's compositions, including the *St. John Passion* (2008), weave many modern trends into a uniquely British lyricism.

The tendency to carry traditions forward while gradually incorporating new elements can also be observed within other national schools. In Germany, for instance, nineteenth-century Romanticism flourished well into the new century in choral works by the aging Max Bruch (1838–1920), Max Reger (1873–1916), Georg Schumann (1866–1952), Hans Pfitzner (1869–1949), Richard Strauss, and others. This was supplanted – just before World War II – by a renewed interest in early Baroque forms and textures, as exemplified by the music of Johann Nepomuk David (1895–1977), Ernst Pepping (1901–81), Wolfgang Fortner (1907–87), and Hugo Distler (1908–42). Their primary inspiration was the early German Baroque composer Heinrich Schütz (1585–1672), and the Passions of Pepping and the smaller motet-like works of Distler are particularly transparent reflections of the earlier master's work. Neoclassical impulses asserted themselves after the war in the work of Siegfried Reda (1916–68) and others. In particular, Reda's impressive motet *Ecce homo aus dem 22. Psalm* (1950) was influenced by Stravinsky as well as by older German masters. The postmodern *Deus Passus* (2000) by Wolfgang Rihm (b.1952), informed by virtually all the compositional techniques associated with twentieth-century German music, perhaps represents the culmination of these tendencies.

In Russia, nineteenth-century nationalism was carried into the new century by Sergei Rachmaninov (1873–1943), Alexandr Kastal'sky, Pavel Chesnokov (1877–1944), Mikhail Ippolitov-Ivanov (1859–1935), and others. Rachmaninov's choral works, which are significant rather than numerous, include the cantata *The Bells* (1913, to a text by Edgar Allan Poe) and the brilliant *All-Night Vigil* (1915), which became internationally popular toward the end of the twentieth century. Kastal'sky, Chesnokov, and Ippolitov-Ivanov focused on the composition of sacred music. Under their guidance, new choral music in the styles of the St. Petersburg School (also known as the Common European Style, established early in the nineteenth century by Dmitri Bortniansky) and the more nationalistic Moscow School (established late in the nineteenth century by Mily Balakirev) continued until the Bolshevik Revolution. Liturgical composition was then severely curtailed until the last decade of the twentieth century. During the Soviet era, however, sacred choral music was still championed by Alexander Gretchaninov (1864–1956), who not only flew in the face of secular authorities but challenged the Orthodox religious establishment as well by calling for the inclusion of instruments in some of his liturgical works. Particularly provocative was *Missa oecumenica* (1944), a Latin mass with orchestra which represented an effort to bring the international religious community together during World War II.

The outstanding Soviet composers Sergei Prokofiev (1891–1953) and Dmitri Shostakovich (1906–75) composed several choral works in which tradition was necessarily viewed through the lens of Soviet realism. Whereas most of Prokofiev's choral music is too narrowly political to warrant much international attention today, the cantata culled from his wonderful score for Sergei Eisenstein's film *Alexander Nevsky* (1939) is still frequently performed. Shostakovich's numerous choral pieces meant to showcase Soviet values were often met with official censure. While his blatantly enthusiastic cantata *The Execution of Stepan Razin* (1964) was popular throughout the country, his 13th Symphony ("Babi Yar," 1962) – a somber reflection on life during World War II, including criticism of Soviet indifference to the slaughter of Jews – was banned from performance until Yevgeny Yevtushenko's text was changed.

Other important Russians whose choral music reflects national traditions include: Dmitri Kabalevsky (1904–87), Georgy Sviridov (1915–98), Rodion Shchedrin (b.1932), Alfred Schnittke, who contributed several important works, and Sofia Gubaidulina (b.1931), whose impressive *Johannes Passion* (2000) appeared at century's end.

In Latin America, composers successfully fused European choral concepts with local musical customs producing a variety of colorful pieces, some of which became internationally popular. Important works include *Chôro No. 10* (1925) by the Brazilian Heitor Villa-Lobos (1887–1959); *El sol* (1934) by the Mexican Carlos Chávez (1899–1978); *Psalm 150* (1938) and *Lamentations of Jeremiah* (1946), by the Argentine Alberto Ginastera (1916–83); *Misa criolla* and *Navidad nuestra* (both 1964) by the Argentine Ariel Ramírez (1921–2010); *Requiem* (1994) by the Puerto Rican Raymond Torres-Santos (b.1958); *Stabat Mater* (1997) and other impressive pieces by the Venezuelan Alberto Grau (b.1938); and the incredible *La passión según San Marco* (2000), by Osvaldo Golijov (b.1960), an Argentine of Romanian heritage who eventually moved to the USA.

In France, Darius Milhaud, Francis Poulenc (1899–1963), and the Swiss Arthur Honegger (1892–1955) – members of the group known as Les

Six – maintained the urbane sophistication associated with French music while incorporating polytonal, Latin American, and jazz elements into their exceptionally colorful choral music. Poulenc and Milhaud were particularly adept choral composers. Poulenc's *Quatre motets pour un temps de pénitence* (1938–39), *Quatre motets pour le temps de Noël* (1951–52), and the cantata-like *Gloria* (1959) are standard repertoire. Milhaud, in addition to enriching the repertoire with numerous part-songs, cantatas and other large choral-orchestral works, was also instrumental in the creation of Jewish liturgical music which could be performed in concert outside the synagogue. Honegger composed a number of large cantatas designed for radio performance, as well as the oratorio *Le roi David* (1921), one of the most popular large choral works of the century's first half, and the masterful and thought-provoking *Une Cantate de Noël* (1953).

Also in France, just after World War I, Nadia Boulanger became the century's most influential teacher of composition. Her students – including the Hungarian Erzsébet Szönyi (b.1924), the Norwegian Øistein Sommerfeldt (1919–94), the Lithuanian Antanas Račiūnas (1905–84), the Portuguese Jorgé Croner de Vasconcellos (1910–74), the Mexican Arnulfo Miramontes (1882–1960), the Canadian Gabriel Charpentier (b.1925), the Australian Peggy Glanville-Hicks (1912–90), and a veritable who's-who of American composers: Aaron Copland (1900–90), Roy Harris (1898–1979), Elliott Carter (b.1908), Daniel Pinkham (1923–2008), Robert X. Rodriguez (b.1946), Donald Grantham (b.1947), David Conte (b. 1955), and others – all returned home with highly individual, often progressive styles, mostly rooted in an affectionate understanding of their own country's traditional music. And all made important contributions to the choral repertoire.

Other composers whose choral music clearly exhibits the influence of national traditions include the Italian church composers Lorenzo Perosi (1872–1956), Domenico Bartolucci (b.1917), and Aurelio Porfiri (b.1968); the Israeli composers Paul Ben-Haim (1897–1984) and Aharon Harlap (b.1941); the Chinese composers Chen Yi (b.1953), Bright Sheng, and Tan Dun (b.1957); and the great Czech composers Jan Hanuš, Karel Husa (b.1921), and Petr Eben (1929–2007).

Ralph Vaughan Williams, Béla Bartók, Leoš Janáček, and the music of Truth

Serious scholarly interest in folk music had begun in Europe during the nineteenth century, and by its end some composers had started viewing folk music, in its purest forms, as the raw material for serious composition. Ralph Vaughan Williams in England, Béla Bartók in Hungary and Leoš

Janáček in Moravia were leaders in these investigations, and each would develop highly individualized styles that absorbed their respective folk traditions completely. Vaughan Williams worked in collaboration with Gustav Holst, Bartók with Zoltán Kodály (1882–1967), in the collection of folk tunes and each produced vivid and often inspiring original choral pieces in addition to superlative choral arrangements of folk songs, many of which became staples of the repertoire. Janáček was equally interested in folk texts. He described the marriage of text and tune in Moravian folk music as "the music of Truth," and he incorporated the spoken inflections of the Czech language into his music, which resulted in one of the most unique compositional styles of the twentieth century.[5] Their efforts were far removed from those who occasionally utilized folk music as a component in the continuance of classical tradition (see above). Rather, the melodic contours, harmonies, rhythmic stresses and formal structures of folk music were actually the bedrocks of their music. Works as varied as Vaughan Williams's *Five English Folksongs* (1913), Bartók's *Three Village Scenes* (1926) and *Cantata Profana* (1931), and Janáček's magnificent *Glagolitic Mass* (1926) and large, dramatic unaccompanied male choruses not only demonstrated, eloquently, the efficacy of their respective musical languages, but also provided inspiration for like-minded composers all over the world. Emīlis Melngailis (1874–1954) in Latvia, Jón Leifs (1899–1968) in Iceland, Lucrecia Kassilag (1918–2008) in the Philippines, Gil Aldema (b.1928) in Israel, Stephen Leek (b.1959) in Australia, Hyo-Won Woo (b.1974) in Korea, and the Haitian-American Sydney Guillaume (b.1982) represent only a handful of those whose choral music is rooted in native musical customs.

Ethel Smyth, Amy Beach, and the emergence of inclusiveness

In 1893, the English Ethel Smyth (1858–1944) composed a Mass in D. Two years later, in America, the slightly younger Amy Beach (1867–1944) composed her *Grand Mass in E-flat Major*. Both works were successful and both women continued to compose, soon earning the respect of their male peers. Smyth's mass was held in such high regard by Sir Donald Francis Tovey that he included a discussion of it in his five-volume treatise on musical analysis,[6] while Beach became one of the most celebrated American composers during the first third of the twentieth century. Both women's music fell into eclipse after their deaths, only to be revived during the last decades of the century.

Their work (which included numerous other choral pieces), though not ground-breaking in any musical sense, was nevertheless of utmost importance in the gradual changing of societal attitudes, not only in regard to gender, but also to race and musical genres. By the end of the twentieth century, women were counted among the world's prominent choral composers, including Rosalina Abejo (1922–91), Thea Musgrave (b.1928), Sofia Gubaidulina, Tania León (b.1943), Margaret Bonds (1913–72), Judith Lang Zaimont (b.1945), Tzippi Fleischer (b.1946), Libby Larsen (b.1950), Nancy Telfer (b.1950), Chen Yi, Sylvie Bodorová (b.1954), Eleanor Daley (b.1955), and Anna Thorvaldsdottir (b.1977).

In the twentieth century, the African-American spiritual, which had become internationally famous during the last third of the nineteenth century, became virtually institutionalized in choral arrangements by Hall Johnson (1888–1970), William Dawson (1899–1990), John Work (1873–1925), Jester Hairston (1901–2000), Moses Hogan (1957–2003), and others. As the century wore on and societal attitudes changed, the genre's stature was elevated from being a merely popular idiom to one of serious artistic utterance.

The other great musical contribution of African-Americans to world culture is jazz. Long before the Nazis' attempt to bind artistic expression in a straitjacket, jazz had been popular in Europe. And it was taken much more seriously there than in the United States, where many people viewed it as something only a notch or two above Devil worship. In Europe, classically oriented composers were experimenting with jazz at least as early as 1927, and since then have produced several interesting choral works incorporating the genre. Among them are: *The Rio Grande* (1927), a piano concerto with choir by Constant Lambert (1905–51); *Das Berliner Requiem* (1928) and *Kiddush* (1946) by Kurt Weill (1900–50); the oratorio *HMS Royal Oak* (1930) by Ervin Schulhoff (1894–1942), who was also bold enough to combine jazz with Schoenbergian techniques; William Walton's *Belshazzar's Feast* (1931); various works by Boris Blacher and Heinz Werner Zimmermann (b.1930); and the *Requiem* (1993) of Nils Lindberg (b.1933).

The first serious American attempts to incorporate jazz in choral music began about 1959 and focused on the introduction of jazz into the Christian liturgy. This was followed by settings of religious texts for concert purposes, including *Jazz Suite on Mass Texts* (1965) by the Argentine-American composer Lalo Schifrin (b.1932) and the important *Sacred Concert: In the Beginning God* (1965, second version 1968, third version 1973) by Duke Ellington (1899–1974). These works were widely criticized at the time,[7] but the concept of choral jazz stuck around, and by century's end vocal jazz ensembles and show choirs were common in American schools. Other American choral jazz works include the oratorios *The Light in the Wilderness* (1967) and *The Gates of Justice* (1970) by Dave Brubeck (b.1920), and the cantata *The Green House* (1991) by the Bulgarian-American composer Milcho Leviev (b.1937).

By the last quarter of the twentieth century, the increasing interest in vocal jazz and an overflow of enthusiasm for spirituals in the United States had resulted in the evolution of the gospel song (a product of nineteenth-century White revivalist movements) into a new genre called Black Gospel, which relied heavily on a call-and-response form ideally suited to choral singing. This genre, primarily influenced by rhythm and blues, also became internationally popular.

Impact of the world wars

The twentieth century's two world wars had a profound impact on choral music. During World War I, composers sought to sow the seeds of patriotism by means of choral works whose sentiments were either blatant (Ives's *They Are There!*) or thoughtful (Ravel's *Trois chansons*). Further, the conscription of young European males into the armed forces resulted in increased composition for women's voices, such as the outstanding series of small works composed by Leoš Janáček in 1916 (*Kašpar Rucky*, *Songs of Hradčany*, and *The Wolf's Track*).

Whereas the eighteenth and nineteenth centuries witnessed celebratory compositions at the conclusion of wars (such as Handel's *Dettingen Te Deum* and Brahms's *Triumphlied*), World War I resulted in a very different kind of musical commemoration. With the possible exception of the Agnus Dei in Beethoven's *Missa Solemnis*, there was scant musical precedent for warning against such events, while traditional requiem settings seemed inadequate to memorialize the enormity of this war's devastation and carnage. Therefore, large cantatas began to appear which often utilized poetry lamenting the waste of war, such as *Morning Heroes* (1930) by Arthur Bliss (1891–1975) and Elgar's *Spirit of England* (1916). This trend culminated in 1934 with Vaughan Williams's thoughtful *Dona Nobis Pacem*. Still, in German choral works from this period, such as Pfitzner's *Von deutscher Seele* (1922), one can sense a veiled resentment at the war's outcome.

During World War II, patriotic (or propagandistic) choral works were composed in all of the combatant countries, good examples being: the *Yellow River Cantata* (1939, revised 1941) by Hsien Hsing-hai (1905–45), *Along the Coast, Conquer the East* (1940) by Kiyoshi Nobutoki (1887–1965), *The Testament of Freedom* (1943) by Randall Thompson (1899–1984), *Six Choral Songs* (1940) by Vaughan Williams, *Das Jahr* (1940) by Ernst Pepping, and Prokofiev's *Alexander Nevsky* (composed shortly before hostilities began in Russia). An interesting twist on the patriotic cantata is Martinů's magnificent *Polni Mše* (Field Mass), composed in 1939 to honor Czech volunteers in the French army. It deals with a Czech soldier, riddled with doubt and hoping that God will recognize him in a foreign land.

Another work in this vein (and from the same time) is Michael Tippett's (1905–98) oratorio *A Child of Our Time* (1939–41), about the young Polish-Jewish assassin whose actions in Paris were manipulated by the Nazis into the nationwide riot on November 10, 1938 known as Kristallnacht, which is now generally viewed as the beginning of the Holocaust. This oratorio still merits attention, not only for its sympathetic treatment of the subject but also for its clever use of African-American spirituals.

Important works of spiritual resistance were also composed in countries occupied by the Nazis, such as Poulenc's *Figure humaine* (1943) and the heartfelt cantata *Lord, Your Earth is Burning* (1944) by the Latvian Lūcija Garūta (1902–77), which contains a particularly poignant setting of The Lord's Prayer.

Choral organizations had long been a part of Jewish life in Eastern Europe. Before, during and after World War I, Jewish worker choruses were occasionally invited by German orchestras to participate in performances of large choral/orchestral works. But when the Nazi era began, the activities of these choirs in Germany were curtailed. In the middle of 1933, the German propaganda ministry organized the Jüdische Kulturbund in order to isolate completely Jewish cultural activities. Within the umbrella of this organization, Jewish choruses, orchestras, and theatrical groups flourished until Kristallnacht and continued to function until early in 1941. While the Jüdishe Kulturbund was rather quickly prohibited from performing music by non-Jewish Germans, its ensembles were the only ones in Germany allowed to perform works by Jewish composers; on occasion, however, it managed without incident to present pieces by German composers, such as Karl Amadeus Hartmann (1905–63), whose compositions the Nazis labeled as "degenerate." Perhaps the Kulturbund's most important choral concert was the February 27, 1941 performance in Berlin of Mahler's Symphony No. 2 ("Resurrection"), given after the performers knew they would soon be transported to concentration camps in the East.[8]

The most heartrending choral activities took place in Nazi ghettos and concentration camps. The eastern ghettos generally maintained some forms of organized music-making (including choral singing) until they were liquidated. In some places, such as Kovno (Kaunas), Lithuania, concerts and plays were controversial,[9] but they were openly embraced in other ghettos. In Warsaw, for instance, concerts were not only publicly advertised but also received critical reviews in the ghetto press. Because of a shortage of performing venues, choruses there gave frequent concerts in any available space, including soup kitchens. Repertoire consisted of works from the standard choral repertoire, opera choruses (a particularly favored genre), and arrangements of traditional Yiddish and Hebrew songs. One of the last concerts before the liquidation of the Warsaw ghetto began in the summer of 1943 was given by a children's choir numbering well over one hundred, and included renditions of "Ani Ma'amin" ("I believe with unshakable faith in Messiah's coming; yet though He tarry, still He will come") and "Hatikvah," which would later become the national anthem of Israel.[10]

Choral activities in concentration camps varied considerably from place to place. In Buchenwald, for example, the commandant ordered a composition contest for the creation of a camp song that could, on his order, be sung by all inmates during morning roll call to drown out frequent spontaneous performances of the "Internationale" by communist inmates; the winning composition was "Buchenwaldlied," by Hermann Leopoldi (1888–1959) and Fritz Löhner-Beda (1883–1942).[11] About the same time (1938) in Dachau, Herbert Zipper (1904–97) and Jura Soyfer (1912–39) composed "Dachaulied," which was performed in secret by a unison male vocal ensemble, accompanied by various rustic instruments made by the inmates. As prisoners were transferred they took this song with them, so that it, like "Buchenwaldlied," became known in several camps.[12] In Sachsenhausen, choral singing, also in secret, is known to have been accompanied by choreography on at least one occasion.[13] In Le Vernet and Ravensbrück, the commandants staged talent shows, with each barracks – which were mostly divided along ethnic lines – producing an act of some kind.[14] Choral singing of folk songs was, therefore, a popular way of carrying out the commandant's orders. While most of these performances were likely sung in unison, the National Holocaust Museum in Washington, DC contains numerous manuscript examples from Buchenwald, and other camps, of TTBB arrangements of folk songs (primarily Yiddish and Polish) and Polish partisan songs.

Highly organized choral singing occurred in Theresienstadt (Terezín). During the war this ghetto camp, some forty kilometers northwest of Prague, contained the highest concentration of Jewish artists, musicians, and intellectuals in Europe. Public concerts, organized primarily by the Czech choral conductor Raphael Schächter (1905–45), ran the gamut of musical genres from opera and symphonic music to cabaret and big band jazz. There were at least nine choirs, including three children's choirs, a male choir, two choirs specializing in liturgical music, a chamber choir specializing in the folk songs of several nationalities, a large Czech-language choir (famous for its performances of Verdi's *Requiem* in 1944),[15] and a large German-language choir that performed, in addition to other works, Haydn's *Die Schöpfung* and Mendelssohn's *Elijah*.[16] Among the inmates were some exceptionally talented composers, including Viktor Ullmann (who also organized concerts), Gideon Klein (1919–45), and Pavel Haas (1899–1944), who each contributed fine choral works which survive, and are only now beginning to enter the repertoire.

The Nazis encouraged musical and theatrical performance in the internment camps established for captured American and British civilians. In Kreuzburg, for example, a Jewish educator named William Hilsley (1911–2003) composed the remarkable *Missa brevis in festo Nativitatis* as a Christmas gift for his fellow inmates. He also composed several cabaret musicals utilizing male-voice chorus.[17] After the war he continued to stage the musicals with his students at the Quaker International School in Utrecht, and allowed for performance of his male-voice mass by three-part treble or six-part mixed choir.[18]

The efforts of English and Dutch women held prisoner by the Japanese in Sumatra must also be mentioned. Under the leadership of Margaret Dryburgh and Norah Chambers, these women created a vocal orchestra that performed not only a variety of folksong arrangements, but also vocal arrangements made from memory of Chopin *Preludes*, Grieg's *Peer Gynt Suite*, and other standards of the European orchestral repertoire.[19]

The war's conclusion elicited numerous commemorative works. Even though not involved in the conflict, the Swiss government commissioned Frank Martin to compose the moving *In terra pax* (1944). Other pieces, such as Hindemith's *When Lilacs Last in the Dooryard Bloom'd: A Requiem for Those We Love* (1946), Milhaud's Symphony No. 3 ("Te Deum," 1946), and Jan Hanuš's *Song of Hope (On the Threshold of Tomorrow)* (1945–48), were also composed close to the war's end (Hanuš's work was actually suppressed by the Czech government until after the Velvet Revolution of 1989).[20] But several important compositions – Dmitri Kabalevsky's Requiem (1961–63), Shostakovich's Symphony No. 13 ("Babi Yar," 1962), and Benjamin Britten's *War Requiem* (1961), for instance – appeared after some time had passed. These pieces came into existence about the same time as works protesting nuclear war, including: *15 June 1960* by Machio Mamiyas (b. 1929) (1961, memorializing a Japanese student killed at an anti-American rally), *Threnody* (1966) by the Canadian R. Murray Schafer (b.1933), and a few years later *Noah* (1976) by Erik Bergman (1911–2006), one of the most important Finnish choral works. More recent additions to this list include the tenth symphony of Robert Kyr (b.1952), *Ah Nagasaki: Ashes into Light* (2005), and two fascinating pieces by Hans Werner Henze: *Orpheus Behind the Wire* (1983) a suite for unaccompanied chorus which places the Orpheus and Euridice tale in a concentration camp, and Symphony No. 9 (1995–96), a setting for chorus and orchestra of segments from Anna Seghers's novel *Das Siebte Kreuz*.

Among the earliest works specifically commemorating the Holocaust are Arnold Schoenberg's great *A Survivor from Warsaw* (1947); the masterful *Requiem ebraico* (1944–45) by his Austrian émigré compatriot Eric

Zeisl (1905–59); and the incredibly moving cantata about the Warsaw ghetto uprising *Di Naye Hagode* (1948) by the Polish-American composer Max Helfman (1901–63). Another important commemorative work is *Song of Terezín*, written in 1964–65 by the film composer Franz Waxman (1906–67). Consisting of gripping and insightful settings of several poems written by children in Terezín, it opened the floodgates for such works, many of which are by composers of marginal talent who somehow felt compelled to set the poem "I Never Saw Another Butterfly." Still, several other fine Holocaust-related choral pieces command attention, not the least of which are Alfred Janson's *Tema* (1966), Sylvie Bodorová's powerful oratorio *Juda Maccabeus* (2002), and the brilliant suite for unaccompanied choir *Chestnut Branches in the Court* (1999) by the young American composer David Cutler (b.1971).

The exemplary *Sacred Service* ("Avodath Hakodesh," 1930–33) by the Swiss composer Ernest Bloch (1880–1959) was the only composition based on Jewish texts that was known to the concertgoing public prior to World War II. After the war, however, a widespread interest in Jewish music developed, attributable not only to the Holocaust but also to a new willingness on the part of audiences to experience more adventuresome and inclusive programming. Liturgical works by composers such as Darius Milhaud and Mario Castelnuovo-Tedesco (1895–1968) began to be publicly performed, while conductors sought out pieces by the Italian Renaissance composer Salamone Rossi (1570-*c*.1630); various giants of nineteenth- and early twentieth-century synagogue music; and prewar émigrés to America, including Max Helfman, Max Janowski (1912–91), and Samuel Adler (b.1928); as well as new works by younger composers such as Malcolm Singer, Michael Isaacson (b.1946), David S. Lefkowitz (b.1964), and Coreen Duffy (b.1976).

Looking ahead

Jewish music was not the only previously marginalized repertoire to reach for the mainstream during the last decades of the twentieth century. As the influence of folk music and jazz continued, conductors were encouraged to program less Eurocentric repertoire. Composers in Korea, Australia, South and Southeast Asia, Venezuela, and Israel – often well known in their own countries – now discovered a rising demand for their music in other parts of the world as well. In the United States, at least, publishing companies flourished through the distribution of choral music from various African countries, Mongolia, and other locales relatively unknown to the West. The African-American spiritual increased in prestige, and minimalism – especially in the hands of John Adams (b.1947) – increased in popularity as it matured through the adaptation of a richer, more Mahlerian harmonic language.

After the explosion of new ideas in the early decades of the twentieth century, and the resistance to them exemplified by traditionalists and later by minimalists, the last third of the century gradually relaxed into an era where virtually nothing new was brought to the compositional table. Rather, choral composers experimented with various combinations of twentieth-century devices, eventually abandoning atonality and dodecaphony in favor of an essentially – but not exclusively – diatonic language (often derived from folk music or chant) which could be manipulated to function in association with any known compositional technique. Arvo Pärt (b.1935), James MacMillan, Tan Dun, and a few others were able to turn this situation to their advantage and create choral works of genuine originality. Some, such as Morten Lauridsen, chose to ignore trends altogether and developed exceptionally distinctive and inviting styles.

But many sought refuge in the harmonies and small forms of earlier centuries, or simply relied on easy aleatoric and/or minimalist gimmicks, interspersed with rich, impressionistic vertical sonorities and otherwise enveloped in unthreatening harmonic environments. A particularly favored device among younger composers of choral music (which threatens to become as common in the twenty-first century as the authentic cadence in the eighteenth) is the gradual creation of a (usually diatonic) chord cluster beginning with a single pitch and fanning outward in one or both directions, as in the impressive *Lucis Creator optime* (published 2001) of Vytautas Miskinis (b.1954). And, while it cannot be claimed that compositions consisting of these procedures necessarily sound alike, it is also true that identifying the work of most current composers through unique stylistic characteristics is frequently impossible. Still, if history is any guide, the strongest artistic personalities will eventually gain prominence, compelling new ideas will emerge and the future of choral composition will remain bright.

5 The nature of chorus

PAUL HILLIER

The English language has two perfectly good words to describe a body of singers: *chorus* and *choir*. They mean almost the same thing and are often used interchangeably, and yet there is a difference between them. Both words derive ultimately from the same source – the Greek χορός – but they entered the English language at different times and for very different reasons.

Choir is derived from the Old French *cuer*. According to the Oxford English Dictionary, the earliest English references to the word date from the fourteenth century. *Choir* refers originally to the place in the church where the service is sung and by extension to those who sing it. *Chorus* came into use during the sixteenth century directly from the Greek, along with many other new words ushered in by the Humanist revival of Greek culture. Its primary meaning is a group of dancers and singers. There is also the closely related meaning (which I will return to later) of the refrain or burden of a song, where those who have been listening join in.

Choir is therefore the thing – the group of people who sing together, and the particular part of a church where they do this. *Chorus* can also refer to a group (though not to a place), but it leads us towards the issue of what the function of a body of singers might be, in both a musical and a dramaturgical sense. In church it is the *choir* we notice processing in at the beginning of a service – we don't usually call them a chorus. In classical Greek drama it is the *chorus* that makes an entrance – we don't call them a choir even though, originally, they sang; if we speak of a Greek *choir* then we are identifying a group of singers by their nationality. In a concert situation these distinctions start to blur. We probably refer to the *choir* coming on stage – even if it's called the LSO Chorus – while those sections of music sung by the choir are called choruses, as in "The choir sang a chorus from Handel's Messiah." Mercifully, the two words are reunited in the phrase *choral music*.[1]

Despite this collision of meanings, which other languages are not troubled by, the underlying distinction is an intriguing one. As it is the nature of *chorus* I want to examine here, in the sense of its function in all kinds of performance contexts, I shall use *chorus* to denote a group of singers, unless some habit of expression redirects me to the monosyllabic *choir.* I crave the reader's indulgence, while assuring him or her that I am not trying to advocate any notion of correct usage!

The Greeks

Ancient Greek drama is the natural place to begin the examination, not because it marks the beginning of an idea, but because it has provided a model that has remained the blueprint for dramatic works with chorus throughout the modern era. When we describe a certain kind of chorus activity we refer to it as being in the manner of a Greek chorus, as found typically in the works of Aeschylus, Sophocles, and Euripides.

In his *Poetics* Aristotle tells us that the art of tragedy grew out of dithyrambs, narratives sung and danced by a chorus at festivals of Dionysos, while comedy (in the form of satyr plays) derived from songs sung around phallic emblems.[2] The actual nature of this evolution from ritual into drama is a matter of considerable scholarly debate, but its results have provided us with a reference point for the idea of the chorus as a defining element in certain kinds of theatrical performance.

The drama festivals, held at special times of the year and incorporating both tragedies and comedies, became competitions as well as celebrations. A wealthy citizen – called the Choregos – was given the honor and cost of selecting, costuming and training the chorus (fifteen persons was the norm in the time of Euripides and Sophocles) while the principal actors (one of whom might well be the author) were financed by the state.

All the performers were masked, but the chorus were usually dressed and masked identically and, once they had made their entrance, normally remained on stage throughout. They thus contributed to the drama at three levels: first, by witnessing and reacting to the action of the play as it unfolded; second, by interacting either as a group or through their spokesman, the chorus leader; and third, by commenting on the action and painting a more general view of the unfolding situation in choral odes that they simultaneously sang and danced.

When it voices its reactions, fears, and hopes, the Greek chorus generally expresses the kinds of things we would feel too if we were in the story with them. In this way we are not only told a tale, but given a point of identification as well, a place in the story. In a tragedy we do not identify with the hero or heroine, however deeply we sympathize with them. The essence of Greek tragedy is that the individual's fate is preordained. Oedipus does not know that he kills his father and marries his mother. But when the truth is uncovered and his wife/mother kills herself, he puts out his own eyes in horror at the actions he has performed. He has transgressed the bounds of what society and the gods can accept as normal. The chorus represents that normality, and the fumbling attempts we all make to try to understand what is happening to us, to fathom what the will of the gods really is.

Today

We can find some of these elements still echoed in modern choral performance, and not only at revivals of Greek drama. Inevitably however, a great deal has changed and, as the title of my chapter suggests, I want to understand the nature of "chorus" as it is today. And so sometimes when I go to a choral concert and sit in the audience, I set aside my professional interest in the music and the performance and focus instead on the chorus. It is after all a curious thing: a collection of individuals who present themselves as a single entity. Why are they there and what do they think they're doing? As a group they seem to represent some kind of authority, but what is the nature of that authority? And for us as audience, what is the nature of our response to this group – for the question is not only how do the singers see themselves, but how or to what extent do we see ourselves in them?

Superficially, of course, the questions can be answered quickly enough. The singers are there because they enjoy it and, if they are professionals, to earn money. Yet what a social microcosm they represent, what diverse roles they play, and what a distinguished history they belong to! – but does any of this matter to them? Usually this is not a question that bothers us, the audience: they are the chorus, and so they sing choral music, the "tuttis." Perhaps they're not good enough to be soloists, and this is one way in which they can still perform music without exposing themselves to individual scrutiny. But is that really all?

To address these questions I think we must go back to the physical core of the matter, which is the actual sound of voices in themselves. When we listen to an individual singer or speaker it is impossible to separate the sound of the voice from the person producing it. It is also impossible to separate any vocal utterance from having some kind of emotional source and carrying some kind of meaning, even if the emotion appears frozen or impersonal, indistinct or insincere, or even when what is uttered is non-sensical. We can never for a moment forget the human being whose voice we listen to. And this is true, I find, whether they are singing or speaking. Singing, however, is something more than speaking.

When we sing we put ourselves, however briefly, into a kind of enchanted place. No matter how self-conscious we are as singers, when we sing we become something other than what we normally are. We put on an invisible mask, which releases us from our normal identity, and leads us towards an expressive state that lies beyond our normal condition. This singing condition manifests itself in many different ways depending on the nature of the event and on the nature of the work. On the one hand we might think of a traditional folksinger, singing as if possessed by a song without necessarily enacting any of the roles or demonstrably evoking any of the emotions it contains. On the other hand we might think of the opera soloist or the Lied singer who aims to embody and enact the music with voice and appearance combined into one affective unity. In the middle we might place the concert singer, whose performance persona may encompass the role of a dramatic character, but is usually a more complex and fluid construction, a blend of the poet, the narrator, and something more generalized than a stage role but still enacted, sometimes to a considerable degree.

A musical event has a social function which ranges from pure theater to pure ritual, but usually partakes of both. In ritual events such as church services the singers fulfill a preordained function. They do not enact this in the way of a theatrical role: they are (we assume) sincere about what they say. If their words make a declaration of belief then, even though it is being said on our behalf, we expect them to believe and mean the words too. Nor do we expect them to interpret their roles in an individually personalized style. Tradition normally ordains the manner in which they sing, and because of their function we do not ask them to convince us of their beliefs.

On stage or in a concert hall our expectations are different, and so is the performance. The singers will use imagination and invention to bring their role to life, and their purpose is to entertain us. We do not expect them to believe what they sing, though we do expect them to convince us that their invented stage persona *does* believe.

But all concerts contain elements of ritual – not just as part of the performance, but in everything the audience experiences as it enters the building; as people take their seats, looking to see who's there, who's wearing what, who's with whom; and as the hush finally descends just before the artists enter. And usually the music itself and its style of presentation also have a certain preordained quality. Symphony concerts and opera performances contain profoundly ritualistic elements, and these are all part of the entertainment, even if we sometimes like to think otherwise. Similarly, one might ask what church service is without its sense of theater.

The nature of all these events is ambiguous and the singer's role in them is difficult to define.[3] Nevertheless, it is perhaps easier to investigate the solo singer's role and come to some conclusions, but the chorus is more mysterious. It is a kind of *community* that exists to sing, that identifies itself by uttering harmonious sounds. Yet the chorus also has its persona, the chorus singers also enter some kind of special state, and the chorus also has something of the same range of dramatic possibilities. But all of these are circumscribed by the fact that the chorus, no matter how few, is a collective entity – otherwise it is not a chorus.

Opera and oratorio

I now want to look more closely at how the chorus functions in various musical situations, beginning with drama (both staged, as opera, and unstaged, as oratorio), then as part of the liturgy, and finally when music is played for pleasure in private or in concert.

Opera and oratorio were created around the same time in late sixteenth-century Italy. Both of them were directly influenced by Greek drama – opera emerging from the work of the Camerata, a group of artists and intellectuals mostly based in Florence, and oratorio in Rome – though in both genres there were other influences at work too.

The Camerata sought to revive ancient Greek tragedy, but they saw themselves first and foremost as being in the musical vanguard, seeing where the future lay and actively working for it. Their research into ancient Greek drama and its music was motivated not only by scholarly zeal, but also as a means of establishing certain priorities that would renew musical style and advance it securely in the right direction. Its leading members – Giovanni Bardi, Giulio Caccini, Vicenzo Galilei, Girolamo Mei – inveighed against the improprieties of imitative counterpoint for the way in which it obscured the sense of the words. The many voices of polyphony, they maintained, prevented the music from moving the listener's affections (to borrow the terminology of that epoch). In a letter to Caccini, Bardi castigates modern composers for apparently thinking it a mortal sin to compose music in which the parts were "heard to move with the same notes, the same syllables of the verse, with long and short notes on the same beats at the same time." In fact he is accurately forecasting what would become one of the hallmarks of choral writing in the first half of the seventeenth century.[4]

The Camerata valued the chorus, provided its music did not obscure the words but arose instead directly from them (as they surmised it had in Greek drama). They also recognized its scenic value: "the chorus is a very great ornament because of both its music and its dancing."[5] And they thought it well worth reviving: "Because Aristotle said that the music given to the chorus was a great enhancement to the tragedy . . . let us do our best to come as close to it as we can."[6] They had clear views on the subject of ensemble singing: "let us now speak of the difference that ought to be observed between solo and ensemble singing, so that we do not do as someone who in part-singing thinks of nothing but to have his own voice heard, as if those who are listening came just to hear his squealing. They do not realize or remember perhaps that singing well in ensemble is simply uniting one's own voice with others, making with them a single body."[7]

The work of the Camerata was transcended by Monteverdi who showed, with unprecedented intensity and psychological depth, how the new musical style could be joined to drama to create a new art form. I want to take a quick look at how Monteverdi uses the chorus, focusing briefly however not on an opera, but on a little chamber work that was published in a book of madrigals: the *Lamento della ninfa* from *Madrigali guerrieri et amorosi* (1638, poem by Ottavio Rinuccini).

This work is sung by four singers: a soprano and a group of three male singers who function as a chorus. The piece has three distinct sections. In the first the chorus sets the scene and describes the nymph emerging from her "humble dwelling" pale and disturbed, crushing flowers as she wanders to and fro, lamenting the loss of her lover who has abandoned her. In the second section the continuo plays a ground bass of four descending notes, above which the soprano sings the nymph's lament. But the chorus watches her, and interjects with cries of sympathy: "*Ah Miserella, sorrowful one! tanto gel soffrir non puó – such coldness cannot be borne.*" The lament ends, and the chorus then sings a short conclusion. It is a very effective little piece, and although it is published in a book of "madrigals," it offers a kind of operatic scene in miniature. Unstaged (though it could easily be staged) it is a representation in the special mode of semi-imaginary theater, and the role of the chorus – here just three singers – is utterly central; indeed the soloist only sings, in effect, because the chorus quotes what she says.

Another chorus work of the same general period but written for a very different context is Schütz's *Sieben Letzte Worte* (c.1658). I call it a chorus work, even though it is mostly sung by individual voices, for it is presented by a chorus whose individual singers take turns to adopt roles – so that the story may be properly presented – but who sing the opening and concluding words altogether. The work does not need a *separate* chorus for this purpose: Schütz carefully designs the work so that all the chorus singers have their individual moments, but the work remains in the keeping of that small group of singers. Whether we see them as soloists who also sing together, or as a group who take solo roles is not important; it is an ensemble piece in the fullest sense of that word.

The most appropriate term for Schütz's work is in fact *oratorio*, though the word did not come into regular use in Germany until around 1700. In their early days opera and oratorio can be seen as two aspects of the same idea, even though they emerged from slightly different backgrounds. The essential difference between them is that an oratorio is usually unstaged and tends to be based either on a biblical story or a mythological story that is strongly ethical in its message, while an opera was most often based on mythology and was, of course, staged. Another strong feature is that most oratorios are built around the use of a chorus. Oratorio is in essence a theater not for the stage, but for the ear and in the mind's eye. Opera too had its chorus, but in time the function of the chorus frequently diminished to a walk-on role, while in oratorio it has remained a defining presence.

The oratorio acquired its name from the place in Rome where such works were first performed: prayer halls or "oratorios." It was the Florentine Philip Neri (canonized in 1622) who in the 1550s began a series of prayer meetings with readings, discussions and the singing of *laude* (the latter also of Florentine provenance). The role of music was encouraged, not least because it attracted listeners who might stay on for other parts of the meeting. One of the most important musical occasions was the *oratorio vespertino*, following Vespers on Sundays and feast days, and held indoors during the winter months. By the turn of the century the musical content had expanded to include the presentation of dialogues, and it is these that contained the seed of the oratorio in miniature: a handful of characters being represented by singers who also sang together in concluding choruses. Eventually longer compositions were presented, either two separate works or one longer piece in two parts, with a sermon in between.

Among the more important composers of these early oratorios are Giovanni Francesco Anerio and, in the next generation, Giacomo Carissimi. The ongoing history of the oratorio is of course far beyond the scope of this chapter, but we should perhaps add that it was with Handel and in England that the later concept of the oratorio, as most of us will have encountered it, took shape. And it was through the process of commemorating Handel (and in England) that the first massive choral gatherings took place and finally severed any lingering connection between the choir standing in massed ranks behind the orchestra, and those mythical beings at the very front of the stage who enter the musical fray only when it is time to sing their arias.[8]

In Handel's time the chorus was still mostly an assembly of professionals, featuring boy sopranos and male altos well into the nineteenth century. In the English provinces too, professionals continued to be engaged for choral work – often a mixture of local cathedral singers and, with the advent of the railway, professionals brought in from London. But inevitably the contribution of amateur singers grew apace, as did the formation of singing clubs and madrigal societies. In many parts of the country, choral singing became a very popular social activity, not only in fashionable places such as London and Bath, but also in the newly industrialized and rapidly expanding urban centres in the Midlands, in and around modern Birmingham, Manchester, and Yorkshire. By the end of the nineteenth century the world of choral music had acquired a resolutely amateur identity, with large amounts of activity well into the early part of the twentieth century. Today the number of dedicated amateur choral singers worldwide remains impressively large, and the variety of countries in which they are active is perhaps even more widespread, but in those places that were formerly the most active centers choral singing has waned in comparison to its former glory, making it hard to imagine now the social prestige of choralism in those days or to appreciate the very deep local pride that was taken in choral singing.[9]

Church music

In dramatic productions – whether staged opera or unstaged oratorio – the role of the chorus is determined both by the requirements of the story itself and by the use made of the chorus as a structural tool that has the flexibility to move outside the story and mediate between the protagonists and the audience. In either case, although the chorus may be used with subtlety to carry out complex musical tasks, the nature of its role is easy enough to ascertain at any given moment, and it remains the task of the chorus singers simply to fulfill their obligations so that the drama can be as effective as possible. A very different kind of chorus serves the needs of the church and its liturgy: different, that is to say, in the nature of its obligations and in the role of the singers.

In a church service, music is first and foremost an extension of prayer. In some services or parts of the service everybody sings, led perhaps by a priest or by a small select group – a choir – which at other times also sings alone. When there is such a choir, the singers are not normally there to entertain; no matter what degree of excellence is expected of them, they are there to take part in a ritual. If there is an audience then it is formed by themselves and those on whose behalf they sing, but ideally their work remains an offering, not a performance. There are of course moments in some services when it is accepted that a performance is given, but these are interludes in the liturgical process rather than an essential part of it.[10]

For centuries the church's music was monophonic chant, sung either responsorially (with a lead singer answered by the full chorus), or antiphonally, with the singers divided in two groups and singing in alternation. Most chants, including psalms chanted antiphonally, are begun by a single voice, whose opening phrase is both the beginning of the song and an invitation to others to continue it. And this basic pattern of exchange, whether responsorial or antiphonal, lies at the core of the liturgy, the act of response acknowledging and affirming what has just been sung. While it is no doubt expedient to share the tasks in such a way, it is also an expression of what the church service is about: a gathering together, a meeting of minds, a sharing of experience.

One can also chant alone of course, but as soon as there are two people then the process begins to make sense in every way. A circle is created and indeed completed; singing that by itself is bare, and simply continues, suddenly has a shape that is musically satisfying; the alternation of two voices, however similar they may or may not be, offers a profound variation from one verse to the next; significantly, there is also the idea that something shared is also something witnessed. Two singers chanting in alternation, not as a performance, or as an entertainment, but as something to be done, and done together, is this not also the beginning of being a chorus? They do not sing at the same time, but they are singing together in the sense that they make one thing, and if one of them stops then the circle is broken.

The song game

We have seen briefly how the chorus functions in a dramaturgical context and also considered its role in the church, in a liturgical context. Now I want to look at what the chorus is when people make music for pleasure: folk music, art music composed for private use as chamber music, and art music for public use as concert music.

In European folk traditions, one of the oldest forms of singing together was the ring dance. It barely survives today, though remnants linger of the tradition of singing ballads in a ring – for example in the Faroe Islands.[11] The ring dance was widely disseminated throughout Europe, and while the manner of it varied from place to place, the essential elements – the circular motion of dancing in a ring, and the division of the group into leader and chorus – were the same.

For its influence on the development of composed music one of the most important examples of ring-dance singing was the *carol*, particularly as found in medieval France and England.[12] The contrast between the solo verse and chorus was reflected in the nature of the dance itself:

> a chain, open or closed, of male and female dancers . . . moved to the accompaniment of the voice . . . the whole procedure was under the direction of a leader . . . who sang the stanzas of the song . . . [while] the ring moved to the left. At the close of each stanza the entire company of dancers would respond with the refrain . . . dancing in place. Then, as the circle revolved again, the leader would sing the following stanza, and so on.[13]

In the later Middle Ages the carol was adopted by Franciscans wanting to use indigenous forms to displace pagan traditions, while yet harnessing their appeal to the common people. The fifteenth-century English poly-phonic carol retained many aspects of the carol's early origins, particularly its form, but gradually acquired more musical sophistication. By the end of the fifteenth century we find that the carol has evolved into a highly developed genre that clearly belongs to court and collegiate circles while still retaining traces of its humble origins. It is particularly in the burden (or chorus) that these traces are most evident.[14]

As in the ring dance, children's singing games blend song and dance together into one activity. The song games are passed down from one generation of children to the next, bypassing the adult world, though the tradition seems to be much reduced nowadays. Some fifty years ago Willa Muir recorded a vivid account of her own experiences, describing the singing games she played in the school playground as a child.[15] She describes the playground as a magic space where the teachers did not come and attempt to control their play. When the children held hands and danced in a circle, or linked arms to advance all together in a row, they established "a common flow of feeling" that in turn released "imaginative energies" that needed to acquire substance. The form of the game was like a shape embodied simultaneously in the song and the dance, and the whole process with its rhythms and waves of feeling was subconsciously felt rather than consciously understood. This shape therefore determined how the children's feelings were expressed, just as the playing of the game engendered the nature of those feelings. "This," Muir reports, "set a distance ... between our ordinary selves and the selves absorbed in the game. In a sense we were liberated from our ordinary selves. That was part of the satisfaction."[16]

This feeling of liberation from one's normal state of being recalls the idea suggested above that to sing is also to place oneself in a special place, and that singing in chorus is if anything more powerful because of its communal nature and the subservience to "a common flow of feeling."

Many of the children's songs Muir describes have the same kind of alternating principle as the ring dances, whether between solo and tutti or a division into two larger groups. She goes on to discuss the ballad repertoire – especially that of the Anglo-Scottish border regions – where again one can observe the structural significance of the refrain, also called the burden or chorus. The lines of the refrain are sometimes in a different meter from the verses and their meaning may be tangential to the story.[17] The words are usually the same from one verse to the next so that in print the refrain is often given only for the first verse, and thereafter one simply has to remember that it's there. In performance of course it is a different matter. We respond to the pattern of alternation as a perfectly natural aural experience, although most of us will skip the refrain when reading to ourselves alone. We may be cheating ourselves, but this is natural enough – with no one else around there is no exchange to be made, no lead singer needing a rest, no dance steps to carry out, and our attention naturally focuses on the story.

In these singing games and other traditional kinds of song closely related to the dance, the function of a singing chorus is clearly reflected in the structure of both the text and the music. The nature of the chorus here is extremely clear, and is built around the same kind of solo/chorus duality that we find also in oratorio, opera, and liturgical music. The chorus represents a communality of feeling, and this is mirrored in the musical and poetic structures where the chorus is the refrain, the constant element returned to between each individualized verse.

The concert game

I have described opera and oratorio, church music, and certain traditional games involving song. But what most choirs and vocal ensembles do is to sing concerts, often alone and unaccompanied by instruments. They draw on a large and widespread repertoire, drawn from many centuries and an ever-growing variety of countries. Some of the music, in being transferred from its original dramatic or ritual context, loses much of the significance that prompted its composition.[18] However a lot of the music – especially from the past two hundred years – was composed directly for concert performance, no other purpose being imagined, and its function is purely aesthetic in the broadest sense.

This repertoire of choral songs is essentially music where the choir sings the whole work. Like the solo art song, choral songs aim to express the mood and meaning of the words, and they stand alone as pieces of music. The choir here presents a self-contained musical world, no longer part of something else, such as an opera, oratorio, or church service. And at this point, with no other performers present, the very notion of "chorus" becomes profoundly ambiguous. It is perhaps this perspective more than any other that has led me to question the assumed identity of choral singers, and to seek to understand what purpose lies behind the use of many voices to project a single text together. Here I find that the element of play, which is present in all music, becomes essential in framing an answer to my questions about the nature of chorus.

To speak of music as play should not be seen as an attempt to trivialize it. Artistic creativity begins and continues in play, and music can only be fully understood by contemplating it as a heightened form of playing a game. We speak of "playing music": and the elements that make up a musical work – its motifs, patterns, rhythms, harmonies, textures, tempos, and dynamics – are the invisible playthings with which a musician plays that game. It is often a serious and profound game, and moves our emotions at depths far greater than those stirred by what we more conventionally call games, but nonetheless music cannot exist without the element of play, properly perceived and evaluated.

In his book *Homo Ludens*, the Dutch historian Johan Huizinga described music as "the highest and purest expression of the *facultas ludendi*."[19] Play is a creative instinct in which we all share. It is something that manifests itself in sacred myths and rituals as well as in the arts, in addition to the more quotidian games we are happy to regard as "mere" play. As Huizinga points out, the phenomenon of play is not simply something we find in human cultures along with other things, but is rather "one of the main bases of civilisation."

Following Huizinga's description of play we can observe that musical activity is something not commonly regarded as materially useful or even necessary. It is an activity that takes place within certain limits of time and space, where accepted rules and procedures are followed, or new ones are freshly invented. The music-making mood is one of rapture and enthusiasm and may be sacred or festive according to the occasion. A feeling of exaltation and tension accompanies the performance, mirth and relaxation follow.[20]

In speaking of music as a game, I am thinking not so much of the exterior, ludic quality of virtuosity, nor of extrovert "playful" styles of expression, but rather of an interior quality of play that operates within the music itself, and of the performers' penetration of this inner world and their bringing it to expressive life so that others can enjoy it too. This is the "game" of music at the highest level, as played by Byrd in his motets, Bach in his cantatas, Beethoven in his piano sonatas, Stravinsky in his ballets, and so on.

Playing music involves an ongoing exchange between the concept of the musical work and the performing of it. A constant flow of tension and release takes place between the elements involved (the musical ideas) and the process of realizing them. Furthermore, this aspect of music as play, as something done for its own sake, only fully emerges where there is an element of performance – an exchange both between performers and between performers and audience – and the more we remove music from a sacred context the more we focus on the element of play.[21] Playing music to oneself, or to friends, or as a public performance, partakes of a game which is more integral than performance as part of a drama or ritual. This game, the concert game, is essentially secular – and sacred music is secularized, and its nature is therefore modified, when presented as a concert.

A lot of the music we perform today, especially "early music," was originally intended for private consumption. The performance of such music makes best sense as a kind of game: a long way removed from the children's singing game or the carol danced and sung in a ring, and the work itself is far more of a self-conscious creation, but ultimately the same purposes are served. The presence of an audience extends the game, giving it a more complex social character, but the fundamental image is still that of play in the sense described by Huizinga. The challenge for today's singers, presenting such vocal chamber music in a public concert, is to find a way of performing that retains the original intimacy, while opening out the circle to include the audience as well.

We do however encounter peculiarities. When a group of singers performs a love song composed, say, for four voices and lute by John Dowland, and performs it to an audience, not just in the presence of others, but necessarily projected outwards to the audience, what is the role of those four singers? How do they see themselves with regard both to what they are doing, singing in a group, and to the audience that is watching and listening? If the same song is sung as a solo with lute accompaniment then we assume and anticipate that the singer embodies the persona of that song, becomes either the poet as maker of the text, or represents (impersonates, imitates) the lover himself. With just one singer this attitude is not only natural, it is expected (in an art song anyway), and the relative success of the performance will be judged in accordance with the manner in which this impersonation takes place. When the four singers perform the same text together, to what extent do they represent the lover? Is it not absurd for each performer to do so simultaneously in front of an audience? Is the lover somehow fragmented into four persons at the same time?

I don't think that singers worry too much about these questions of identity, and neither does the audience. We all accept the conventions involved. But clearly there is a marked difference between the solo and the quartet performance, though the music used is basically the same. In the quartet version the performance is more about the text, as poetic construction, than it is a dramatic impersonation. In fact as a quartet the singers are singing as a chorus. They present the material that joins the text together musically, which has indeed become the means of realizing the text. The music has perhaps even displaced the text and become the main reason for the performance and the text has become only an accident, each vocal part contributing differently to the whole.

If the Dowland song is sung not by four singers but by a choir of twenty or forty, what happens to it, and what do the singers make of it? The sound will inevitably thicken and a greater range of dynamics becomes possible (this may be stylistically anachronistic, but that is not the point.) It becomes a choral part-song, and the performance will tend towards something a bit different. The soloist's performance identified the singer with the song, either as lover, or narrator, or something of both. The quartet may have partly achieved this kind of identity, but the performance will also have become more of a game – the performance will be partly about the quartet performing together. The fully choral performance will be about the choir as a community performing the song; identity and meaning will have shifted away somewhat from the poetic substance towards something more objective and, in a sense, more purely musical.

The chorus game

What "game" does a chorus play that other musical performers cannot? First let us be clear that by "chorus" here I mean either a group of solo voices, or several voices, or many; second, that it is the collective nature of the group that matters, not the actual number of people in it; and third, even so, that there is of course a vast difference between a quartet and a massed choir of four hundred.

The chorus shares with the solo singer and the actor the use of voice and the presence of language, and therefore plays some of the same language games that constitute the art of poetry and acting. But a solo singer is usually heard with accompaniment of some kind, whereas a chorus often sings alone and makes all the music itself. In a cappella music the chorus can be both theme and accompaniment, foreground and background, melody and harmony, tune and counterpoint. But, accompanied or not, a chorus can intensify the meaning of a text in ways that a single singer cannot. It can present multiple versions of the same idea (which is usually verbal as well as musical), and it does so through various kinds of repetition, variation, and contrast, and by sheer weight of numbers. Even when a musical idea is imitated but not actually altered, the entrances of different voices always introduce some new element and change our sense of what has gone before. The multiple and sometimes simultaneous repetition of words expands their rhetorical significance, which is further enhanced by the authority that emanates readily from the presence of a group or crowd, be it threatening or reassuring, lamenting or celebratory.

The chorus that sings a love song sings the details, tells the story, but offers it as part of a shared experience. This manifold style of utterance magnifies the experience for performers and audience alike. It is not a private utterance, even when the song text would suggest otherwise. The singers may sing for themselves, but the experience is always a collective one as well, and the song is experienced as a social act, a shared reenactment of the story – though of course this does not negate the individual reactions and feelings of each singer and listener. As the number of singers increases, the subject matter may become of secondary importance. This usually means that the social ingredient has become more significant – the game starts to change. The music and the words still "matter," they are still being "played," but they are being used for another purpose, in a game that is more social and socializing.

Endgame

Until around 1800, choral music retained its intimate relationship with the solo voice.[22] The disposition of voices in terms of range and number was typically the same for both solo and tutti sections, and there is plenty of evidence to show that the chorus consisted simply of the soloists.

This arrangement existed not as a matter of convenience, but by intention and as standard practice. A few more singers might be added in the tuttis, perhaps to mark an important occasion, but this was usually just one of several options. Even when a chorus in the modern sense of several singers to a part was used, it was normally small by later standards.

Early in the nineteenth century the meaning of *chorus* started to change. A fertile tradition of large choirs developed in which the singers were mostly or even wholly amateur. The nature of oratorio composition adapted itself so perfectly to this new kind of instrument that the word *chorus* became identical with the idea of a large group of singers of miscellaneous abilities. To the extent that earlier music continued to be performed, it became normal to sing it with the newer type of large chorus. Even madrigal societies customarily sang what had once been chamber music in gatherings of forty or fifty people.

Fundamentally this is still how most people outside the music profession see the chorus, as a large motley collection. The truth of course is far more nuanced and complex. Thanks in part to the revival of earlier performance practices, and to the rise of smaller professional ensembles who commission new works to suit their new identity, and thanks also to the bewildering range of music now being contemplated (whether rooted in jazz, pop, or non-Western musics), the repertoire is now more diverse than ever.

Nonetheless, today most choral music has become detached from any social purpose it might once have belonged to, and must make its effect in one rather specific arena: the public concert. At the same time, and perhaps accordingly, professional choruses and ensembles find it increasingly difficult to maintain a place for themselves in the modern market.

For some of them the situation is even critical. I think the way forward lies, not in commissioning more new works that depend on the status quo, but in reimagining what it is the chorus does, or can do, and shaping new works accordingly. Choral music as a *repertoire* is one thing, a list of pieces. The *nature* of chorus is something more mysterious, more intricate, more polyphonic in its implications than the words *choral music* suggest. The nature of chorus is like the refrain in a song: it represents what is known, the place for everyone to join in, the marker of sections, the place where the group says "yes" to the individual, the beginning of the circle and the end.

PART II

Choral music the world over

6 Choral music and tradition in Europe and Israel

LEO SAMAMA

A quick personal scan of the choral world in Europe at large, between Moscow (Russia) and Reykjavik (Iceland), indicates that more than 30 million Europeans, approximately 4 percent of the population, participate in choral music at the beginning of the twenty-first century. Europe's long-standing choral tradition has consisted since as early as the 1830s until well after World War II of both a musical and a socio-political component. These components are largely interconnected, as for example when a composer writes choral music in which the social and political circumstances of its performance – for example, singing together for a political event or singing in a choir which is formed by a specific professional group such as firemen or diamond cutters – are incorporated. Since the 1960s this socio-political tradition has diminished.

Well into the twentieth century, most choirs, except for opera choruses and later radio choirs too, were composed of amateurs. Before World War II, some professional chamber choirs were founded primarily to perform a cappella music. After the war, however, some of the best amateur choirs (for example, the Berlin-based Ernst Senff Chor, which is now semi-professional, the Arnold Schoenberg Chor in Vienna, and the London Philharmonic and the London Symphony choirs) began to perform on a level that is difficult for even professional choirs to attain. The main difference between amateurs and professionals is that professional symphonic and professional chamber choirs offer full seasons and perform a broad repertoire, and are thus comparable to professional symphony

For this chapter I am indebted to the following: Veronika Bvrar, Mihela Jagodic and Marko Studen (Slovenia), Inara Jakubone and Elina Karaseva (Latvia), and Hild Borchgrevink (Norway). Babette Greiner (Netherlands) has been an informative and critical colleague for several years within the Tenso Network. With her help all members of Tenso and associated choirs have sent necessary and useful information about their choirs and the choral world in their respective countries. And last but certainly not least I thank John Lydon, who made me aware of what I meant to write but too often missed by an inch because of my lack of fluency in English. He proofread and corrected the text with wisdom and insight.

Most information in this chapter has been brought together from either the websites of the departments of culture of each country or the Music Information Centers (MIC) of these. Apart from these, some websites of major choral foundations or European platforms for choral singing provide figures on choral singing in Europe and several individual countries. Major surveys on the situation of choral music in Europe during the last decades of the twentieth century have not yet been undertaken.

orchestras. Another difference is that professional choirs employ only fully trained professional singers.

A further difference between amateur and professional choirs lies in the repertoire they perform. Although the situation has begun to change in recent decades, most amateur choirs focus on traditional repertoire, while professional choirs, certainly those connected to broadcasting companies, devote most of their seasons to contemporary repertoire. Due to this specialization, and because of the skill of these professional choirs, the musical demands of contemporary choral works have become greater than ever. From the 1950s to the 1980s, many composers began to experiment with new vocal techniques, new sounds, and new structural principles. These experiments considerably changed the repertoire and sharply sepa-rated professional choirs from the amateur choral world.

In the late twentieth century, the repertoire of the thousands of choirs in Europe began to broaden. Composers and conductors could now draw inspiration not only from the classical Western canon, but also from the music of new immigrant populations and from contemporary Western popular music, resulting in a plethora of musical styles. Many composers devote themselves exclusively to choral music, and amateur and profes-sional singers throughout Europe participate in a variety of choral ensembles.

Choral music since 1945: Janus's head

Shortly after 1945, many composers started to experiment with new vocal techniques and the limits of the new vocal ensembles' virtuosity. With their brilliant scores for twelve singers, the French composers Olivier Messiaen and André Jolivet invented what they called the "orchestre vocal," each singer being a soloist and an ensemble singer at the same time. Messiaen's *Cinq rechants* (1949) and Jolivet's *Épithalame* (1953) were the first of many demanding scores for such an ensemble. Beginning in the late 1950s, composers such as Luigi Nono (*Il canto sospeso*, 1956, and *Cori di Didone*, 1958), Dieter Schnebel (*Für Stimmen [... missa est]*, 1958–67, *Maulwerke*, 1968–74), Hans Werner Henze (*Jüdische Chronik*, 1960, and *Orpheus behind the Wire*, 1983), Krzysztof Penderecki (*Stabat mater*, 1962; *Passio Secundum Lucam*, 1966, and *Canticum canticorum Salomonis*, 1970), György Ligeti (*Lux Aeterna*, 1966, and *Drei Phantasien nach F. Hölderlin*, 1983), and Heinz Holliger (*Die Jahreszeiten*, 1975–79) continued to develop new vocal techniques. Many sounds produced by the human voice were researched and incor-porated into new scores. By 1980 many of these new techniques had been introduced into new choral music for amateurs through the music and didactic writings of composers such as R. Murray Schafer (*The Tuning of the World*, 1977, and the theatrical piece *Jonah*, 1979).

During the last quarter of the twentieth century, even more styles and techniques became available to composers, who became increasingly interested in researching past techniques and incorporating them into new ones. Styles and techniques of all sorts competed as well as coexisted with one another. From the 1970s onwards, composers, performers, and audiences alike could discern an ever-larger repertoire consisting of (a) new new music (the contemporary avant-garde), (b) new old music (the results of ongoing research into unfamiliar music from the past), (c) old new music (the output of contemporary composers uninterested in writing avant-garde music) and (d) old old music (the known and proven fruits of the Western canon). Thus the choice of repertoire became an increasingly complex issue for composers, conductors, educators, and singers. By the end of the century, the controversies yielded a thrilling but overwhelming amalgam of possibilities; amateur and professional choirs alike began to specialize in the music of a particular style or time period in order to give their repertoire a sense of focus.

During the last quarter of the twentieth century, classical choral music has been augmented by choral arrangements of popular music. Since the choral conductor and educator Clytus Gottwald asked in the early 1990s how it was possible that a conductor who performed Krenek's masterly *Lamentations* (the summit of dodecaphonic vocal music) "could descend to Bortnyansky and nineteenth century Russian church music," one may wonder what Gottwald's reactions would have been to so many choirs and their conductors performing all sorts of pop music with the greatest conviction and joy. Gottwald's answer would probably be, as he remarked in *Choral Music and the Avant-Garde*: "Possibly the causes of such contradictions lie in the music itself. Again and again one sees top-rank musicians get carried away when in cheerful company. They sing or play the most tasteless pieces, or freely express their admiration for some pop star or other – as Ligeti did for the Beatles."[1] However, the "new" folk music of the second half of the twentieth century is in fact that same pop music Gottwald mentions, that is, everything written between the Beatles and today's rap music, between early rock and roll and an endless stream of musical melodies by Rodgers, Sondheim, and Lloyd Webber, between beat masses, gospels, and modern anthems and the New Spirituality of some of the great masters of today, such as Arvo Pärt and Eric Whitacre.[2]

Some internationally renowned choral conductors and teachers, including Felix de Nobel, Marinus Voorberg, Eric Ericson, Uwe Gronostay, Clytus Gottwald, James Wood, Frieder Bernius, Paul Hillier and Tõnu Kaljuste, were also important in the development of choral music during the second half of the twentieth century. With their expertise and with the choirs they founded, their influence endures in the twenty-first century and has resulted in an enormous increase in new music and of vocal ensembles, professional, semi-professional, and amateur. Europe boasts some of the best vocal ensembles in the world, wonderful examples of the musical potential of amateur and professional choirs alike.

Professional choirs in Europe

At the beginning of the twentieth century, the professional choral field was made up primarily of opera choruses. All other choirs consisted of amateurs. The most important development in Europe after World War II was the founding of professional radio choirs. Virtually every broadcasting organization sought to have its own symphony orchestra and its own choir. Famous choirs established during this period included those of the German Südwestfunk (SWR), Westdeutsche Rundfunk (WDR) and Radio in the American Sector in Berlin (RIAS; after 1993, Deutschlandfunk), the British Broadcasting Corporation (BBC), the Danish, Swedish, Finnish and Latvian radio, the Dutch public radio, and the Netherlands Christian Broadcasting Society (NCRV). Many of these choirs still exist today, although their positions are financially less secure than a few decades ago. The repertoire of these choirs was generally determined by the artistic vision of their respective broadcasting organizations. The choirs serving broadcasting companies that gave special attention to contemporary art (e.g. RIAS, SWR, and WDR), specialized in new music and had the opportunity to commission many works. Most of these ensembles are chamber choirs, with the notable exception of the philharmonic choir (Groot Omroepkoor) of the Dutch radio.

While many of Europe's professional choirs are affiliated with a radio station, there are also a number of independent professional choirs and vocal ensembles. Eric Ericson's Eric Ericson Choir in Sweden, Felix de Nobel's Nederlands Kamerkoor in the Netherlands, Laurence Equilbey's Accentus and Roland Hayrabedian's Musicatreize in France, Harry Christophers' The Sixteen and Stephen Layton's Polyphony in England, and Tõnu Kaljuste's Estonian Philharmonic Choir in Tallinn are examples of such ensembles. These choirs are either supported by governmental subsidies together with some sponsoring and box office sales, or funded by more incidental local subsidies. Some have a full season; some are organized to undertake a limited number of projects per season.

The repertoire of these independent ensembles is often either more specialized or more diversified than that of most radio choirs. Musicatreize, for example, specializes in contemporary repertoire, primarily performing works that the ensemble itself has commissioned. On the other hand, the

Nederlands Kamerkoor's repertoire ranges from the early fourteenth century to the present; the ensemble performs early music under the direction of period musicians and commissions a handful of new works each year. Similarly, though The Sixteen's reputation is largely based on its performance of Renaissance music, the ensemble also sings contemporary British music such as the works of the Scottish composer James MacMillan. Paul Hillier's Theatre of Voices and the Hilliard Ensemble have set the standard for smaller vocal ensembles, performing a broad range of music dating from the early Renaissance to the twenty-first century.

Although several choirs specializing in music before 1750 already existed earlier in the twentieth century, the 1960s and 1970s saw an increase of period instrumental ensembles (for example, Concentus Musicus conducted by Nikolaus Harnoncourt, the London Classical Players by Roger Norrington, the Amsterdam Baroque Orchestra by Ton Koopman). With them, equally specialized choirs were founded. Among the most well-known are the Monteverdi Choir conducted by John Eliot Gardiner, the Amsterdam Baroque Choir by Ton Koopman, and the Huelgas Ensemble by Paul Van Nevel, dedicated solely to the music of the Middle Ages and the Renaissance. By the end of the century, some similar choirs such as the New Siberian Singers conducted by Teodor Currentzis in Novosibirsk (Russia) and Collegium 419 in the Czech Republic were established in the former Eastern European countries too.

The main distinction between these specialized choirs and the others lies in their extensive knowledge of historical performance practice and in their vocal technique, which emphasizes non-vibrato singing. Although most vocal ensembles until well into the eighteenth century used only male singers and boys for the top parts (famous boys, choirs, singing with the professionals, are the Wiener Sängerknaben and the Tölzer Knabenchor), most modern and even specialized ensembles nowadays also use female singers while trying to retain the crystal-clear sound of the boys.

In 2003, a new organization, called Tenso, was founded to provide support to the best of professional chamber ensembles. Tenso brings together knowledge and research, exchanges management information, co-commissions new music, organizes masterclasses for young composers, and bridges the gap between the professional and the amateur choral world. Most important, Tenso organizes an annual conference, called Tenso Days, in one of its members' cities. As of 2010, these members are: Accentus (Paris), Latvijas Radiokoris (Riga), Det Norske Solistkor (Oslo), Musicatreize (Marseille), Nederlands Kamerkoor and Cappella Amsterdam (Amsterdam), and RIAS Kammerchor (Berlin). Tenso Days have been held in Paris, Berlin, Riga, Amsterdam, Oslo, and Marseilles, and since 2009, Tenso has been supported by the European Union.

Amateurs choirs in Europe

Today, with some 30 million amateur singers in Europe, each country has its own structures and various platforms to promote choral singing nationally and internationally. Added to the nineteenth century's amateur choirs (church or temple choirs, oratorio choirs, operetta and opera choruses, municipal choirs of a more general kind, and the newly emerging socialist choirs), the later twentieth century yielded a plethora of new choral groupings, such as gay and lesbian choirs, school and university choirs, amateur chamber choirs, jazz, swing, and gospel choirs, pop, folk, and show choirs, and many more. These choirs could further be broken down into different types: mixed choirs, men's and women's choirs, and children's choirs, again to be divided into boys' and girls' choirs.

After World War II, most European countries established programs to support the arts. Amateur and professional organizations alike benefited from such initiatives. In the Soviet and communist countries, choral singing was considered by the government to be an important unifying activity. In the West, by contrast, singing was seen as the voice of each individual cultural identity, as Goethe noted in his essay "Einfache Nachahmung der Natur, Manier, Stil."[3] And yet, despite the acknowledged benefits of musical involvement, many governments decided to reduce subsidies for most cultural activities in the 1980s. By cutting funding for the arts, some nations sought to balance their budgets and to force taxpayers and communities to involve themselves more directly in the production of regional and national culture.

After the fall of the Berlin Wall in 1989, choral music and choral singing were once again seen, especially in the former communist countries, as the voice of regained cultural identity. The Baltic countries, most Balkan countries, Hungary, Slovakia, and the Czech Republic, and Poland invested much in amateur and professional choral music initiatives. However, within a decade and especially after the worldwide financial crisis of 2008, another round of severe cuts in the arts was implemented. In consequence, choral societies, choral platforms, and national and international associations for choral singing worked harder than ever to demonstrate, through research and outreach, the importance of singing for children and adults, for amateurs and professionals alike.

Today, there exist many supranational entities created to support amateur choral music initiatives in Europe. The most important currently are Europa Cantat (European Federation of Young Choirs) and the AGEC (Arbeitsgemeinschaft Europäischer Chörverbände), which together comprise some 20 million amateur singers in registered choirs. In 2011, these two organizations joined forces to create the new European Choral Association, which covers virtually all national platforms and all specialized international European platforms. They organize festivals, competitions, and supranational youth choirs, such as the European Youth Choir. The most important event is the triennial Europa Cantat festival, when thousands of young singers come together, each time in a different city, and sing in a variety of styles for and with each other.

Across Europe, the main efforts for the next decade will be on attracting more young people, on improving music education in elementary, middle, and high schools, on the healing, social, and psychological aspects of singing alone and in groups, and on interculturality, especially with so many "new" Europeans in every country. Several countries have recently started research programs meant to bring the diverse cultural groups within their borders together through community singing, and at the same time to halt the decline in music education. By emphasizing the social and community-building benefits of choral music, music educators hope to legitimize choral singing in the eyes of politicians and funding organizations. At the same time, through radio and television, but also through movies, with their never-ending flow of old and new musicals, the breadth of choral music is still growing, even among the younger generations. In several European countries, choirs of all sorts compete with each other on television, singing anything from the lighter classical repertoire to the latest arrangements of pop songs, for a very broad and general audience.

A brief survey of European choral music

Russia, Belarus, and Ukraine

The recent development of choral music within the former communist states of Eastern Europe has been as varied as it has been in Western Europe. These Eastern European nations, however, share one important common denominator: the influence of the former Soviet regulation of the arts, particularly music, is still felt, especially within academic institutions. Though these nations' post-communist economies cannot provide comprehensive support for the arts, music has become more important than ever as a promoter of national unity and identity.

At present, no information is available on the number of amateur choirs in Russia, Ukraine, or Belarus. With the decline and abolition of the communist system, the typical socialist choirs have disappeared, but not the desire of many to sing in choirs. Opera choruses have survived, liturgical choirs, especially within the Orthodox Church, have been founded, folk music is still much loved, and some specialized choirs demonstrate that the latest developments in Western Europe are closely followed in Russia too. Thus the Kyiv Chamber Choir sings Russian baroque as well as traditional Russian music, Vasilii Titov made quite a name with his Moscow Baroque, and the New Siberian Singers in Novosibirsk, founded by Teodor Currentzis, proved themselves to be on a level with similar ensembles in the West. Quite well-known in addition to these are, among others, the Moscow State Chamber Choir, the Russian State Symphony Cappella, and the St. Petersburg Chamber Choir.

Baltic states

Although the Baltic countries (Lithuania, Latvia, and Estonia) are now connected with the Scandinavian countries through the Nordic Houses for Culture, they were ruled for most of the twentieth century by the Soviet Union Consequently, singing, and especially choral singing, continues to be and still is an important part of the cultural identity of the Baltic countries. Music education, particularly singing, is obligatory in all primary schools, and the nations host choral festivals together and separately every year.

At the famous annual Song and Dance Festivals, founded in the nineteenth century and which are now considered to be an important part of UNESCO's Oral and Intangible Heritage of Humanity, tens of thousands of singers of all ages come together to sing and compete with one another. For example, in 2003 some three hundred choirs came together at the Latvian Song and Dance Festival. A choir of 20,000 sang national songs, while many of the individual choirs presented new repertoire. At the Nordic-Baltic Festivals, which include the Scandinavian countries and Iceland, the social and cultural exchanges are as important as raising the general level of singing. Composers and conductors alike achieve national and international recognition at these festivals, which in some cases draw more than 100,000 visitors. And yet, despite this deep interest in choral singing and the enormous impact of the festivals, the number of amateur singers in each of the Baltic countries does not greatly exceed the European average of 4 percent of the population.

The Baltic countries have few professional choirs, the most famous of which are the Latvijas Radiokoris and the Estonian Philharmonic Choir. In addition to opera choruses and academic choirs, some semi-professional chamber choirs, such as the Jauna Muzika in Vilnius, are rather competitive and have recorded interesting programs. These new ensembles, along with a number of amateur choirs, have inspired many composers to write new music. Thus, because the number of composers writing vocal and choral music is extremely large relative to the rather small populations of these countries, there is a very active contemporary music culture. Composers such as Arvo Pärt, Veljo Tormis, Erkki-Sven

Tüür, and Peteris Vasks have built national and international reputations with their music, which incorporates elements of folk music and New Spirituality.

Poland

As in the other former Eastern Bloc countries, Poland boasted many academic, symphonic, opera, school, factory, and folk music choirs during the period of communist cultural policy. Since the 1960s, when public performance of avant-garde music was first allowed in Poland and the Warsaw Autumn Festival attained an international reputation, many choirs, including foreign ensembles, have become acquainted with the music of such important composers as Witold Lutosławski, Henrik Górecki, and Krzysztof Penderecki. These composers' mixture of sound exploration, harmonic clusters, and (especially with Penderecki) a new Roman Catholic ecstasy expressed in musical terms, exerted a great influence on the choral world. At the same time, new research into the vast repertoire of Polish Renaissance and baroque music led to the establishment of several choirs specializing in this repertoire.

Since the 1990s, the number of official choirs seems to have decreased. In 2009, 63 choirs were registered with the Polish Music Information Center. However, in addition to these, Poland has many 'unofficial' choirs, since almost every church, academy, school, community center, or foundation has its amateur choir. Poland is also home to nine professional choirs: in addition to the Polish Radio Choir, there are six official symphony choirs, one of which is the National Choir of Poland, and two chamber choirs, of which the Polish Chamber Choir (also known as Schola Cantorum Gedanensis) in Gdansk is the most famous. The other is the chamber choir of the Capella Cracoviensis in Cracow.

Czech Republic, Slovakia, and Hungary

Czechoslovakia, now divided into the Czech Republic and Slovakia, and Hungary have a long tradition of adult and especially children's choral singing. The choral and vocal training programs for children are world-famous, and many youth choirs in this region still win first prizes at international competitions. Since the 1990s, however, a certain decline in the number of choirs and the investment in choral singing has been obvious; the financial support provided by the new economies cannot match that of the communist era. Still, as in most former Eastern Bloc countries, choral singing is thought to strengthen national unity and identity.

The Czech Republic, Slovakia, and Hungary each have hundreds of amateur choirs; the Union of Czech Choirs (Unie českých pěveckých sboru) alone comprises more than 350 ensembles. Throughout the region, children's and amateur choirs compete with one another at annual choral festivals. The three countries have extensive vocal training programs for children: the Hungarian choral education system became popular even in Western Europe after World War II, although in the last quarter of the twentieth century most Western European countries developed their own pedagogical methods or shifted their focus more toward Anglo-American systems such as that of Murray Schafer, which is based on soundscaping and the exploration of sounds, on improvisation and composing by amateurs in choirs and schools. However, the Kodály system has remained popular and paved the way for a spectacular increase in children's choirs throughout Europe, performing more daring repertoire than ever.

Among the best-known professional choirs of the Czech Republic are the Prague Philharmonic Choir, the Czech Philharmonic Choir Brno, the Prague Chamber Choir, and Collegium 419, which specializes in music dating from the Renaissance through the eighteenth century; in the Slovak Republic the most noted choirs are the Slovak Philharmonic Choir in Bratislava and the Bratislava City Choir. In Hungary, the National Choir in Budapest, the Chamber Choir of the Hungarian Radio, and the Debrecen Kodály Chorus are the best known and of the highest quality.

Serbia, Slovenia, Croatia, and the Balkans

Slovenia, Serbia, Croatia, and the other countries of the Balkans share much in common with Poland, the Czech Republic, Slovakia, and Hungary. In many of the former Yugoslavian and other Balkan nations such as Bulgaria, the musical world is not yet organized at such a level that details about choral singing and music education for amateurs and children are available. Most of these countries are not yet connected to the International Association of Music Information Centers, or have only limited data available for research. However, Bulgaria boasts many choral festivals, and many Bulgarian amateur choirs travel to festivals throughout Europe, as can be seen by leafing through the brochures of most Western European festivals.

In terms of figures, Slovenia serves as an example of the interest in choral singing throughout the region. The Public Fund of the Republic of Slovenia for Cultural Activities reports that some 100,000 amateurs (5 percent of the population) and children sing in more than 2,500 public, children's, and church choirs. Male double quartets are particularly popular. Some 600,000 people annually attend the many concerts of these choirs at government-supported choral festivals. Slovenia also has three professional choirs: the Slovenian Chamber Choir and two opera choruses. Croatia has a handful of professional choirs, one of which is the Croatian Radio and Television Choir.

Israel

Although Israeli choral music was influenced almost exclusively until the 1970s by European tradition or by traditional liturgical music for the synagogue, the current singing culture presents a unique mixture of Russian and Central European, Mediterranean and North African elements. With the immigration of many Russians to Israel and the younger generation of Israeli composers' interest in their nation's Middle Eastern cultural heritage, the vocal music, and thus the choral music too, has changed considerably. In 1952, the founding of Zimriya, a triennial international choral festival, provided opportunities for Israeli singers to work with conductors from around the world. Several years later the nation's first major choir, the Rinat National Choir of Israel, was established by the conductor Gary Bertini. During the 1950s and 1960s, the singing and choral training at kibbutzim was supported by the founding of the Israel Kibbutz Choir for talented singers. Many initiatives followed, resulting in a plethora of chamber choirs, some of them professional, such as the Tel Aviv Chamber Choir, the Ramat-Gan Chamber Choir, and the New Israeli Vocal Ensemble, which performs a broad, eclectic repertoire from Renaissance to modern times and features conductors from around the world.

Accurate figures on the number of amateur choirs and singers are not available. The two largest organizations are the Tel Aviv Philharmonic Choir, which has some eighty amateur singers and is connected to the Tel Aviv Opera, and the Jerusalem Oratorio Choir, which contains the Jerusalem Oratorio Chamber Choir. Recently, the latter has proved the value of searching for new modes of bridging cultural divides: made up of Christian and Muslim singers, the JOCC has demonstrated choral music's ability to cross cultural borders. In addition to these Israel has a considerable number of choirs for children and teenagers, such as the Ankor, Efroni, Moran, and the Li-Ron choirs.

Recently, efforts have increasingly been made to bring Israeli and Palestinian cultures together, also through choral singing, as for example by the Voices for Peace Choir. Founded in 2002 by the composer Shlomo Gronich and the Arab Community Center in Jaffa, this choir consists of pre-teen and teenage Israeli and Arab girls, which made quite a name for itself with the bilingual song "Hevenu Shalom Aleinu / Ana Ajmal Min Salam" (We brought peace upon us / There is nothing more beautiful than peace). Similar projects have been set up by the Efroni and the Sawa choirs, from Emek Hefer and Shfar'am respectively; the latter city has a mainly Arab community. Although the results of these exciting projects have still to be evaluated, the first reactions from within the choirs are positive.

Southern Europe

In the Greek folk music tradition and in that of the Greek Orthodox Church, choral singing is fundamental. Though precise figures are unavailable, the Hellenic Choirs Association reports that there are some 2,500 singers in 120 choirs across the country. As in most European countries, the repertoire of these choirs is derived from three basic sources: liturgical music, folk music, and the more international body of choral music dating from the Renaissance to the present. The chamber choirs show particularly broad musical tastes. One look at the programs at the choral festivals of Karpenisi (Evrytania) or Preveza (Epiros) will demonstrate the international scope of the Greek choral world nowadays.

Italy's many professional opera choruses create a choral music culture strikingly different from that of Greece. Though the Coro dell'Accademia Nazionale di Santa Cecilia in Rome is the only Italian concert choir that performs on an international level, there are more than 2,500 listed amateur choirs throughout the country, most of which are associated with the Federazione Nazionale Italiana Associazioni Regionali Corali (Feniarco). In Milan, the Associazione Culturale Cantosospeso offers a full curriculum of choral singing, beginning with training for very young children, who then progress step by step through choirs until reaching a chamber choir, Coro 1492, mainly dedicated to contemporary choral music, a women's choir, and a mixed choir which performs over fifty concerts per season. Italy has several extensive educational programs and masterclasses for young choral music composers. Despite the success of these programs, a recent poll shows that most young choristers prefer to sing a lighter repertoire of pop, musical theater, folk, spiritual, or jazz music rather than classical or modern polyphony.

In Spain, most professional choirs also serve the many opera houses. However, unlike Italy, Spain also has a large number of professional choirs. Some three thousand amateur choirs, comprising over 300,000 singers, are listed. The Federació Catalana D'Entitats Corals (Catalan Federation of Choral Entities), the Confederación de Coros del País Vasco, and the Federación Coral de Madrid are examples of regional platforms for all sorts of choral activities. Spain even has a lively community of barbershop choirs. Among the more professional organizations are the Coro Nacional in Madrid, the choirs of the Prince of Asturias Foundation in Oviedo, and the Cor de Cambra del Palau de la Música Catalana in Barcelona.

Since the restoration of democracy in Portugal in 1974, the development of a structured music education program has led to the emergence of hundreds of amateur and semi-professional choirs across the country. Approximately 10,000 singers perform in amateur ensembles, and Portugal also boasts three internationally renowned professional choirs: the Coro Casa da Música in Porto; the Coro do Teatro Nacional São Carlos, mainly an opera chorus; and the very successful Coro Gulbenkian in Lisbon.

France

French choral ensembles are organized into national and regional foundations on all levels. With so many platforms for choral music in France, it is not easy to determine how many people sing in choirs, but different figures suggest that at least 2 to 3 million people participate in choral activities across the nation. Since the 1980s, some thirty *maîtrises*, educational choral institutes for youths up to age 18, have trained young musicians with a daily mixture of music and regular school classes. These *maîtrises* organize many concerts and are considered stepping stones to the conservatories. Next in importance is the institution of the Petits Chanteurs, the boys' choirs (now also with girls) linked to the churches. More than eighty of these ensembles, comprising some 2,500 singers, belong to the federation of Pueri Cantores. The Missions Voix en Région, the organization for the support and advancement of choral and vocal practice in the French provinces, lists some 12,000 choirs and nearly 500,000 singers, another 2,500 federal choirs with some 100,000 singers, and 5,000 school choirs with another 200,000 singers.

For all these choirs, France has about fifty music schools and conservatories with educational programs for choral conductors. Since 1972, choirs have competed at the Florilège Vocal de Tours. The triennial Choralies festival in Vaison-la-Romaine is also well known; there many choirs from France and abroad come together to sing and for training. À Coeur Joie (the federation for amateur choirs) and the Association Nationale des Chorales Liturgiques are brought together on a national level by the Institut Français d'Art Choral in its dedication to sharing information, boosting education and pursuing research in choral music.

In addition to the roughly twenty-five independent professional choirs with specialized repertoire, there are professional choral ensembles affiliated with each of the roughly twenty opera houses and as part of French radio (Choeur de Radio-France, with 110 vocalists). The repertoire of these professional ensembles is diverse, but the quality is consistently excellent. While the opera choruses perform mainly nineteenth- and twentieth-century repertoire, the choral groups affiliated with period ensembles such as Marc Minkowski's Les Musiciens du Louvre and William Christie's Les Arts Florissants specialize in early music, and many other professional choirs perform a broad range of rather advanced repertoire. At the highest level are the vocal ensembles and chamber choirs Accentus (Paris), Musicatreize (Marseilles), Les Éléments (Toulouse), Sequenza 9.3 (Pantin) and Les Solistes de Lyon. These ensembles consist entirely of professional singers, though the musicians, unlike those of the opera choruses or Radio-France, are untenured and are paid per production. Most of these choirs commission new works regularly; the young ensembles Jeune Choeur de Paris and Les Cris de Paris present brilliant new compositions together with music from the Renaissance onwards. Through this artistically rewarding policy, these organizations serve as examples to many adventurous amateur choirs and have set a high musical standard in France.

Switzerland and Austria

On June 3, 2008, the president of the Austrian Choral Federation (Chorverband Österreich) spoke on invitation to the Austrian Parliament in relation to a governmental inquiry on the situation of the arts, noting that, though the nation has 3,200 choirs with more than 82,000 members, governmental support for choral music is only a fraction of what the 2,000 soccer clubs receive. Every year over 3 million people attend choral concerts, many more than the number attending soccer games. As in most countries, the organization of these choirs is defined on a regional level. These regional organizations as well as the national federation regularly organize masterclasses for conductors, choral festivals, conferences on choral music, and professional days for young composers.

Compared to some European nations such as Germany and Switzerland, the number of men's choirs in Austria is a rather small 20 percent of the total. Mixed choirs are the most common, women's choirs the least. Because only 14 percent are children's choirs, Chorverband Österreich invests a great deal in this important group, especially as subsidies for the arts are diminishing. Although Austria has a world-famous choral ensemble, the Arnold Schoenberg Chor, a fully professional chamber choir does not exist. Two notable amateur groups are the Wiener Singverein, which has existed since Beethoven's time, and the Wiener Kammerchor.

In Switzerland, the situation is only slightly different. As of 2009, the country had four ensembles with professional singers: in the German-speaking part, the Basler Madrigalisten and Schweizer Kammerchor; in the French-speaking part, the Ensemble Vocal de Lausanne; and in the Italian-speaking part, the Coro della Radiotelevisione Svizzera in Lugano. However, in February 2010, the City Council of Zürich decided to cancel its financial support to the Schweizer Kammerchor, a decision that gives credence to recent concern that interest in choral music is declining. Still, Switzerland officially has 1,740 amateur choirs. These consist of some 500 mixed choirs (29 percent), 220 women's choirs (13 percent), 840 men's choirs (48 percent), 140 children's choirs (8 percent) and 40 church choirs (2 percent), altogether comprising 54,000 singers.

These choirs are assembled in the Schweizerische Chorvereinigung, founded in 1977 through the merger of three older federations, the Eidgenössischer Sängerverein (men's choirs), the Schweizerischer Verband Gemischter Chöre (mixed choirs) and the Verband Schweizerischer Frauen- und Töchterchöre (women's choirs). The number of church choirs is astonishing, though many churches seem to have lost interest in the classical choral tradition. On the other hand, men's choirs, nearly half of the total number of choirs, are still flourishing.

Germany

In the 1960s, the former West Germany counted over 16,000 choirs, of which three-quarters were men's choirs. Nowadays, according to the 2010 figures of the Arbeitsgemeinschaft Deutscher Chorverbände (ADC, Federation of German Choral Societies), Germany boasts more than 2 million singers in some 50,000 choirs, comprised of 22,000 general amateur choirs and over 28,000 church choirs. A quarter of all singers are younger than 25. However, another 16,000 choirs, with more than 600,000 members, are not part of the ADC. Of the more than 66,000 choirs, mixed choirs account for 45.2 percent of the total, children's and youth choirs for 30.9 percent, men's choirs for 15.9 percent, and women's choirs for 8 percent. About 4 percent of the population sings in some sort of choir or vocal group.

Virtually all of these choirs rehearse weekly and organize either weekly or monthly performances or several concerts a season. Exceptions are to be found among the hundreds of concert choirs around the country. In addition to their own concerts, they often perform with the local city orchestra too. Some have acquired impressive reputations, even abroad; they include the Philharmonischer Chor Duisburg, the Gürzenich-Chor Köln, and the Gewandhauschor Leipzig, but also the Dresdner Kammerchor and the Kammerchor Stuttgart, and of course the famous Tölzer Knabenchor.

Germany has five professional radio or former radio choirs. The best-known are the Rundfunkchor Berlin, the Chor des Bayerischen Rundfunks, the RIAS Kammerchor, and the SWR Vokalensemble Stuttgart. The first two work with the symphony orchestras of Berlin and Munich and sing mostly oratorios; the others have broader repertoires: RIAS is extremely versatile in every field from the Baroque onwards, and the SWR is by far the ensemble most dedicated to contemporary music. As an independent professional vocal ensemble, the Deutscher Kammerchor is a partner of the Deutsche

Kammerphilharmonie. Finally, most opera houses have their own opera choruses, yielding another eighty choirs.

For those many thousands of choirs, a well-organized educational system is a necessity. Music schools, conservatories, masterclasses for singers, composers and conductors, summer schools, festivals, and competitions provide whatever is needed. The education of young conductors and composers is taken especially seriously. Since 66,000 choirs need guidance, training and repertoire on every imaginable level, several associations for professionals and for amateurs provide the necessary input. Recently, an increasing number of masterclasses for young composers focus on choral music, both sacred and secular.

Northern Europe

The comprehensive attention given to choral music in Germany is found in most of Northern Europe as well as in the Netherlands and Belgium. Denmark, Iceland, Norway, Sweden, and Finland have extensive programs for young choral singers and conductors. For several decades, the attention given to educating young composers with a special interest in writing choral music for amateurs has been increasing. Still, most composers prefer writing for the best professionals and underestimate the challenge of composing for amateur choral singers.

Denmark has a long tradition of choral music and choral singing going back to the beginning of the nineteenth century, as do most central and northern European countries. Some 80,000 Danish music lovers sing regularly in choirs. Each city has several secular choirs, church choirs, and children's choirs, and the universities are active centers of choral singing, with large symphonic choirs and smaller a cappella choirs. In addition, Denmark has two opera choruses, an internationally renowned radio choir (currently resized into an eighteen-voice chamber choir: DR Radiokoret VokalEnsemblet) with its own choir school, an equally internationally renowned vocal ensemble (Ars Nova), and a few project choirs consisting of mainly young professional singers.

Belief in the importance of musical and especially vocal training for young people has led to some interesting arts initiatives in Denmark. The oldest is the founding in 1924 of the Copenhagen Boys' Choir, also known as the Copenhagen Royal Chapel Choir. The young singers are trained at the Sankt Annæ Gymnasium and discharge their duties at Copenhagen Cathedral. The gymnasium's pupils are recruited from talented eight-year-olds. They receive a complete school education plus comprehensive vocal and musical training. The gymnasium houses two well-known choirs, the Sankt Annæ Pigekor (St. Anne's Girls" Choir) and the Sankt Annæ Gymnasiekor (St. Anne's Gymnasium Choir).

In Denmark, 2008 was proclaimed the Sangens År (Year of Song). During that year a special songbook was created for elementary schools, extra money was provided for choral singing in schools and churches, and special programs for singing were developed. The success of these events led to another initiative: the Ministry of Education, the Ministry of Social Welfare, and the Ministry of Culture joined forces to create a new project, the Syngelyst (Joy of Singing). The organizers note that "Singing ought to be a natural part of everyday life for children and young people, who should sing much more than they do today, and sing together, sing for themselves, write songs and have ideas about singing." Syngelyst has been funded with €6 million for a period of three years.

Finland has some 3,000 amateur choirs, mostly men's or mixed choirs, followed by church, children's and women's choirs. The Tapiola Children's Choir, one of the best of its kind, occupies a special position. The training concept of this choir is based on the natural use of each child's voice. Each child must play one or more instruments too, and movement, dance, and drama are incorporated into their performances. The choir works regularly with contemporary composers, who write sophisticated works for these children.

The Finnish Radio Chamber Choir was originally part of the Finnish Broadcasting Company; when the radio withdrew its funding, the ensemble changed its name to the Helsinki Chamber Choir. The National Finnish Opera in Helsinki also has a professional chorus. Better known today is the Tapiola Chamber Choir, which works with most of Finland's professional orchestras. Screaming or shouting choirs are also fairly popular; originally developed so that the shouts would carry long distances over lakes or in the countryside, the technique was adopted by groups of singers in a choral setting; the style of immensely loud rhythmically structured shouts is now exemplified by the internationally successful Mieskuoro Huutajat (Men's Choir of Shouters) from Oulu.

Sweden is traditionally a stronghold of choral singing. Music education is well established from elementary schools up to the music academy, and choral conducting holds an important place in the pedagogical field. Like other Scandinavian countries, Sweden has an extensive choral curriculum for youth, exemplified by the efforts of organizations such as SWICCO (the Swedish International Choral Center in Örebro). With their Uniting Youth in Song project, in cooperation with the Regional Music Institute in Örebro as well as with several branches of Europa Cantat and comparable organizations in Italy (Feniarco) and Spain (SCIC), Swicco strives to create amateur choral festivals and to support and enhance the field by training children's choir directors, founding youth choirs, and researching the field of choral music. Another example of Swedish music education is the Adolf Fredriks Musikklasser in Stockholm, a singing school with one thousand pupils aged 10 to 16; it is a normal primary and secondary school with regular singing and music classes. The school has eighteen choirs, of which the Adolf Fredriks Girls" Choir represents the top echelon.

The main organization for choirs is the Federation of Swedish Choir Associations (Körsam), bringing together some twenty regional platforms and well over 100,000 singers. The other main platform, the Korforbund, has over 300,000 singers in their member choirs. Recent studies indicate that nowadays, in total, between 600,000 and 900,000 people sing in choirs. At the top of the list of choirs in Sweden stand the Swedish Radio Choir and the Eric Ericson Chamber Choir. Both are the result of the training of master specialist Eric Ericson, who put the extraordinary Swedish choral tradition on a more professional and international track. His cooperation with composers, first in Sweden and later throughout the world, has inspired many other conductors. There are also some superb semi-professional and amateur chamber choirs, mainly connected to universities or churches, including Lunds Vokalensemble in Lund, St. Jakobskor in Stockholm, and Göteborgs Kammarkör in Göteborg.

In Norway, the choral world still needs professionalization though, on a purely creative level, the choral scene is remarkable. For example, the composer Lasse Thoresen has developed the Concrescence project, which brings together innovative sounds based on the latest vocal techniques and international folk music with educational principles for amateurs and professionals; the result is a true "concrescense," a growing together of traditional cultures and the newest musical expressions. Recently, the professional situation of the choral movement in Norway seems to have improved, after the government decided to support fully one independent professional choir, the Norwegian Soloists' Choir (Det Norske Solistkor). Currently, the only salaried professional choir is the Norwegian Opera Choir. Over 200,000 people throughout Norway sing in choirs, with a repertoire ranging from folk music to the most adventurous works of the avant-garde.

The Netherlands and Belgium

The Netherlands and Belgium have an extensive choral singing tradition dating back to the glorious music of the Franco-Flemish Renaissance, which was brought into the concert hall in the last quarter of the nineteenth century. In Belgium, the many choirs are divided between the Walloon, the Flemish, and the German-speaking regions of the country. In all, over a thousand choirs are registered with Fédération Chorale Wallonie (Brussels), also known as the foundation À Coeur Joie, and the Koorfederatie Vlaanderen, together again with the Vlaamse Federatie van

Jonge Koren (Flemish Federation of Youth Choirs). Together, the two regions have four professional choirs, of which the best-known are Philippe Herreweghe's celebrated Collegium Vocale in Ghent and the Flemish Radio Choir.

The oldest existing professional chamber choir in Europe is the Nederlands Kamerkoor, founded in 1937 and since considered one of the best all-round chamber choirs. The radio choir (Groot Omroepkoor) in Hilversum, with more than seventy professional singers, has become one of the very best professional symphonic choirs in Europe. The same holds for the slightly smaller opera chorus in Amsterdam. Since the 1970s, when the Netherlands became a world center for contemporary ensemble music, several amateur chamber choirs have slowly evolved to a more professional status. The Nederlands Kamerkoor currently has a competitor in Cappella Amsterdam, both in Holland and internationally. Both are examples for half a dozen semi-professional chamber choirs all around the country. Alongside these are professional and semi-professional vocal groups such as the experimental Vocal Lab and the very successful Netherlands Youth Choir.

With such high-quality exponents of choral singing, it is not surprising that some 1.6 million people in the Netherlands, according to recent figures, sing weekly; of these, nearly a million are choral singers. Indeed, every village has its choir, and many of these choirs spend much of the season preparing for a performance of Bach's *St. Matthew Passion* in the weeks before Easter. In addition, ensembles perform cantatas and chorales during the weekly religious services, and for several decades now, an ever-larger number of contemporary pieces, sacred and secular. Haarlem and Utrecht have excellent choir schools, and the Haarlem Choral Biennale and Eric Ericson Master Class offer high-profile programs with the best of professional choirs and special courses for young conductors. Together with the Swedes and Germans, the Dutch play an important part in the training and organization of amateur choirs in Europe.

The United Kingdom and Ireland

In 2008, the Arts Council of Ireland reported that more than 10,000 people sing in some four hundred choirs served by the Association of Irish Choirs. This makes singing in a choir one of the country's most popular arts activities, though only 0.15 percent of the population is involved. With a special state-funded program, Raising Your Voice, the arts council is working to promote choral singing. The program demonstrates that people across a wide social spectrum enjoy singing in choirs; it aims to provide training and to lead children into the joy of singing while also promoting initiatives for people of all ages. Ireland has only one state-funded professional choir, the National Chamber Choir, and its singers are part-time. This also holds for the choirs engaged by the National Opera and the Wexford Festival Opera.

In England, the rich choral singing tradition goes back to the four-teenth century. The foundation of this rich choral scene was first of all the over thirty cathedrals with their schools, followed later by the educational system at universities and elementary schools. Though there has in recent years been a certain decline in attention to music in general and singing in particular, a plethora of mostly private foundations continues to provide financial support for such arts organizations. The professional infrastruc-ture in England is different from that found in most European countries, as the country counts only a few professional choirs with salaried singers; the sole chamber choir with salaried singers is the BBC Singers, funded by the British Broadcasting Corporation (BBC). However, scores of vocal ensembles and choirs consist of professional singers engaged on a free-lance basis, project by project. From the King's Singers and The Sixteen to Polyphony, from Ex Cathedra to the London Concert Choir, from the Holst Singers to the New London Chamber Choir on the one hand and New London Chorale on the other, all of these choirs and vocal ensembles exist thanks to an infrastructure that remains without comparison.

There are now some fifty cathedral and choir schools around the country. The most distinguished among them is the King's College Choir, Cambridge, under the direction of Stephen Cleobury. Described by the composer Peter Maxwell Davies as "a crowning glory of our civilisation," the choir was established in the fifteenth century and has served as an international role model for its musical excellence and distinctively fresh and beautiful sound. More than thirty university choirs provide vocal training and regular practice for students; about 150 Anglican choirs are registered and receive mostly private funding. Youth Music distributes millions of euros annually to a large number of youth choirs. One exceptional organisation is the National Youth Choirs of Great Britain, founded in 1983 and comprising an educational structure of three junior choirs, a choir for boys with changing voices (Cambiata), two training choirs, the National Youth Choir itself, and the graduate chamber choir (Laudibus).

In the 1990s, when a decline in interest in choral music was apparent, the government departments of Children, Schools and Families (DCSF) and Culture, Media and Sport (DCMS) joined forces with the music industry at large to stimulate youth involvement in music. One conse-quence of this was the start in 2007 of the Sing Up initiative, which promotes singing as a cross-curricular tool in schools, provides training opportunities for teachers to lead inspiring singing activities with young people, gives every child the chance to sing and opportunities to develop their vocal and performance skills, and runs successful projects that place singing at the heart of communities. An exemplary organization, the Voices Foundation offers in-school programs, professional development training for both classroom teachers and specialists, and quality resource materials.

A final word on English choral singing may be necessary, since the English sound is different from what can be heard elsewhere in Europe. Based on the tradition that girls and women should not sing in worship, the English have developed a strong predilection for boys' voices in general. This certainly has affected the sound still prevailing in English choirs, even nowadays when more and more girls join the boys: a crystal-clear, slightly sharp, but extremely well-projected choral sound. Together with music by hundreds of British composers, from Henry Purcell, Herbert Howells, Benjamin Britten, and John Rutter to James MacMillan and Julian Anderson, and the strong support of the record industry, this sound has influenced choral singing all over the world and has meant that British choral singing and the British choral scene set a standard for many millions of music lovers and singers.

Conclusion

Today, some 30 million singers perform in nearly a million European vocal ensembles led by at least three-quarters of a million conductors. From music publishing to concert sales, a thriving industry has been built up around amateur choral music. However, even with several positive initiatives, and many major festivals and competitions all over Europe and recently also on television, the general impression is that governments at large need more pressure based on evidence about the necessity of music in general and choral singing in particular, in order not to cut their budgets.

Indeed, the multicultural society that Europe is increasingly becoming does need new policies for the arts, new ways to energize music (also with the help of new media), new views on arts education, and, with regard to choral music, a better integration of choral singing through all social and cultural layers. Many are concerned that the position of music in our society is changing for the worse, and that an ever larger number of people who once were amateur music makers have become rather passive consumers. It may be true, too, that the attention given to music and music education in schools, from elementary schools to the universities, is declining in consequence of budget cuts and changing opinions on the role of arts education in general and music education in particular in modern-day schools. However, one should also acclaim those many new initiatives that have recently been started to recapture the attention of educators, young people, and lovers of music, especially of singing.

Some recent experiences in choral singing as mentioned above have resulted in positive side effects beyond merely acquainting people with music: for example bringing people together, improving social behaviour (such as through choral singing in prisons), transcending national or regional borders, racial and religious differences, and enhancing children's learning abilities and social skills. In short, more and more people could and should be convinced that singing is a necessity for the future of a healthy and united Europe.

Resources

Documents

Bastian, H. G. *Kinder optimal fördern – mit Musik*. Mainz: Atlantis-Schott, 2001. *Musik(erziehung) und ihre Wirkung: Eine Langzeitstudie an Berliner Grundschulen*. Mainz: Schott, 2000.

Fischer, E. (ed.). *Chorgesang als Medium von Interkulturalität: Formen, Kanäle, Diskurse*. Stuttgart: Steiner, 2007.

Geisler, U. and K. Johansson (eds.). *Choir in Focus 2010*. Göteborg: Bo Ejeby Förlag, 2010.

Goethe, Johann Wolfgang von. *Einfache Nachahmung der Natur, Manier, Stil* [1789]. In Goethe *Werke* 6 vols., ed. E. Staiger. Frankfurt am Main: Insel Verlag, 1965, vol. VI: *Vermischte Schriften*, pp. 252–56.

Gottwald, Clytus. "Choral Music and the Avant-Garde," in L. Reimers and B. Wallner (eds.), *Choral Music Perspectives: Dedicated to Eric Ericson*. Stockholm: Royal Swedish Academy of Music, 1993, pp. 119–34.

Jagodic, Mihela (ed.). "Choral Music in Slovenia." Datasheet provided by Marko Studen, Inge Breznik, Tomaž Faganel, and Karmina Šilec. Ljubljana, 2010.

Reimers, L. and B. Wallner (eds.). *Choral Music Perspectives: Dedicated to Eric Ericson*. Stockholm: Royal Swedish Academy of Music, 1993.

Taruskin, Richard. *Music in the Late Twentieth Century. The Oxford History of Western Music*, vol. V, Oxford University Press, 2005.

Walker, R. *Music Education, Cultural Values, Social Change and Innovation*. Springfield, IL: Charles Thomas Publisher, 2007.

Documents available online

Deslandres, G. *Choral Life in France*. Barcelona, November 11, 2006. www.xtec.es/entitats/rmcc/mediterrania/Choral_Life_in_France.pdf.

Hedell, K. *Svenska körer sjunger svenskt?* Uppsala: Institutionen för musikvetenskap, 2007. www.korcentrum.uu.se.

Lindholm, S. *Children's Choir – a Serious Medium*. 2004. www.listento.no/mic.nsf/doc/art2004011611272498600595.

ICCM General Report 2005–2008 (International Center for Choral Music). www.ifcm. net/public/doc/476.pdf.

Kultur in bewegung. Das Programm "Kultur" 2007–2013. European Union 2009. ec. europa.eu/culture/.

Kunst, Kultur und interkulturelle Dialog. Vienna: EDUCULT – Institut für die Vermittlung von Kunst und Wissenschaft, 2008. www.bmukk.gv.at/medienpool/ 16159/kkid.pdf.

Kunstfactor, *Monitor amateurkunst in Nederland 2009* Utrecht: Kunstfactor, 2009. www.kunstfactor.nl/.

Skyllstad, K. "Creating a Culture of Peace: The Performing Arts in Interethnic Negotiations," *Intercultural Communication* 4 (November 2000). www.immi.se/ intercultural.

Statistics published by, among others, the Deutscher Musikrat, the British Arts Council, the Irish Arts Council, the Italian State Department for Culture, and diverse music information centers.

Websites

General

Europa Cantat = europacantat.org

International Association of Music Information Centers = www.iamic.net (with links to most European Music Information Centers)

International Federation for Choral Music = www.ifcm.net

Global Choral Community = www.choralnet.org

Austria

Austrian Federation of Choirs = www.chorverband.at

Czech Republic

Czech Choral Society = www.ucps.cz

Denmark

Danish Amateur Music = www.danskamatormusik.dk

Danish Music Center = www.musiskcenter.dk

Finland

Finnish Amateur Musicians' Association = www.sulasol.fi

France

À coeur joie (French Choral Network) = acj.musicanet.org

Musical Confederation of France = www.cmf-musique.org

Germany

Chordatenbank = www.chordatenbank.de

Deutscher Chorverband = www.deutscher-chorverband.de

German Music Council = www.musikrat.de

Stiftung Dokumentations- und Forschungszentrum des Deutschen Chorwesens
= www.chorwesen.de

Verband Deutscher Konzertchöre = vdkc.de

Great Britain

Association of British Choral Directors = www.abcd.org.uk

British Choirs on the Net = www.choirs.org.uk

Making Music = www.makingmusic.org.uk/

National Association of Choirs = www.nationalassociationofchoirs.org.uk

Royal School of Church Music = www.rscm.com

British Choral Institute = www.britishchoralinstitute.co.uk

Greece

Hellenic Choirs Association = www.stegi-chorus.gr

Hungary

Association of Hungarian Choirs, Orchestras and Folk Ensembles = www.kota.hu

Ireland

Association of Irish Choirs = www.aoic.ie

Italy

International Association of Friends of Religious Music = www.amicimusicasacra.com

Italian National Federation of Regional Choral Organisations = www.feniarco.it

Solevoci Community = www.solevocicommunity.it

Latvia

Intangible Cultural Heritage = www.nkmva.gov.lv

The Netherlands

General article on the choral scene in the Netherlands: retro.nrc.nl/W2/Lab/Profiel/Zingen

Organization for Amateur Arts = www.kunstfactor.nl

Norway

Norwegian Choir Association = www.kor.no

Poland

Federation Caecilianum = www.caecilianum.eu

Federation of Pueri Cantores = www.puericantores.opoka.org.pl

Polish Choir and Orchestra Association = www.zgpzchio.pl

Slovenia

Choral singing in Slovenia = www.jskd.si/english/choral_singing/choral_singing_slovenia.pdf

Republic of Slovenia Public Fund for Cultural Activities = www.jskd.si

Spain

Federació Catalana d'Entitats Corals = www.fcec.info

Sweden

Federation of Swedish Choir Associations = www.korsam.se

Switzerland

Schweizerische Chorvereinigungen = www.usc-scv.ch

7 Canada's choral landscape

PATRICIA ABBOTT AND VICTORIA MEREDITH

Canada's choral culture is vibrant, diverse and widespread. Choral music is an integral part of every village, town, and city in this geographically large (just under 10 million square kilometers) but population-small (just over 33 million) country. Canada boasts world-class choirs and choral composers, whose works have gained international recognition.

What makes the Canadian choral scene unique and different from that of our southern neighbors, the United States? Is it our colonial past? Our bilingualism? Our geography? Our weather (a favorite Canadian topic of conversation)? Our collective desire to be distinct, in a polite and peaceful way? The impact of immigrant cultures and our concept of a diverse society? After all, the concept of Canada as a multicultural society is embodied in the Canadian Multiculturalism Act of 1985, which proclaims multiculturalism to be a "fundamental characteristic of the Canadian heritage and identity." No doubt the answer lies in all of these influences and more.

While many Canadian choral works are solidly rooted in the folk, classical, and sacred music traditions of its founding peoples (primarily settlers from France and Britain), there is no doubt that immigrant communities, such as the Irish, the German-speaking Mennonites, Ukrainians and Eastern European Jews who came to our country in the nineteenth and early twentieth centuries, have also had an influence on composers and the way in which we approach choral music making. In recent decades, a greater respect of and appreciation for the culture of Canada's indigenous peoples, formally identified as First Nations,[1] have also had an impact on mainstream choral music.

And then there is the land itself: the majestic Rockies, endless stretches of prairie land and sky, remote northern forests and the Northern Lights, the Great Lakes, the mighty St. Lawrence Seaway, our Atlantic and Pacific Coasts, the "Rock" (as Newfoundland is known) ... Composers write about the land, the sea and sky, and Canadian choirs want to sing about them.

The choral landscape

Amateur activity

Performing choral music is a widespread and grassroots activity in Canada. There is virtually no place in Canada where choral music is not practiced. From church and school choirs to independent community choirs of every size, type, and style of repertoire, there is a choir for every skill level and every music preference, including groups that are professional in all but name. The Association of Canadian Choral Communities estimates that there are some 38,000 choristers singing in choirs that are members of their provincial choral federations. If we consider the many choristers singing in non-affiliated choirs, this number is easily doubled or tripled. The city of Winnipeg, Manitoba, with a population of about 720,000, holds an annual ChoralFest organized by the Manitoba Choral Association which attracts the participation of more than 100 school and community choirs over an eleven-day period each fall. Choral music is clearly important in this central Canadian city with strong French, Mennonite, and Ukrainian roots. An annual sacred music festival each fall in Montreal regularly attracts ten to twelve choirs – some 500 choristers – who perform some of their own repertoire and unite their voices in a massed choir to sing masterworks by composers such as Berlioz, Franck, Handel, and Mozart. These festivals are just a few examples of the thousands of choral events that take place every year in which choirs perform in addition to their own concerts. University and college campuses also offer numerous choral performances on a regular basis.

The growing importance of children's and youth choirs

While there have long been children's and youth choirs affiliated with schools and religious institutions in Canada, such as Les Petits Chanteurs du Mont-Royal (Montreal), the late 1970s and early 1980s saw the establishment of independent children's choirs that sought to bring the performance of choral music by young voices to a new level of excellence. One such choir was the Toronto Children's Chorus (TCC) founded in 1978 by the talented, hardworking, and very determined Jean Ashworth Bartle. Her vision for the TCC – to make it the best children's choir in the world – provided leadership throughout the Canadian choral community, demonstrating that it was possible to present professional-level concerts with young voices. Inspired by Ashworth Bartle and the TCC, others followed suit and established excellent choral programs across Canada. Many of these – Shallaway (St. John's, Newfoundland, and Labrador), the Amabile Youth Choir (London, Ontario), the Saskatoon Children's Choir and the Cantilon Choirs (Edmonton, Alberta), to name but a few – have earned

national and international recognition and awards. Each of these programs includes several levels of choirs, providing training to new singers
and greater musical challenges for the more experienced. These choirs,
and many others in every region of Canada, produce several concerts per
season, engage professional instrumentalists and vocal soloists, record,
commission new works, and travel internationally, thus contributing to
the overall health of the choral community and making Canadian music
known abroad. It is largely thanks to some of these ensembles that the
works of composers such as Nancy Telfer, Stephen Hatfield, and Ruth
Watson Henderson have made their way across the country and beyond.

Professional activity

Amateur choirs greatly outnumber professional choirs, which we can
loosely define as those ensembles whose singers are paid for their services.
Although few in number, Canada's professional ensembles contribute
substantially to Canada's choral culture setting standards for excellence,
commissioning and premiering new music, and providing outreach and
educational activities in their communities and on tour. Prominent
Canadian professional choirs include the Vancouver Chamber Choir
(VCC), Pro Coro Canada in Edmonton, the Winnipeg Singers, the Elora
Festival Singers of Elora, Ontario, the Elmer Iseler Singers based in
Toronto, and Montreal's Studio de musique ancienne. In addition, professional choristers are engaged on a contract basis for ensembles such as the
chorus of the Orchestre symphonique de Montréal and L'Opéra de
Montréal. Historically, professional chamber choirs in Canada can trace
their roots back to the 1930s, when the Canadian Broadcasting Corporation
(CBC) began to engage already-formed choirs or professional singers for
regular and special radio broadcasts notably in Vancouver, Winnipeg,
Toronto, and Montreal. Other ensembles which made a significant impact
on choral music in Canada were the Montreal Bach Choir, conducted by
Georges Little (1920–95), and the Festival Singers of Toronto, founded in
1954, who changed their name to the Festival Singers of Canada in 1968
when they became the country's first choir to attain professional status.
Led by Elmer Iseler (1927–98) for most of its duration, this ensemble
formed the basis for the Elmer Iseler Singers, founded in 1979. Another
influential ensemble was the Tudor Singers of Montreal under the direction
of Wayne Riddell. Both Iseler and Riddell, through their programming,
commissioning, symposiums, and masterclasses, became icons of choral
music in Canada, mentoring and inspiring several generations of conductors right across the country. Jon Washburn continues to be a leader in
commissioning new works and in providing training through an annual
National Conductors' Symposium with the Vancouver Chamber Choir.

Newer on the scene is the Nathaniel Dett Chorale, a professional chamber choir based in Toronto and named after the African-Canadian composer. Its mandate is to perform and promote the music of the African diaspora in its many forms.

The role of federations and associations

Aided by government grants in the 1970s and early 1980s, amateur choral activity began to benefit from structured services as provincial choral federations and a national association for conductors were formed. Today, eight of Canada's ten provinces have a provincial choral federation. From west to east, they are the British Columbia Choral Federation, the Alberta Choral Federation, the Saskatchewan Choral Federation, the Manitoba Choral Association, Choirs Ontario, the Alliance des chorales du Québec, the New Brunswick Choral Federation, and the Nova Scotia Choral Federation. Among the activities and services they offer to their members are conducting courses for beginners, choral music lending libraries, the organization of festivals, conferences and honor choirs, group insurance, conductor mentoring programs, concert listings, newsletters, and much more. At the national level, the Association of Canadian Choral Conductors (ACCC) (now the Association of Canadian Choral Communities) was formed in 1980. This association holds a biennial conference called Podium that focuses on professional development, with workshops, masterclasses, reading sessions, and concerts. The ACCC also sponsors the National Youth Choir (NYC) every two years for top singers between the ages of 17 and 25, publishes lists of recommended Canadian choral repertoire, an information magazine called *Anacrusis*, and a membership and professional directory, and organizes the National Choral Awards and a conducting apprenticeship program linked to the NYC. It collaborates closely with the provincial choral federations and other national and international music organizations to promote the performance and creation of choral music, particularly Canadian music.

Canada's festivals and competitions

Nearly every town in Canada, regardless of size, hosts its own annual music festival, of which choral singing is a major component. Since 1944, when the first Kiwanis Music Festival was launched in Toronto, most festivals have been sponsored at least in part by local service organizations such as Kiwanis or Lions Clubs and engage both paid and volunteer staff members as well as professional musician adjudicators. Performances are assessed and ranked and prizes are awarded, with top competitors advancing to the provincial level of competition, from which those identified as the very best will compete again at the national level. There are ten different choral prizes awarded nationally, based on age, size, and type of choir. Singers and conductors credit participation in local music competitions with inspiring their singers to prepare their best performances. Not only is the competitive element inspiring to many singers, they are also presented with the opportunity to learn from an expert adjudicator, the chance to hear other choirs perform in the festival, and the pride and prestige of having performed their best, and sometimes of winning.

In addition to local music festivals, Canada is home to numerous national and international festivals and competitions. Both the east and west coasts of Canada offer long-standing, high-quality, international choral festivals in beautiful coastal settings. In Powell River, British Columbia, the International Choral Kathaumixw, Sliammon for "a gathering together of different peoples," was established in 1984 with the goal of creating a festival of a quality that would be on a par with festivals in Europe. It attracts about thirty choirs biennially and includes choral and solo competitions, orchestra, workshops, communal song singing, and seminars. Since the inaugural festival in 1984 in which there were four hundred participants, this biennial gathering has attracted more than twelve hundred singers from around the world who gather to share their music, culture, and friendship, and to perform for a distinguished international jury. Not all Canadian music festivals are competitive. Festival 500 is a non-competitive, international choral festival, held in North America's oldest city, St. John's, Newfoundland and Labrador. Festival 500 was established in 1997 as an anchor event in the John Cabot Anniversary Celebrations, to commemorate 500 years of European discovery in North America and as an effort to boost a depressed economy through increased tourism in an area boasting rugged coastal views, rich history, whale watching, and icebergs. Unique aspects of Festival 500 include the highlighting of a particular global culture at each festival, the opportunity for individual singers to attend without a choir and participate in a massed choir setting, and the academic symposium that parallels the festival, bringing together singers, conductors, audience, and scholars. Both of these international events project a hospitality typical of their gracious coastal regions, featuring the participation of numerous volunteers, home stays for performers, interaction between local residents and visitors, and tours of the region.

The influence of the Canadian Broadcasting Corporation

From 1976 to 2008, the CBC and its French-language counterpart Radio-Canada, in cooperation with the Canada Council for the Arts, sponsored a biennial National Radio Competition for Amateur Choirs aimed at promoting amateur choral singing and Canadian choral repertoire. In 2009, responsibility for this national choral initiative shifted to the ACCC, in collaboration with the Canada Council for the Arts and CBC Radio, and it was renamed the National Competition for Canadian Amateur Choirs. Choirs in various categories compete for monetary prizes as well as national radio broadcasts. The competition encourages the performance of Canadian repertoire by requiring that one of the four pieces submitted by each choir must be an original Canadian composition. It is not unusual for new Canadian works to result from this requirement. Through CBC radio broadcasts of the national semi-finals and national finals, a pan-Canadian listening audience has the opportunity to listen to choirs and repertoire from across the country. In addition to chamber and concert choirs, choirs from a myriad of cultural traditions abound in Canada, each continuing to specialize in its own distinct repertoire and language. Hence, the National Competition includes a separate category for cultural choirs where listeners are exposed to Ukrainian, Finnish, German, Chinese, and many other choral traditions. The CBC also supports Canadian choral music through regular broadcasts of Canadian professional and amateur choral concerts, notably on the weekly *Choral Concert*, and by making many of these concerts available on its website (Concerts on Demand). The Canada Council for the Arts provides financial support to professional and amateur choirs on a competitive, juried basis.

Forging a unique choral voice: Canada's choral composers
Pre- and post-confederation composers
There is ample evidence in historical accounts that the early French settlers sang masses and motets in church services as well as music for entertainment, including choral music, in the colonies that were to become Canada. There are collections of polyphonic music in Montreal and Quebec City that date back to the early 1700s. The arrival of British settlers and the establishment of Anglican and other Protestant congregations further increased the types of choral music in the colonies, with metrical psalms, hymns and anthems sung in addition to the high masses and vesper services of the Roman Catholic Church.

By the early nineteenth century, choral activity was growing, especially in churches and, even in smaller towns, and published materials, such as hymnals and books of chant, became available. By mid-century and in the period around the time of Canadian Confederation (1867), the arrival of European musicians, the influence of the singing school movement and the establishment of choral societies and music schools all helped to foster the growth of choral music and provide opportunities for Canadian composers.[2] The Toronto Mendelssohn Choir, founded in 1894, is credited with being the oldest Canadian choir still active today. Among the better-known composers of choral music from this period were the French-born Antoine Dessane (1826–73) and Quebec-born Ernest Gagnon (1834–1915), both of whom wrote sacred works and arrangements of French-Canadian folk songs. Among those writing some of Canada's first large-scale choral-orchestral works were Guillaume Couture (1851–1915) (*Jean le Précurseur*) and Alexis Contant (1858–1918) (*Caïn*).

The early twentieth century

By the late nineteenth and early twentieth centuries, Canadian-born musicians began to seek formal training abroad with noted French and British pedagogues, while many more composers born and trained in Europe established themselves permanently in Canada. Noted for their choral works, including masses, cantatas, and oratorios, are Charles A. E. Harriss (1862–1929) and the prolific Claude Champagne (1891–1965), who also penned some very sophisticated arrangements of folk songs. Also noteworthy is the African-Canadian composer and conductor R. Nathaniel Dett (1882–1934), born in what is today Niagara Falls, Ontario, who studied in the United States and with Nadia Boulanger in Paris, and who became one of the most highly acclaimed composers and pedagogues of his generation.

Mid and late twentieth-century voices

"Hands across the sea"

Some of Canada's most significant composers immigrated to Canada, bringing with them musical styles of their homelands. European influence remained strong as many composers returned to artistic centers such as London and Paris for formal composition training. One such pillar of Canadian choral music was Healey Willan (1880–1968), considered by many to be the "father of Canadian choral music," whose early training was in the British choir school tradition. Willan was best known for his liturgical output, and his motets, masses, and anthems exhibit a proclivity for elegant counterpoint, modality, and melismatic, linear writing. Another early Canadian composer who maintained close ties with Britain was W. H. Anderson (1882–1955), who sang at St. Paul's Cathedral before immigrating to Canada in 1910 where he became particularly well known for the natural lyricism of his choral compositions, many of which are well-suited for young, amateur choirs. Under the pseudonym Michael Bilencko, Anderson also arranged a large number of Ukrainian, Czech, and Icelandic folk songs, using primarily those versions sung by settlers in his new home of Manitoba.

The French-Canadian composer Lionel Daunais (1902–82) received the Prix d'Europe, which allowed him to study in Paris before returning to Canada where he maintained parallel careers as a singer and composer of French-language choral and solo works. Similarly, Pierre Mercure (1927–66) studied in Paris with Nadia Boulanger. Jean Coulthard (1909–2000) received her early training in composition in Canada before going to England to study with Ralph Vaughan Williams, later working with Aaron Copland, Darius Milhaud, Arnold Schoenberg, and Béla Bartók. Violet Archer (1913–2000) studied with Bartók and Paul Hindemith. Derek Healey (b.1936) studied with Herbert Howells at the Royal College of Music in London before moving to Canada, bringing with him an intense interest in music of various cultures. Derek Holman (b.1931) served as music master at Westminster Abbey Choir School and Warden of the Royal School of Church Music before immigrating to Canada where he is a highly respected church musician and composer whose *Night Songs* received the 1988 Association of Canadian Choral Conductors National Choral Award for Outstanding Choral Work. The highly influential Quebec composer Claude Vivier (1948–83) was a student of Stockhausen who employed twentieth-century compositional techniques, frequently setting texts derived from ancient and medieval literature.

Typical of Canada's character of "cultural mosaic" rather than "melting pot," many Canadian composers brought with them the cultural and musical influences of diverse homelands and heritages. The music of Malcolm Forsyth (1936–2011), who was born in South Africa, combines African and North American folk music within his own unique style. Srul Irving Glick's writing (1934–2002) displays a significantly Jewish idiom.

New directions

Regardless of their place of birth, Canadian composers have established distinct compositional styles, often closely related to the landscape of the country's vast and diverse terrain. R. Murray Schafer (b.1933) holds a reputation as one of Canada's most creative composers whose choral music paints vivid sound portraits of the Canadian landscape. His concept of "soundscapes" influences music classrooms across Canada in an attempt to increase listeners' awareness of sounds of all types in the world. Schafer's dramatic approach to composition extends to music to be performed from different sides of a lake, or the placing of multiple choirs surrounding the audience. *Epitaph for Moonlight* and *Miniwanka* have become Canadian standards with their evocative texts and aleatoric opportunities for participants. Schafer's unique non-traditional scores have captured the interest of visual artists as well as musicians, resulting in their display in art galleries. Brief aleatoric passages and tonal depictions of Canada's natural beauty are also found in works such as *Keewaydin* by Harry Freedman (1922–2005) and *The Blue Eye of God* by Nancy Telfer (b.1950). Canadian geography has been the inspiration for Stephen Chatman's (b.1950) *Due West*, *Due East*, and *Due North* choral settings depicting such typically Canadian phenomena as mosquitoes and trains. Stephen Hatfield (b.1956) is recognized as one of Canada's most dynamic, imaginative composers. His music is frequently grounded in native and global ethnic traditions. Ruth Watson Henderson's (b.1932) *The Song My Paddle Sings*, Lydia Adams's (b.1953) *Mic'Maq Honour Song*, and the settings of poetry by native poet Pauline Johnson by Jeff Smallman (b.1965) and James Rolfe (b.1961) are a few examples of the influence of First Nations culture on Canadian choral tradition.

Folk song settings form a significant portion of Canadian choral repertoire. Most "classical" composers have also written concert arrangements of Canadian folk songs. Some of the best-known of these composer/arrangers include Ruth Watson Henderson (b.1932), Harry Somers (1925–99), Godfrey Ridout (1918–84), Donald Patriquin (b.1938), and Stuart Calvert (b.1933). Compositions by maritime composers of Canada's east coast, such as Allister MacGillivray's (b.1948) *Away from the Roll of the Sea* and *Song for the Mira*, have a particularly appealing quality as they express a closeness to the land and sea found in this part of the world, as the line between original compositions in a folk style and true folk songs becomes blurred.

The twentieth and twenty-first centuries have produced world-class Canadian composers whose music is known and performed globally. While these composers write in their own styles, there is a freshness about many Canadian choral compositions that makes them particularly appealing to choirs and audiences internationally. Imant Raminsh (b.1943), Eleanor Daley (b.1955), Ruth Watson Henderson, Stephen Chatman, Nancy Telfer, Mark Sirett (b.1952), Donald Patriquin, Allan Bevan (b.1951), and Stephen Hatfield have attracted the attention of conductors and choirs around the globe. Works such as Daley's *In Remembrance* and Raminsh's *Ave Verum Corpus*, Sirett's *Thou Shalt Know Him*, and Willan's *Rise Up My Love, My Fair One* have become part of the standard repertoire. Perhaps one explanation for the vocally idiomatic writing in so much of Canadian choral repertoire can be found in the fact that a large number of the composers are also choral conductors who work regularly and closely with voices and have a strong understanding of the medium.

Several of Canada's most prolific composers are women. Ruth Watson Henderson, Nancy Telfer, Eleanor Daley, and Ramona Luengen (b.1960) have all received international acclaim and have had a substantial number of compositions published in Canada, the USA, and Europe.

The new millennium

Competitions, commissions, and such prestigious initiatives as ACCC's National Choral Awards help to bring the work of established and emerging Canadian composers to the attention of the choral community.

Events such as the biennial composition competition sponsored by the Association of Canadian Choral Communities have resulted in high-profile performances and publication of winning compositions. Composers such as Allan Bevan, Eleanor Daley, and Jeff Smallman have gained increased public exposure through such competitions. They are representative of a talented cadre of composers who are taking Canadian choral composition into the new millennium with ever-widening creative techniques as they build their own portfolios and reputations.

A select list of Canadian choral repertoire

Daley, Eleanor. *In Remembrance* (SATB or SSAA)

Daunais, Lionel. *Figures de danse* (SATB)

   Le Pont Mirabeau (SATB)

Freedman, Harry. *Keewaydin* (SSA)

Glick, Srul Irving. *The Hour Has Come* (SATB)

Hatfield, Stephen. *La Lluvia* (SATB, also SSA)

Henderson, Ruth Watson. *Missa Brevis* (SATB)

Lang, Rupert. *Agneau de Dieu* (SATB)

   Cantate Domino (SSAA)

Luengen, Ramona. *Salve Regina* (SSAA)

Mercure, Pierre. *Cantate pour une joie* (SATB)

Patriquin, Donald (arr.). *J'entends le moulin* (SS or SATB)

Raminsh, Imant. *Ave Verum Corpus* (SATB)

   Magnificat (SATB)

Schafer, R. Murray. *Epitaph for Moonlight* (SATB)

   Gamelan (SATB or SSAA)

   Miniwanka (SATB or SSAA)

Sirett, Mark. *Thou Shalt Know Him* (SATB)

Somers, Harry. *Five Songs from the Newfoundland Outports* (SATB)

Telfer, Nancy. *Missa Brevis* (SSA)

Tilley, Alexander. *In Flanders Fields* (SATB or SA)

Vivier, Claude. *Jesus Erbarme Dich* (SATB)

Willan, Healey. *Hodie Christus natus est* (SATB)

   I Beheld Her, Beautiful as a Dove (SATB)

   Rise Up My Love, My Fair One (SATB)

Additional resources

Association of Canadian Choral Communities www.choralcanada.ca

The Canadian Encyclopedia www.thecanadianencyclopedia.com. This website includes the online version of Helmut Kallmann, Gilles Potvin and Kenneth Winters, *The Encyclopedia of Music in Canada*. University of Toronto Press, 1981.

Canadian Music Centre www.musiccentre.ca. Visitors to the website now have access to hundreds of archival recordings.

Choral Works by Canadian Composers: A Selective Guidelist of Published Choral Compositions by British Columbia Composers. Vancouver, BC: British Columbia Choral Federation, 2004.

Jonas, Holly Higgins. *In Their Own Words: Canadian Choral Conductors.* Toronto: Dundurn Press, 2001.

Kallman, Helmut, Gilles Potvin, and Kenneth Winters (eds.). *Encyclopedia of Music in Canada.* University of Toronto Press, 1981, 1992.

McGee, Timothy J. *The Music of Canada.* New York: W.W. Norton & Company, 1985.

Pitman, Walter. *Elmer Iseler: Choral Visionary.* Toronto: Dundurn Press, 2008.

Recommended Canadian Choral Repertoire, ed. V. Meredith, P. Abbott, and B. Clark. Montreal, QC: Association of Canadian Choral Conductors, 2002.

Recommended Canadian Choral Repertoire, vol. II: *Sacred,* ed. V. Meredith, P. Abbott, and B. Clark. Montreal, QC: Association of Canadian Choral Conductors, 2004.

Recommended Canadian Choral Repertoire, vol. III: *The Folk Song,* ed. P. Abbott, and J. Hawn. Montreal, QC: Association of Canadian Choral Conductors, 2006.

Recommended Canadian Choral Repertoire, vol. IV: *Sacred, Secular and Christmas,* ed. P. Abbott, and J. Hawn. Montreal, QC: Association of Canadian Choral Conductors, 2008.

Recommended Canadian Choral Repertoire, vol. V: *Seasonal Favourites,* ed. J. Hawn, and C. Murray. Halifax, NS: Association of Canadian Choral Conductors, 2010.

8 A multiplicity of voices: choral music in the United States

KATHY SALTZMAN ROMEY AND MATTHEW MEHAFFEY

Drawing on a diverse and evolving population, the choral culture of the United States reflects the multiplicity of contemporary American society. Whether in worship, protest, recreational, or concert settings, people of all ages, ethnic backgrounds, and creeds comprise the country's dynamic singing community. According to the 2009 Chorus Impact Study published by Chorus America, more people in the United States are involved in choral singing than in any other performing art. Approximately 22.9 percent of American households have at least one member in a chorus. An estimated 42.6 million singers participate in one or more of 270,000 religious, academic, children's, community, and professional choirs.[1] This abundant choral landscape is enriched by America's diverse population of composers and supported by a variety of service organizations and advocacy groups.

Religious communities

Singing was an important part of religious life in the colonial era, but was largely unorganized. In the eighteenth century, musicians such as composer William Billings (1746–1800) spearheaded the establishment of "singing schools." These traveling schools, lasting from a few days to several weeks in length, moved from town to town with the aim of improving the quality of congregational singing. Participants learned rudiments of vocal production, solmization, and part-singing. Alumni of the schools established church and community choirs throughout New England and the northeast United States. By the 1780s, organized choirs had become very widespread across New England.

In the early nineteenth century, Lowell Mason (1792–1872) and members of the Better Music Movement led a mission to permeate the culture with more complex music. This movement resulted in the establishment of music programs within the public schools, higher standards of church music, and the founding of the Boston Academy of Music in 1833. The rustic style of Billings's music was abandoned in New England in favor of a more European manner of composition. Singing school masters were relegated to rural areas in the south and west, where their style of singing, known as shape-note singing, used geometric shapes on a staff as visual cues to assist singers in learning to read music. *Sacred Harp* and *Southern Harmony* were two of the most popular collections of the folk songs and hymns of the era. Both are still used by shape-note singing societies across the country today.

Choral singing also flourished in insular populations such as the Shakers, Moravians, and Mormons. Music from the Shaker communities tended to be simple and was derived from the prosody of the chosen text. Thousands of Shaker tunes survive today, many of them standards of modern hymnody. The Moravians, immigrants from central Europe, developed an advanced musical culture in Bethlehem, Pennsylvania. This community had ready access to contemporary music from Europe and performed the American premieres of masterworks such as Haydn's *The Creation* as early as 1811. The Bethlehem Bach Festival, which presented the first American reading of Bach's Mass in B minor, BWV232, in 1900, is an outgrowth of this strong tradition. At the edge of the western frontier, the famed Mormon Tabernacle Choir was founded in 1847, just one month after the Mormons settled in Utah. This choir of over three hundred volunteer singers has gained worldwide fame, in part because of *Music and the Spoken Word*, its weekly program that has been broadcast on the radio since 1929 and televised since 1962.

The fervent religiosity of nineteenth-century America coincided with the development of gospel hymns: simple catchy songs with sacred texts and folk-based melodies. Gospel hymns were used at denominational camp meetings to teach Bible stories, particularly to the young. White gospel songs from this era, such as "Jesus Loves Me," are common additions to today's mainstream denominational hymnals. White gospel music continues to be used in worship by evangelical communities and has maintained wider popularity through recordings and radio broadcasts.

The style known today as "black gospel music" developed from a melting pot of styles, ranging from the hymnody of both black and white congregations to the camp-meeting spiritual songs composed by slaves in the early nineteenth century. Black musicians began combining these elements with the popular styles of jazz, ragtime, and blues to create a new genre of religious music that would have a lasting impact on music worldwide. By the turn of the twentieth century, black gospel music was a thriving art form, particularly in Pentecostal and Baptist churches in large urban centers such as Chicago and Detroit. The advent of radio and the recording industry greatly increased the audience for gospel music in the early 1900s. Groups such as the Golden Gate Quartet, along with gospel artists like Thomas A. Dorsey and Sallie Martin, propelled black gospel music into the mainstream of American culture. Many of today's popular musicians and contemporary musical styles trace their roots to gospel music.

Choral music in modern American churches and synagogues varies greatly among and within denominations. Whether small or large, choirs play an important role in American religious communities. Religious choirs tend to be made up of volunteer singers of all ages and ability levels. Larger congregations often have graded choral programs of children's, youth, and adult choirs. Churches may also employ a small number of professional singers to augment volunteer choristers. A select number of churches and synagogues, often based in larger city centers, have fully professional choirs to sing for worship. Some churches have organized choirs that developed into some of the country's leading professional and community choral organizations. These include Voices of Ascension, founded by Dennis Keene at Church of the Ascension in New York City; Musica Sacra, founded by Richard Westenburg at New York City's Central Presbyterian Church; and VocalEssence (formerly the Plymouth Music Series), founded by Philip Brunelle at Plymouth Congregational Church in Minneapolis, Minnesota. Many religious choirs incorporate popular styles of music into their repertoire. Regardless of style, choral music continues to be a vital part of worship and liturgy in the United States.

Academic choirs

Of the millions of adults singing in American choirs, the 2009 Chorus America Chorus Impact Study indicated that approximately 65 percent began singing when they were in primary or middle school. The study also revealed that, for many adults, this connection to choral music was cultivated early in life through exposure in the home to familial singing, radio broadcasts, recordings, and live performances. According to Chorus America, "introducing children to choral music opportunities when they are young develops future performers, audience members, and consumers of arts and culture well into adult years. Choral singing is an activity that fosters personal fulfillment and an appreciation of beauty for a *lifetime*. Moreover, singing with a chorus has life-long collateral benefits including fostering behaviors that lead to good citizenship."[2]

Choral music in public schools
Music programs in public (i.e., state non-feepaying) schools vary dramatically throughout the United States. National standards for music education were developed by the Music Educators National Conference in 1994, and accompanied by legislation in the form of the Goals 2000: Educate America Act, which included the arts as a core academic subject. The

United States, however, does not regulate musical standards on a national level. American public schools are part of individual districts within each state. These districts are independent in policy and funding, and governed at the local level. Consequently, music programs differ greatly in scope depending on the traditions, culture, and values of each state, region, district, and school. In any given district, there may be public schools with flourishing choral and instrumental ensembles in close proximity to schools with limited or no musical opportunities.

Primary and secondary music programs serve students ages five through eighteen in kindergarten, elementary school, middle school, and high school. Depending on funding and staff, schools include a variety of curricular offerings including general and specialized music classes; children's, men's, and women's choruses; mixed choirs, chamber ensembles, and madrigal groups. School districts with greater activity and administrative support may host annual district festivals, clinics, or honors ensembles. At the state level, professional service organizations also sponsor annual events such as the State Solo and Ensemble Contest or All-State music ensembles that bring together students from all districts in competitive and collaborative music-making forums.

School choral programs also provide opportunities to explore such American genres as musical theater, vocal jazz, and show choir.[3] Musical theater, which has as its centerpiece the popular song, offers students a more contemporary, interdisciplinary experience. Many high schools present elaborate annual productions ranging from such traditional shows as Rodgers and Hammerstein's *Oklahoma!* to more modern hits such as Stephen Sondheim's *Into the Woods* and Jonathan Larson's *Rent*.

Vocal jazz distinguishes itself from musical theater and show choir in several ways, the most important being the absence of choreography. According to Michael Weaver, "vocal jazz, in the purest sense, is about harmonic singing, improvisation and syncopated rhythms."[4] Often considered the only musical form to have originated in the United States, jazz plays an important role in American music education. The activities of composer/educator/performers such as Phil Mattson, Kirby Shaw, Steve Zegree, and Bobby McFerrin have contributed to the widespread growth of vocal jazz education.

The study of jazz, musical theater, and show choir within public school programs has enriched the educational experience and increased student participation in music. However, Ronald McCurdy, president of the International Association of Jazz Educators from 2000 to 2002, challenged teachers and administrators to think more broadly about music education in the future: "If we subscribe to the notion that "As we live, so do we sing," then we must listen to the lyrics of today's global society! Leaders must acknowledge technology and music business, remain open-minded as to other genres of music ... rather than teaching only what is familiar to them."[5]

This shift towards a more open-minded, multicultural perspective in teaching dates back to the civil rights movement of the 1960s and government reform of education during the 1970s, which served as social catalysts in the globalization of American music education.[6] National conferences such as the Tanglewood Symposium of 1967 provided a professional forum to evaluate the current and future state of music education up through the twenty-first century.[7] The final recommendations of this conference were summarized in the influential Tanglewood Declaration, which states that "music of all periods, styles, forms, and cultures belong in the curriculum."[8] Over the next thirty years, major advances were made in the areas of teacher training, curriculum development, published resources, recordings, and media programs, all of which furthered a more global approach to music education. Multicultural advocates such as Mary Goetze have continued to challenge current thinking and practice around issues of authenticity, enculturation, and ownership.[9]

Choral music in higher education

Singing has long been popular on American college campuses. Student-governed ensembles were some of the first choirs in higher education. Harvard University's Glee Club was founded in 1858, followed by the University of Michigan's in 1859, Yale University's in 1861, and the University of Pennsylvania's in 1862. These glee clubs were founded as men's choruses, but over time many of them became coeducational or were complemented by female counterparts such as the Radcliffe Choral Society, founded in 1899 at Harvard.

During the first quarter of the twentieth century, music studies at the university level became more formalized with the founding of such conservatories as the Juilliard School in 1905, Eastman School of Music in 1921, and Curtis Institute of Music in 1924. Many of America's most influential collegiate choral ensembles were founded during this period. In 1906, Peter Lutkin founded the A Cappella Choir of the Northwestern University Conservatory of Music, making it the first permanent organization of its kind in America. F. Melius Christiansen (1871–1955), a Norwegian Lutheran immigrant, established the St. Olaf Choir in Northfield, Minnesota in 1912. Since its inception, this college choir has toured the world, setting new standards for choral excellence and instituting a tradition of distinctive choral music at Lutheran colleges throughout the country. Likewise, John Finley Williamson (1887–1964) – a Presbyterian church musician from Dayton, Ohio – became convinced that professionally trained ministers of music could best serve the needs of church music programs. In 1926, he founded what is now Westminster Choir College to train a new breed of choral musicians. The Westminster Choir gained great repute through radio broadcasts, international touring, and performances with the world's finest orchestras and conductors. These early conductors and institutions were important proponents of the American a cappella choir movement that established regional choral traditions and schools of choral philosophy, influencing generations of students and audiences to come.

African-American institutions of higher learning made equally important contributions to the field of choral music. Through concert touring, the Fisk Jubilee Singers of Fisk University in Tennessee introduced the world to the concert spiritual in the 1870s. The famed Tuskegee Institute Choir, founded in 1886 by Booker T. Washington, reached international fame under William Dawson (1899–1990) and established traditions that have been adopted by the Morehouse and Spelman College Glee Clubs in Atlanta, Georgia; the Morgan State University Choir in Baltimore, Maryland; as well as community and professional ensembles across the country. Spiritual arrangements have continued to evolve under such later composers as Moses Hogan and André Thomas, and are an established part of the American choral canon.

In addition to those mentioned previously, numerous faculty members in choral music have made significant contributions to the development of the choral art in the United States. In California, Howard Swan (1906–95), known as one of the founding fathers of American choral music, conducted the renowned Men's and Women's Glee Clubs at Occidental College from 1934 to 1971. Swan's student Charles Hirt (1911–2001) established the University of Southern California departments of Church and Choral Music in 1946. Hirt toured extensively, espousing the belief that music can be used as a force for social good. He was perhaps most influential as the teacher of noted conductors such as William Dehning, Dale Warland, and Lynn Whitten.

Another significant conductor-teacher was Harold Decker (1914–2003), who led the graduate program in conducting at the University of Illinois from 1957 to 1981. He also co-authored the preeminent resource book, *Choral Conducting: A Symposium*, with noted teacher Julius Herford (1901–81), who himself led the conducting program at Indiana University from 1964 to 1980. Influential conductors taught by Decker include choral leaders Anton Armstrong, René Clausen, Joseph Flummerfelt, and Jameson Marvin.

Herford's influence extended beyond the academy to impact such recognized conductors as Robert Shaw, Roger Wagner, Elaine Brown, Fiora Contino, and Margaret Hillis. Other historic collegiate choral leaders include: Lorna Cooke deVaron at New England Conservatory of Music from 1947 to 1988; Robert Fountain at Oberlin College from 1948 to 1970, and at University of Wisconsin, Madison from 1971 to 1994; Weston Noble of the Luther College Nordic Choir from 1948 to 2005; and Lloyd Pfautsch at Southern Methodist University from 1958 to 1992.

Community organizations

Children's and youth choirs

While many school districts across the nation reflect healthy choral and instrumental music programs, an ever-increasing number of districts have been forced to reduce or even eliminate music from their curriculum due to financial constraints. In response, many civic arts organizations have garnered private and corporate support to develop educational programs that partner with public schools through artist residencies, in-school performances, music festivals, and curriculum workshops for classroom teachers.

In 1999, the Choral Arts Society of Washington, DC, discovered that only 40 percent of public schools in the city employed a music teacher. In collaboration with the District of Columbia Public Schools, this chorus developed an elementary music curriculum entitled *artsACCESS* (Arts for Children Creates Educational Success in Schools) to reinstate music strategically in four schools each year. Likewise, the Weill Institute of Carnegie Hall in New York City engages over 50,000 students and teachers annually in educational offerings for pre-school (Carnegie Kids), elementary school (Musical Explorers / LinkUP!), middle school (Perelman American Roots), and high school students (Citi Global Encounters / Cultural Exchange).

Professional music organizations such as the Cleveland Orchestra have developed tiered choir programs for singers from primary through secondary school to support music making and training within the public schools. Colleges and universities are also extending their outreach to include choral training for children and young adults. The Michigan State University Children's Chorus (MSUCC), based in East Lansing, Michigan, is a Grammy-award-winning program founded in 1993. MSUCC focuses on the comprehensive education of choral musicians from early grade school through high school. Similar programs include the Indianapolis Children's Choir at Butler University, the Indiana University Children's Chorus, and the Syracuse Children's Chorus, which works in collaboration with Syracuse University (New York).

Major city centers are also home to innovative community choral programs for children and youth. These organizations are leaders in fund-raising, membership, and educational outreach, and are known for creative programming, which often emphasizes global repertoire and commissioning. The Chicago Children's Chorus administers a program that serves thousands of inner-city children through choirs in numerous Chicago schools, after-school neighborhood choirs, and a select Concert Choir. On the east coast, the Young People's Chorus of New York City serves over a thousand children of diverse ethnic backgrounds in public schools through its Core After-School Program, the Satellite Program, and an affiliate program in Erie, Pennsylvania. The mission of the American Boychoir – a private boarding school for boys in Princeton, New Jersey – is to "sustain and move forward with a distinctively American voice the one-thousand-year-old boychoir school tradition."[10] In the west, the internationally recognized San Francisco Girls Chorus serves as a regional center and training model "to create outstanding performances featuring the unique and compelling sound of young women's voices through an exemplary music education program."[11]

Amateur community choirs

The tradition of amateur choral singing can be traced back to early musical societies, which emerged during the nineteenth century with the growth of population and industry in northeastern urban centers. The Handel and Haydn Society of Boston, founded in 1815, grew out of the Better Music Movement (see page 115). Other choirs – such as the German-inspired singing society Deutsche Liederkranz (founded in New York in 1847) and the English glee club-inspired Mendelssohn Club of Philadelphia (founded in 1874) – reflected the diverse cultural backgrounds of American immigrants. Many choral groups were originally established as men's clubs, but a shift in focus to European art music soon brought women into these ensembles. By the late nineteenth century, choirs such as the Oratorio Society of New York, founded in 1873, were formed with the intent of singing large choral/orchestral works. These organizations became leading cultural institutions in their cities, introducing American audiences to such masterworks as Handel's *Messiah*, Brahms's *Ein Deutsches Requiem*, and Mahler's Symphony No. 8.

Today, a vast array of volunteer community choral organizations serves the millions of amateur vocalists living in the United States. Community ensembles range in size from small choirs that perform for local civic events to large artistic institutions. These ensembles perform a diverse range of choral repertoire spanning classical, jazz, barbershop, pop, folk, and global music. Many community choirs perform at a level similar to that of their professional counterparts. The Cleveland Orchestra Chorus, which gained repute under first Robert Shaw and later Robert Page, maintains the highest standards of performance and training while retaining its status as an entirely volunteer ensemble. Amateur singers also participate in seasonal and yearlong festivals such as Cincinnati's historic May Festival Chorus and the Berkshire Choral Festival in Massachusetts.

Some community choirs extend their mission beyond high standards in concert performance to education and cultural preservation. For many singers, "the bridging of social gaps, the opening to different perspectives on life, even apart from the music itself, is one of the most rewarding and sustaining aspects of their choral singing."[12] Through musical and educational programming, these ensembles strive to build community, and to raise awareness around such contemporary issues as the celebration of cultural heritage, social justice, interracial collaboration, and affirmation of sexual orientation.

The Zamir Chorale in Boston raises "awareness of the breadth and beauty of Jewish culture through performances, recordings, symposia, publications, and musical commissions."[13] Welsh *Gymanfa Ganu* – festivals devoted to the singing of Welsh hymns – are popular annual events throughout the United States. In 1963, the country-and-Western singer Tennessee Ernie Ford released an album with the San Quentin Prison Choir. The growing number of choirs in American prisons connects singing with issues of social justice, providing inmates with a positive outlet for interaction, socialization, and enrichment. Singing City, founded in 1948 by Elaine Brown as an integrated choir in the inner city of Philadelphia, embodied the vision that racial, cultural, religious, and economic barriers could be overcome by the shared experience of choral singing. In the 1950s and 1960s – a time of deep racial conflict across the country – Singing City joined forces with the civil rights movement to present concerts to integrated audiences throughout the southern United States.

In the 1970s, choral music became a powerful tool for the gay and lesbian communities. This began with the founding of two organizations: the feminist vocal ensemble Anna Crusis Women's Choir of Philadelphia (1975), and the Gotham Male Chorus in New York City (1977). In 1978, the San Francisco Gay Men's Chorus became the first openly gay ensemble in the United States. Over the next several years, gay/lesbian/bisexual/transgender (GLBT) choruses were founded in major metropolitan centers nationwide, including the Seattle Men's Chorus (1979), the Turtle Creek Chorale in Dallas (1980), and MUSE – Cincinnati Women's Choir (1980). As of 2011, almost two hundred ensembles are listed as members of GALA Choruses, the national service organization of GLBT choirs.

Professional choirs

Professional choirs in America differ from those in other parts of the world. Unlike countries in Europe and East Asia, where governments may support full-time professional choirs, the United States government provides very limited funding to the arts as a whole. Financial support for American arts organizations comes from a combination of federal and state grants, corporations, private foundations, and individual donors. As a result, the number of full-time, professional choruses is comparatively small. Among these ensembles are the Metropolitan Opera Chorus, military choruses such as the Air Force Singing Sergeants and Navy Sea Chanters, the male vocal chamber ensembles Chanticleer and Cantus, and popular groups such as the Manhattan Transfer and Rockapella.

A broader definition of professional choirs in America includes organizations that pay a designated core of their membership, or the entire ensemble, for selected artistic activity at various points throughout any given season. Examples include the Kansas City Chorale, the Miami-based Seraphic Fire, and the Austin, Texas ensemble Conspirare. There are also organizations with a largely volunteer membership supplemented by a core of professional singers. The Mendelssohn Club of Philadelphia and the Pacific Chorale in California are among the many organizations that use this model.[14] Additionally, professional ensembles are often assembled to serve the needs of seasonal music festivals such as the Carmel Bach Festival in California, the Santa Fe Desert Chorale, the Oregon Bach Festival, and Spoleto Festival USA in Charleston, South Carolina.

The spread of professional and volunteer choirs during the twentieth century was a result of the work of visionary conductors who established ensembles and raised performance standards and public awareness through innovative programming, commissioning, recording, touring, and outreach. These conductors included: Fred Waring (1899–1986), founder of the Pennsylvanians and the Fred Waring Glee Club; Eva Jessye (1895–1992), conductor of the Eva Jessye Chorale and noted for her work on George Gershwin's opera *Porgy and Bess*; Robert Shaw (1916–99), leader of the Collegiate Chorale, the Robert Shaw Chorale, and the Atlanta Symphony Orchestra Chorus; Roger Wagner (1914–92), founder of the Roger Wagner Chorale and the Los Angeles Master Chorale; and Margaret Hillis (1921–98), founder of the Chicago Symphony Chorus. In addition to their musical responsibilities, these individuals were composers, arrangers, collaborators, administrators, and choral ambassadors. Their individual and collective passion for the advancement of the choral art resulted in myriad opportunities for the next generation of choral musicians. The torch lit by these seminal figures has been passed on through the history of American choral music, linking future conductors to a heritage that continues to grow and evolve.

Composers

The foundation of choral repertoire in the United States extends back to African-American field hollers, European art music, gospel and folk songs, Native American chant, sacred music of all denominations, western ballads, and music of America's diverse immigrant populations, informing an evolving body of traditional and contemporary music.

Through an initiative entitled American Masterpieces: Three Centuries of Artistic Genius, the National Endowment for the Arts (NEA) began awarding major grants in all areas of the arts to preserve and further the cultural heritage of the United States. Beginning in 2006, these funds supported composer residencies, workshops, concerts, and regional choir festivals presented by academic and community organizations from coast to coast. The initiative supported performances of works by American composers from all eras, including music by the composers listed below:

- eighteenth- and nineteenth-century composers William Billings and Stephen Foster;
- twentieth-century composers Samuel Barber, Leonard Bernstein, Harry T. Burleigh, Aaron Copland, William Dawson, R. Nathaniel Dett, Charles Ives, Norman Luboff, Gian Carlo Menotti, Alice Parker/Robert Shaw, William Schuman, Randall Thompson, and Virgil Thomson;
- contemporary composers Dominick Argento, William Bolcom, Brent Michael Davids, Jennifer Higdon, Moses Hogan, Aaron Jay Kernis, Libby Larsen, Morten Lauridsen, Stephen Paulus, Ned Rorem, Conrad Susa, Eric Whitacre, and Chen Yi.[15]

In the program overview, conductor Philip Brunelle wrote:

> The composers in this compilation represent some of the finest musicians devoted to the choral art; they were chosen for their noted affinity for writing for voices coupled with their masterful sense of textual relationship to the music they compose. There are, of course, thousands of American choral composers down through history, and this roster of twenty-nine composers represents an important introduction to the richness and diversity of American choral music.[16]

Other prominent American composers include John Adams, Amy Beach, Lukas Foss, Norman Dello Joio, Kirke Mechem, Meredith Monk, Vincent Persichetti, Daniel Pinkham, Undine Smith Moore, William Grant Still, Steven Stucky, and Gwyneth Walker. Twentieth-century immigrants such as Paul Hindemith, Ernest Bloch, Arnold Schoenberg, and Igor Stravinsky, along with jazz/Broadway music legends such as Dave Brubeck, Duke Ellington, George Gershwin, Jerome Kern, and Richard Rodgers, also made significant contributions to the American choral art. These artists, as well as countless others, have become part of the many stylistic traditions represented on contemporary concert programs.

Increasingly, many choirs have championed new music through the commissioning and performance of works by established and emerging composers. Community and professional choirs including the San Francisco Girls Chorus, the Young People's Chorus of New York City, Chanticleer, the Esoterics, Gregg Smith Singers, and the former Dale Warland Singers have placed the cultivation of new music at the center of their mission. These choruses alone have commissioned and premiered hundreds of significant works for children and adults by many of the preeminent American and international composers of the twentieth and twenty-first centuries. The practice of commissioning and performing new music has become so much a part of the American choral culture that school, volunteer, and religious choirs of moderate size are now frequent supporters of living composers.

Service organizations

The cultivation of choral music across the United States is supported by numerous organizations that serve every aspect of the profession. The American Choral Directors Association (ACDA) was founded in 1959 as a non-profit organization to promote excellence in choral singing and to advocate for the choral art in American society. With over 20,000 active members among conductors, teachers, students, and church musicians representing more than one million singers nationwide, ACDA is the world's largest choral organization. The association consists of fifty state chapters divided into seven geographic regions, which support the membership through newsletters, festivals, workshops, and conventions.

Chorus America was founded in 1977 by twenty-four of America's most prominent choral conductors to serve the needs of professional choruses. Today, Chorus America represents both volunteer and professional ensembles, supporting over 1,600 choirs, businesses, and individual members through a diverse offering of services and resources. Additionally, the organization has undertaken significant national surveys documenting the impact of choral singing throughout the United States. Both ACDA and Chorus America sponsor annual conferences that involve professional training, performances, commissioning, and repertoire sessions.

GALA Choruses Inc., an international association of GLBT choruses, was founded as a musical and advocacy organization in 1982 to serve the GLBT community through a broad offering of publications, leadership conferences, programs, and annual festivals. Its mission is to support the growing number of GLBT choruses as they "change our world through song." In addition, the organization provides grants for the commissioning of new works, and sponsors an international festival that draws five to six thousand singers from North America and abroad.

The American Guild of Organists (AGO), founded in 1896, promotes the scholarship of organ and choral music. MENC: The National Association for Music Education, founded in 1907, supports the activity of music teachers at every level. The National Convention of Gospel Choirs and Choruses (NCGCC) established in 1933 by Thomas A. Dorsey, Willa Mae Ford Smith, and Sallie Martin, furthers the mission and education of gospel music. Founded in 1938, the Barbershop Harmony Society – formerly the Society for the Preservation and Encouragement of Barber Shop Quartet Singing in America, Inc. – promotes the art of barbershop singing. The Choristers Guild, organized in 1949, supports children's and youth choirs within the school and church; and the National Collegiate Choral Organization (NCCO), founded in 2005, focuses on research and performance opportunities for college and university conductors. Many choral professionals in the United States are also members of the International Association for Jazz Education (IAJE), the International Federation for Choral Music (IFCM), and the National Association of Teachers of Singing (NATS).

Publishers

The United States is an international leader in the area of music publishing, generating and distributing professional materials that reflect all stylistic periods and musical traditions. The Music Publishers Association of the United States, founded in 1895, includes over seventy-five member organizations, including Boosey & Hawkes, G. Schirmer, Inc., and Theodore Presser Company, which have affiliate companies and/or agents around the globe. During the latter part of the twentieth century, new publishing companies were established to address the growing need for multicultural repertoire, world music resources, and original works by international composers. World Music Press (1985), Earthsongs (1988), Alliance Music Publications, Inc. (1994), and Mj Publishing (2000) are some of the many publishers that focus on music of diverse cultures through specialized series and educational resources. Likewise, individual composers have provided broader access to their music through self-publishing and private web distribution. The American Society of Composers, Authors and Publishers (ASCAP) represents the greater community of creative artists. ASCAP was founded in 1914 and serves as the leading performing rights organization in the United States with over 380,000 member-owners. The organization encompasses every style of music and monitors the licensing and royalties connected with performances of all copyrighted works affiliated with its membership.

Summary

The choral culture of the United States continues to evolve as communities forge collaborative artistic and social relationships locally, nationally, and internationally. Twentieth-century choral leaders such as Elaine Brown, Howard Swan, Charles Hirt, and Robert Shaw cultivated the idea that choral music could be used to promote the common good. Building on this legacy, conductors, composers, and singers in the twenty-first century are expanding the scope and reach of choral music in the United States by looking to ethnic identity, cultural heritage, and social engagement, in addition to the Western classical canon, as they compose and program repertoire.

Despite this impressive vitality, the choral field, like most other artistic disciplines in the United States, faces significant financial challenges. The 2008 Congressional Arts Report Card published by Americans for the Arts indicated that "Congress woefully underfunds the arts despite the proven return on investment in communities, giving the National Endowment for the Arts (NEA) a budget of just 48 cents per American – a little more than the cost of a first class [postage] stamp."[17] Fluctuations in government, corporate, foundation, and private funding require that choral organizations increasingly diversify their financial base in order to remain viable. Additionally, many choral ensembles continue to grapple with issues related to audience development and the relevancy of choral music in today's world. As Ann Meier Baker and Todd Estabrook of Chorus America assert:

> One of the most surprising things about choruses may be that even though their effects are all around us – with an impressive number of beautiful concerts being sung by an enormous number of talented singers – their many positive attributes are often overlooked. In a society that seeks to enhance civic engagement and student achievement, the data [in the 2009 *Chorus Impact Study*] suggests that it would be a mistake not to leverage the benefits that choruses bring to children, adults, and the communities they serve.[18]

The twenty-first century offers choral musicians around the world resources heretofore unknown – the technology to communicate directly with one another, expanded performance opportunities, and global access to repertoire, publishers, research, and professional organizations. Today's musical world is measured not by distance, but by the quality of the community and relationships it engenders. The outgrowth of these connections, combined with America's diverse choral heritage and the efforts of civic, academic, and religious music organizations, will shape the future of choral music and the significant role it can play in contemporary society.

Select bibliography

Conlon, Joan (ed.). *Wisdom, Wit, and Will: Women Choral Conductors on Their Art*. Chicago, IL: GIA Publications, 2009.

Decker, Harold A., and Julius Herford (eds.). *Choral Conducting: A Symposium*, 2nd edn. Englewoods Cliffs, NJ: Prentice Hall, 1988.

DeVenney, David P. *American Choral Music since 1985*. New York: General Music Publishing Co., 1999.

    Source Readings in American Choral Music. Monographs and Bibliographies in American Music, vol. XV. Missoula, MT: College Music Society, 1995.

Glenn, Carole (ed.). *In Quest of Answers: Interviews with American Choral Conductors*. Chapel Hill, NC: Hinshaw Music, 1991.

Hitchcock, H. Wiley and Stanley Sadie (eds.). *The New Grove Dictionary of American Music*. London and New York: Macmillan Press, 1986.

Mussulman, Joseph. *Dear People . . . Robert Shaw: A Biography*. Bloomington: Indiana University Press, 1979.

Paine, Gordon (ed.). *Five Centuries of Choral Music: Essays in Honor of Howard Swan*. Stuyvesant, NY: Pendragon Press, 1988.

Web resources

American Choral Directors Association www.acda.org

American Guild of Organists www.agohq.org

The Barbershop Harmony Society www.barbershop.org

Choristers Guild www.choristersguild.org

Chorus America www.chorusamerica.org

GALA Choruses, Inc. www.galachoruses.org

National Association for Music Education www.menc.org

National Association of Teachers of Singing www.nats.org

National Collegiate Choral Organization www.ncco-usa.org

National Convention of Gospel Choirs and Choruses www.ncgccinc.com

9 A hundred years of choral music in Latin America 1908–2008

MARÍA GUINAND

In order to understand the choral activity of the last hundred years in Latin America, it is important to summarize the history that shaped this region since the sixteenth century.

Choral music, understood as organized part singing, did not exist in any of the indigenous civilizations of the American continent. This art was established by Spanish immigration, through the Catholic Church, because its missionaries were responsible for education in general and particularly for musical training. During colonial times, choral music developed in the cathedrals, missions, brotherhoods, and religious societies.

The development of music in these territories took place between 1500 and 1820.[1]

Cathedrals

Cathedral choral music was highly developed in the Virreinato de Nueva España in Mexico City, Puebla, and Guatemala, and later in Cuba; in the Virreinato de Nueva Granada in Bogotá and later in Caracas; in the Virreinato of Perú in Lima and Cuzco; and in the Virreinato del Río de La Plata in La Plata.

Most masses, magnificats, requiems, laments, and motets (many of them polychoral) were composed in Latin for church services, following the Renaissance and baroque styles of the music from the cathedrals of Seville and Toledo in Spain. It is not surprising, therefore, that works by Morales, Victoria, Guerrero, and Palestrina, among many others, are found in the archives of the cathedrals in Santa Fé de Bogotá, Lima, and Mexico City. Other works composed in Spanish or in Amerindian languages were inspired by the *villancico*, a Spanish genre, allowing for the incorporation of new rhythmic and contrapuntal patterns.

Missions

Missionaries used music as a way of teaching Christian ideas to native populations. They praised the ability of indigenous people to assimilate the European cultural traits, especially in music, since natives were particularly skillful at building and playing musical instruments.

The social structure in Latin America did not allow natives to take high-level positions in the musical scene. Only some "mestizos," of mixed Spanish and indigenous ancestry, held important positions during the mid-colonial times (1650–1750). In Mexico and Peru, natives of noble descent were educated in special music programs. In Quito, the Franciscans founded the San Andrés School (1550–81) for the sons of indigenous chiefs. Music education aimed to familiarize the natives with Gregorian chant and later with polyphonic singing. The Jesuit and Franciscan orders were the most connected to musical activities. The latter made a major impact on the native groups of North and Central America. The writings of Franciscan monk Juan de Torquemada, in his *Monarchia Indiana* (or 'Indian monarchies'), give evidence of this reality.[2]

During the seventeenth and eighteenth centuries, Jesuits were very active in the missions of Paraguay, Bolivia, Argentina, and Brazil until they were expelled from Brazil in 1759 and from Hispanic America in 1767.

The most outstanding missionary composers were Domenico Zipoli, Juan de Araujo, and Manuel de Mesa (1725–73).

Two musical miracles in America

The musicologist Curt Lange (1903–97) described the Escuela de Chacao organized in Venezuela in the eighteenth and nineteenth centuries, and Escola Mineira in Brazil, as the "two musical miracles in America."[3]

The main characteristic of these two centers of musical activity and choral composition was the social diversity of their members. Many of them were free mulattos ("pardos," or "blancos de orilla"), placed below the hierarchy of the white population in the case of the Escuela de Chacao and the Escola Mineira. Being musicians allowed them to enjoy a privileged social position. Thus, it is interesting to reflect on the extent to which attitudes of racial superiority were reflected in musical composition, first, within the European styles of that time, and later making way for a very rich explosion of new rhythms, melodies, colors, and instruments that characterize today's Latin American music.

The Escuela de Chacao flourished in the second half of the eighteenth century and the early nineteenth century and stretched into the postcolonial period, under the encouragement of Pedro Palacios y Sojo (1739–99), priest and composer, who was influenced by the works of Pergolesi, Haydn, and Mozart.[4]

Most works were written for the Latin liturgy, but there were some Christmas and funeral tunes, carols, and patriotic songs as well, showing musical activity outside the ecclesiastical domain.

The Escola Mineira was founded in the Capitanía General of Minas Gerais, Brazil, in the early eighteenth century. The development of architecture, sculpture, and music was in part the work of mulatto artists.[5] With Portuguese colonial organization as a precedent, the region's musical life was organized around the different *Irmandades* or religious associations. The composers cultivated the pre-classical style like their fellow composers of the Escuela de Chacao. Most of the new works were sacred and in Latin.

The nineteenth century: the new free nations of America and the development of their music

The wars of independence occurred in Latin American countries during the first four decades of the nineteenth century, but civil wars and conflicts continued throughout the century. Nonetheless, in some countries such as Mexico, Cuba, Argentina, Venezuela, and Brazil, philharmonic societies and some charitable music societies were created in the middle of political and social uncertainty. These countries were undoubtedly important locations for trade, cultural, social, and political exchange in Latin America during the nineteenth century, and were visited by many great virtuoso musicians who encouraged the development of opera, symphonic, choral, and chamber music.

Argentina enjoyed an economy that allowed greater cultural development in some cities thanks to its agricultural activities. In Buenos Aires, there were eight important theaters; Teatro Coliseo, the most famous venue, had thirty Italian and French operas performed there in 1854. The Nuevo Teatro Colón was built in 1902 with an established program of great artists. The philharmonic society premiered Beethoven's *Missa Solemnis* in 1836.

In Cuba, a country that was part of the Spanish empire until the end of the nineteenth century, as well as in Mexico and Brazil, important theaters were built for intense operatic activity. In Caracas, a theater was built in 1881 under the French influence and named after President Antonio Guzmán Blanco.

At the same time, musical soirées were abundant in the haciendas and mansions of the educated high society, where attendants used to listen, to play, and to sing ballroom music. Styles such as the *habanera* (in Cuba), the *modinha* (in Brazil), the *waltz* (in Venezuela), the *cadomblé* (in Uruguay), and the *zamba* (in Argentina), became very popular.

This elitist musical activity took place alongside the creation of conservatories and music schools in several countries; there was constant exchange with Europe in the mid nineteenth century and early twentieth century, which stimulated younger musicians to study abroad. Most of the works written at the turn of the century were symphonic works or operas of nationalist nature, deeply influenced by the French and Italian styles.

The choral activity related to the Catholic Church that had continually developed from the sixteenth century until the end of the colonial period (early eighteenth century) diminished considerably during the nineteenth century, with only a handful of composers writing sacred music in this period.

The twentieth century

Despite the scant importance that choral music was given in the nine-teenth century, a renaissance of choral music took place in the twentieth century in consequence of musical exchanges with Europe and later with the United States. These initiatives helped to develop national conserva-tories, and to enhance the work of some religious centers where the chapel master tradition still existed, thus stimulating new compositions for the services.

The development of music in these new countries from the colonial period up to the present day has not been uniform. Some countries have had more or less steady musical growth that can be seen through the history of their music education institutions, their symphonic and choral organizations, their encouragement to composers, and their concert activities. Other countries have been more subject to the ups and downs of politics that have characterized the region. Consequently, we cannot talk about systematic growth in Latin American choral music, with con-sistent educational plans to train ensembles and conductors, but rather only about a choral movement in which the individual initiatives of conductors, composers, and promoters have been decisive in achieving what we can showcase nowadays as the result of this process. What is certain is that in Latin America, choral music has become part of cultural and community life in many diverse institutions such as schools, uni-versities, music conservatories, public offices, private companies, and community centers.

In the choral history of the region at the begining of the twentieth century, Argentina and Brazil can be considered the musical pivots, later joined by Venezuela, Chile, Mexico, Cuba, Colombia, and Uruguay, and successively and at a different pace, by the other countries. This is not an absolute classification but it allows for the organization of very vast information that exists on Latin American choral singing.

In the first half of the twentieth century the new a cappella repertoire was inspired by the madrigal and choral song tradition and the new sacred music modeled on the neoclassical style. Later, popular, folk, and Indian music were stylized into the nationalistic music of the nineteenth century. The interest in ethnomusicological research gave rise to new choral repertoire consisting of arrangements and choral versions of traditional music.

The birth and establishment of choirs and the subsequent development of choral institutions that allowed exchanges, organization of events, professional development of conductors and the dissemination of Latin American choral repertoire contributed to the rapid deepening of the choral culture.

The first part of the twentieth century: 1900–60

The first quarter of the twentieth century was influenced by European nationalism and the first attempts to establish vernacular forms of composition. It was not until the 1930s and 1940s that a new era began, influenced by European trends in composition. As Juan Orrego Salas has written:

> In the first half of the twentieth century, the most significant phenomenon in Latin America was the fast growth of nationalism in the social and political development of the continent. Music was an important part of this current . . . While in some manifestations of musical nationalism, the indigenous vernacular element was more evident (in Mexico, Central America, Ecuador, Bolivia, and Peru), in others African-American traditions prevailed (in the Caribbean and Brazil); for a third group, the dominant element was the Hispanic traditions (in Argentina, Chile and Uruguay).[6]

Many composers of this period actively participated in initiatives for improved music education in their countries. The search for roots and identity was more vigorous in Brazil, Argentina, Mexico, Venezuela, and Cuba, resulting in a more developed choral art in these countries.

Argentina

Musical nationalism in Argentina evolved differently than in other Latin American countries. The so-called *gauchesca* tradition caught the attention of most composers, as did the Andean traditions of the Western provinces and the *porteño* urban culture.[7] All these trends are present in many choral compositions of the twentieth century. However, we can also find choral works that reflect European compositional styles which are remote from nationalist aesthetic.

The work of Juan José Castro (1895–1968) includes several symphonic choral compositions, such as *Elegía a la muerte de García Lorca* (1945) and *De tierra gallega* (1946), based on the poems of the Spanish writer Federico García Lorca. The compositions of Luis Gianneo (1897–1968), particularly *Agnus Dei*, in the form of a cantata, and the *Tres canciones corales*, follow a nationalist trend. A more contemporary harmonic language is found in the motets of Roberto Caamaño (1923–93) and in the compositions of Alberto Ginastera (1916–83) such as *Lamentaciones del Profeta Jeremías*, Op. 14, and *Salmo CL*, Op. 5 (1938), for children's choir, mixed choir and orchestra, and *Turbae ad passionem gregorianam*, a theatrical setting of the Passion, for mixed choir, soloists, and orchestra.

Undoubtedly, the leading exponent of Argentinian Romantic nationalism is Carlos Guastavino (1912–2000), who became a role model for a generation of Argentinian choral and vocal composers because of his sensitive treatment of poetry. Among his a cappella choral works are *Se equivocó la paloma* (1941) on a poem by Rafael Alberti, and the *Indianas*, a series of compositions based on the poetry of Leon Benarós. In all of them, poetry is expressed through an exquisite but simple musical language. Other composers worth mentioning are Pedro Valenti Costa (1905–74), Felipe Boero (1884–1958), Emilio Dublanc (b.1907), Carlos Tuxen Bang (b.1931), Alfredo Donno, Athos Palma (1891–1951), and Eduardo Grau (1919–2006).

During this period, some important figures such as the musicologist Carlos Vega (1898–1966), the Austrian-born pedagogue Guillermo Graetzer (1914–93), and the conductor and pedagogue César Ferreyra (1926–2001), founder of the Coro de Cámara de Córdoba (1956) and Coro Municipal (1970) and author of the book *Juegos corales* (choral games), had an enormous impact on choral life.

The work of Casa Editorial Ricordi Argentina, the only music publishing company in the region, was instrumental in the dissemination in Latin America of choral music from Argentina and other places.

Brazil

In this early period, the growth and development of Brazilian choral music can be seen through the compositions of some of the most distinguished composers, who were also widely recognized in Europe and United States. Unlike most Latin American countries which had centralized the development of music in their capitals, Brazil extended its musical activity to different cities: São Paulo, Río de Janeiro, Recife, Salvador, Curitiba, Minas

Gerais, and Belo Horizonte. The prolific compositional activity that developed in Brazil in the first half of the twentieth century is unparalleled in the Latin American continent. The constant exchanges with Europe, the ethnomusicological projects of the likes of Heitor Villa-Lobos and Mario Andrade established the basis of the music development of this huge and diverse country.

During this period, there was continuing debate and tension between nationalist music with folkloric and ethnic roots, and the music inspired by modernism. This polarization reached its peak between the 1940s and the 1960s with a strengthening, practically a renaissance, of a deeper nationalism that is expressed through new musical languages. Some of the most important composers of this period, whose works include a cappella or symphonic choral music, were Heitor Villa-Lobos (1887–1959), Mozart Camargo Guarnieri (1907–93), Francisco Mignone (1897–1986), Claudio Santoro (1919–89), and César Guerra Peixe (1914–93). However, the most far-reaching compositional innovations between 1930 and 1940 came from Grupo Musica Viva under the leadership of the German composer Hans Joachim Koellreutter (1915–2005). In a 1946 manifesto, the Grupo proclaimed its opposition to the folkloric elements of nationalism.

Heitor Villa-Lobos was the leading figure in Brazilian choral music. His four-year administration as the head of the music program and artistic superintendent of the Department of Education of the Federal District was a great boost to the dissemination of the Canto Orfcônico (choral singing). Through mass choral gatherings with over 30,000 choristers, Villa-Lobos brought "an educational element to refine the good taste in music, by forming elites, contributing to the musical elevation of the people and developing interest in national artistic matters."[8] His numerous choral compositions and arrangements for equal voices and children's choirs originated from his goal of integrating choral singing into formal education.

Villa-Lobos's diverse body of choral music encompasses only a small portion of his output. Significant among his a cappella works are his *Missa São Sebastião* (1937) for female voices and a piece for mixed choir on biblical texts, *Bendita Sabedoria* (1958). In both pieces, his characteristic harmonic and melodic language of unstable tonality, unresolved dissonances, the systematic use of altered or incomplete chords, and parallelisms are all present. His most important choral symphonic works are *Choros no. 3* (1925) for orchestra and male voice choir and *Choros no. 10* (1925) for orchestra and mixed choir. Others are *Bachiana no. 9* (1944), the secular cantata *Mandu Çarará* (1940), the *Missa Vidapura* (1919) and *Magnificat-Gloria* (1958).

The compositional work of Villa-Lobos in Rio de Janeiro was paralleled only by Camargo in São Paulo. Perhaps the most prolific composer after Villa-Lobos, as a founder of the Coral Paulistano in 1936 he was crucial to the choral life of São Paulo. Camargo wrote over fifty a cappella pieces for this choir, based on African-Brazilian and indigenous music.

The Coral Paulistano, one of the most emblematic choral ensembles of Brazil, was one of the outcomes of the Semana de Arte Moderno in 1922, which encouraged nationalism. Therefore, a large number of choral works at the end of the 1930s, 1940s, and 1950s, were dedicated to this ensemble, becoming a creative springboard for conductors and the composers who frequented their rehearsals. Fructuoso Vianna, who wrote 25 pieces, and Miguel Arquieróns, who conducted over 800 concerts and premiered about 340 pieces, were the other conductors of this ensemble. The creation of genuinely Brazilian choral music was one of the most important achievements of this ensemble.

Other composers such as Mignone and Santoro made important contributions to the choral repertoire of Brazil. Guerra-Peixe, from Petrópolis, gave new energy; he became very impressed with a folk dance called the *macaratú*, in Recife, and did exhaustive research on this genre. Some of his most representative works are *Serie Xavante* (1972) for mixed choir and *Temas de carimbó* (1973) for mixed choir.

Venezuela

As evidenced in the chronicles gathered by José Antonio Calcaño, the quality of music making in the country was poor at the beginning of the twentieth century. "After its fantastic and surprising birth in colonial times, Venezuelan music was on a downward spiral until almost disappearing at the beginning of Gomez's regime. This sad path is parallel to the country's general life . . ."[9]

It was not till 1919 that the renaissance started in Venezuela, first with the Escuela de Bellas Artes and then with the Círculo de Bellas Artes, which became important centers of debate about the most recent European aesthetic theories.

Vicente Emilio Sojo (1887–1974) received his first music lessons from Régulo Rico (1878–1960) but he was clearly an example of the truly self-taught musician. He founded both the Orfeón Lamas, an emblematic choral ensemble and seed of the Venezuelan choral movement, in 1929, and the Symphony Orchestra of Venezuela in 1930. Orfeón Lamas was the country's first choral ensemble of mixed voices and its cultural ambassador during the 1930s, 1940s, and 1950s, until its disappearance in the sixties. This ensemble was devoted to the performance and dissemination of choral works written mostly by musicians and composers who were part of the choir and were also in Sojo's composition class. These young composers created a compositional style with nationalist elements, remarkably influenced by the Italian madrigal. Part of the Orfeón Lamas's repertoire consisted of sacred music by composers from the Escuela de Chacao. Sojo's choral output consisted of madrigals, arrangements of Venezuelan popular music, and sacred works for choir and orchestra. *Misa cromática* (1922–33), and *Hodie super nos fulgebit lux* (1935) are two of the most noteworthy works.

Juan Bautista Plaza (1898–1964) studied at the Pontifical Institute of Sacred Music in Rome with the aim of becoming qualified to introduce the reforms in ecclesiastical music decreed by Pope Pius X in his *Motus Proprio*. Plaza was chapel master at the cathedral of Caracas for twenty-five years and one of the founders, together with Sojo, of the Orfeón Lamas. He devoted himself to the rescue and classification of the Venezuelan colonial music archive. His substantial compositional output of 107 pieces falls principally into the genre of sacred music, including *Misa de requiem* (1933) and several motets for Holy Week. He also composed over fifty-five secular a cappella works.

With the creation of the Orfeón Lamas, an active generation of choral composers grew up under Sojo's leadership. They used selected poems by the best Ibero-American poets, modeling on polyphonic madrigals and choral songs of the Renaissance, sometimes using romantic and impressionistic harmonies, and incorporating elements of folklore and traditional music.

Other composers, all members of the Orfeón Lamas and pupils of Sojo, whose body of choral work has been influential in Venezuela, were Antonio Estévez (1916–88), founder of the Orfeón Universitario (1942); Angel Sauce (1911–95), founder of Coral Venezuela (1943); Evencio Castellanos (1915–84), organ player and pianist; Inocente Carreño (b.1910); Antonio Lauro (1917–86), an outstanding guitar player and one of the principal Latin American composers for guitar; José Antonio Calcaño (1900–78), diplomat and founder of the Creole Corporation Choir (1952); and Gonzalo Castellanos (1926), founder of the Philharmonic Choir (1968).

In the younger generation were Modesta Bor (1926–99), a student of Aram Khachaturian; José Antonio Abreu (b.1939), founder of El Sistema (Fundación del Estado para el Sistema Nacional de los Coros y Orquestas Juveniles e Infantiles de Venezuela); and Alberto Grau (b. 1938), founder of the Schola Cantorum de Caracas (in 1967).

The creation of these choral ensembles established the country's choral music scene in schools, universities, communities, companies, and public institutions. At the end of World War II, many artists and intellectuals arrived in Latin America, and Venezuela in particular, and some of them helped to enrich choral singing. They founded the choirs of the Basque and Catalan centers, the chorus of the Caracas Opera with Primo Casale, the Cultural Association of Ancient Music with Ruth Gosewinkel, and many other choirs.

Mexico

The Mexican Revolution started in 1910 and lasted for over ten years, with a nationalist fervor permeating all forms of artistic expression in the country. Manuel Ponce (1882–1948), considered a pioneer of nationalist Romantic music, was inspired by different styles of mestizo folk music, popularizing genres such as *corrido*, *jarabe*, *son*, *huapango*, and many others. He was also interested in Aztec music which emerged during the Aztec renaissance in the 1920s. After his studies in Europe, Ponce's composition style developed, but his interest was more towards folk music and piano, guitar, and symphonic music; he also composed a number of songs arranged for choirs.

After Ponce, Carlos Chávez (1899–1978) was the most influential composer between the 1920s and 1950s. He was a promoter of the Aztec musical heritage, believing that indigenous music was very vigorous and one of the most creative periods of Mexican culture. He studied Aztec instruments and music in the documents of the colonial archives of the sixteenth century and developed a theory of the Aztec melodic system. His style incorporated folkloric elements through the use of melodies, harmonies, and rhythms through which he built a national identity for his repertoire. Like Villa-Lobos, Chávez asserted that art should have a national identity but be universal at the same time. One of his pieces in which the choir plays an important role is the ballet *El fuego nuevo* (1921), written for female choir and orchestra.

In this period, some important figures shaped Mexican choral music. Miguel Bernal Jiménez (1910–56), born in Morelia, wrote traditional sacred vocal music and pieces combining the Italian *verismo* style with nationalist elements. Morelia, earlier named Valladolid, was the city where the first music conservatory of the Americas was founded in 1743, as well as the first cathedral children's choir. This tradition, lost during the nineteenth century, was restored in 1914, and the Conservatorio de las Rosas, the cathedral children's choir and the concert choir Niños Cantores de Morelia enjoyed immense recognition during the 1950s and 1960s. Luis Sandi (1905–96), a composer and conductor, was director of choral activities at the Conservatorio Nacional de México and founded the

Coro de Madrigalistas (1938). His body of work includes indigenous music aligned with Chávez's concept. Rodolfo Halffter (1900–87), born in Spain, spent most of his life in Mexico and wrote several lyrical works, the most important of which is his *Tres epitafios* (1937?) based on parts of Cervantes' *Don Quijote*.

The Caribbean, Cuba, the Dominican Republic, and Puerto Rico

Ever since the eighteenth century, Cuba has led the musical culture in this region. At the end of the nineteenth century, some important composers from the Dominican Republic and Puerto Rico followed Cuba's lead. Because of their provincial nature, the other Caribbean islands had a slower development and did not make any significant contribution to choral music. Both in Cuba and Puerto Rico, nationalist music and Italian opera gradually came to dominate the scene at the end of the nineteenth century, and at the beginning of the twentieth century.

Cuba

Eduardo Sánchez Fuentes (1874–1944), whose approach to nationalism was based on indigenous music, contributed to the development of vocal and choral music. He cultivated the Italian *verismo* style combined with Amerindian music. In 1923, the Grupo Minorista was established in Havana and included young poets, artists, and musicians who encouraged the revitalization of Cuban music and research work on everything related to African elements present in Cuban culture. Fernando Ortiz (1881–1969), the most important Cuban ethnomusicologist, coined the term "Afro-Cubanism." Amadeo Roldán (1900–39), Alejandro García Caturla (1906–40), and Argeliers León (b.1918), all three representatives of Cuban nationalism, included many Afro-Cuban elements in their music, particularly in the treatment of rhythm.

Puerto Rico

Ballroom music was the most important genre in the nineteenth century. The most noteworthy composers of this genre were Manuel Tavárez (1843–83) and Juan Morel Campos (1857–96). The choral works of the distinguished cellist, Pablo Casals (1876–1973), born Catalan but Puerto Rican at heart, are considered an important contribution to the choral repertoire. Héctor Campos Parsi (1922) was active in music education programs and composed numerous choral pieces.

The Dominican Republic

Activities related to music, particularly choral music, on this part of the island shared with Haiti, were practically nonexistent in 1900. However, there were two prolific composers, Clodomior Arredondo-Muira (1864–1935), and the main chapel master, José María Arredondo (1840–1924). The latter left an impressive legacy of sacred works, among them 135 masses and a number of motets.

Andean Region (Bolivia, Colombia, Ecuador, Peru, Chile and Uruguay)

Bolivia, Ecuador, and Peru

Of these three countries, Peru was the most musically developed in the first half of the twentieth century. Rodolfo Holzmann (1910–92) and Andrés Sas (1900–67) were the most influential composers, followed later by Edgar Valcárcel (b.1932). In Bolivia, two composers, Eduardo Caba (1890–1953) and Simeón Roncal (1870–1953), were the pioneers of musical art and both stood out for their nationalist instrumental works. In Ecuador, the Italian Domenico Brescia (1866–1939) helped to develop music education in Quito, and developed a nationalist musical identity. Some of his most outstanding students were the ethnomusicologist Segundo Luis Moreno (1882–1972) and Luis Salgado (1903–77). However, choral music had almost no importance in the musical life of these countries until the second half of the century.

Colombia

Musical activity in Colombia at the beginning of the twentieth century was mainly associated with the Conservatorio Nacional de Música in Bogotá, where Guillermo Uribe-Holguín (1880–1971) headed the Sociedad Sinfónica de Conciertos, promoting new composers and leaving an important legacy of works of different genres, including choral music, many of them of a nationalist nature. Antonio María Valencia (1902–52), a student of d'Indy, wrote a considerable number of choral works, both sacred and secular, characterized by the use of counterpoint, and an imaginative harmonic language influenced by impressionism and popular music. His main work is *Misa de requiem* (1943). Other composers of this generation with an important legacy in choral music were Blas Emilio Atehortúa (b.1933) and Luis Antonio Escobar (1925–93), whose *Canticas colombianas* (1969) are miniature choral treasures by virtue of their selection of poems and structure.

Chile and Uruguay

In Chile and Uruguay, nationalism was weaker because of European immigration. In Chile, Pedro Humberto Allende (1885–1959), Carlos

Lavín (1883–1962), and Carlos Isamitt (1885–1974) were composers and ethnomusicologists who had great influence on the musical scene in the 1950s, not only because of their compositions, but also through their contribution to music education. In the next generation, those who contributed greatly to choral music were Alfonso Letelier (1912–94), Luis Advis (1935–2004), and Gustavo Becerra Schmidt (1925–2010) whose oratorios *La araucana* and *Machu Picchu*, based on Neruda's texts, are among the most important. The composer who had the widest reputation outside his country was Juan Orrego Salas (b.1919). His catalog of cantatas, oratorios, and a cappella works is vast. Together with Mario Baeza (1916–98), founder of the Coro Universitario de Chile, he contributed to give an international dimension to Chilean choral life.

In Uruguay, Carlos Estrada (1909–70) and Héctor Tosar (1923–2002) were the most significant.

The past fifty years: 1960–2010

The first sixty years of the twentieth century, as previously noted, created the basis for the further development of choral music in Latin America. New repertoires were generated, and many choirs and orchestras were founded. Music schools and conservatoires, particularly those following European models, taught new generations of musicians. The exchange with Europe and North America continued in different ways. On the one hand, many fine musicians emigrated to Latin America after World War II, and several European opera companies and orchestras toured in the main cities. On the other hand, a substantial number of Latin American musicians went abroad to study. Also during the late 1950s and early 1960s some choirs started to participate in international choral events and to compete in prestigious international contests.

Those who won first prizes in the Concorso Polifónico Guido d'Arezzo were the Conjunto Pro Música de Rosario (1967) and Coro Estable de Rosario (1981) from Argentina, conducted by Cristian Hernández Larguía (b.1921); the Coral Ars Nova (1972) from Brazil conducted by Carlos Alberto Pinto Fonseca (1933–2005); the Schola Cantorum de Caracas (1974) from Venezuela, conducted by Alberto Grau; Cantoría Alberto Grau (1989), conducted by María Guinand (b.1953); and the Coro Universitario de Mendoza UC Cuyo (1975) from Argentina, conducted by Felipe Vallesi (1931–97), which also (2009) won the European Grand Prix conducted by Silvana Vallesi (b.1962).

Alongside this group of fine choral conductors, who also joined international choral organizations and fostered cooperation, were others who were devoted to the same mission such as Maria Isabel Soler (Argentina), Amalia Samper (Colombia), Waldo Aranguiz (Chile), and Edino Krieger (Brazil).

In the decades since 1990, many more choirs have won international recognition and have contributed to the strengthening and stimulation of choral music in their countries. It is an almost impossible task to mention them all, but some of the most representative choirs, with their conductors, are as follows:

Argentina
: Estudio Vocal de Buenos Aires (Carlos López Puccio), Coro de Cámara de Córdoba (César Ferreyra), Grupo de Canto Coral (Néstor Andrenacci), Coral Femenino San Justo (Roberto Saccente), Coro Universitario de Mendoza UC Cuyo (Silvana Vallesi), Coro Nacional de Jóvenes (Néstor Zadoff), Coro de Niños y Jóvenes Ars Nova (María Beatriz de Briones), Coro de Cámara de la Provincia de Córdoba (Gustavo Maldino), Coro de Jóvenes (Hugo de la Vega);

Bolivia
: Sociedad Coral Boliviana (José Lanza Salazar);

Brazil
: Canto em Canto (Elza Lakschewitz), Coral Brasilia (Emilio de Cesar), Madrigal de Brasilia (Eder Camuzis), Camerata Antigua de Curitiba (Helma Heller), Coro Orquesta Sinfónica del Estado de São Pauloi (Naomi Munakata);

Chile
: Coro de la Universidad Católica (Víctor Alarcón), Coro de Cámara de la Universidad (Guido Minoletti, b.1937);

Colombia
: Ensemble Vocal de Medellín (Cecilia Espinosa), Coro de la Universidad de los Andes (Amalia Samper), Coro de la Universidad Javeriana de Bogotá (Alejandro Zuleta);

Cuba
: Exaudi (Maria Felicia Pérez), Entrevoces (Digna Guerra), Schola Cantorum Coralina (Alina Orraca);

Mexico
: Capilla Virreinal de la Nueva España (Aurelio Tello, b.1951), Coro de Cámara de la Schola Cantorum de México (Alfredo Mendoza), Voce in tempore (Ana Patricia Carbajal), Coro del Teatro de Bellas Artes (Alfredo Domínguez);

Peru
: Coro Nacional (Andrés Santa María and Antonio Paz), Coro de Niños del Perú (Osvaldo Khuan);

Puerto Rico
: Coro de la Universidad de Puerto Rico (Carmen Acevedo Lucio);

Uruguay
: Coro de la Universidad de la República (Francisco Simaldoni);

Venezuela
: Cantoría de Mérida (José Geraldo Arriechi), Camerata de Caracas (Isabel Palacios), Schola Juvenil de Venezuela (Luimar Arismendi), Aequalis (Ana María Raga), Cantoría Alberto Grau (María Guinand), Orfeón Universitario Simón Bolívar (Alberto Grau and María Guinand).

A consequence of this explosion of choral enthusiasm was the need to create national and regional organizations in order to develop further professional development activities and to build a regional network. Many national and international festivals have been created, but it is the

America Cantat festival that is the most important choral event in the region. It was the initiative of Asociación Argentina para la Música Coral (AAMCANT), joined by the Fundación Schola Cantorum de Venezuela (FSCV) which launched this event, inspired by the Europa Cantat festivals. So far, six festivals have taken place: Mar del Plata (Argentina 1992 and 1996), Caracas (Venezuela 2000), Ciudad de México (Mexico 2004), Havana (Cuba 2007) and Juiz de Fora (Brazil 2010). Other relevant organizations that have taken the lead nationally and internationally are ADICORA (Argentina), the Colombian Choral Corporation, and the Central America and the Caribbean Choral Federation.

Initiatives to support choral music such as journals and the preparation of editions of Latin American choral repertoire are still scarce, but it is worth mentioning the journal *O Arruia* of the Associaçao de Canto Coral de Rio de Janeiro, edited by Elza do Val Gomez (Brazil) and active since 1961, and the editions of Argentinian music of Grupo de Canto Coral.

Composers

In the past forty years, the growth of choral music in the region has gone hand in hand with the enthusiasm of composers to write for different ensembles. This has not happened in all countries with the same vigor, but in those countries where there was at least one fine choir, composers were motivated to write more challenging and fascinating music. In Latin American choral literature one can find a wealth of music, which ranges from newly composed pieces using diverse contemporary compositional techniques, to others that incorporate popular and folk materials into new formal concepts, and which also includes a wide variety of arrangements and choral versions of popular tunes. Most composers have worked in either one of the first two categories, and almost all in the last one. Few major symphonic choral works have been produced in this period.

There are numerous prolific composers who have written works in all three categories. A list, not exhaustive, follows.

In Brazil, the tonal language of Marlos Nobre (b.1939), through which he continues exploring the possibilities of the chromatic scale, moves him away from tonality, which he considers anachronistic. His music is influenced by African-Brazilian rhythms of Recife (*maracatu, frevo, caboclinhos, candomblé* and the *cirandas*). His most important works are *Cantata del Chimborazo* (1982) and *Columbus*, Op. 77 (1990) .

Alberto Grau, a leading figure of the Venezuelan choral movement, has a vast catalog of sacred and secular a cappella music especially for mixed choirs, female choirs, and children's choirs. Grau created the school of choral conducting in Venezuela and worked closely with José Antonio Abreu to develop the choral symphonic repertoire of El Sistema. Grau has always composed with a pedagogical purpose and with a specific choir in mind. This is why his music is so rich and varied, full of color and rhythmic interest. One particular aspect of his compositional language is the use of eurhythmics in many of his compositions, to enhance the interpretation of rhythms. Some important works of this kind are his *Opereta ecológica in 4 acts*, *Binnamma*, *Mi patria es el mundo*, and *Caracolitos chicos*. His ballet *La doncella* (1977) and his childen's opera *Balada del retorn* (2009) for choir and instrumental ensemble are his most extended works.

Antonio Russo (b.1934), an outstanding conductor himself, has a musical style filled with innovative harmonies and a transparent use of counterpoint. He has an extensive oeuvre of a cappella music, but his major contribution has been to the symphonic choral repertoire with cantatas such as *Eros, Selene, Eros*, *Pequeños blancos amores*, *Magnificat*, *Misa Corpus Christi* and *Passio secundum Johannem*.

Other notable composers are Alberto Balzanelli (b.1941) from Argentina, Aurelio Tello (b.1951) from Peru, and the Venezuelan composers Cesar Alejandro Carrillo (b.1957), Miguel Astor (b.1962), and Francisco Rodrigo (b.1938).

In Brazil Ernst Widmer (b.1927) conducted the Grupo Madrigalista (1958–67). His prolific choral output in a modernist style explores diverse vocal techniques. Others who wrote in a more conservative manner, but very effectively for choirs were Henrique de Curitiba (Zbigniew Henrique Morozowicz) (1934–2008), a very prolific composer of choral songs and sacred music; Ernani Aguiar (b.1950), a conductor, composer and musicologist who specialized in reviewing, editing, and reinterpreting the music of the eighteenth century and produced several renowned masses and motets; Ronaldo Miranda (b.1948); Osvaldo Lacerda (b.1927); and Edino Krieger (b.1928).

In Cuba, Harold Gramatges (1918–2009) wrote some works for mixed choir and soloists using Ibero-American poetry. Aurelio de la Vega (b.1925), Julián Orbón (1925–91), Leo Brouwer (b.1939), guitarist and orchestral conductor, and Roberto Valera (b.1938), have all enriched the choral literature.

Others in Cuba who also have contributed to the choral repertoire are Alfredo Rugeles (b.1949), director of the Festival Internacional de Música Contemporánea, Mario La Vista (b.1943), and Jorge Córdoba Valencia (b.1953).

The following is a representative listing of the large category of notable composers whose works are based on popular traditions.

Argentina: Ariel Ramírez (b.1921) composer, *Misa criolla* (1964), *Navidad nuestra* (1964), and Misa por la paz y la justicia (1980); Damián Sánchez (b.1946), Dante Andreo (b.1949), Oscar Escalada (b.1945), Fernando Moruja (1960–2004), Liliana Cangiano, Ángel Lasala, Rubén Urbiztondo, Hugo de la Vega, and Néstor Zadoff.

Brazil: Aylton Escobar (b.1943), conductor and composer; Carlos Alberto Pinto Fonseca (b.1933), who founded the choir Madrigal Ars Nova which was an influential model in Brazilian choral music. Inspired by the traditions and rituals of the different African people who live in Brazil, he wrote works such as *Misa Afro-Brasileia* and *Jubiaba* for mixed voices.

Cuba: Guido López Gavilán (b.1946) is one of the energetic promoters of Cuban culture. As an instrumentalist and choral composer he supported the Festival de Música Contemporánea in Cuba. His main choral works relate to Cuban rhythms, and require great vocal virtuosity. Electo Silva has been director of the Orfeón Santiago and has had a very active life as a pedagogue. His compositions and arrangements are characterized by a highly personal and unique lyricism. Conrado Monier (b.1952) is well known for his many arrangements of popular songs, as is Beatriz Corona (b.1950) for her melodious compositions inspired by the Trova Cubana.

Venezuela: Federico Ruiz (b.1948) is one of the leading figures in Venezuelan choral composition today, together with Beatriz Bilbao (b.1957).

Other composers are: in Mexico, Carlos Jiménez Mabarak (1916–94), Ramón Noble (1920–99), Blas Galindo (1910–93), Mario Kuri Aldana (b.1931), Sabina Covarrubias (b.1980); in Peru, Rosa Alarco (1911–80); in Ecuador, Luis Gerardo Guevara (b.1930) and Eugenio Auz (b.1958); and in Colombia, José Antonio Rincón (b.1937), and Alberto Carbonell (b.1932).

New dimensions for choral activity

Choral singing in today's Latin America is a powerful tool of social integration and cohesion through the practice of values such as solidarity, teamwork, achievement and motivation of the collective, and discipline, which are fundamentals of this art. Perhaps, after four centuries, Latin Americans are retrieving the teachings of so many missionaries who taught through the arts. Since 2003, the Andean Corporation of Development has worked closely with El Sistema and the Fundación Schola Cantorum de Venezuela, with the support of the International Federation for Choral Music, to create a regional program Voces Latinas a Coro. Its mission is to develop a network of children's and youth choirs especially in the most deprived areas of cities such as La Paz, El Alto, and Santa Cruz (Bolivia), Quito (Ecuador), Lima (Peru), Bogotá, Medellín, and Cali (Colombia), São Paulo and Río de Janeiro (Brazil), Caracas, Mérida, Trujillo, and Ciudad Bolívar (Venezuela), and to strengthen choral life by training choral teachers and conductors and sensitizing them to the idea of working with choral music as a tool of social integration, education in human values, and cooperation.

The results have been very rewarding. In Venezuela, through El Sistema and the Fundación Schola Cantorum a new generation of young singers is growing up in more than 200 centers, called "núcleos," that are placed in the favelas or deprived areas of the country. Some of these are for children with special needs, and several have been placed in detention centers.

In Ecuador, Peru, Colombia, and Bolivia, alliances have been made with several educational initiatives such as the Jesuit schools of Fe y Alegría, or municipal schools. Working towards the same goals, these programs operate under different names such as Construir Cantando Program in Venezuela; Um Canto en Cada Canto in Londrina, Brazil; Instituto Baccarelli in São Paulo, Brazil; Academia Brasileira de Orquestra e Coros Sinfônicos (Orquestrando a Vida), Campos, Brazil; Juventudes Unidas (Instituto Distrital para la Protección de la Niñez y la Juventud, Idipron, Bogotá, Colombia); Fundarboledas (Cali, Colombia); Fundamadeus (Medellín, Colombia); Música en los Templos (Bogotá, Colombia).

Many massed choral symphonic concerts have taken place in each country, thus showing politicians and authorities the potential that choral music has to keep youth away from lives of drug-taking, crime, and prostitution and the many problems that beset the fabric of everyday life. This is only the beginning of a long road that we believe can give new meaning to choral life in our times and in our region.

Select bibliography

Aretz, I. (ed.) *America Latina en su música*. Mexico: Siglo XXI Editores, SA, 1977.

Asuaje de Rugels, A., M. Guinand, and B. Bottome. *Historia del movimiento coral y de las orquestas juveniles en Venezuela*. Caracas: Departamento de Relaciones Públicas de Lagoven, 1986.

Béhague, G. *Music in Latin America: An Introduction*. Englewood Cliffs, NJ: Prentice-Hall, 1979.

Calcaño, J. A. *La ciudad y su música*. Caracas: Crónica Musical de Caracas, 1956.

Chase G., Pan American Union, and Library of Congress. *A Guide to the Music of Latin America: A Joint Publication of the Pan American Union and the Library of Congress*. New York: AMS Press, 1972.

Grau, A. *Choral Conducting: The Forging of the Conductor*. Caracas: GGM Editores, 2009.

Milanca Guzmán, M. *La música venezolana: de la Colonia a la República*. Caracas: Monte Avila Editores Latinoamericana, 1994.

Plaza, J. B. and N. de Plaza. *La música en nuestra vida: escritos 1925–1965*. Caracas, Venezuela: Fundación Vicente Emilio Sojo, Fundación Juan Bautista Plaza, Ministerio de Educación, Cultura y Deportes, Consejo Nacional de la Cultura, 2000.

Ramón y Rivera, L. F. *La música colonial profana*. Caracas: Instituto Nacional de Cultura y Bellas Artes, 1966.

Tiemstra, S. S. *The Choral Music of Latin America: A Guide to Composition and Research*. New York: Greenwood Press, 1992.

10 Choral music in East Asia: China, Japan, and Korea

JING LING-TAM AND GENE J. CHO

Prelude: cultural and historical perspective

It is often said that music is universal, that the entire human race possesses musical instinct. If music is humankind's shared instinct and, as several recent scientific studies in anthropology seem to suggest, the earliest form of humans' spoken language was monosyllabic and tonal, what Mithen called "infant-directed speech" or IDS, then the Sinitic (that is, Chinese) language may be seen as a remnant of humanity's earliest speech, since it is the only monosyllabic and tonal language in the modern world.[1] From there, one may conjecture that, as a tribe began to develop a shared vocabulary however simple, and as tribal life became more organized, there would arise a need for concerted voices in communal gatherings. It follows that responsorial and antiphonal chanting or singing may have developed and gradually become humankind's earliest vehicle of group communication, as in burial (compare evidence of Neanderthals' burial rituals more than 70,000 years ago) or other rituals such as moon and harvest festivals.

Indeed, human history abounds with ancient tales of choral singing. Christian music historians point to certain biblical passages as the earliest references to group or choral singing, such as the song of triumph uttered by the Israelites on the shores of the Red Sea, with Miriam, Moses' sister, as the first choral conductor or, more properly, the first cantor (the "Psalm of Victory" from Exodus 15). In China, there is also a famous story from the Warring States Period (early third century BCE) of soldiers singing the Chu (楚) folksong in order to weaken the fighting spirit of the enemy. This particular tale has been told and retold in many of China's historical chronicles as well as portrayed in *Jingju* (or *Jingxi*, often erroneously referred to in the West as "Chinese opera"), and in the award-winning Chinese movie *Farewell, My Concubine*. Large gatherings of Taoist monks singing and chanting in the enormous courtyard of the Forbidden Palace were an integral part of the imperial rituals in China (and Korea), as, for

The authors acknowledge the contributions of Saeko Hasegawa, Lee Hae-Jong (Youngstown State University), Tsutsumi Mihoko (University of Florida, Gainesville), and Lei Ray Yu (Boston University).

example, depicted in the movie *The Last Emperor*. Choral singing as a vehicle for supplication to a higher power is not just a practice in ancient times; in 1941, the Nationalist Party of China organized a thousand-person choir in Chongqing to heighten the anti-Japanese sentiment among the masses, and the Chinese Communist Party also used choral music as a tool to raise the fighting spirit of the populace.

While such mass singing may not belong to the subject matter proper of this chapter, we can gain from these examples a greater measure of appreciation that choral singing has long been regarded as having a function in warfare, socio-political reform, and ritual oracle; for music was regarded as a channel of communication not only for and between people but also between terrestrial beings and celestial spirits – hence, the theory of the harmony of the spheres, a belief that was sustained from the days of Pythagoras to Kepler (*harmonice mundi*).

The organized curriculum of music education in East Asia – here in reference only to three countries: China, Japan, and Korea and, more specifically, the art of modern choral singing – is inseparable from the history of Christian missions in the East. As the historical tradition of choral music can be traced to early European liturgical practice (for example, the *schola cantorum*), so the development of choral music in these Asian countries was no less than the fruit of early missionary endeavors beginning in the last decades of the sixteenth century. However, the development of choral music in China, Japan, Korea, and Taiwan has been anything but uniform. While these nations are close neighbors geographically, China, Japan and Korea are culturally, socially, politically, and religiously (not to mention ethnically) dissimilar. They are fiercely independent, and each of them has followed different developmental paths in politics, economy, industry, and commerce; in all, however education and the arts are supervised by the national government and are part of the political agenda in times of peace and of war. This was particularly evident in the decades before and after the turn of the twentieth century. In Japan, it was during the period of the emulative pro-Western policy of Emperor Meiji that the first Western-style music schools were opened. In contrast, China followed a slower pace of acceptance of and development in Western music education, as the posture of the Chinese polity had been one of deep-seated suspicion toward the political-cultural intent of the West. This is partly because China had suffered greatly in the concerted invasion by the eight Western countries' military alliance during this period. This attitude has lingered, and came to the fore during the decade-long Cultural Revolution period; as recently as 2008, China's Ministry of Culture issued a ban on public performance of Handel's *Messiah* and Mozart's *Requiem* by a visiting ensemble.

It is true that in these and all other East Asian countries (as well as elsewhere in the world), mass singing has long been an integral part of cultural heritage. Every spring, huge masses engage in the "song-and-dance festival" on the hills of Yunnan and Guangxi provinces and elsewhere in southern China, and in the *bon matsuri* Buddhist festival in the countryside and smaller townships all over Japan. Due to space limitation, the traditional or indigenous choral music heritages of these countries will not be addressed here. Instead, this chapter will focus on the choral music that generally integrates certain "shared" performance considerations in the Western choral music traditions. These may include: (1) the ability to maintain independence in voice parts (that is, polyphonic, as opposed to unisonal and heterophonic); (2) proficiency in shared notational systems for pitch and rhythm; (3) accuracy in singing "in tune" (versus the habitual portamento/glissando and improvisatory – heterophonic – manner in East Asian vocal music); and (4) training in vocal production, including vocal blending, diction, and articulation.

It must be noted that many of these aspects of performance practice were not native to East Asian vocal traditions, but became a part of the curriculum in Western-style music institutions, in Christian missionary schools (many for female students) before World War II, and in national music conservatories established in the more recent past by these countries' ministries of education.

Japan was the first country in East Asia to open Western-style music schools – as early as 1887, compared to China's opening of its first national conservatory in 1927. It was in the decades after World War II, however, that glee clubs on non-musical college campuses flourished, soon becoming mixed-voice choral activities, whereas in the years before the war none of the secondary schools were coeducational, and few female students attended tertiary institutions. In contrast to the primary emphasis that was placed on training in solo performance (in violin, piano, voice, etc.), choral activity was not given priority in the educational curriculum in the conservatories, often being relegated to the status of extracurricular activity.

The People's Republic of China

After the founding of the People's Republic of China (1949), many aspects of the music curriculum followed the tradition of Russian conservatories, and many Chinese musicians were educated in the former Soviet Union. After the end of the Cold War and with the ensuing contact with the West, Chinese composers were eager to emulate the latest European compositional idioms (for example, serialism and electronic media), few of which were readily applicable in vocal/choral composition or performance by average choral ensembles. Hence, few composers made any significant and lasting contributions to choral literature. For example, Chou Wen-Chung, one of the most widely recognized Chinese composer-scholars, who resides in the United States, wrote only one seldom-performed choral work, *Poems of White Stone* (1959), for mixed chorus and chamber orchestra.[2] Xien Xinghai (or Hsien Hsing-Hai, a student of d'Indy and Dukas), a preeminent composer, contributed to the repertoire with many part-songs but, because of the political nature of their lyrics, these works are seldom performed today, with perhaps the sole exception of his *Yellow-River Cantata* (1939, rev. 1941). If there has ever been a choral work from the past that still enjoys any degree of currency, it is "Moli-Hua" (Jasmine Flower), a simple folk song with an undiminishing popularity, many arrangements of which have been published in China and the United States. Created during the Qing dynasty (1644–1912), it was the first Chinese song ever to be introduced to Europe, and the melody was made familiar to Western audiences through Puccini's adaptation of it in *Turandot*. Its sustained popularity was demonstrated in a performance by the Beijing University chorus at the summer Olympics of 2004 in Greece. Indeed, many composers arrange or make use of China's folk melody material; notable among them are Qu Xi-Xian and Zhang Yi-Da.

The earliest choral curriculum in China's tertiary institutions was in the women's teacher training colleges in 1907, preparing students to teach singing, instruments, and music fundamentals to children in primary schools. The impact of music became notable with the return of foreign-educated intellectuals, among them Huang Zi (from the USA), Xiao You-Mei (from Japan and Germany), and Chao Yuen-Ren (from the USA). In 1927, Chao's *Hai Yun* was the first oratorio-like composition and his solo song "How Can I Not Think of Her?" retains some degree of popularity. Huang Zi produced numerous choral works during his short life (1904–38), greatly contributing to choral music in China, and he wrote the first multi-movement piece – *Chang Hen Ge*. Even though China's Ministry of Education and Culture did not give strong support to promoting the choral curriculum during the warring years, mass singing was often employed by the Kuomintang and the Chinese Communist Party as a powerful political and specifically, anti-Japanese tool. More recently there has been a shift in the government's regard for choral music and its benefit to society. Today, every sizeable city has its own municipal philharmonic orchestras and choral organizations, with programming that strongly favors works by national and local composers. Even so, concerts devoted entirely to choral music are relatively rare; choral selections are often programmed as a part of "variety show" musicals. Choral compositions by Chinese composers active in international arenas are also few. Among the younger generation of Chinese composers who have made notable contributions to choral literature are Chen Yi and Zhou Long. Worth mentioning also is Tan Dun; although not primarily known as a composer of choral works, his choral symphony *Heaven, Earth, Mankind* (1997) for solo cello, children's choir, and Chinese bronze bells deserves to be included in the programming of choral concerts in the West.

Promotion of amateur choral music is slow, mainly because of the general lack of music literacy. The amateur Chinese populace's ability in music reading is by way of "simplified notation" or *jianpu* (简谱), a system that uses Arabic numerals to signify scale degree positions with no distinctions between different modalities (for example, 6, sung to the syllable LA, is used to denote the tonic of a minor mode). Many older Chinese possess an uncanny ability to sing music notated in *jianpu* with solmization syllables, but have difficulties in singing from staff notation. While *jianpu* is a powerful and eminently practical tool for sight-singing, and is comparable with the solmization-syllable system, this mode of *jianpu* notation is not readily adaptable for scoring multi-voiced harmonized choral music, especially where tonal and modal shifts abound, containing thereby many accidentals.

To avoid potential conflict with the authorities, composers have been selecting uncontroversial texts while still maintaining a strong creative element. For example, Qu Xi-Xian (1919–2010) wrote several folk song arrangements, one of which, the *Pastoral*, is published in the USA. Other composers have also been published in the USA, such as Se Enkhbayar and Liu Wenjin. In spite of restrictions, Chinese choral culture is advancing rapidly. Composers are rapidly finding ways to represent the diversity of China's multi ethnic, multi linguistic society. Contact with the West has resulted in aspirations on the part of Chinese choirs and conductors to employ their substantial resources to create high-quality choral musicianship. The leaders of Chinese choral music, such as Ma Ge-Shun and Wu Ling-Fen, are being joined by a new generation of choral conductors and choral educators, such as Yalun Gerile and Wang Jin. It is only a matter of a few years before China becomes a major player in the world's choral culture.

Taiwan (Republic of China)

The choral landscape in Taiwan – the "other China" – has been decidedly different from that on the mainland. Choral activity thrives on campuses and in municipal and industrial sectors. In the 1950s and 1960s, the glee clubs on college campuses – extracurricular organizations that were once for males only – began to expand their membership to include treble voices, and choral organizations grew rapidly, providing students with an excitingly new avenue of coeducational extracurricular activity. Subsequently, many of the graduates who were members of choral organizations during their college years began to form amateur choral organizations in many sectors, including private, municipal, industrial, and civic enterprises. Most prominent in the international choral world is the Taipei Philharmonic Chorus led by Dirk DuHei that has built a reputation for the highest standards of the choral art. Choral competitions have become annual events that attract widespread attention and approval, further promoting this genre across the island. The extent of Taiwanese choral music in recent years can be substantiated by its hosting of international choral festivals in 2009 – the tenth such undertaking.

Among the composers of the past generation, Chuan-Sheng Lu and Fu-Yu Lin have made notable contributions with their many arrangements of Taiwanese folk songs. Dai Keong Lee, a Hawaiian Chinese, also contributed repertoire with compositions such as *Canticle of the Pacific* (1943, rev. 1968) and *Mele Olili* (Joyful Songs, 1960), a work utilizing characteristic Hawaiian idioms.

Japan

Under the pro-Western policy of the Meiji government (1868–1912), shōka (singing) became mandatory from primary to secondary schools. Western music, particularly popular English and German art and children's songs, were included in school songbooks. The Meiji government also sent young students to Western countries to study music, perhaps the most famous of whom was Taki Rentaro. Soon, Western-educated composers such as Taki were contributing their compositions in Western idioms to these *Monbusho* songbooks approved by the ministry of education. Much of this early choral music used in the non-coeducational secondary school system was for either all-male or all-female voices, a tradition still observable in today's choral compositions. It was only with the admission of Christian missionaries into Japan and with the opening of missionary schools that choral singing became an accepted part of Japan's cultural modernization. It is worth mentioning that the introduction of Western music in Japan did not arouse any resistance from Japanese people because of its strangeness. While the typical traditional system of Chinese music is *anhemitonic* pentatonic (containing neither semitones nor the syllables *fa* and *ti*), the Japanese tonal system possesses – alongside the *anhemitonic* patterns – the *hemitonic* penta- and hexa-tonic patterns (containing either one or both *fa* and *ti* syllables). This feature of Japanese native music prompted the Japanese ethnomusicologist Kishibe to remark that Japanese music is "harmonic" in nature as compared to Chinese music which is "non-harmonic."

Tangible evidence of the ready acceptance and popularization of Western choral music in Japan was the early publication of a comprehensive anthology of Western choral works. For example, the anthology *One Thousand Years of Church Music: The Church Anthem Book* published in 1939, included selections from the late Renaissance to the Romantic period. Within a decade or so after World War II, publication of Western choral anthologies not only resumed but also increased noticeably.

After the period of relative eclipse during World War II, choral music and all genres of Western music saw a dramatic revival soon after the war. In fact, even during the war, German music – art songs, choral, instrumental, and orchestral works – was not officially banned because Germany and Japan were wartime allies. The Japan Choral Association (JCA) was established in 1948 and has had a major impact on the growth of choral culture. The Little Singers of Tokyo was founded in 1951 to give Japanese children the opportunity to sing Gregorian chant and polyphony in Latin. Performances of Beethoven's Ninth Symphony (a work which is said to have been introduced to Japan by German soldiers during the war years) have become year-end events in many Japanese cities. In one account, orchestras in the Tokyo area gave seventy-seven performances of Beethoven's Ninth during December in one year; the audience is often invited to sing along during the "Ode to Joy" chorus. Japan boasts more concert halls than any other nation in the world; in the Tokyo area alone, there are about 150, many with state-of-the-art acoustics.

Choral organizations exist in each prefecture with hundreds and thousands of amateur choirs, while professional choirs are few in number, only in the large cities numbering five or six in total. Choral singing has become a national pastime not only for its cultural and educational benefits (music is a compulsory class from primary through junior high although the number of teaching hours has been halved in recent years – and it is optional at tertiary levels). It is also promoted as pleasurable and healthy. Civic support for choral music is widespread; generous financial sponsorships by the business sector such as by the *Asahi Shimbun* newspaper to the JCA help to promote nationwide choral competitions and other events. In recent years, the JCA's program has expanded to cover a wide range of activities, from choral festivals and competitions to choral workshops and *cantats* for mothers' choruses, junior or *kodomo* (children's) choruses, men's choruses, and silver choruses (for the elderly).

Prior to the establishment of the JCA, and in spite of the popularity of choral music, relatively few notable composers contributed to choral literature. For example, Takemitsu Toru, the preeminent modern Japanese composer, wrote twenty works for solo voice, twelve of which he personally arranged for mixed voice chorus. However, his most famous choral composition undoubtedly is *Kaze-no-uma* (Wind Horse). There has been a marked increase in choral compositions since the founding of the JCA and its public solicitation of choral compositions for its national competition that began in 1971, with the winning works being awarded Asahi prizes and publication contracts. Notable choral composers are Chihara Hideki, Hosakawa Toshio, Suzuki Teruaki, Kanno Shigeru, and Matsushita Ko; many of their works set Christian or Western lyrics (for example, *Canticum Sacrum*; *Ave Maria*; *Die Lotusblume*; *Missa Brevis Beati Pauperes Spiritu*; *Antiphona Beatae Mariae Virginis*). Also notable is that, even with such Western lyrics, their compositions often exhibit a distinctly Japanese character in poetic use of the otherwise Western music idiom. Worthy of mention among many choral conductors are: Tanaka Nobuaki, the first professional choral conductor in Japan and a driving force for Japanese choral works; and Suzuki Masaaki who has attained international status as a Bach authority. Noteworthy also are Imai Kunio (Shokei Gakuin University) and Sasaki Masatoshi (Iwate University). The latter is particularly renowned for his performances of baroque music, and both are also accomplished singers.

Korea (South Korea)

In East Asia, Korea must be regarded as the most active and advanced in choral music, with the artistic level of performance equal to or exceeding that in many Western countries. This may be due, at least in part, to the complex phonetics in the Korean spoken language (far more complex than in Chinese or Japanese). However, it is undeniable that the choral tradition and a high regard for choral music are deeply rooted in and derived from the church music heritage in Korea, in percentage terms the most Christian country in East Asia. Catholic, Protestant, and other denominational churches command a large segment of the population. The works of the following composers deserve particular note. La Un-Yung (1922–93), a prolific composer and choral conductor as well as a theorist and church musician, skillfully combined Western idioms (such as church modes) with Korean folk-music elements, contributing to date nine cantatas and well over one thousand compositions. From the same generation Kim Byong-Kon's treble-chorus anthem "My Heart is Steadfast" is exemplary. Among the younger generation of choral composers, Park Jung-Sun (b.1945) should be noted, for while he is known internationally as a composer of orchestral works, he is much more highly regarded in his native Korea as a choral composer; his Inchon Mass (1996) for unaccompanied chorus is regarded as one of his best works.

One indicator of the popularity and importance of choral music is the number of Korean students majoring in choral conducting in the United States and elsewhere, far greater than the numbers from any other Asian countries. Another tangible indication of this popularity is the frequency of international choral festivals held in Korea, with several foreign choirs participating. In the first decade of the twenty-first century, there were nearly a dozen major international choral festivals.

Among notable Korean choral conductors with international status, two should be mentioned as having attained undisputed recognition: Yoon Hak-Won, the artistic director of the renowned Incheon City Chorale, and Lee Sang-Kil, the artistic director of the Anyang City Choir. The extent and the level of choral music in Korea have been such that it enjoys generous financial support from both government and corporate sectors.

Postlude: future perspectives

In spite of the vigor of choral culture in this part of the world, its compositions and choral cultures are not yet part of the mainstream. In the American Choral Directors Association guide, *Twentieth Century Choral Music: An Annotated Bibliography of Music Appropriate for College and University Choirs*, not one East Asian choral composition is mentioned.[3] However, international choral festivals hosted by Korean, Japanese, and Taiwanese organizations continue to raise greatly the status and visibility of East Asian choral music. China is increasingly active, hosting a 2010 international choral festival in Shaoxing (Zhejiang province), an ancient city famous for its poetic beauty with bridges and calligraphy. The world is changing rapidly, and it is only a matter of time before East Asia will play a dominant role in the world's choral culture.

Select bibliography

Bloesch, R., and W. Weyburn. *Twentieth Century Choral Music: An Annotated Bibliography of Music Appropriate for College and University Choirs.* American Choral Directors Association Monograph, No. 9. Lawton, OK: ACDA, 1997.

Kioka Eizaburo, (ed.) *One Thousand Years of Church Music: The Church Anthem Book.* Tokyo: Kyokai Ongakuu Shuppan Kanko Kai, 1939.

Kishibe, S. and K. B. Shinkokai. *The Traditional Music of Japan.* Tokyo: Kokusai Bunka Shinkokai, 1969.

Liu, Ching-chih and C. Mason. *A Critical History of New Music in China*. Hong Kong: Chinese University Press, 2010.

Mithen, S. *The Singing Neanderthals: The Origins of Music, Language, Mind and Body*. London: Weidenfeld and Nicolson, 2005.

Mittler, B. *Dangerous Tunes: The Politics of Chinese Music in Hong Kong, Taiwan, and the People's Republic of China since 1949*. Wiesbaden: Harrasowitz Verlag, 1997.

Palmer, A. *Contemporary Japanese Choral Music*. Clarence, NY: Mark Custom, 1992.

Strimple, N. *Choral Music in the Twentieth Century*. Milwaukee, WI: Amadeus Press, 2002.

Tsutsumi, M. "A History of the Japan Choral Association," Ph.D dissertation, Florida State University, 2007.

11 New voices in ancient lands: choral music in South and Southeast Asia

ANDRÉ DE QUADROS

Context and origins

The continent of Asia has always been something of a mystery to those in the West. Even by knowledgeable people, it is perceived as exotic and far too complex to be understood completely. With choral music it is no different. Questions that are often asked concern the types of choir that exist, what repertoire these choirs sing, in which contexts they function, what the composers write, and so on. These questions are partly being answered by the increasing global presence of South and Southeast Asian choirs, many of them participating in international festivals and competitions. The ones that travel are, however, representative of only a small number of choirs with the aspirations and resources to undertake such ambitious endeavors. The subcontinent of South Asia (where over one-fifth of the world's population lives) along with the Southeast Asian region encompasses twenty-one countries and a population of well over 2.5 billion. Group singing traditions were rich and varied well before the onset of Western contact. Even part-singing, not in the way that we understand Western choral music, but in various forms of antiphonal, call and response, and parallel intervallic singing, predates the colonial period. One only needs to examine Yampolsky's treasure trove collection of Indonesian field recordings,[1] some of which he describes as "choral", the *bodu beru* group singing with drum ensembles in the Maldives, or the Buddhist temple chants in Laos and elsewhere in Southeast Asia, to begin to appreciate this rich landscape. Nevertheless, the dual remarkable inventions of Western music – harmony and staff notation – combined with

The author acknowledges the rich contribution that Jamie Hillman made to the research, data collection, and assembling of information for this chapter. A number of colleagues provided information through interviews and correspondence. They are: Sureka Amerasinghe, Mark Blanford, Andre David, Dinali David, Miguel Felipe, Rapti Fernando, Anthony Frans, Bernard Tan Tiong Gie, Pham Hong Hai, Willie Godridge, Isabelle Jaitly, Sanjeev Jayaratnam, Tommyanto Kandisaputra, Nelson Kwei, Juliette Lai, Ishan de Lanerolle, Earl Stanley Lazo, Indra Listiyanto, Sri Manthakas, Kristianto Meike, Blossom Mendonca, Nani Muljana, Moe Naing, Joel Navarro, Tian Hui Ng, Neil Nongkynrih, Oscar Pantaleon Jr., Bagus Paradhika, Charith Peiris, Eshantha Peiris, Philippine Choral Directors Association, Chew Hock Ping, Susanna Saw, Sri Senanayake, Virgil Sequeira, John Sharpley, Situ Singh, Sili Suli Limbong, Aida Swenson, Bernard Tan Tong Gie, Kittiporn Tantrarungroj, Jennifer Tham, Garry Thin, Jonathan Velasco, Nariman Wadia.

the forces of Christianization, colonization, Westernization, and, most recently, globalization, have resulted in a rich choral culture in this region that is unlike anywhere else. Indeed, even the choral cultures of individual countries in the region are unique and different as a consequence of the varying impacts of Christianization and Westernization. A few examples will suffice to explain this variety.

Colonial India, after the departure of the British, was divided into the modern independent nations of Afghanistan, Burma, Bangladesh, India, Nepal, Pakistan, and Sri Lanka. In none of these countries do you see a majority Christian population. Contrast this with the experience of Spanish colonization of the Philippines, where Christians comprise nearly 85 percent of the total population. The Spanish fervor of Christian conversion stands in stark contrast to British policy in India, where there was no serious official imperative to conduct large-scale Christianization. In India, there is one example of Iberian missionary force – on the west coast of India, in the small enclave of Goa, colonized by the Portuguese between 1510 and 1961. Here, the Roman Catholic population, at one third of the total, is higher than anywhere else on the subcontinent. What, then, have been the consequences of these differences on the origins and development of choral music?

Remember that we are speaking here about a specific type of choir, the choir forged in the crucible of European experience of church, state, and community, taken in the baggage of colonizers and missionaries, and planted firmly on foreign soil. There is very little early data on the development of choral music in Asia, but we can make several reasonable assumptions.[2] Wherever colonization took place, churches and schools were built. Colonizers sought to replicate their cultural habits – food, religion, and the entire panoply of cultural behaviors – wherever they went. In churches, singing took place as part of the liturgy. Thus, the liturgy, and its music, were usually copies of the liturgical rites of the old country. Imagine, therefore, the surprise of the seventeenth-century traveler Sebastiani at the musical accomplishments of native Indians upon visiting Goa, the seat of Portuguese power:

> . . . and when I said that it was like being in Rome, I was told that I was not mistaken, because the composition was that of the famous Carissimi . . . I cannot believe how musically proficient are the Canarini [Goans and Konkanis]. . .[3]

Schools were typically built to perpetuate the colonial mission. Churches, religious orders, or other Christian authorities ran most schools, and group singing was generally included as part of the curriculum. Even now, in Muslim-majority Malaysia, Christian schools form choirs that participate regularly in choral competitions.

Although the British, Portuguese, Dutch, Spanish, and French placed a heavy footprint on indigenous cultures, this footprint was far from uniform. The nation-states of South and Southeast Asia, molded through colonization, reflect vastly different levels of industrialization, education, and Westernized civic life. By World War I, Thailand was the only country not to have been colonized; the British ruled the Indian subcontinent, Burma, Malaya, and Borneo; the Dutch controlled what was then the Netherlands East Indies (now Indonesia); the French ruled Indochina, now Cambodia, Laos, and Vietnam; the Portuguese had been reduced to minor footholds in Goa and East Timor; and Spain had sold its longtime colony, the Philippines, to the new ruler, the United States. By this time, an entrenched middle class of Europeans and local people had absorbed the cultural norms of the European middle class. The "weekend" had been established, leisure time was created, and European civic life had taken hold through, for example, operetta companies, orchestras, and choral societies. The Bombay Madrigal Singers Organisation, the Singapore Musical Society, and the Philharmonic Society of Selangor (Malaysia) are examples of the latter.

Tracing the development of Asian choral music, while an engaging and worthwhile pursuit, is a scholarly enterprise in its own right, going far beyond the scope of this chapter, so I am going to move rapidly to the modern, postcolonial period.

The current state of the art

The recent period, which is the primary focus of this chapter, is associated with the globalization of choral music starting after World War II, with increasing cultural exchanges, international educational opportunities, and the rise of international festivals, competitions, and cultural events. There is no information on the traveling of choirs from this region to international events before World War II. The first Filipino choir to travel abroad was the University of the Philippines Madrigal Singers in 1969. The Paranjoti Academy Chorus from Mumbai have thrilled European and American audiences also since the 1960s. Indonesian choirs started traveling around 1980, and are now among the most active choral travelers.

The development of choral music in each country is directly connected to situated socio-political and religio-cultural constructs. In Indonesia, for example, the rise of choral music is a direct consequence of the marginalization of the minority Christian community and the consequent bonding of churches, in which choral music plays a central role. Even with the democratization of Indonesia, choral music belongs mainly to Christian life; there are very few community choirs, or choirs that represent the majority Muslim community. The most distinguished choirs and conductors not part of churches are the Batavia Madrigal Singers (Avip Priatna), the Cordana Youth Choir (Aida Swenson), and the Elfa Singers founded by the late Elfa Secioria. A different example exists in the little-known northeastern states of India – Assam, Manipur, Meghalaya, Nagaland, and Tripura – where the missionary presence built on an already strong group vocal tradition, leading to an active hybrid choral culture.

The education of Asian conductors in the United States and Europe not only brought Asian, regional, and Western choral cultures into increasing contact, but also played a major role in the formation of choral life and organizations in this region. Conductors such as Andrea Veneracion brought her education at Indiana University directly into the shaping of the University of the Philippines Madrigal Singers, among the best-known of Filipino choirs. A case in point, Veneracion and the Madrigal Singers generated a laboratory both for creating the distinctive Filipino choral sound and for composers to write music combining indigenous rhythms, melodies, and musical forms. There is a broad base of enthusiasm for choral music in the Philippines unusual for Southeast Asia. Not only is choral music widely encouraged in churches and educational institutions, but there is also some degree of government support. For example, the approval by the Philippine Congress for the National Music Competition for Young Artists (NAMCYA) has enabled the initiation of several children's choirs. This competition attracts nationwide interest and provides an environment for the aspiration and exhibition of excellence for choirs of all configurations.

Apart from the Philippines, the two countries that enjoy the most visibly vigorous choral life are Singapore and Indonesia. Singapore is the only country in the entire region to have successfully reached the same socio-economic stratum as the majority of industrialized countries in the Western world. There is a strong choral culture at almost all levels of Singaporean life, with the possible exception of tertiary institutions; there is still no substantial university program for the education of choral conductors and composers. But in schools, churches, and the community, choirs are of exceedingly high quality. Unlike in other parts of the region, Singaporean choirs represent all sectors of its rich demographic of Chinese, Malay, and Indian peoples. The role of the Singaporean government in supporting the rise of choral music has been of crucial importance. With the establishment in 1991 of the National Arts Council's Choral Unit, financial support and an awareness of the advantages of choral life have enabled the continuing rise in quality of Singaporean choirs, many of which tour internationally. In this small country, the choral leaders are Jennifer Tham, Lim Yau, Nelson Kwei, Lim Ai Hooi, and Toh Ban Sheng.

Indonesian choirs, competitive in orientation and strongly spiritual in mission and repertoire, usually attract substantial support from their churches. The education and professional development of choral musicians has occurred outside educational institutions. In the early days, the Dutch missionary H. A. van Dop trained several conductors in the Jakarta Theological Seminary; more recently, Catharina Leimena and Esther Nasrani have nurtured most of the important choral leaders. Apart from the regular choral events that church communities organize, Indonesia has a number of national and provincial competitions, symposia, and festivals. The church music society YAMUGER, founded in 1968, has a wide network of Christian singers and conductors. Several successful symposia and festivals have been organized by the LPNN (the National Foundation of Choral Music Development), founded in 1983, and by Tommyanto Kandisaputra with the Bandung Choral Society. Special mention must be made of the Cordana Choir's innovative blend of choreography and secular song from Indonesia's various Muslim and other traditions, a blend that has enabled it to carve a special place in the choral performing world.

One might expect there to be a strong similarity between the various Muslim-majority countries of this region – Bangladesh, Indonesia, Malaysia, and Pakistan. In fact, there is little in common. Pakistan and Bangladesh, formerly one country, have a limited choral life, mainly confined to Christian and expatriate communities. In these countries, church choirs have developed hymnology and repertoire that effectively use local languages. The IGM Choir in Karachi sings Pakistani traditional music in antiphonal style, while the choir of the Shurer Dara Music School in Dhaka, Bangladesh, sings Bengali devotional music.

Throughout Asia, there is an increasing unity between local languages, liturgy, and music. Protestant and other non-Catholic churches had no official barrier to blending language and culture with liturgy, so this has happened seamlessly and has been facilitated by the increasing availability of biblical translations. After the Second Vatican Council enabled Catholic usage of the vernacular, the Philippines, in particular, saw a sharp increase in compositional activity for ritual. In this regard, the Asian Institute of Liturgical Music in Manila, under the leadership of the composer Francisco Feliciano and the conductor Jonathan Velasco, has served as a training ground for Christian choral composers and conductors from all over the continent.

Whether for lack of an extensive body of works written by local composers or simply as an act of preference, most Asian choirs sing

Western choral music. Structured as Western choirs, it is only natural that Western art music, African-American spirituals, and arrangements of popular and jazz standards form the core of the repertoire. Even where local composers have produced works, they are frequently arrangements of traditional folk songs, or pieces accompanied by instruments, and use Western chord progressions. The more sophisticated creative voices of composers such as Vanraj Bhatia and Victor Paranjoti (India); Daud Kosasih, Subronto Atmodjo, Binsar Sitompul, Frans Haryadi, and Alfred Simanjuntak (Indonesia); Americ Goh, Zechariah Goh Toh Chai, John Sharpley, Phoon Yiew Tien, and Leong Yoon Pin (Singapore); and a host of Filipinos, Fabian Obispo, Francisco Feliciano, Rodolfo Delarmente, John Pamintuan, and Ryan Cayabyab are relatively few in number but their compositions have traveled all over the world. Other than these, prominent composers are as follows: Tim Jenkinson (Brunei); Nariman Wadia (India); Christian Isaac Tamaela, Budi Susanto Yohanes, E. L. Pohan, Bonar Gultom-Gorga, Pontas Purba, and Ivan Yohan (Indonesia); Joyce Koh, Kelly Tang, Ho Chee Kong, and Hoh Chung Shih (Singapore). The compositions have traveled with their choirs, for while a choir may sing Western repertoire at home, on an international tour, it seeks to invite audiences into its distinct musical culture.

The world has discovered small and large Asian choral cultures mainly through international encounters. Take, for example, the travels of the Gitameit Choir from Myanmar, formerly known as Burma, and the Revelations and Soul Sounds from Sri Lanka. Until these international appearances took place, the world knew very little about these choral cultures.

In spite of severe restrictions in educational infrastructure, access to publishing, and a scarcity of performing venues of reasonable quality, there has been a sharp rise in the quality of choral performance throughout the entire region. South and Southeast Asian choirs, particularly from Indonesia, the Philippines, and Singapore, are consistently winning major international prizes. The work ethic, taxing rehearsal schedules, and communal loyalty are frequently of a different order of magnitude when compared with Western counterparts. It is common to find Indonesian choirs that rehearse at least fifteen hours per week. These factors may account in part for a kind of sound quality that amazes international audiences. The Indonesian and Filipino choirs possess similar vocal qualities: a light, easy, free, and essentially naturally beautiful sound, not produced through years of vocal training, but more as a result of participating in a vibrant singing culture.

While choirs are typically found in educational institutions, in churches and in the community at large, choirs with a different mission are also being organized. This is further evidence that choirs discharge a vital community-mobilizing function, one of compassion and expressive humanity. In Nepal, Poesie and the Fags gives transgendered people an artistic voice. One of the world's most successful prison choir programs is run by the Christian Prison Ministry in Bangkok, and in the Philippines (BuCor Love Foundation Choir in the Maximum Security Camp of the New Bilibid Prison) and Indonesia (Bogor Prison), similar programs exist.

The most active Asian choirs and conductors on both national and international levels are listed below.

Afghanistan	Children's Choir from the Afghanistan National Institute of Music (Adriana Mascoli).
Brunei	Magna Voce, Serunai Singers (Garry Thin).
Bangladesh	Joyful Sound Choir.
Cambodia	Cambodia Baptist Bible College Choir; Cambodian Christian Children's Choir.
India	Cadenza Kantori; Cantata Choir, Mumbai; Gleehive; Goa Choral Symphony; Delhi Chamber Choir (Gabriella Boda-Rechner); Living Voices (Blossom Mendonca); Nagaland Choir; Navrachana School Choir (Madhumeeta Majumdar); Newman Choir; Paranjoti Academy Chorus (Coomi Wadia); Shillong Chamber Choir (Neil Nongkynrih); Stop-Gaps Choral Ensemble (Alfred D'Souza).
Indonesia	Angelorum Choir (Anthony Frans); Batavia Madrigal Singers; Cordana Youth Choir (Aida Swenson); Institut Teknologi Bandung Choir (Indra Listiyanto); Manado State University Choir (André de Quadros) (see Figure 11.1); Maranatha Christian University Choir (Bambang Jusana); Paduan Suara Gema Sangkakala Manado (Melky Sikape and Ivan Besau); Paragita Choir of Universitas Indonesia; Parahyangan Catholic University Student Choir (Paulus Yudianto); Studio Cantorum (Fatmawati Djunaidi).
Malaysia	Dithyrambic Singers (Ian Lim); Johor Bahru Chamber Choir (Raymond Lee); Kuala Lumpur Children's Choir (Susanna Saw); Malaysian Institute of Art Ladies Choir (Susanna Saw); Seremban Chung Hua Alumni Choir (Chew Hock Peng); Young Kuala Lumpur Singers (Susanna Saw).
Myanmar	Epiphany Catholic Choir (Naw Lar Hay); Gitameit Voices (U Moe Naing); Univoice (Sayarma Say htoo loo).
Nepal	Nepali Christian Chorus; Poesie and the Fags.
Pakistan	All Saints Choir; IGM Choir of Karachi; St. John's Choir; St. Patrick's Cathedral Choir.
Philippines	Ateneo de Manila College Glee Club (Marilou Venida-Hermo); De La Salle University Chorale (Rodolfo Delarmente); Himig Singers (Alvin Aviola); Novo Concertante Manila (Arwin Tan); Philippine Normal University Chorale (Luzviminda

Figure 11.1 Manado State University Choir, North Sulawesi, Indonesia

	Modelo); University of the East Chorale (Anna Tabitha Abeleda-Piquero); University of the Philippines Concert Chorus (Janet Sabas-Aracama); University of the Philippines Madrigal Singers (Mark Anthony Carpio); University of the Philippines Manila Chorale (Nikos Ibarra R. Mante); University of the Philippines Singing Ambassadors (Edgardo Manguiat); University of Santo Tomas Singers (Fidel Calalang, Jr.).
Singapore	Anglo-Chinese Junior College Choir; National University of Singapore Choir (Nelson Kwei); Philharmonic Chamber Choir (Lim Yau); Singapore Symphony Children's Choir; Singapore Symphony Chorus; SYC Ensemble Singers (Jennifer Tham); Victoria Chorale (Nelson Kwei); Victoria Junior College Choir; The Vocal Consort.
Sri Lanka	Choir of Visakha Vidyalaya; Colombo Philharmonic Choir (Manilal Weerakoon); Contempo (Eshantha Peiris); Holy Family Convent Choir (Rapthi Fernando); Ladies College Choir (Sureka Amerasinghe); Lylie Godridge Singers (Willie Godridge); Merry An Singers (Andre David and Mary Anne David); Methodist College Choir; Peradeniya Singers (Bridget Halpe); Soul Sounds (Soundarie David); St. Benedict College Choir (Krishan Rodrigo); St. Joseph's College Choir (Francis de Almeida); St. Thomas' College Choir; Revelations (Sanjeev Jayaratnam).
Thailand	AMAS Choir; Bangkok Music Society Choir; Bangkok Voices (Kittiporn Tantrarungroj); Siam Harmony Choir (Jose Librodo); Siam SuanPlu Chorus (Kaiwan Kulwattanothai); Wattana Girls' Chorus (Satit Sukchongchaipruek).
Vietnam	Vietnam Children's Choir (Pham Hong Hai); Vietnam National Opera and Ballet Choir.

A bright future

If the recent past is anything to judge by, South and Southeast Asian choirs will play an increasingly large part in influencing choral life in the twenty-first century and beyond. One can see a certain coming of age in this region, a self-awareness and pride in the sound, the movement, and the song; these ancient lands are transforming a European genre of music, making it into their own.

Bibliography

Coelho, V. A. "Kapsberger's Apotheosis . . . of Francis Xavier (1622) and the Conquering of India," in R. Dellamora and D. Fischlin (eds.), *The Work of Opera:*

Genre, Nationhood, and Sexual Difference. New York: Columbia University Press, 1997, pp. 27–47.

De Quadros, A. "Choral Life in India," *International Choral Bulletin* 122 (1993), 33–37. "From Old Ragas to New Voices: Experiencing Contemporary Indian Choral Music." In Brian A. Roberts and Andrea Margaret Rose (eds.), *Sharing the Voices: The Phenomenon of Singing 2: Proceedings of the International Symposium, St. John's, Newfoundland, Canada, 1999.* St. John's, NL: Memorial University of Newfoundland Faculty of Education, 2000, pp. 178–83.

Mulyadi, M., M. Satiadarma, and A. Soemantri "Choral Life in Indonesia," *International Choral Bulletin* 30, 2 (2011), 9–13.

Navarro, J. "Music in the Philippines Protestant Church: 1960–2000," in Brian Roberts (ed.), *Chapters in Philippine Church History*. Manila: Memorial University of Newfoundland Faculty of Education, 2001, pp. 451–62.

Saw, S. "An Overview of Choral Activities in Malaysia," *International Choral Bulletin* 30, 2 (2011), 5–7.

Sheng, T. "A Choral Miracle on Our Tiny Island: Singapore Choirs," *International Choral Bulletin* 30, 2 (2011), 14–17.

Shzr Ee, T. "Story of Choirs in Singapore," National Arts Council.www.nac.gov.sg

Veneracion, A. "Choral Music in the Philippines," *International Choral Bulletin* 20, 3 (2001), 4–5.

Yampolsky, Philip *Vocal Music from Central and West Flores*, Washington, DC: Smithsonian/Music of Indonesia, 9. Folkways Recordings, 1995.

12 From chanting the Quran to singing oratorio: choral music in West and Central Asia

AIDA HUSEYNOVA

Historically, West and Central Asia has been considered a region with a less developed choral music tradition. This lack of choral development had many causes, such as limitations put on music activities by Islam, the main religion for the Arab, Persian, and Turkic ethnic groups predominantly living in this part of the world; focus on individual rather than collective musical self-expression; the prevalence of monodic forms; improvisation as the key element of the music. Nonetheless, it would be simplistic to ignore unique forms of choral music that have emerged in this region since antiquity. These forms have later become sources for creative exploration by national composers. Arab, Persian and Turkic music traditions are distinct from each other and diverse within themselves. However, they underwent long historical periods of convergence and mutual influence which caused the presence of many common traits.

The earliest forms of choral music in the region go back to Zoroastrianism, the oldest of the revealed religions, which emerged in Iran and later spread out to the subcontinent, including territories of the present-day Azerbaijan, Uzbekistan, and Tajikistan. Zoroastrianism considered music as a sacred channel, a means of communication between human beings and the divine. In combination with the idea of collectivism essential for this faith, this belief was responsible for the important role of choral singing in Zoroastrian rituals. Prophet Zoroaster is believed to be the author of *gathas*, the hymns of praise that date to the second millennium BCE and have been included in *Avesta*, the holy book of faith. Seventeen *gathas* are a part of *yasna*, Zoroastrian liturgy, being arranged according to meter in five groups[1].

The emergence of Islam imposed a new role for music in society and culture. *Tajwid*, or chanting verses of Quran, the holy book of Islam, or of any other religious text has been recognized as among a few legitimate musical activities (although not regarded as music). Usually performed solo by a *muezzin (muadhdhin)* or *mullah*, those who come to the mosque to pray can join in. In early Islamic rituals, an ensemble or a choir of *muezzins* could participate in collective prayer[2]. *Adhan*, the call to prayer usually sung solo, could also be performed by two *muezzins* antiphonally[3].

Nowadays, the Umayyad Great Mosque in Damascus, Syria preserves this rather unique tradition of collective call to prayer.

Some rituals of Islam include choral music as a necessary component, such as *taziye* (*taziyeh, taaziye*), also known as *shabih* (*shabeh*), the religious mystery about the martyrdom of Imam Hussein, the grandson of the Prophet Muhammad. *Taziye* is performed during Muharram, the month of mourning according to the Hijri (Islamic) calendar, in areas with large Shia populations, including Iran, Azerbaijan, Iraq, Afghanistan, Tajikistan, southern Lebanon and Bahrain. The performance involves a group of men, some presenting the main characters of the drama, and others singing *marsiyya*, choral songs. *Marsiyya* are performed a cappella, mostly in unison or with simple elements of heterophony. During Muharram, men also sing responsorial songs, *nowheh*, to express their anguish at the martyrdom of saints. The leader vocalizes in a variable pulse and the group responds in a heavily metrical manner, accompanying singing by rhythmic breast-beating and often self-flagellation with chains. The latter, however, has recently been banned by some members of the Shia clergy.

Choral performance plays an important role in the rituals of dervishes, religious mendicants, and followers of Sufism, a mystical branch within Islam. Dervishes perform *sama*, literally "listening," when "musically embellished mystical poetry" is chanted by a group led by one or two singers[4]. During the *sama* ritual, singing is accompanied by handclapping and metric patterns kept by *daf* (*def, duff*), a large tambourine without metal jingles. *Zikr* (*dhikr, zikir, zekr*), literally "remembrance" of God, is associated with Sufism but, however, is also related to Islam in general. It is usually implemented on various holiday occasions, and may also serve healing purposes. *Zikr* can be performed by men or women, in either solitary or collective ways, softly or aloud. Collective loud *zikr* has developed into a liturgy that may include recitation, singing, playing non-pitched percussion instruments, as well as body and head movements. The main focus of this ritual is chanting God's many names which leads to a ceremonial climax marked by the collective cries "Allah! Allah!" or "Hu! Hu!" (He! He!) when all participants experience the state of trance. The performance of *zikr* involves a specific breathing technique which according to the Sufi philosophy facilitates spiritual union of the individual with the divine. Participants of *zikr* also perform *qasida*, the song praising God. It is strophic and written in a responsorial form with the call part introduced by a leader or leading group, and the response performed by others. The choral singing is accompanied by a set of instruments, usually frame drums or cymbals.

Choral songs known as *tahlil* and accompanied by the *mizmar* (conical oboe) and frame drums also honor Allah; their performance is not restricted to specific times and places. During Ramadan, the month of fasting, children and teenagers go to the neighbors' doors and sing greeting songs, hoping to receive sweets and coins. Festive songs are performed collectively in the mosques on the occasion of Islamic holidays, such as the end of Ramadan (*Eid al-Fitr*) and the Feast of the Sacrifice (*Eid al-Adha*). Choral singing is a feature of *mawlid* (*mawled, mevlut, mevlit*), the Prophet Muhammad's birthday. It is usually accompanied by frame drums and includes the litany and hymns[5]. In the litany, the soloists perform improvisatory melodic phrases praising the life and deeds of the Prophet Muhammad while the choir may stay silent or keep up a drone. Hymns have a metric base and are sung by the choir in unison.

Choral singing is a feature of many genres of folk music in the region. *Mayda*, a threshing song in Uzbekistan, Kazakhstan, Kyrgyzstan, Tajikistan, and Turkmenistan, *bekbekey*, performed by women shepherds, and *shyryldang*, sung by horse herders in Kyrgyzstan, are chanted responsorially and antiphonally. *Fidjri*, a work song of pearl-divers in Iraq and the Persian Gulf area, presents a unique type of group singing that includes *khrab* where the soloist sings the melody and the rest of the seamen sustain a vocal drone two octaves beneath the melody. A remarkable style of vocal polyphony considered as "one of the most isolated and interesting traditions of polyphony on our planet" emerged in Nuristan, a mountainous part of East Afghanistan.[6] This three-part vocal polyphony is principally dissonant, with a dronelike bass part. It is performed by either men or women and can be accompanied by drums, *wadzh* (bowed harp), clapping, and dancing.

Wedding celebration seems to be among the main occasions for collective singing. In most Arab cultures, women sing wedding songs in a fast *parlando* style combined with ululation that is produced by tremolo-like tongue vibration. Women and men perform wedding songs: *zhar-zhar* in Kazakhstan and Kyrgyzstan, *yor-yor* in Uzbekistan and Tajikistan, or *halay* in Turkey, Iran, Azerbaijan, and Turkmenistan. *Halay*, where people form a circle or a line, usually holding hands, is representative of the collective dance songs performed on festive occasions, just as *yalli* and *yalla* are representative in Azerbaijan and Uzbekistan respectively, *chobi* in Iraq, *arda, ayyala*, and *samri* in the southern part of Iraq and the Persian Gulf area. At wedding ceremonies in Tajikistan, a male choir sings *naqsh*, a recitative-like song. Many dance songs in the Arab tradition, such as *radih* or *dahhiyya*, are performed responsorially by a singer (or two) and a group of people, both males and females. *Dahhiyya* includes a theatrical element: the performance reaches its climax at the appearance of a female dressed in black and holding a sword. *Pesta* (*basta*) is a song about love and separation in Iraq, performed by a singer and choir with the accompaniment of the oud, a pear-shaped plucked string instrument, and drums. Many love songs in Arab folk music, such as *ataba, murabba*, and *muthamman*, are in a strophic form where soloist(s) perform the stanza, and the audience repeats the final line or sings a refrain while accompanying the entire performance by hand-clapping.

Choral singing is involved in the celebration of pre-Islamic holidays, such as *Navruz* (*Novruz*, *Nauruz*), the New Year in many Central Asian countries, that occurs on the day of the vernal equinox – March 20 or 21. Songs that praise the awakening of nature are sung in a responsorial form with the soloists performing the verse, and the choir singing the refrain. *Sumalak* songs are performed collectively by women while they cook a holiday meal. Choral singing is a part of the *Boychechak* (Snowdrop) festival spring holidays appraising the beauty of flowers and celebrated in Uzbekistan and Tajikistan. A group of boys and girls holds a branch of sycamore decorated with snowdrops, irises, and tulips and walk around the village handing out flowers and performing songs praising their beauty; the soloist sings the verse, and the rest of the group joins in the chorus. The *Lola* or *Binafsha* (Tulip) festival, includes a men's antiphonal song performed by several groups sitting in the teahouses, sometimes joining each other in a large choir of several hundred people.

Since the mid nineteenth century, the musical traditions of the region have encountered a rapid integration of Western musical practices, including Western forms of choral singing. During the modernization era in Ottoman Turkey in the nineteenth and early twentieth centuries, and at the time of the Turkish Republic (since 1923), as well as in Iran under the Gajar (1794–1925) and Pahlavi (1925–79) dynasties, a cohort of national composers emerged that contributed to the development of choral music as well. The Iranian composer Ali Naqi Vaziri (1887–1979) included choral episodes in his operettas and incorporated choral singing into the national schools' curricula. Ahmad Pejman (b.1937) wrote choral episodes for his opera *Rustic Festival* (1967) and created the oratorio *Khorramshahr* (1992). *Twelve Anatolian Folk Songs* (1926), by the Turkish composer Cemal Reshit Rey (1904–85), was among the first works combining authentic Turkish folk music traditions with the stylistic constructs of Western music. Ahmed Adnan Saygun (1907–91) wrote his first choral works in the 1930s; his masterpiece, the oratorio *Yunus Emre* (1946), is based on the poetry of the eponymous thirteenth-century Turkish philosopher. This work was translated into several languages and has received performances worldwide, including one in New York by the NBC Symphony Orchestra under Leopold Stokowski (1958).

In the part of Central Asia that was part of the Russian Empire from the early nineteenth century and then part of the Soviet Union (1920–91), the process of mastering forms of Western choral music was facilitated by close contacts with Russian music and strongly stimulated by the national and cultural policy of the communists. From the late 1940s onward, the

Kazakhs Ahmed Zhubanov (1906–68) and Latif Hamidi (1906–83), the Kyrgyzs Abdylas Maldybaev (1906–78), Uzbek Mukhtar Ashrafi (1912–75), Yunus Rajabi (1897–1976), Tolib Sadykov (1907–57), and Mutal Burkhanov (1916–2002), the Turkmens Dangatar Ovezov (1911–66) and Veli Mukhatov (1916–2005), and the Tajiks Azam Kamalov (1912–71), and Ziedullo Shahidi (1914–85) accomplished syntheses between indigenous music idioms and forms of Western choral music. Burkhanov, for example, wrote pieces based on Uzbek, Tajik, Uyghur, Kazakh, and Iranian folk tunes, such as *Six Choruses a cappella* (1954) where he incorporated folk melodies in the homophonic and modest polyphonic texture.

Unlike in the rest of Central Asia, in Azerbaijan the forms of Western music, including choral forms, had been mastered before the Soviet era. Uzeyir Hajibeyli (1885–1948) included choral episodes in his opera *Leyli and Majnun* (1908). They were written under the influence of *taziye* and were based on traditional and folk melodies. Furthermore, Hajibeyli created mature choral works, such as the chorus "Chanlibel" from the opera *Koroghlu* (A Blind Man's Son) (1937), in which he incorporated modal rules of Azerbaijani traditional music within fugue and sonata forms.

The development of choral music in the Soviet part of Central Asia suffered as a result of the impact of communist ideology. All religious rituals and associated choral singing were severely discriminated against. In the meantime, the Soviet regime encouraged the idea of collective singing, as it corresponded with the imperatives for collectivism and grandiosity essential for Soviet aesthetics. Thus a large number of choral works glorifying communism and its heroes were written by Central Asian composers during the Soviet era. They featured stylistic clichés typical of Soviet choral music, such as march-like rhythms, simple melodic patterns, and massive chordal texture. However, there are gems, such as the choral *mugham* created by the Azerbaijani composer Jahangir Jahangirov (1921–92) in his chorus "Chahargah" from the opera *Azad* (1956), or the choral *kuu* based on the main instrumental genre of Kazakh and Kyrgyz music introduced by the Kazakh composer Bakhitzhan Baykadamov (1917–77) in his a cappella choral pieces (1971–72).

During the past few decades, choral music in West and Central Asia has experienced ups and downs caused by various social, political, and military factors. The 1979 Islamic revolution in Iran, the 1978 war, and events of the 1990s in Afghanistan, the Iran–Iraq war of 1980–88, and military operations in Iraq since 1991 have caused a negative impact on musical life in general and have reduced the role of Western choral genres in the panorama of musical life. At the same time, military conflicts stimulated the appearance of choral works of a patriotic nature. Furthermore the productivity of the composers in the post-Soviet countries of Central Asia dropped after the collapse of the Soviet Union in 1991 because of the breakup of the system of governmental support of arts and music. Nowadays, as the turmoil of the post-Soviet period is over, composers continue writing choral pieces exploring genres of traditional music previously rejected by the Soviets.

In Turkey and in many Arab countries, particularly, Lebanon, the period since 1980 has been marked by increased interest in Western musical genres including choral ones. To facilitate this, composers, choral conductors, and educators from Soviet (subsequently post-Soviet) Central Asia representing a more mature level of the art music tradition have been invited to work in these countries, which has resulted in an increased integration of cultures. Performing traditions enjoy growing professionalization and popularity as well. For instance, the independent consortium Luna in Syria includes five choirs founded between 1999 and 2007 that aim to promote treasures of Arab choral music along with pieces from Western repertoire within the country and abroad.

In 2008, the choral festival Aswatuna ("Our Voices") took place in the ancient city of Petra, Jordan, a UNESCO World Heritage Site. The festival, directed by André de Quadros and Shireen Abu Khader, happened to be the first choral encounter between Arab choirs and Western musicians, and brought together about two hundred choral singers and conductors. Among festival participants were the Sharagan choir from Iraq, the Magnificat Choir of the Custody of the Holy Land from Palestine, the choir of students at the Conservatory in Damascus, Syria, the Fayha Choir from Lebanon, the Dozan Wa Awtar Singers from Jordan, and Voces Nordicae from Sweden. The Aswatuna festival demonstrated the role of choral music as an effective means to build bridges between countries and cultures. For example, the Magnificat choir performs music from Palestine including pieces of Islamic and Christian heritage, and collaborates with Israeli choirs, thus showing historical links between the various cultures in the Middle East.

Despite differences in styles and techniques, certain paradigms in choral works penned by composers from West and Central Asia stem from common sources of their creativity. The first source is the *maqam/ makom/mugham/mukam* tradition which determines the importance of call–response relations between vocal and instrumental parts and the extensive use of imitative technique. The melodic patterns of traditional modes are incorporated into the harmonic and polyphonic texture. The second source is the music of Islamic rituals with the predominance of male choirs, the principle of alternating soloist and choir, and mainly unison singing. The third source is traditional instrumental music, where the main melody can be duplicated in fourths or fifths and combined with the bourdon tone. In choral pieces written in the first half of the twentieth century, these sources were juxtaposed with the stylistic properties of Western music in a spirit of late Romanticism. Choral pieces created since the 1960s feature more recent developments in Western choral music found in the works of Stravinsky, Orff, and Bartók.

Bibliography

Abasova, Elmira. *Uzeir Gadzhibekov: Put' Zhizni i Tvorchestva* [Uzeyir Hajibeyov: His Life and Music]. Baku: Elm, 1985.

Abdullaev, Rustambek. *Obriad i Muzyka v Kontekste Kul'tury Uzbekistana i Tsentral'noi Azii* [Ritual and Music in the Context of the Culture of Uzbekistan and Central Asia]. Tashkent: Swiss Agency for Development and Cooperation, 2006.

Ammar, Faruk Khasan. "Rannee Mnogogolosie na Vostoke" [Early Polyphony in the East]. *Sovetskaia Muzyka* 7 (1975): 112–16.

Beliaev, Viktor. *Central Asian Music: Essays in the History of the Music of the Peoples of the USSR*. Middletown, CT: Wesleyan University Press, 1975.

Boyce, Mary. *Zoroastrians: Their Religious Beliefs and Practices*. London and New York: Routledge, 2001.

Chelkowski, Peter (ed.). *Tazieh: Ritual and Drama in Iran*. New York University Press, 1979.

During, Jean. "What is Sufi Music?" in Leonard Lewisohn (ed.), *The Legacy of Mediaeval Persian Sufism*. London: Khaniqahi Nimatullahi Publications, 1992, pp. 277–87.

al-Faruqi, Lois Ibsen. "The Mawlid," *World of Music* 28, 3 (1986): 79–89.

Feldman, Walter. "Musical Genres and Zikr of the Sunni Tarikats of Istanbul," in Raymond Lifchez (ed.), *The Dervish Lodge: Architecture, Art, and Sufism in Ottoman Turkey*. Berkeley: University of California Press, 1992, pp. 187–202.

Jordania, Joseph. *Who Asked the First Question: Origins of Vocal Polyphony, Human Intelligence, Language and Speech*. Tbilisi: Logos, 2006.

Levin, Theodore. *The Hundred Thousand Fools of God: Musical Travels in Central Asia (and Queen's, New York)*. Bloomington: Indiana University Press, 1996.

Mamedova, Leyla. *Khorovaia Muzyka Azerbaidzhana* [Choral Music of Azerbaijan]. Baku: Adiloglu, 2010.

Mez, Adam. *The Renaissance of Islam*. New York: AMS Press Inc, 1975.

Nizomov, Asliddin. *Sufizm v Kontekste Muzykal'noi Kul'tury Narodov Tsentral'noi Azii* [Sufism in the Context of the Musical Culture of the Peoples of Central Asia]. Dushanbe: Irfon, 2000.

Qureshi, Regula Burckhardt. "Sounding the Word: Music in the Life of Islam," in Lawrence Eugene Sullivan (ed.), *Enchanting Powers: Music in the World's Religions*. Cambridge, MA: Harvard University Center for the Study of World Religions, 1997, pp. 263–98.

   "Sufi Music and the Historicity of Oral Tradition," in Stephen Blum, Philip Bohlman, and Daniel Neuman (eds.), *Ethnomusicology and Modern Music History*. Urbana and Chicago: University of Illinois Press, 1991, pp. 103–20.

Sakata, Hiromi Lorraine. *Music in the Mind: The Concepts of Music and Musician in Afghanistan.* Washington, DC: Smithsonian Institution Press, 2002.

Say, Ahmet. *The Music Makers in Turkey.* Ankara: Music Encyclopedia Publications, 1995.

Seyidova, Saadat. *Gadim Azerbaijan Merasim Musigisi.* [The Music of Ancient Azerbaijani Rituals]. Baku: Mars-Print, 2005.

Shiloah, Amnon. *Music in the World of Islam: A Socio-Cultural Study.* Detroit: Wayne State University Press, 1995.

Tadzhikova, Zoia. "Svadebnye Pesni Tadzhikov" [Wedding Songs of the Tajiks], in *Istoriia i Sovremennost': Problemy Muzykal'noi Kul'tury Narodov Uzbekistana, Turkmenii i Tadzhikistana* [History and Modernity: The Problems of the Musical Cultures of Uzbekistan, Turkmenistan and Tajikistan]. Moscow: Muzyka, 1972, pp. 249–66.

Touma, Habib Hassan. "The Fidjri, a Major Vocal Form of the Bahrain Pearl-Divers," *World of Music* 19, 3–4 (1977): 121–33.

The Music of the Arabs. Portland, OR: Amadeus Press, 1996.

Yanov-Yanovskaya, Natalia. *Mutal' Burkhanov: Vremia, Zhizn', Tvorchestvo* [Mutal Burkhanov: Epoch, Life, Works]. Tashkent: Media Land, 1999.

13 Voices of the Pacific: the (ch)oral traditions of Oceania

KAREN GRYLLS

In the beginning . . .

From the time that the ancient voices of Oceania were first heard, tens of thousands of years ago, there was singing.[1] The songs belonged to the indigenous cultures that inhabited the many islands of the Pacific. They sang about their ancestors, their relationship with the land, their daily lives, and they told their Creation stories and communicated with their deities.[2]

In the Pacific, singing represented an elevated form of verbal utterance. Singing, chanting, or intoning was deemed the most effective way to communicate with the deities, and the one sure way to appeal to the human appetites of the Polynesian pantheon was through good singing. Poets, composers, and choreographers (often one and the same person and highly regarded) wrote songs and choreographed dances, which added the visual dimension to the expression of the words. The singing traditions in Eastern Polynesia were unison, while those in the Western Polynesian tradition were choral, that is, they sang in parts.[3] The songs were part of daily life and, more important, ritual, and the ability to sing was a part of the individual's self-identity.[4] So great was the power of the uttered word expressed in both song and dance that the role given to instrumental music was comparatively small.

Songs were defined essentially by their function, and great expectation and importance were attached to the singing of them.[5] Performances were socially significant, and ridicule and shame were attached to anyone who did not perform with style and excellence; for example, when a leader failed to start the group together. Group performances at festivals and special occasions created a degree of friendly rivalry and competition. Songs (in both recited and sung styles) were categorized according to their purpose, and chant formed the basis of much of their musical content.[6] Like the Polynesian songs, the Aboriginal songs were defined by function.[7] Inherited networks of songlines, the songs and verses that acted as maps and guides across the land, had to be preserved.[8]

I am very grateful to Faye Dumont (Melbourne) and Richard Moyle (Auckland) for their generous and sage advice during the writing of this chapter.

McLean refers to the "choir" in the Pacific as "a group of singers."[9] Singers sang in groups dedicated either to sacred or to secular music. These groups had leaders, but not conductors in the European sense. Those who led (*fuatai mi* [Samoa] and *tahiva* [Tonga]) kept or beat time, and did so with a unique style and grace. The stylized and rather exaggerated gesture comprised movement that indicated and controlled the rate of clapping, and contained elements of mime (not regarded as dance) and sometimes humor, which gave a visual dimension to the words.[10] The leader faced the audience (it was considered rude to do otherwise) and performed the role with appropriate style. Voice parts are described with a mixture of local and English terms,[11] and there are clearly identifiable vocal qualities, although the manner of singing is more difficult to describe.[12] The vocal quality, often related to the function of the chant and the role of the person who sang it, is generally one that can be heard outdoors; consequently there is a degree of nasality and pure chest tone used in the singing.[13] The *imene tuki*, the traditional hymns of the Cook Islands, display loud, piercing, shrill tones.[14] This same shrillness and nasality are the qualities also most admired by the Australian Aboriginals.[15] (The sound essentially comes from the throat and the nose.) By comparison, the Hawaiian sound is sweeter, possibly influenced by the European style.

The traditions of learning the songs were oral.[16] An exception to this is the Tongan notation system, a variant of solfa based on Tongan numerals with durations indicated by standard punctuation marks.[17] Solfa was also used almost a century later in New Zealand by Sir Kingi Ihaka to teach his compositions, the *waiata* from his hymnbook, to the members of the Auckland Anglican Māori Club.[18] Nonetheless, the Oceanic traditions were oral, and those who sang the songs considered them *taonga* or treasures for the generations to come.[19]

Newcomers

The first European contact in Oceania began in the seventeenth century, and it was the arrival of the immigrants and missionaries from Europe that rather changed everything.[20] One of the first musical contacts between the Europeans and the Polynesians was in New Zealand, an exchange of trumpet calls between one of Tasman's crew and the local Māori at Golden Bay in 1642.[21] A century later, in 1769, Cook's ship the *Endeavour* arrived in New Zealand. Cook found the Māori *waiata* "harmonious enough but very doleful to the European ear."[22] Nicholas, in his narrative of a voyage to New Zealand with Samuel Marsden on the *Active* in 1815, described the singing of the Māori on board as "a plaintive and melodious air and seemed not unlike some of our sacred music ... as it forcibly reminded me of the chanting in our cathedrals, it being deep, slow and extended ... It was divided into parts, which the chiefs sang separately, and were joined in chorus, at certain intervals, by the other New Zealanders; while they all concluded it together."[23] In 1773, James Burney, a young officer on the *Adventure*, observed that the performance of Te Rangihouhia and his party also demonstrated singing in harmony.[24]

Missionaries

The missionaries discovered very quickly that singing was a means to conversion, and the single most important European influence on the musical traditions of Oceania was hymn singing. This came at a price, however – the indigenous singing and dancing traditions suffered as a result "[since] anything relating to 'heathen' religion or ceremony was resolutely opposed [by the missionaries]."[25] The explicit sexual nature of some of the dance forms and the warlike dances, such as those of the New Zealand Māori, were hugely at odds with the missionaries' puritanical, Victorian ideals.

There was, as a result, a tragic loss of traditional repertoire. English tunes were set with local language texts, yet as McLean points out, "Nowhere did the missionaries enjoy immediate success."[26] In 1839 the missionary Richard Taylor wrote of the Māori singing: "The native airs embrace no more than three or four notes and they carry no more into the hymns they sing, indeed it is the most discordant singing I have ever heard, no country choir in England being worse ..."[27] In Australia, the Lutheran clergy founded the Mission at Hermannsburg, Inkat'irbirberintjaka (in Ntaria, west of Alice Springs) in 1877. From the early days there, the traditions of Christian congregational singing coexisted with the songs of the Arrente. "The musical impact on the indigenous community was significant, with the community taught Bach chorales translated into their own Aranda language. Today the members of the Ntaria ladies' choir perform no pre-Lutheran music, but sing chorales in a highly emotive manner, importing fluid aboriginal vocal styles into the metrical structures of the chorale."[28] The Aboriginals found the Western music easy to learn since it had none of the microtonal complexity found in their own music. Moses Tjalkabota,[29] the Aboriginal evangelist, who recalled learning the hymns as a child, remembers being taught the melodies from the violin. Torres Strait Island was so heavily missionarized that it is now difficult to know what indigenous music there may have been.[30]

New Zealand's first missionaries were Anglican and French Catholic.[31] In 1859 the Reverend J. W. Stack established the Māori Mission[32] at the

Māori Pa, Kaiapoi Nature Reserve. This mission boasted a fifty-strong choir at St. Stephen's Anglican Church; there was seating for two hundred people at the regular choral services and the choir (nearly all Māori) sang the hymns and chants for the Anglican services. In Hawaii, through the work of the Hawaiian Congregational Missions from 1820, the *himeni* were little more than "the ancient spirit of the Hawaiian tradition clothed in European harmony."[33] Throughout Oceania, the trend from the 1830s onwards was for indigenous choirs to sing music more and more influenced by the European choral traditions.

Immigrants

The music and traditions that the German, Irish, Welsh, English, and Scottish immigrants brought with them significantly influenced the musical life of cities and towns in New Zealand, Australia, and Polynesia from the 1830s onwards. In 1836, with the settlement of German Lutheran immigrants on Kangaroo Island, South Australia, came German vocal traditions. In 1858 Lutherans founded the Adelaider Liedertafel,[34] the oldest male choir in Australia.

Cathedral musical traditions, Catholic and Protestant, played a large part in the development of church choral music. Irish-born Catherine Fitzpatrick, regarded as the first Australian choral conductor, was a schoolteacher who arrived in New South Wales in 1811. She organized a small group of singers to sing at mass, and when the church was finally built she became the first woman conductor at St. Mary's Cathedral, Sydney (1818–43), the first Catholic church in Australia.

The Welsh brought with them their great hymn singing festivals and eisteddfods.[35] There were also Scandinavian choirs which sang songs and hymns from their religious traditions, while others embraced their own folk music traditions.[36] In Australia, the early songs recalled the hardships of convict life; by the late nineteenth century, the songs recounted the adventures in the lives of the farmers and herders. Folk music from the British Isles formed a large part of the repertoire of songs sung in schools and communities in the colonies well into the twentieth century.

The musical influences

Alfred Hill (1869–1960),[37] born in Melbourne and educated at the Leipzig Conservatory of Music, was one of the most influential musicians in New Zealand and Australia in the late nineteenth and twentieth centuries. As well as his study of European music at the Leipzig Conservatory, Hill's fascination with Māori *waiata* resulted in numerous compositions; *Waiata poi*,[38] the cantata *Hinemoa* (1896),[39] and his opera *Tapu* (1902–3) attracted much attention and critical acclaim. It was a bold move to compose with indigenous song; it worked for Alfred Hill perhaps because the Māori *waiata* had already been impregnated with European musical language, and the lilting melodies were well suited to the Romanticism of the late nineteenth century. This was less the case in the decades that followed.

From the start of the twentieth century, musicians arrived in Australasia from England,[40] many to work in the churches, community choirs, and universities.[41] Peter Godfrey's arrival in New Zealand in 1958 transformed choral singing and laid the foundations for the years that followed.[42] The choral sound, aesthetic, and repertoire were from the finest English cathedral tradition; the didactic models and music were European. These musician immigrants worked tirelessly to establish conservatories and university schools of music, to establish and conduct choirs and orchestras, and to compose new music.

In turn, local musicians went to Europe and England to train;[43] they were encouraged by their teachers to establish and explore their own national identities.[44] In one of Douglas Lilburn's successful early works, *Prodigal Country* (1939) for baritone, SATB chorus and orchestra, the choice of Robyn Hyde's poem *Journey from New Zealand* was particularly apposite in this respect.

Percy Grainger (1882–1961), sometimes called the Charles Ives of Australia, had a great interest in folk songs from the British Isles and arranged many of them for choir. By the twentieth century, the folk song was a genre that told stories: the stories of the convicts' lives, of the gold rushes, of the hardships endured by the immigrants, of the lives of the whalers and sealers.[45] They were the stories of colonial life, often sung to familiar melodies from the homelands.

Choirs and composers

Choral societies,[46] harmonic societies, and philharmonic choirs abounded in Australasia from the mid nineteenth century, and their repertoire was largely oratorio. Common fare included works such as Handel's *Messiah* and Mendelssohn's *Elijah*, and sometimes glees, madrigals, and excerpts from oratorios.[47] As well as the Victorian choral societies, antipodean ensembles also included glee clubs,[48] madrigal societies, male choirs and Liedertafeln. By 1930 the Rotorua Māori Choir and the Tahiwis, a Māori male quartet, were recording for the Columbia label in Australia. There were also Māori church choirs.[49] The music sung by the Māori artists sometimes included the traditional *waiata* but with European-style melodies and harmony. From the 1980s in New Zealand, there was an upsurge of smaller ensembles, chamber choirs, vocal ensembles, and early music groups that continue to flourish. So too do the gay and lesbian choirs which were established in the 1990s.[50]

As early as 1979, national choirs were formed first in New Zealand and then in Australia. These included: the New Zealand Youth Choir (1979) and the New Zealand Secondary Students' Choir (1988) founded by Dr. Guy Jansen, whose vision and entrepreneurial spirit have given young singers in New Zealand excellent choral singing for three decades; Voices New Zealand (1998) founded by Karen Grylls and Jacqui Simpson; Australian Voices (1993) founded by Stephen Leek and Graeme Morton; the Sydney Children's Choir and the Gondwana Choirs founded by Lyn Williams; the National Māori Choir (active around 2000), and various national male choirs. Immigrant choirs and choirs with a social or political emphasis have added to the colorful choral canvas that exists today.[51] One of the newest choirs in Auckland is the CeleBRation (CBR) Choir, a singing group for people with neurological conditions.[52]

Once there were choirs,[53] composers could write for them, and this is essentially how the corpus of choral music developed from the mid twentieth century. Tongan *punake* had long understood the importance of commissions for occasions.[54] Composers in the Western traditions now had the chance to engage with new initiatives and enterprises; the remoteness of the Pacific gave those who put together their musical ideas the opportunity to explore their own identities with considerable freedom. After World War II, eastern and southern Europeans made their way to Australia, and in the 1970s immigrants came from Asia and the Pacific. From the middle of the twentieth century, composers began to write choral music that reflected the landscape and the many musical traditions of those who called the islands of the Pacific home.[55]

A group of composers embraced the traditions of Asia – Anne Boyd and Jack Body had interests in both the gamelan and medieval music.[56] In *As I Crossed the Bridge of Dreams* (1975) Boyd adopts a Japanese compositional structure, basing the piece on three different pitch-sets and groups of *gagaku* instruments.[57] The text is from the writings of an eleventh-century Japanese noblewoman. David Hamilton's *Rakiura* (1993) tells a true story of a Japanese woman living in a cave on Stewart Island and the work is based on the stylized character of the Noh drama.[58] With invented languages for each movement, Body's *Five Lullabies* (1989) creates different ethnic atmospheres, and his musical textures are "inspired by the vocal polyphonies of China's minority cultures."[59]

The compositions of Eve De Castro-Robinson and Stephen Leek explore the natural world with the sounds and colors of the land; Leek's impressive aleatoric textures draw upon the stories of the Dreamtime with

Aboriginal texts. Birdcalls have inspired some of his work as they have for De Castro-Robinson in *Chaos of Delight III* (1998).[60] Poets, too, provided inspiration. Griffiths and Farquhar were drawn to the writings of A. R. D. Fairburn, James Baxter, Charles Brasch, Denis Glover, and Hone Tuwhare. For her song cycle *The Poet* (2007), Jenny McLeod set Janet Frame's witty, bittersweet poems about the life of the poet as artist.

Lilburn's *Prodigal Country* (1939) and Sculthorpe's *Port Essington* (1977) and *Child of Australia* (1988) reflect on the landscape, life in the colonies, and the pride in one's native land. At the start of *Child of Australia* Sculthorpe used an indigenous melody but, as Shearer observes, it little resembled the melody in its original context.[61] Douglas Mews begins *The Lovesong of Rangipouri* (1974) with a complete Māori chant recorded by Hone Crown at Makara in 1963 and transcribed by Mervyn McLean.[62] Hopkins asks that the second melody in *Past Life Melodies* (1991) be sung with an appropriate nasal, strident tone. Increasingly, permission to use indigenous material in composition and performance comes as a result of the relationships built between individuals and performing groups. Without such a relationship, Anthony Ritchie avoids integrating authentic *waiata* in *Ahua* (2000).[63] Instead, like Marshall in *Tangi* (1999), he has used some of the conventions from the indigenous tradition.

Who we are . . .

At the start of the first movement of *Journey to Horseshoe Bend* (2003), Andrew Schultz combines the sounds of the Ntaria Women's Choir singing Aboriginal words to the Lutheran chorale "Wachet auf" with those of a symphony chorus and orchestra. For the Ntaria women, it was a long journey from Alice Springs to the stage of the Sydney Opera House. In 1996, the New Zealand Youth Choir and Te Waka Huia traveled from New Zealand and stood on that same stage for the first performance of a New Zealand choir and *kapahaka* group.

Gillian Whitehead showed the author the first copy of *Taiohi taiao*, (2004) some months before the first rehearsals: "There are no corners in this piece," she said, "it needs to flow just like the water from the spring." The piece is about water as the life-giving force, the spiritual essence that pervades every part of life. The music, the songs are that essence, the *taonga*, the treasures that the composers will write, that the voices of Oceania will sing out. The ancient voyages of the Pacific, the *Malaga*, will continue. There are stories not yet told . . .

Select list of choral works

Atherton Michael (b.1950) *The Mahogany Ship* (1994) SSA choir, string quartet and
   percussion
   Kalliopeia sopha (2000) SSA choir
Body, Jack (b.1944) *Carol to St. Stephen* (1975) three soloists and
   SSSSAAAATTTTBBBB choir
   Five Lullabies (1989) SATB
Boyd, Anne (b.1946) *As I Crossed the Bridge of Dreams* (1975) a cappella choir
De Castro-Robinson, Eve (b.1956) *Chaos of Delight III* (1998) SSA and metal clickers
Ete, Igelese (b.1968) *Malaga* (2002) chorus, dancers, and instrumental ensemble
Farquhar, David (1928–2007) *The Islands* (1967) five settings of poems by Charles Brasch,
   A. R. D. Fairburn, and James K. Baxter for unaccompanied SATB choir
Fisher, Helen (b.1942) *Tete Kura* (2000) Text Ngapo Wehi; *Pounamu* (1989, rev.
   1997) SSAATBB and koauau (nose flute)
Griffiths, David (b.1950) *Lie Deep My Love* (1996) Text: J. K. Baxter SSATTBB and
   SATB quartet
Hamilton, David (b.1955) *Missa Pacifica* (2005) soprano and alto soloists, SSATB
   youth choir, large mixed-voice choir, 3 trumpets, 3 trombones, 5 percussion, 2
   harps and strings
   Rakiura (1993) alto solo, SSAATTBB
Hopkins, Sarah (b.1958) *Past Life Melodies* (1991)
Leek, Stephen (b.1959) *Knowee* (1988, arr. 2008) SSAATTBB a cappella
Lilburn, Douglas (1915–2001) *Prodigal Country* (1939) baritone solo, SATB chorus
   and orchestra
Marshall, Christopher (b.1956) *Tangi* (1999) mezzo-soprano solo, SATB
   To The Horizon: Images of New Zealand (1990, rev. 1997) SATB mixed choir
McLeod, Jenny (b.1941) *The Poet* (2007) chamber choir and string quartet
Mews, Douglas (1918–93) *Lovesong of Rangipouri* (1974) baritone and SATB choir
Ritchie, Anthony (b.1960) *Ahau* (2000) soprano, mezzo-soprano, two tenors, bar-
   itone, and orchestra
Schultz, Andrew (b.1960) *Journey to Horseshoe Bend* (2003) symphonic cantata for
   solo voices, narrators, choirs, and orchestra
Sculthorpe, Peter (b.1929) *Child of Australia* (1988) speaker, soprano solo, SATB
   chorus, and orchestra
   Night Piece (1966) SATB chorus and piano
   Sun Music for Voices and Percussion (1966)
Walker Dan (b.1978) *Ngailu Boy of the Stars* (n.d.) SSA (premiered by the Torres
   Strait Island and Sydney Children's Choirs), piano, percussion and electronic
   sounds
Whitehead, Gillian (b.1941) *Taiohi taiao* (2004) SSAATBB and koauau (nose flute)

14 Choral music in Africa: history, content, and performance practice

RUDOLF DE BEER AND WILSON SHITANDI

Introduction: a historical overview

Singing as a group activity existed in Africa long before colonization. A few anthropological and archeological sources as well as analysis of oral history recordings provide clear evidence of a long-standing quasi-choral music culture in Africa. For instance "an African style of singing based on vocal homophony or polyphony has been demonstrated for many years" by communities such as Ijesha-Yoruba of Nigeria, Nguu of Tanzania, Zulu, Xhosa, and Swazi of South Africa.[1] Nketia argues that although there is no information on how this style of singing originated and developed, it seems clear that it existed before Western influence. The use of polyphonic and homophonic choruses among the Maasai people of Kenya is further evidence of the existence of choral singing in Africa before the colonial establishment. These group activities were and still are primarily part of the social activities of the African communities where music making is generally social. The presence of choral forms of African traditional music is exemplified by its social and communal aspects. Indeed, in most indigenous African communities, music making was and still can be conceptualized as choral. Euba notes that "choral music in African traditional cultures was utilized as a strong indicator of communal approach to music making and its importance in modern culture shows a bond with [African music] tradition."[2]

Despite the vastness of the continent in geographical and cultural terms, data on the structures of choral organization in Africa is scarce. It has been difficult for musicologists to establish historical facts about indigenous African group music traditions of the pre-colonial period because of the lack of written documentation, recordings, and music notation. This chapter will therefore focus on choral activities in Africa during the postcolonial era and is also limited by the fact that there are as many different musical cultures as tribes in Africa and one cannot provide a comprehensive coverage of the choral activities of each of these cultures and tribes. The content will therefore focus on the choral activities of sub-Saharan Africa. North Africa will nonetheless be referred to in the context of individual persons and the musical trends in some countries where choral activities are noticeable.

Admittedly, choral performances became more modernized and formalized with heightened colonial, missionary, and religious activities in large parts of the continent.[3] Kidula notes that different social constructs such as the Anglophone, Francophone, and Lusophone can now be associated with the emergence and practice of certain innovative ways of recognizing and doing choral music.[4] Nonetheless, Africans easily adopted the Western tradition of choral music brought into Africa by missionaries because of the number of concurrences, including the social nature of singing together, polyphonic structures in the music, and the function of music as an enhancement for a social (religious) activity, such as the congregational singing of Christian hymns. These hymns were later transformed into new African choral styles by being adapted to African practices, including language, parallel movement between voices, responsorial elements, and rhythmic alterations, through the inclusion of dances or instrumental accompaniments. This even had an influence on the new folk songs which were sung in four-part harmony, referred to as neo-traditional choral music.[5] However, non-African choirs in Africa did not adapt to this new form of choral music, and function in a typically European tradition.

Forms of choral music in Africa

Modern African choral music (MACM) emerged at the end of the nineteenth century but only began to be appreciated on a wider scale in the 1950s. This appreciation has given rise to an enormous number of literary choral works with a significant number of ardent enthusiasts.[6] The contemporary choral music tradition in sub-Saharan Africa is the result of African indigenous elements encountering Euro-American Christianity and educational systems. Thus, Euro-American structures and elements continue to be applied even as African ethos, structures, and performance styles are practiced and solidified. For political and historical reasons, the choral tradition in the eastern and southern parts of the continent has a strong European influence, and some choirs only perform art music from European traditions. More and more Africans have recently studied music in academies within and outside Africa. Consequently, choral experimentation with Western musical forms has become increasingly intensified. Forms of choral music with artistic, creative, intellectual, and philosophical expression continue to emerge with varying degrees of religious and socio-political roles and influences.

In some instances, Western-based anthems or hymns have been translated into African indigenous dialects, which has led to the reorganization of their original melodic and rhythmic ideas to conform to the speech rhythm and tonal inflection of the African languages. The products have been hybrids of Western and African musical elements, with the latter not being consciously introduced into the compositional and performance processes. As spiritual or gospel songs, they are sung in a choral format accompanied, in some instances, either by Western musical instruments such as electric bass guitar, accordion, keyboard or by African instruments, or a combination of both.

In other instances, African melodies have been harmonized in Western style thus generating genres combining African traditional tunes and Western choral idioms. In Nigeria, such choral genres are referred to as "native airs."[7] A good example of such an anthem is the hymn "Aleluia" derived from a Chechewa tune from Malawi, arranged in four-part harmony by Rev. Father Emmanuel Mlenga (as in Example 14.1).

Another form of choral music that appeals to a wider audience continentally and perhaps internationally is the adaptation and arrangement of African folk melodies using Western harmonies. Examples of such works include *Missa Maleng* and *Centenary Mass*, composed by Anthony Okelo from Uganda and Samuel Ochieng' Mak'Okeyo from Kenya respectively. The composers have derived melodies from their traditional musical expressions (e.g. Acholi and Luo) and have creatively reorganized them using Western harmonies and fugal techniques.

Closely related to these forms of choral music are compositions that use new material by way of melodic and textual ideas but rhythmically organized and performed in an African idiom. Some of these works are sung in foreign languages (Latin, English, French, German, Arabic, Chinese, etcetera) rather than the indigenous local languages. Use of foreign languages is more often dependent on whether the composer hails from Anglophone, Francophone, Lusophone, or Arab areas of Africa or had hitherto set lyrics learned from a foreign language. A classic example of this form of choral music is *Missa Luba*, a mass that was jointly composed by students of Father Guido Haazen at the Roman Catholic Mission in Kamina in the Democratic Republic of Congo (formerly Zaire). The work employs Latin text while ingeniously fitting it into local melodic styles. Another example is *Missa Kenya* for four voices and instrumental accompaniment composed by Paul Basler. Because of the political history of many countries such as South Africa, most African composers wrote in their native languages while African composers of Western origin (for example Arnold van Wyk and Hubert du Plessis) used not only European languages but also strict Western classical compositional techniques.

Another form of African choral music that deserves mention here is the "folk opera," which is believed to have sprung out of the "Native air

Example 14.1. "Aleluia"

Aleluia

Music and Text: Chechewa
Father Emmanuel Mlenga

opera."[8] It is a neo-African style that blends African styles with Western theatrical forms. Fundamentally, scenes from diverse sources are dramatized alongside choral compositions in the opera. They are essentially multi-artistic in nature, combining music, dance, drama, poetry, costumes, and visual arts. Formal opera with major chorus parts also emerged, and Mzilikazi Khumalo's *Ushaka* and *Princess Magogo* are examples of the formal opera that were performed internationally.

In an attempt to describe these choral music genres, African scholars have generated terms such as "neo-African art music" and "Afro-classics."[9] This is perhaps aimed at distinguishing the choral works exhibiting an African originality and depth from the purely classical repertory performed widely in sub-Saharan Africa. Despite the lack in many countries of modern auditoriums that are acoustically designed for choral and orchestral performances, large musical works by classical Western composers continue to be performed in many parts of Africa, a legacy of the colonial era where traditions from the English choral societies spilled over into Africa. For instance, Handel's *Messiah* has featured prominently in many concerts and festivals across Africa and has even been translated into the eleven official languages of South Africa and into Kiswahili, spoken in most parts of East Africa. This phenomenon has not changed through the past few decades, but this has not hindered the development of new choral music traditions in Africa. In fact, the Western choral music phenomenon has for many years continued to inform emerging trends in the creation and performance practice of choral music in several parts of Africa.

General choral music performance practice

In sub-Saharan Africa, choral singing has become both a formal and an informal way of negotiating cultural and contemporary spaces. In the precolonial period, choral and vocal music created an avenue through which people learned the beliefs and values of the society with its aesthetic values, all of which helped the culture of the community to survive. Although choral activities are more defined and organized in contemporary African societies than they were in early communities, choral music was and continues to be cultivated as a group activity. It is probably the musical activity in which the most people on the continent actively take part either as amateurs or as semi-professionals. There are choral groups ranging from small ensembles to large choirs of one hundred participants or more. The spectrum ranges from children to adults singing in all possible voice distributions from unison to multipart singing. Many contemporary choral groups are urban and secular, such as the Cantare Audire, Gauteng Choristers and Muungano National Choir from Namibia, South Africa, and Kenya respectively. Others are affiliated to churches or educational institutions. In South Africa, all tertiary institutions have choirs, and there are festivals for these groups, such as the KUESTA University Choir Festival (the longest-running festival in South Africa) and SATICA (South African Tertiary Institutions Choral Association).[10] In addition, there are Christian youth association choirs, otherwise called "praise and worship teams." For instance, Kayamba Africa and Kenya Boys Choir are groups of young artists from Kenya who are renowned for fusing together tunes from traditional, contemporary, and religious musics and performing them in four-part Western harmonies accompanied by electronic instruments.

Certain choral expressions, sprung mainly from the choral and congregational singing favored by Christianity in sub-Saharan Africa, have subsequently moved beyond churches to secular concert halls, as with the Winneba Youth Choir of Ghana. Choral performances in all spheres are now organized at multiple levels. At present, there are musical concerts, cultural festivals and music competitions organized by different Christian denominations, and by government and non-governmental (private) institutions. Two such choral events are the Kenya Music Festival (KMF) and the South African Old Mutual/Telkom National Choir Festival. These festivals are acknowledged as the biggest annual cultural activities on the African continent. KMF brings together school, college, and university choirs for musical contests. It should be noted that in most parts of Africa the word *festival* is used interchangeably with *competition*. In East Africa, such competitions are referred to as *mashindano ya kwaya* (choir competitions, as in Figure 14.1).[11] In Durban, among the Zulu people, there is an all-night choral contest, where *isicathamiya*, is performed, from which groups such as Ladysmith Black Mambazo were born.[12] In Mali, one finds yet another huge cultural and music competition called the Tuareg Festival. Many of the music competitions occur annually or biennially. The competitions are organized as church, educational, or private music events in most cases. For example in Tanzania, Baraza la Muziki la Taifa (BAMUTA; National Music Council) organizes a national music festival, while the Lutheran Church organizes youth festivals.

Customarily, during formally organized choral music performances singers may be clad in long robes, an African traditional or contemporary African outfit (see Figure 14.1), or according to a Western dress code of their choice, or simply in a combination of black trousers or skirts and white shirts or blouses. It is also common to see singers standing in two or more rows, slightly curved, preferably with male behind female singers. If the singers are few, they often stand in a single straight or slightly curved line. The conductor or song leader always positions himself or herself in front facing the performers. In choral performances that are structured on the African solo–chorus delivery style, soloists or a song leader will spearhead the performance while facing the audience. In many instances, choirs may rehearse and perform music without an accompanist, because of the scarcity of pianists in some parts of Africa. For high-profile performances, such as major competitions or formal concerts, the choirs sing with an accompanist but sometimes without rehearsing with the accompanist. In South Africa and Namibia, many choirs from a Western background

Figure 14.1. St. Cecilia Holy Cross Choir, Nairobi, Kenya

approach performances in a similar fashion to the performance practice of their European counterparts.

Many choir competitions in Africa have been held over time to foster the spirit of communal pleasure and learning or as a means of reviving, stimulating, or sustaining interest in certain social issues. In addition to stimulating local musical tastes, the competitions are also meant to raise standards in musical performances where competing groups are required to perform prescribed works and, like in the Western traditions, are adjudicated by a jury of practicing musicians. The jury is normally entrusted with the responsibility of giving encouragement and guidance in the form of constructive criticism (adjudication/appraisal) to the performers. The panel is also expected to come up with a ranking of the participating choirs. In the final analysis, the prizewinners are assured not only of silver trophies but also of certificates of merit or certificates of participation, a tradition adopted from English choral societies. In some instances, cash prizes are given to winning teams. Unfortunately, because of the lack of professionally educated musicians, the prescribed pieces are in many instances too difficult, and the adjudicators' comments can be unprofessional.[13] Many choirs take part in international competitions; these choirs include the TUKS Camerata, Stellenbosch University Choir, and the Tygerberg Children's Choir from South Africa, as well as the Maskato Youth Choir from Namibia, Christ the King Choir from Uganda, and St. Stephen Jogoo Road Choir from Kenya.

Choral festivals have been formalized in most of Africa's contemporary societies as forums for avant-garde artists to display their musical prowess and choral skills. The resulting impact of the music festival phenomenon has been an immense output of choral works, enthusiastic audiences, and high-quality choral performances. It should be noted that in some areas of Africa, choral festivals may occur as events that include several performing arts including music, dance, elocution, drama, and even theater. Some commercial endeavors are to be found, such as the *Feste de Corais* (choir festival) on Mozambique's national television with trainers and judges who enhance the educational aspect of choral music[14]. Festivals like these are the cause of many new choirs being founded.

Although music festivals, especially those oriented towards church and school, account for the bulk of choral music performances in Africa, there are other choral activities mounted by private or government institutions. In South Africa, *The Sowetan* newspaper sponsors the Sowetan Nation-Building Massed Choir Festival. It is common to find church choirs or private choral entities mounting concerts during festive seasons. Choral organizations such as the Nairobi Music Society and National Symphony Orchestra from Ghana are but a few of such private choral groups. In

Nigeria, the Musical Society of Nigeria (MUSON) promotes Western-oriented choral music through concerts in various parts of the country. Other choral music performances take place during state functions, for instance, during national holiday celebrations or political gatherings. During such functions, choirs sing to entertain dignitaries as well as the public. Choral performances have over the years informed the evolution of dance hall concerts by many popular artists.

Many choral musicians feel the need for a structured regional or national choir organization, but because of political difficulties there are still only a few of these existing. In the Democratic Republic of Congo, the International Federation for Choral Music (IFCM) assisted in the formation of the first national organization of its kind, La Fédération Congolaise de Musique Chorale (FCMC).

Adapted Western hymns are a widely performed choral genre, particularly in the liturgy. In southern Africa some choirs tend to focus on performances of new choral music composed mainly by European and American composers, but many choirs also perform new choral music by African composers. In addition, new secular works are performed by church or secular choirs as special anthems at secular or other religious occasions, or during competitive music festivals. Both sacred and secular choral works can be heard via FM radio stations or CD and DVD recordings. Some of this music is performed live on stage or television. These modern presentation and recording opportunities have inspired abundant creativity. Inspirational praise-and-worship choruses, otherwise known as "pop gospel music," have increasingly been adopted in Christian revival or fellowship prayer meetings. Probably the most famous choir in this genre is the Grammy-awarded Soweto Gospel Choir.

Choral music continues to hold a significant place in the churches and entertainment industry in Africa. Consequently, the music is used as a means of articulating and informing the general public about social and political issues such as the fight against the spread of HIV/AIDS. For instance, Edzimkulu (a Canadian non-governmental organization) in collaboration with volunteers from Edmonton (Alberta) and the Underberg region (South Africa) has initiated Music in AIDS education projects aimed at destigmatizing people living with HIV/AIDS in South Africa.[15] In neighboring Mozambique, the national television utilizes choral music to warn society about the dangers of malaria and other social issues such as HIV/AIDS and domestic violence. When music is used as a means of communicating to the general public, composers are commissioned to write songs on topical issues such as HIV/AIDS; it is customary to witness choral groups performing such songs on 1 December of every year to mark World AIDS Day. Not only on the occasion of World AIDS

Day, choirs through their music transmit vital information on the global challenges being posed by the disease. In some instances, music festivals assign themes based on HIV/AIDS, and choral groups with songs that relay the HIV/AIDS messages effectively are awarded monetary incentives or prizes.

African politicians realized the value of choral music during the struggles for independence, and they also discovered its evident communicative and influential power. The music was, and is still, used to advance political ideologies and propaganda. Patriotic and political songs may use themes based on nationalism, good governance, corruption, and social or economic development. In Kenya, choral music is considered by the ruling parties and government as instrumental in propagating the parties' ideologies or government policies. During state or national celebrations, choirs sing to praise the country's leaders. Others narrate accounts of the history of their countries through music.

The musical and textual themes of African contemporary choral works are varied and wide-ranging. There are those, like works from Justinian Tamusuza from Uganda, which are based on tunes and texts that are traditional in character. Others are often textual ideas extracted from biblical stories. One such work is *Barali ba Jerusalema* by Michael Mosoeu Moerane (1909–81) from South Africa. In southern Sudan, Archbishop Zubir Wako uses liturgical themes in his Roman Catholic hymns but chooses to use Arabic text to be more communicative (as in Example 14.2).

Secular texts may include themes that are related to topical issues such as environmental conservation, prevention of malaria, peace and conflict resolution, HIV/AIDS, poverty, literacy, and so on. Performances with such thematic messaging are usually sponsored by world organizations or international agencies affiliated with the United Nations. Patriotic and political songs may use themes based on nationalism, good governance, and social or economic development.

Large choral works are performed for general entertainment and appreciation in most cases. In South Africa, the existence of professional orchestras means that choirs such as the City of Tygerberg Choir, Johannesburg Symphony Choir, and the Drakensberg Boys' Choir regularly perform most of the well-known Western oratorios. Choral performances may include traditional or Western musical instruments or even a combination of both types of instruments. As early as 1950, African choral works had begun exhibiting compositional styles rooted in indigenous musical expression. Songs in local languages that were arranged in four-part harmony became common. Fusions of different styles in a choral performance were evident, and a considerable number of composers

Example 14.2. "Arsala-l Llah Daniel Comboni"

ARSALA-L LLAH DANIEL COMBONI
(God sent Daniel Comboni)

Choir Group Composition–Khartoum

Arr. Zubir Wako

began experimenting with a wide spectrum of African idioms, providing expanded rhythmic and aesthetic identities. Mensah attests to this fact when he records that "a spate of songs with (sometimes) instrumental support was largely generated through the activities of choir and schools, which also developed a tradition of staging musical plays."[16] In South Africa, composers with a Western orientation also incorporated African elements in their choral compositions. Amongst these works were *Firebowl* by Hans

Roosenschoon and *Horizons* by Peter Louis van Dijk. This spread African cultural identity across the world as their works were performed and recorded by groups such as the King's Singers. Other world-famous composers of choral music from southern Africa include Hendrik Hofmeyr, Peter Klatzow, and Roelof Temmingh. A number of choral works can now be found that use more elaborate forms instead of the popular verse–refrain or stanza–chorus structure with homophonic texture.

As more choral composers from different parts of Africa and different musical backgrounds continue to emerge, the compositional base expands to include even arrangements of African popular tunes. As mentioned in the preceding paragraphs, these innovative compositional ventures have widened the scope and corpus of choral music to include roles that are not only confined to churches and schools but also include political arenas, entertainment centers, international forums, and other performance venues.

Choral composers

To provide a list of African choral composers with their profiles, respective works and contribution to choral traditions in Africa exceeds the scope of this chapter. Instead, we have focused on a few composers within a historical perspective.[17]

From a historical and stylistic perspective, African choral composers can be categorized in different groups. In each region or country, there is a category of composers who can be referred to as the pioneers of MACM. This is a group of traditionalists who were schooled in early mission schools, acquired music literacy, and used traditional Western musical ideas to awaken cultural nationalism or traditional musical expression in their compositions. Names that surface in this respect include Ephraim Amu (1899–1995), of the Ghanaian composition school, and Youssef Greiss (1899–1961), who is seen as the father of Egyptian choral composers; according to Kamal, Greiss is perhaps the pioneer of composition in all of Africa.[18] Fela Sowande (1906–87) is acknowledged as the father of Nigerian art music.

In East Africa, one personality stands out as the architect of the MACM. Although choral music existed as a church genre and as entertainment/leisure music for colonial settlers, it was the efforts of Graham Hyslop, an English Episcopalian (Church Mission Society) who in 1950 became the music and drama officer of the British colony, that saw the birth of a choral movement aiming at adapting and arranging African folk tunes.[19] Thereafter, his students and disciples such as George Senoga-zake (who was born in Uganda but worked in Kenya), Peter Kibkosya, and

Chris Adwar from Kenya took the effort a notch higher when they fought for the inclusion of this new choral music genre into the Kenya music festivals. The efforts of Joseph Kyagambiddwa in the development of Ugandan choral music cannot go unmentioned. Performances of his *Ten African Religious Hymns* were well received by German audiences in the 1960s during his sojourn abroad.

In South and Central Africa, we acknowledge Enoch Sontonga and Reuben T. Caluza (pianist and organist) as the first school-educated Africans in South Africa to have continued the tradition of composing in the late nineteenth century. From the same country we find clergymen-composers such as Tiyo Soga (one of the first Xhosa missionaries) and John Knox-Bokwe are noted by Mensah as the pioneers of art music in the modern sense of the word.[20] The works of some composers who lived and worked in exile, such as Todd Tozama Matshikiza (1921–68), were influenced by political realities. In the Democratic Republic of Congo-DRC (the former Zaire), according to Turino, pioneers of choral music include Mwenda-Jean Bosco and Father Guido Haazen (the composer of *Missa Luba*).[21] Probably, the most famous African composer and collector of choral music is James Stephen Mzilikazi Khumalo, who also published African choral music in dual notation. Most African choirs utilize the tonic sol-fa notation system, which prevents them from reading music in staff notation. However, there also exist choirs with fairly well established choral music traditions that read staff notation.

Prominent choral modernists came in good numbers, widening the boundaries of choral expressions by venturing into and experimenting with atonal aesthetics. Composers such as Akin Euba with his concepts of "African pianism" and "creative musicology" could serve as a model for composers under this category. Kwabena Nketia (b.1921) is another household name through his immense contributions in the area of Africa musicology. He is generally regarded as the father of African musicology.

The last category of composers comprises contemporary avant-garde choral artists. The characteristics of their compositions are conditioned by a wide variety of cultural differences and perhaps also by social and political considerations. In the contemporary African choral soundscape, there are composers whose works exhibit such characteristics and who even may qualify as members of the Western avant-garde by virtue of their use of non-tonal idioms. One famous South African is Bongani Ndodana-Breen, though such composers with an African background are, however, few in number. In Kenya, Arthur Kemoli, Boniface Mganga, Fredrick Ngala, George Mwiruki, Henry Wanjala, Ken Wakia, Mellitus

Wanyama, Richard Khadambi, Sylvester Oteno, Timothy Njoora, and Wilson Shitandi are the leading avant-garde choral artists.

Conclusion: challenges and prospects

As already noted, the information discussed in this chapter is not exhaustive because of the vastness of the African continent. Prominent composers and excellent choirs that began creating great choral sensations in the 1950s have generated a huge amount of choral music of lasting significance. Despite variations from one region to another, the choral tradition in Africa continues to be vibrant. Furthermore, the choral enthusiasts, academies, private research organizations, and government institutions may forge a common front in confronting modern challenges that tend to create impediments to steady development in the African choral music industry. For instance, there is a need for a concerted effort to ensure that copyright laws are enforced to guarantee royalties to composers and performers of choral music. Piracy is still rampant, and performers are occasionally duped into offering performances without receiving any proceeds from the concerts. In addition, most choral artists (composers, conductors, cantors) work in many institutions without pay because they are not educated in this field due to the lack of adequate relevant courses in choral music at universities. This trend has deterred many choral artists who would otherwise have contributed positively to a more rapid growth of the genre. However, SAMRO is probably the leader on the continent in copyright issues.

Lastly, there is a need to document lives and works of prominent choral composers and artists in Africa. Due to the lack of adequate financial resources for publishing, great works are often heard only once. Apart from this, much of the music exists in loose scores that eventually get misplaced or disappear when the composers die. It is imperative that the current boom in choral repertoire in Africa is preserved for posterity because the music is not only impacting the lives of people across the continent, but it is also a discourse of the history of these people. This cultural material has been fascinatingly repackaged and fused with musical ideas from outside the continent, thus creating a music that is not only intercultural in nature but also relevant in many spheres of life of the people in Africa.

Select bibliography

Basler, P. *Missa Kenya: for SATB Chorus and Tenor Solo with Horn, Percussion and Piano Accompaniment.* Fort Lauderdale, FL: Plymouth Music Company, 1996.

Barz, G. F. *Performing Religion: Negotiating Past and Present in Kwaya Music of Tanzania.* Amsterdam: Rodopi, 2003.

"Politics of Remembering: Performing History(-ies) in Youth Choir Competitions in Dar es Salaam, Tanzania," in F. Gunderson and G. Barz (eds.), *Mashindano! Competitive Music Performance in East Africa.* Dar es Salaam: Nyota and Mkuki Publishers, 2000, pp. 379–406.

"*Tamati*: Music Competition and Community Formation," in F. Gunderson and G. Barz (cds.), *Mashindano! Competitive Music Performance in East Africa.* Dar es Salaam: Nyota and Mkuki Publishers, 2000, pp. 421–28.

Bokwe, J. K. "Vuka Debora," in J. S. M. Khumalo (ed.), *South Africa Sings*, 2 vols., Braamfontein: SAMRO, 1998, vol. I.

De Beer, R. "The Origins, Developments, and Current Performance Practices of African Neo-Traditional Choral Music of Southern Africa." Unpublished PhD thesis, Nelson Mandela Metropolitan University, Port Elizabeth, 2007.

Detterbeck, M. "South African Choral Music (Amakwaya): Song, Contest and the Formation of Identity." Unpublished Doctoral thesis, University of Natal, Durban, 2002.

Ekwueme, L. E. N. "Composing Contemporary African Choral Music: Problems and Prospects," in C. T. Kimberlin and A. Euba (eds.), *Intercultural Music.* Richmond, CA: MRI Press, 1999, vol. II, pp. 77–88.

Euba, A. *Essays of Music in Africa*, vol. II: *Intercultural Perspectives.* Lagos: Elekoto Music Centre Lagos, 1989.

"Nketia, J. H. K. and the African Avant-Garde," in A. Euba and C. T. Kimberlin (eds.), *Composition in Africa and the Diaspora.* Richmond, CA: MRI Press, 2008, vol. I, pp. 143–54.

Guettat, M. "The State of Music in the Arab World," in R. Letts and K. Fahkouri (eds.), *The State of Music around the World.* Paris: International Music Council, 2007.

Herbst, A., A. Zaedel, J. Rudolph and C. Onyeji "Written Composition," in A. Herbst, Meki Nzewi, and V. Kofi Agawu (eds), *Musical Arts in Africa: Theory, Practice and Education.* Pretoria: Unisa Press, 2003.

Huskisson, Y. *The Bantu Composers of Southern Africa Supplement.* Pretoria: Human Sciences Research Council, 1983.

El-Kholy, S. "Traditional and Folk Idioms in Modern Egyptian Composition since the Fifties," in C. T. Kimberlin and E. Euba (eds.), *Intercultural Music.* Richmond, CA: MRI Press, 1999, vol. II, pp. 33–44.

Kidula, J. N. "Making and Managing Music in African Christian Life," in R. King (ed.), *Music in the Life of the African Church.* Waco, TX: Baylor University Press, 2008, pp. 101–16.

"Music Culture: African Life," in R. King (ed.), *Music in the Life of the African Church.* Waco, TX: Baylor University Press, 2008, pp. 37–56.

"The Choral Arrangements and Performance Practice of Arthur Kemoli," in A. Euba and C. T. Kimberlin (eds.), *Composition in Africa and the Diaspora.* Richmond, CA, MRI Press, 2008, vol. I, pp. 109–30.

Kidula, J. N., H. Wanjala and W. Shitandi "Setting Indigenous Melodies for Concert Performances: A Historical Outline on the 'Adaptation and Arrangement of African Tunes.'" Paper presented during an international music symposium at Kenyatta University, 2002.

King, R. "Beginnings: Music in the African Church," in R. King (ed.), *Music in the Life of the African Church*. Waco, TX: Baylor University Press, 2008, pp. 1–16.

"Music Culture: Euro-American Christianity," in R. King (ed.), *Music in the Life of the African Church*. Waco, TX: Baylor University Press, 2008, pp. 17–36.

Klatzow, P. *Composers in South Africa Today*. Cape Town: Oxford University Press, 1987.

Mbuyamba, L. et al. "Dossier Africa," in J. Tagger (ed.), *International Choral Bulletin*. Louvigny: IFCM International Office, 2006, pp. 5–17.

Mensah, A. A. "Compositional Practices in African Music," in R. Stone (ed.), *The Garland Encyclopaedia of World Music: Africa*. New York: Garland Publishing, 1998, pp. 208–31.

"Music of the South Sahara," in E. May (ed.), *Musics of Many Cultures*. Berkeley: University of California Press, 1980, pp. 172–94.

Njoora, T. "Music Composition and Its Awesome Responsibilities: Some Hard Issues that Frame Creativity and Output," *Journal of East African Musical Arts Education* 2 (2005), pp. 62–72.

Nketia, J. H. K. *African Art Music*. Ghana: Afram Publications, 2004.

African Music in Ghana: A Survey of Traditional Forms. Accra: Longmans, 1963.

The Music of Africa. London: Gollancz, 1974.

Nzewi, M. "African Music Creativity and Performance: The Science of the Sound Voices: A World Forum of Music Therapy," 2006. www.voices.

"Challenges for African Music and Musicians in the Modern World Music Context," in C. T. Kimberlin and A. Euba (eds.), *Intercultural Music*. Richmond, CA: MRI Press, 1999, vol. II, pp. 201–28.

Musical Practice and Creativity: An African Traditional Perspective. Germany: Iwalewa-Haus, University of Bayreuth, 1991.

Okafor, R. "Types of Music in Nigeria," in R. C. Okafor and L. N. Emeka (eds.), *Nigerian Peoples and Culture for Higher Education*. Enugu: New Generations Ventures Limited, 1994, pp. 140–66.

Olaniyan, O. "A Discourse of Yoruba Lyrics (Otherwise Known as Native Airs) as Contemporary Art Music for Christian Worship," in M. A. Omibiyi-Obidike (ed.), *The Art Music of Nigeria: Prospects and Problems*. Ibadan: Stirling-Horden Publishers, 2001, pp. 58–69.

Olwage, G. E. "Music and (Post) Colonialism: the Dialectics of Choral Culture on a South African Frontier." Unpublished Doctoral thesis. Rhodes University, Grahamstown 2003.

Rieth, D. E., Jr. *A Study of Choral Music in Kenya: The Contribution of Its Composers and the Influences of Traditional and Western European Musical Style*. Michigan: UMI Dissertation Services, 1998.

Turino, T. *Nationalists, Cosmopolitans and Popular Music in Zimbabwe*. University of Chicago Press, 2000.

PART III

Choral philosophy, practice, and pedagogy

15 Globalization, multiculturalism, and the children's chorus

FRANCISCO J. NÚÑEZ

Choruses are transforming. In many parts of the world, new communities create new vocal ensembles to reflect their own identities and passions. As populations shift, and communities expand to include a diverse range of people, choirs seek to span conventionally unbridgeable borders such as rich–poor, East–West, North–South, or Christian–Muslim. Likewise, concert audiences are changing, and increasingly demand repertoire that is relevant to their respective cultures and experiences. The younger generations, which have grown up in the digital age and with globalization, also seem to be more open and receptive to different cultures than some of the older generations.

In this chapter, I will focus on the children's chorus and its future in an increasingly globalized society. This discussion will be based on my artistic and social philosophy – one that has been strengthened by personal experience as founder and conductor of the Young People's Chorus of New York City (YPC), an organization which began as an after-school program and is designed to thrive in a diverse, but still largely segregated city. In this environment, I learned a great deal from the children as I observed how they changed both socially and musically, and how they learned to interact comfortably with peers from diverse backgrounds. I will also examine the state of the youth chorus today, its place in the community, and the challenges it faces in organization, advocacy, and audience development. I will argue that choruses should strive for both artistic excellence and diversity: the dual mission that has propelled me to question the relevance of the children's chorus in a global community – one that is faced with ever-changing attitudes, new trends and audiences, and many opportunities for non-traditional avenues for performance and outreach.

Background

Before founding the Young People's Chorus over twenty years ago, I studied the mission statements of many choirs that were already in existence. I noticed that most of them had a common theme – to create a chorus capable of attaining the highest levels of artistic achievement in performance. These thoughts immediately came to mind: What constitutes artistic excellence in children's choruses? Who are the children receiving music performance opportunities and education? How do family resources affect membership? How does membership affect repertoire? How does membership attract an audience?

In order to answer these questions, we must dispel some misconceptions and understand the impact that numerous, newly formed community-based choruses have in neighborhoods and concert halls, and will eventually have on the political stage. I have tried to answer these questions by reenvisioning the repertoire, membership, and organizational practices of the chorus. How these three aspects evolve will determine the nature of the children's chorus as it matures in the twenty-first century.

Establishing a choir is not difficult. One does not need a substantial amount of money. One can expect quick results and can achieve excellence with almost any skill level. With great singers, a chorus can easily be superb, but even with inexperienced singers one can create a chorus that is capable of inspiring audiences. The resource needs are simple: a tuning fork or pitch pipe, a piano or guitar, and a space in which to rehearse.

Music making can be easy. You can teach by rote. You can call several people together and decide on repertoire that can easily be performed by all involved. Developing an audience is just as simple; invite the friends and family members of the singers to a local social hall or church for the performance and hold a post-concert reception. In some instances, the social purpose may take precedence over musical aesthetics. One can be forgiven for a mediocre performance if the message is sufficiently impactful. The human voice is such an inspiring and expressive instrument that, outside of the professional concert hall, people are often willing to overlook the technical shortcomings of singers. A solid technique and musical literacy do not necessarily supersede singing with passion, gusto, or joy.

However, if the conductor's purpose is both social awareness and musical excellence, the challenges are obviously more demanding. To illustrate these ideas, I offer an example from my personal experience.

In 1988 I formed the Children's Aid Society Young People's Chorus, which later became an independent organization called the Young People's Chorus of New York City. The Children's Aid Society is a not-for-profit program that serves the 100,000 very needy children in New York City each year. When I began working with this group, their programs took place in specific, separate neighborhoods. Yet, I was convinced that the children in the various choral programs could learn much from each other. I offered the Children's Aid Society the idea of gathering children from all their after-school neighborhood centers and bringing them together with children from other centers – children from different ethnic backgrounds, as well as children from both below-poverty and well-to-do families. At the same time, I wanted to create a children's chorus that would use its cultural diversity to reach greater heights of artistry.

I received some basic funding, a beautiful rehearsal room and buses to bring the children from different parts of New York City – Harlem, Greenwich Village, Spanish Harlem, the Lower East Side, the Bronx – to meet on the Upper East Side, one of the city's posh neighborhoods. The initial chorus was composed of nearly seventy singers, ages 8–14, who came to the group from all walks of life.

On my first day of rehearsal, a reporter from the *Upper East Side Resident* interviewed me in the hallway. Several children were already waiting for rehearsal to begin, while other children and their parents were still streaming in from the elevator and the stairs. During the interview, a twelve-year-old girl from Spanish Harlem with shabby clothes and unkempt hair was pulling on my jacket, trying to get my attention. Suddenly the door of the elevator opened and out stepped a very tall woman in a mink coat, carrying several shopping bags bearing the names of French boutiques. With her twelve-year old daughter in tow, she hurried towards me to explain why they were late. She and her daughter had spent the weekend shopping in Paris for new clothes for school, but her plane had been delayed coming back because of inclement weather. In the meantime the young girl by my side who had been pulling on my jacket finally spoke up, "Mr. Núñez, don't forget I need $1.50 to buy a bus token to get home tonight. My mom doesn't have any money."

The reporter was quick to notice what he later referred to as the "juxtaposition" in the Young People's Chorus, not just of ethnicities, but of classes too. This was exactly what I wanted to create. If I could bring urban children of different racial, economic, and religious backgrounds to work together, barriers would fall and the youngsters would realize how much they had in common. I was also convinced that, with proper training, these children could be excellent and enthusiastic musicians. Singing in a chorus would lose its traditional stigma among young people, and would actually be thought of as "cool."

Such was the reality I dealt with during my first few years as a children's chorus conductor. It reflected a reality that was prevalent and pervasive in New York City and around the world. There were immense social gaps and wide disparities of wealth, color, and beliefs. But seeing the initial results, I was convinced more than ever that music would be an effective way to bridge these gaps. I looked at similar previous efforts around the world. Twenty years ago, there were very few models to which I could aspire. Today there are numerous parallel endeavors around the world that can be held up as models of success, such as El Sistema, the visionary global movement started in Venezuela in 1978 that has transformed the lives of thousands of children, while transforming the communities around them.

YPC proved to be an ideal laboratory for me. I took the traditional format of the American children's chorus and adapted it to an environment that was unique to New York City, where diversity was a microcosm of a global world. If I could successfully create an excellent chorus with such a diverse membership – something I realized had not been pursued with deliberation before – it could serve as a model for other groups with similar intentions. I took the same care and technical considerations founded in eighteenth-century choral education and tried to keep the best of those traditions alive. Yet I adapted the methodologies and techniques to create a pedagogy that seemed to suit the choir members.

My philosophy has grown out of my personal background. I was raised in the Dominican Republic and in the New York City neighborhood of Washington Heights. While I was studying classical piano, I was constantly exposed to Latin rhythms on the streets. My life was infused with the very distinct culture around me. When I started composing, my music naturally reflected a fusion of all the styles I learned and grew up with. My fascination with this cultural mix carried over to adulthood, when I tried to recreate the same experience for the children with whom I was working. These students were young, eager, and open-minded, and served as the perfect group for my new endeavor. Together we sought to break new ground in the realm of the children's chorus, as I considered new ideas for membership, repertoire, and vocal styles, and how these ideas could evolve and be developed in communities where social barriers had been broken.

There is a lingering condescension towards children's choruses because of the traditional role children's choruses have played throughout history. In essence, they have played a supporting role. Over the centuries, the most influential composers of serious music did not devote much time to writing music for children's choruses except for a rare few, such as Vivaldi, Kodály, and Britten. Others wrote music for children as minor characters or as metaphorical elements in opera or oratorio. Latin American and Asian composers usually just arranged folk songs for children instead of writing extensive works exclusively for children. Therefore, audiences had very few opportunities to hear children sing in a capacity equal to their adult co-performers. This problem still exists today, in that most of the people who attend performances of children's chorus music are not lovers of that music in its own right: they are there because they are the parents or friends of the singers. While there are a few esteemed choirs that have been able to reach a larger audience, such as the Hong Kong Children's Chorus, the Tapiola of Finland, or the internationally renowned Vienna Boys Choir, serious music-goers (those who purchase subscription tickets to ballets, orchestras, dance companies, professional new music ensembles, and chamber ensembles, or even professional choirs) are not the same audience who attend children's chorus concerts. The fact is that most children's chorus concerts are marketed as family concerts (that is, simply family endeavors) or as a minor part of a larger festival. Few concert series or subscriptions of a children's ensemble, if any, exist. To some listeners, the children's chorus has not reached comparable levels of artistic legitimacy to other choirs. In many countries, the children's chorus is an extension of the schools, an educational addendum. This prejudice is persistent; the children's chorus is perceived as an amateur ensemble, which at best hopes to mold undiscovered talent. Audiences and critics may be kinder to children's choruses because children are not perceived to be truly capable of being excellent: the process of trying is seen as enough.

Taking these facts into consideration, I find the traditional label of "children's chorus" rather limiting, and I struggled for some time to redefine it. When I started my own chorus, I knew that I needed to question certain terms. I didn't want a "choir," nor did I want to call it a "children's chorus." From the general public's perspective, the "children's chorus" label remains the catch-all term that includes any amateur singer who is of pre-college age. As a general rule, the children's chorus is defined as a group of singers with unchanged voices (treble), and the youth chorus as a group that includes voices that have changed (girls and boys with changed voices). Among many choruses around the world, a youth ensemble may often include members up to age thirty. But despite the fact that I started YPC with only fourteen-year-olds as the oldest members, I envisioned the chorus growing to include older singers and boys with changed voices. Although this idea would take all of ten years to accomplish, I was aware at the choir's inception that there were no similar choruses for young men in New York City. Many of these young men lived in disenfranchised neighborhoods and were vulnerable to gangs, drugs, and violence. If any lives could be changed by music, this group needed the most help.

Some choruses have managed to skirt the issue of perceived legitimacy by adopting more organic names, ones that refer neither to "children" nor to "youth." Examples include Amabile (Canada), which is made up of girls and boys (changed and unchanged voices) ages 6–18; Shallaway (Canada), made up of girls and boys (with unchanged voices) up to age 18; Carmina Slovenica (Slovenia), made up of girls and women up to age 22; Cantamus

(UK), made up of females ages 13–19; Anima (USA), made up of girls and boys (with unchanged voices) up to age 18; and Angelica (Japan), girls ages 13–18. I am not comparing the original concerns and motivations of these choirs with mine, but I knew in the early days I was working with a stigmatized perception. I ended up with *Young People* as a name, which I find respectful and inclusive of a wider range of ages, from 8 to 26; however, the name continues to pose challenges since it connotes youth.

Historically, the children's chorus evolved from an "affinity-based" to an "identity-based" group. Affinity-based groups – mainly church or community children's choirs – were the most popular until recently, given the ease with which they could be formed, connecting people from the same communities, in small homogeneous towns and cities, with common interests and backgrounds. Over time, as shifting populations changed the face of communities, identity-based groups with stronger social agendas and more specific missions, often focused on social equity, began to emerge.

There is an increasing interest in the creation of choruses that reflect a wider educational and social agenda. The Dominican Republic, for example, is beginning a national program that will bridge the rich and the poor, something that has never been accepted in the past. In 2010, the country began a national choral program with a mission of inclusion. The program, called Uno a Uno (One by One), is a non-governmental effort to unite the country's children, rich and poor, as a first step in building a community of diverse economic backgrounds. In 1984, in the midst of Uganda's civil war, human rights activist Ray Barnett started the African Children's Choir. He was inspired by the singing of one small boy, and formed the first African Children's Choir "to show the world that Africa's most vulnerable children have beauty, dignity and unlimited ability." In 1989, the World Youth Choir was established; it has became one of the most remarkable musical and intercultural experiences offered to young musicians, with a message of "international peace and tolerance in perfect artistic unity."[1]

Creating a multicultural environment

Establishing diversity in a youth chorus is not difficult since today's youth have grown up in a multicultural society that took older generations longer to develop and longer to accept. Today's youth take multiculturalism as a matter of course. They know of no time when the Internet, social media, and mobile phones did not exist, and information was not as readily accessible as nowadays. Moreover, throughout Europe, North America, and practically any area where immigrants comprise a substantial part of the demographics and infuse the mainstream with their own cultures, schools are enrolling children from diverse backgrounds at a rapid rate. It is regrettable that there has been an anti-immigrant backlash recently which has targeted immigrant school-children everywhere from the US to France and Sweden, but the mere proximity of children to others from different cultures is exposing them to new cultures and values at a much more accelerated pace than their parents ever encountered. Young people learn to juggle social identities and roles. They interact in an inclusive, structured world at school and then adapt their behavior to different worlds after school. It is common to find that in most immigrant families, parents feel a certain duty to defend their national heritage – an instinctive reaction to the environment in which the immigrants find themselves – and strive to teach their children about their own history and language. Consequently, both the "host" and "new" communities are being asked to adapt or to risk isolation.

The arts are perhaps the most visible manifestation of this adaptation. One can see it in the cross-cultural fusions of styles that have created many new captivating rhythms and forms that have become part of the main-stream musical vocabulary: *salsa*, a fusion of Cuban-African *son* devel-oped by Cuban and Puerto Rican immigrants in New York City in the 1960s and 1970s; *bhangra*, folk music that originated from the Punjab region of India and Pakistan, with a back beat; *reggaeton*, salsa mixed with rap and reggae, popular among Afro-Latino youth in the early 1990s. One can hear it in *beur* hip-hop in France and urban *desi* music, which takes pride in its Bollywood roots. Different cultures expect to represent them-selves differently through cultural vocabularies that are familiar and rele-vant to them.

The fusion of musical styles in new choral repertoire is already hap-pening, and will continue to impact repertoire in the future with an influx of newly composed music influenced by multiple traditions. Likewise, concert audiences are changing, increasingly demanding musical reper-toire that is relevant to their cultures and experiences. Surely, performing multicultural music has been a wonderful introduction to new cultures. It has given most programs the impression of being open and inclusive. But multiculturalism in repertoire is only the beginning of an unpredictable and musically uncertain future, where ideas of *unity* quickly become outmoded, if not overused, and professionals in the field must form a new choral *universality*. For, as inspiring as the songs may be, the perfor-mers and audiences may be at cross-purposes; there is no denying that the act of inclusion is not always visible in terms of membership.

As young singers – the true offspring of the twenty-first century, steeped in the openness of cultures and ideas that have been laid out before them through decades of cultural innovation and social struggle – look to the future, many choirs find themselves in a state of transition. How, then, can youth choruses deal with rapidly changing demographics, cultures, ideas, and tastes? As the world becomes more multiracial, and cultural hybridity becomes the norm, we will need to reconsider three areas where these changes will have the most impact: repertoire and the changing face of musical styles, membership and diversity of both the ensemble and its audience, and management practices.

Repertoire and new musical styles

In order to prepare for a diverse future, children's choirs must develop new approaches to pedagogy and technique in order to include and not isolate. Over the years, many children's choruses have evolved slowly and some have changed little from their roots. Some examples of change might include transitions from exclusive boys' or girls' choirs to mixed-gender choirs, or from purely classical repertoire to include multicultural music, jazz, or gospel. To paraphrase Igor Stravinsky in his Norton Lectures, tradition is something we receive from past generations, but we must promise that it will bear fruit. Once we accept an idea, we must speak it, change it, and adapt it before passing it on.[2]

We must, in this sense, keep ourselves within tradition and make it our own. We must continually explore the past while seeking a new future; our individual sense of self must be managed to take on the rapidly changing world. We must discipline ourselves to accept new ways of conducting the chorus, auditioning singers, choosing repertoire, and staging, and new ways of using technology and reaching out to an ever-evolving, more enlightened audience.

As repertoires evolve around the globe, music becomes an effective medium to represent unique perspectives and reinterpretations of distinct cultures. If choirs choose to change their mission to diversify their membership to include children from cultures outside the mainstream, the concept of excellence should also change to include performing a globalized repertoire. This notion goes beyond multicultural pieces of certain cultures; it encompasses the fusion of different rhythms, harmonies, languages, and basic musical harmonic language. I do not know what is coming musically, but I do know that we must be ready for new musical concepts that will employ new vocal techniques, new ways to perform, and alternative ways to communicate with the audience. If conductors focus on performing only one style of music, they are forced to look for a certain voice that fits within the box of that particular genre and anything outside the box will be rejected. However, within musical multiplicity comes fluidity of vocal techniques and different vocal backgrounds become an asset.

Children's choirs never get old; the children graduate and move on and new voices replace them. Conductors, unfortunately, do age, and it is essential that they figure out how to stay in touch with musical transformations in both the classical and the non-classical realms. Meanwhile, as globalization continues to break boundaries and exposes societies to cultural treasures that have previously been arcane, composers are absorbing the world's sounds and young people are soaking up the new dances and rhythms at a very fast rate. Such conditions are the perfect incubator of new musical ideas. From musical diversity, we can reinvent the use of the concert stage or churches for concerts. Why not sing in museums, galleries, in restaurants with dinner being served as great jazz artists do, or in the Apple store?

As we train our singers for a new musical tomorrow, we need to incorporate techniques that allow singing with different colors, degrees of vibrato, ability to manipulate weight and pitch. We also need to build a better ability to work with any musical genre and with different conductors. If a choir has a mission of diversity to include children from different backgrounds and different musical traditions, we are bound to hear vocal production that is not founded on Western choral traditions. This discovery may affect the concept of excellence for the educated music lover. How can one achieve conventional choral excellence with children who have neither heard nor experienced the technique of the most basic choral music by Brahms, Bach, or Purcell?

As we move towards a pluralistic future, we must figure out how to teach music from the classical tradition as well as music from other cultures to children who have little or no training in these areas. In a sense, our options are greatly expanded. As we broaden the scope of our repertoire, we also raise the bar, expecting musical skills that are demanding in their own way. With commitment and an understanding of diverse cultures, we can teach any young child the proper techniques necessary to produce a beautiful, healthy tone able to perform an authentic interpretation of classical literature as well as any style of music. Any child from any part of the world can be trained to sing beautifully in any style of music.

Let me conclude this section with another anecdote. Recently I was asked to write a new song to celebrate the twenty-fifth anniversary dinner for the Japanese Chamber of Commerce in New York City, an organization that helps to deepen ties between US and Japanese businesses in the United States. The Japanese, who are deeply rooted in tradition, were enthusiastically open to the idea of creating new songs that would bring together our two cultures. The new song, entitled "Building Bridges", was based on Japanese pentatonic melodies with American pop rhythms. The words were co-written with a Japanese business professional and were sung in English and Japanese. The instrumentation included piano, koto, taiko drums, and drum set and bass. While this style may not sound unusual when viewed in the context of other contemporary children's choral works, not so long ago this idea would have been unthinkable at such a prestigious dinner with such important businessmen and-women. Yet the ties between cultures transcend conventional attitudes about music, and the boundaries of nation-states and transnational corporations, once insurmountable, are now blurred.

Membership and diversity

Using children to bridge cultures is an effective route to take as they have fewer preconceptions on race and color. Young people who are living in a diverse world at school are more open to the idea of allowing a diverse membership into the choir. However, it is often the case that the inflexible, fixed attitudes of privileging among some adults spill over into their own families, thereby perpetuating misconceptions that hinder the growth of these mission-based choirs.

Adult choirs that have a difficult time changing their roster are also forming children's choirs within their ranks. This concept allows open-minded adults to participate in crossing into other cultures and to build a new sense of themselves through such connections. Here they allow diversity in membership, repertoire, and mission to grow. Viewed from this perspective, the future appears to rest on the ideas acquired and developed by young people today. In time this new direction can affect the adult choirs as the young people grow up and become singing adults and audience members.

When I started YPC, there were no guideposts or benchmarks available to indicate how to achieve "artistic excellence" with young voices. It took me years of study to know what I wanted to achieve with the children's chorus. I listened to dozens of choirs before I could begin to hear the nuances in skill level, vocal quality, and abilities. In order to achieve what constituted choral excellence, I needed to make a decision on what vocal techniques and which educational model worked best for me from among all the different choral programs I heard worldwide. I also learned that prior vocal training, family values, and finances had a greater impact on musical education and excellence than I had expected.

I learned early on that the quality of choral education varied all around the world, with a dramatic difference between boys' and girls' choirs and even more when they were combined. I heard unique vocal techniques in Eastern and Western Europe, throughout Asia and different parts of North and South America. Most of these ensembles were comprised of a homogeneous blend of voices from a particular region, with only a few choirs with a little diversity in their membership. I believe the only commonality between choirs was the training of the conductor in the Western model. Otherwise, choirs perform traditional choral works from the European tradition, and music of their culture. The essence of each choir comes through when they sing "their" music or music from their particular region. Only then can choirs show varied timbres, ease of performance, language facility, and a charm that cannot be matched by others.

It seemed to me that it was much easier to teach a group of children with similar backgrounds and experiences a certain kind of music on a regular basis. In addition, most members of conventional community choirs are involved in music making either during the day in school or studying voice or taking instrument lessons privately. Theory, technique, and discipline are likely already taught and ingrained in students prior to chorus rehearsals. Many choirs also have a rigorous audition process. Once enlisted, the children are put on a level system that allows them to learn and grow within a prescribed educational paradigm before reaching the highest choral division. The final choral division usually has the oldest and most advanced students who are the ones being heard in public. This conservatory style of education can lead to a very high level of musicianship, but only certain types of families are able to participate in such a rigorous system for years – families with a strong appreciation for music education and an understanding of discipline and the effect of consistency of effort, which have the time and the means to support their children, and which are financially secure. A chorus that aims to transcend social and economic barriers, therefore, will need to consider the basic concerns of members who are not as privileged.

Management

The twenty-first-century children's choral conductor faces the major challenge of understanding change. It is important to note that the changes are not just cultural or ethnographic. The expectations of managing such ensembles are also changing. Choirs managed in an "autocratic" manner will see young people yearning to work in more democratic forms of participation, following the lead of many of their popular and inescapably visible idols. Young people forming their own groups – whether they are a cappella groups or garage bands – appear to follow this model, with no one person in full control. Each member takes turns leading or conducting, and the group votes on musical choices. An example of this social equality is the Orpheus Chamber Orchestra, a Grammy award-winning classical music chamber orchestra based in New York City. Orpheus is well known for its collaborative leadership style, in which the musicians, not a conductor, interpret the score.[3]

Changes in membership and audience necessitate changes in traditional financial management models. The traditional tuition-based chorus might not survive in this new environment, as new members, especially those from disenfranchised communities, may not be able to afford the tuition costs. Individual and corporate support is still needed to support substantial scholarship programs. In addition, these ensembles need new strategic and financial business plans that include innovative fundraising campaigns that accommodate post-recession strategies and redefine grassroots donor cultivation and marketing, such as the use of social networking websites. Recently, philanthropy has been leaning more favorably towards collaborative efforts among various organizations. In the absence of sufficient funds, collaborations are seen as a more effective way to share resources and best practices, and even, in some cases, office and rehearsal space. Growth strategies must be carefully considered. Most choirs survive with only a skeletal staff; however, as membership, commitments, and responsibilities grow, these ensembles also need to redesign their staff models. Some groups may need full-time staff to help them learn about commitment, discipline, and rehearsal attendance. Moreover, a large volunteer force is essential to the overall management of a chorus. How much of a social function you are willing to offer your members will determine what areas of expansion you will need to address, and what kind of staff you will employ.

Given the usual funds available, scholarships and other forms of support barely cover many other needs, such as transportation, food, touring, uniforms, additional music education, supplemental mentorship, or even just complimentary tickets to allow all members of the family to attend performances that are not free of charge. While this final detail may seem small, widening the social mission of a chorus also means addressing the economic realities of its membership, such as single-parent households or the ability to pay a babysitter. At the same time, financial assistance should be given discreetly so as to preserve a sense of equality among the children. I have found that providing something as simple as free tickets to the entire family could be crucial to their child's participation. Eventually, families see the impact that the chorus has on their children and they become the best resource to ensure that the child goes to rehearsals and concerts.

With new membership, new audiences also emerge. The parents of the singers are the most fervent supporters. Family education is a very important aspect of running a diverse music program. Not only will we add one or two multicultural pieces to our programs, our audiences will demand a more global view. In my experience, parents of some singers were more than willing to share new music with the conductors and even offered to help teach the ensemble techniques that were unique to the particular work. As adults marry outside their own culture, biracial and multiracial children will demand new music that reflects their complex identities – new rhythms, melodic and harmonic styles, and instruments that combine uniquely diverse cultures. As we change our membership and repertoire, we must train ourselves to work within the new community and to be flexible enough to accept new rhythmic and melodic directions with no preconceptions or prejudice. Conductors must not come with preconceived notions and expectations; they must be open to new ideals and cultural nuances, so that in the end, both they and the families learn from one another.

Beyond the family needs at concerts and at home, extra-familial audience expectations are also changing. What do audiences with no relation to your choir expect from this new model of diversity? Will *their* concept of excellence be met? When there is diversity, the audience will not expect your chorus to perform masterworks. They may have different expectations based on stereotypes. And one of the greatest challenges is not merely to create an excellent chorus, but to shatter these stereotypes.

It took years to educate and convince a largely skeptical New York City public that even though the children come from diverse backgrounds, they are able to sing music of all styles, including classical repertoire, at a very high level; it was not until the *New York Times* reviewed YPC concerts and wrote a superb review, followed by several national articles, that we were able to attract the general public. To achieve musical excellence per se is one thing; to change the mindset of the general public is a larger, more extensive, and unavoidably collective endeavor.

We live in a multicultural world that, in a sense, is still experiencing growing pains and is learning to function with a redefined identity. In such a world, the children's chorus can proactively be a vehicle for change, understanding, tolerance, and inclusion. At the same time, the children's choir has reached a point in which it no longer plays a supporting role, but has become a performing instrument capable of artistic excellence in its own right. The children's choir has reached its prime. The demands are great, but the rewards are rich.

16 Exploring the universal voice

MARY GOETZE, CORNELIA FALES, AND
WOLODYMYR SMISHKEWYCH

Few things come more naturally to us humans than producing vocal sounds. Beginning at birth with our first breath and cry, we use our voices to express ourselves and convey our needs. Babies instinctively explore a wide array of vocal sounds, sometimes for the sheer joy of hearing their own voices. As they are enculturated, children are encouraged to imitate the spoken and sung sounds they hear. This universal process has yielded not only different languages, but also an array of vocal timbres used in speaking and singing around the globe, each reflecting cultural preferences and context.

The vocal timbre that evolved to dominate Western choral music is rooted in the Italian vocal technique called *bel canto*. Today *bel canto* (discussed below) is employed around the globe, leading Western musicians to assume that it thrives because it is the preferred vocal technique across cultures. However, its wide dissemination results from its alignment with European colonization, Christianization, and imperialism. In many countries, a Western musical education is the only formal accredited study of music available, and the only option for voice training is with teachers trained in *bel canto* technique.[1]

Despite this, numerous other singing traditions around the globe – including in the United States and Europe – have thrived for centuries. Once never heard outside of their native contexts, today diverse vocal styles are finding their way into the Western choral repertory as a result of travel by individual musicians and touring ensembles. Published songs are typically transcribed and notated by Western-trained musicians. Melodies and harmonies are assigned to standard soprano, alto, tenor, and bass ranges, and tuned to intervals of diatonic scales. Rhythms are notated in conventional durations, and grouped into common meters. Scores may include a brief pronunciation guide, a translation and a paragraph about the song. However, notation includes only those aspects of the songs for which there are Western musical symbols. Thus, without having heard a native performance, a Western choir rendering a notated song may only faintly resemble the way that song is performed within the culture.

Today, technology is facilitating musical connections between cultures, making it possible to know how a song is sung in the original culture.

Some songs are sold as sheet music in Western notation with an audio recording featuring natives of the culture pronouncing the lyrics and singing the song. Emerging technology presents vocal music solely through model performances on DVDs, allowing a choir to learn the song aurally from the native singers rather than from notation. Some DVDs include recordings of isolated vocal parts and pronunciation, with movement instruction as well as cultural information.[2] Furthermore, it is possible for musicians in remote locations to interact in real time as they view and hear one another over the Internet.

Having audio and visual vocal models of diverse singing styles makes possible the transmission of the subtleties of style for which there is no notation. Hearing such aspects as timing, tuning, and vocal timbre presents a new challenge for directors: they must decide whether or not to ask their choirs to match these non-notated aspects of native model performances – especially the vocal timbre. Even with a native model available, some choirs choose to perform such songs with *bel canto* technique. Their directors may believe that singing in any other way will alter the sound they have developed with the choir, or that it will damage the singers' voices (a view long held by *bel canto* pedagogues).

In his 1968 book *Folk Song Style and Culture*, Alan Lomax wrote: "voice qualities frowned on by Western teachers are important in the aesthetics of other singing styles. Rasp and nasality, qualities which are anathema to the European voice teacher, play an essential part in certain singing styles."[3] A conductor would never substitute a clarinet for an oboe solo in a symphonic work, yet vocalists and choral directors freely change vocal timbre when performing non-*bel canto* vocal styles – a practice that is inconsistent with Western musical values.

There are additional reasons why, in our view, it is appropriate for twenty-first-century choirs to consider singing diverse musical styles with diverse vocal timbres. First, performing music as it is performed in the culture of origin shows respect for the people of that culture – a gesture that can contribute to good relationships between cultures, ethnicities, and racial groups. (A culture's preferred vocal timbre is as important to its people as a *bel canto* sound is to most Western-trained classical musicians.) Second, listening with the intent to match vocal timbre enhances choristers' aural perception, as singers attend keenly to perceive and produce myriad variations of such elements as color, pitch, accent, consonants, ornaments, and nuance. Last, it provides singers the opportunity to develop vocal versatility, as they explore a range of ways to vocalize and then return to a Western choral sound. For students, such experiences complement the technical training they receive in voice lessons.

The issue of performing – vocal or any other music – in the traditions of other cultures has always been controversial in the field of ethnomusicology. Traditionally, ethnomusicologists study indigenous musical behavior as it occurs within the culture where the music originates. Learning to perform indigenous music was, and is still, regarded as a method of learning about its cultural significance, the aesthetics that govern it, and other factors crucial to its consumption. From this point of view, when ethnomusicologists study technique and style for the sake of performance (usually to non-indigenous audiences), it is considered tangential to the ethnomusicological enterprise. Many of the controversial elements of the argument find their substance in the representation of the music in question: the most objectionable performance of a non-indigenous music is one that announces itself as "authentic" to the tradition of origin.

The production of traditional vocal techniques as advocated in this chapter, however, is a different venture from the performance criticized by ethnomusicologists. We do not claim here that singing non-*bel canto* styles will produce an "authentic" vocal timbre. No matter how diligent the effort to teach a *bel canto*-trained singer to produce a non-Western style, the result will be a vocal timbre that is to some degree non-authentic. The subtle features necessary to achieve a truly authentic sound are often absorbed slowly and unconsciously as part of indigenous enculturation into a musical tradition. No amount of deliberate training can replace that process. To describe the exploration of non-*bel canto* vocal styles, we use the word *approximation*. The notion of approximation calls attention to the difference between indigenous and non-indigenous production of vocal timbre, and expresses a deference to the process by which a sound is refined within a culture.

This chapter is intended to provide an overview of vocal production in order to lay the groundwork for understanding the array of approaches to singing found around the globe, and to suggest ways these might be approximated by choirs. We begin with a concise overview of aspects that are common to all singing. Then we outline some defining characteristics of *bel canto* technique, not as an instructional resource, but rather for purposes of comparing it with selected aspects of non-*bel canto* vocal techniques – the topic of the subsequent section. This final section includes suggestions for approximating these diverse techniques and caring for the singing voice.

Vocal production

Our discussion begins with five fundamental aspects of vocal production that are common to any style of singing: respiration, phonation, registration, resonance, and articulation.

Respiration

The sustained stream of breath that starts the process of vocal sound is dependent upon a posture that allows for efficient lung expansion and diaphragmatic mobility. The posture for singing that is embraced in many cultures is uncomplicated and natural with a tall stance and a somewhat elevated sternum (breastbone). Whether seated or standing, the singer keeps his or her head directly above the spine.

Exceptions to this posture often reflect the function of the song and the activity it accompanies. Webster Stech reports this suggestion for acquiring a Balkan sound: "Bend over from the waist as if you were cutting grain or weeding or working in the garden, and sing."[4] The posture of some Japanese traditional singers subtly reflects picking low-growing rice in fields. As they lean forward with knees slightly bent, the resonance in the chest area – and thus vocal timbre – is affected.[5]

While efficient and quiet respiration with an open throat is preferred in many cultures, intentional noisy inhalation is also found. Such practices suggest resistance to the stream of air in the vocal tract as a result of partial closure. Singing is typically done as the air is expired, although there are practices in which the vocal folds produce a tone on the intake of breath.[6]

If the sternum is high, the inhaled breath fills the lungs inside the lower ribs causing a lateral expansion. In this position, the abdominal and intercostal muscles (those in the rib cage) are free to "support" – in actuality, to dynamically resist against – the breath during singing.[7] When airflow and support are controlled, a clear tone is produced. In some non-classical and popular styles, breathiness or raspiness is preferred. In this case, it is not the result of intentionally poor vocal technique, but simply a valued quality. An intense constant or pulsed contraction of the intercostal and abdominal muscles is used in some traditions to generate pressure on the vocal folds – called *subglottic pressure* – resulting in a louder and more complex sound, while also impacting the behavior of the vocal folds.

Phonation

Phonation begins in the larynx, which is comprised of vocal folds or vocal cords, the *glottis* (the space between the vocal folds), and the muscles and cartilages that support them. The larynx is housed in the thyroid cartilage which is sometimes called the Adam's apple. During phonation, the pliable vocal folds are in constant motion: opening, releasing a puff of air, and closing in a periodic vibratory pattern. It is not the coming together of the folds that creates the sound, but rather "the varying pressures resulting from the bursts of air escaping through the glottis" that are perceived by the ear.[8] If these puffs of air could be heard outside the vocal tract, they would sound like a buzz.

The rate of opening and closing of the folds (measured in cycles per second) determines what the ear perceives as pitch. The action of the vocal folds is analogous to a brass player's embouchure: just as their lips extend and tighten in order to produce a higher-pitched buzz, so the vocal musculature controlling the vocal folds responds to the singer's intent, lengthening and tightening for higher pitches or shortening and releasing tautness for lower pitches.[9]

We attribute vocal pitch to the fundamental frequency of the complex waveform, within which are higher frequencies called *overtones*. The combined properties of the harmonic frequencies that comprise a complex wave are what we hear as timbre, and allow us to recognize different vowels in speech and singing.

The intensity of the vibration is a product of breath pressure, and, together with the resonance, determines the loudness level we perceive.

Registration

Different vocal registers, with their concomitant timbres and ranges, result from different vibratory patterns of the vocal folds. The two registers most commonly used for both speaking and singing are referred to as *chest voice* or *heavy mechanism*, and *head voice* or *light mechanism*. The term *falsetto* is sometimes used instead of head voice in males and females, but in this chapter we use the term *falsetto* to refer to a register above the head voice used only by men.[10] Other registers – the lowest register sometimes termed vocal fry, *Strohbass*, or pulse phonation, and the high-pitched range called the *whistle* or *coloratura* register – are not included in this discussion (although the style of Tuvan throat singing known as *kargyraa* is an example of cultivated pulse phonation technique).

During phonation in the *chest voice*, the full mass of the folds vibrates from end to end, laterally and vertically. The name is derived from the rumble or sympathetic vibration felt in the chest while singing in this register. During phonation the folds are closed more than half of the time.[11] This results in resistance to the airflow, so the chest voice requires more substantial breath flow than the head voice. The sound is relatively loud and has a richer array of overtones.

During phonation in the *head voice*, only the inner edges of the vocal folds vibrate and the outer mass is less active. Waves travel from end to end and from the outside toward the inner edges. The sensation of vibrations in the chest is reduced as the pitch level of phonation ascends, while sensations in the resonating areas in the head increase. The folds are closed approximately 30 to 40 percent of the time, resulting in less sub-glottal breath pressure.[12] As a product of its simpler overtone structure, the pure head register has a flutelike quality, especially in women.

The male *falsetto* register is used in numerous cultures. In Western art music, it is sometimes considered the register of the countertenor, though there is debate as to whether the Western countertenor uses a "developed falsetto" or simply has a head voice register that extends higher than other males. According to Miller and other *bel canto* pedagogues, the vocal fold action in falsetto is "not identical to that of legitimate head voice – indeed it exhibits quite a different behavior."[13] As in the head voice, the thin edges of the folds vibrate and come together, but the remainder of the folds are firm and do not vibrate.[14] Given the quality and high range of this register, it is used in many cultures for comedic effect or by men imitating women in drama, which is common in both Chinese and Japanese opera.[15] In the history of Western music, there have been repertoires devoted to *falsettists*, singers specializing in falsetto, but these repertoires were distinct from those sung by male altos or sopranos.

Resonance

The source waves originating in the larynx become amplified in the throat, mouth, and nasal cavities resulting in vibrant and varying vocal colors analogous to the transformation of the brass player's lip buzz when it enters a trumpet. Certain overtones present in the original buzz are amplified and others muted, and the resulting combination of overtones determines the *timbre* (tone color) of the instrument. The size and shape of the resonating chamber (the bore) combined with the filter effect of the instrument itself contribute to each brass instrument's unique timbre.

While the resonating chamber of a brass instrument is fixed and solid, the human resonators are soft and changeable. Certainly, a singer's bone structure contributes to some aspects of vocal timbre, but modifying the shape and size of the flexible resonating spaces makes a wide range of vocal colors possible. In addition to opening the throat and mouth, the larynx can be lowered or raised to change the length of the vocal tract, muscles can be tensed or relaxed, and the inner surfaces of the mouth and pharynx can be made taut or lax. McKinney writes that the throat's "vertical and horizontal dimensions can be increased or decreased, the tension in its walls is highly variable, and the size of the orifices leading to the mouth and nose can be varied, as can the entrance to the larynx itself."[16]

How the sound exits the body also plays a role in the timbre. "Since the lips serve as a preliminary determinant of the type of external orifice on the resonator system, they will have a strong effect on the timbre of the voice."[17] Lip position can darken and brighten the tone, and when the lips are protruded like a megaphone, they add ring (characteristic of higher overtones in the sound) and carrying power to the voice.

/I/ (h<u>e</u>)   /u/ (t<u>o</u>)

  /i/ (<u>i</u>t)   /ʊ/ (h<u>oo</u>k)

   /ɛ/ (g<u>e</u>t)   /o/ (<u>o</u>h without diphthong)

    /æ/ (c<u>a</u>t)   /ɔ/ (s<u>a</u>w)

      /ɑ/ (f<u>a</u>ther)

Figure 16.1 English vowels

In essence, vowel color is dependent on the shape of these resonating areas. "All vowels, per se, have resonance but each vowel has its own distinct pattern of resonance that is the result of the number, frequencies and energy distribution of the overtones that are present. It is by means of these differences in the overall patterns of resonance that we are able to hear and discriminate one vowel from another."[18] These bands of energized overtones that define vowels are called *formants*.[19]

Many aspects of vowel color reflect the language being sung, and to some degree a singer's native language. In addition, the production of the consonants plays a role in the color of the vowels they precede.

Singing and language

The vowel chart in Figure 16.1 is included to illustrate the relationship between the shape of the pharynx and vowel color. While a vast array of vowel colors are sung in myriad languages of the globe, for the sake of simplicity we include only pure Latin vowels, written in the International Phonetic Alphabet, with the closest English equivalent in parentheses. The vowels are arranged with [a] (as in *father*) at the lowest point on the triangle. To sing a pure [a], the most open of these vowels, the jaw is lowered, the throat and the mouth are open and the forward part of the tongue is flat and low in the mouth. Moving up the left side of the triangle, each vowel is created by a different tongue position, as the tongue's center approaches the roof of the mouth. Similarly, moving up the right side, the vowels are produced by reducing the opening of the lips.

Articulation

Consonants are the wonderful array of hisses, snaps, clicks, and hums that combine with vowels to create words. They are created by partial or complete closure of the vocal tract above the larynx by the lips, tongue, soft and hard palate, teeth, uvula, glottis, or epiglottis. Consonants without phonation are called *unvoiced* consonants, while those that include it are called *voiced*. Additionally, some consonants – categorized as stops, affricates, fricatives, and plosives – are formed by stopping, partially stopping, or stopping and then releasing the airflow. Typically, consonants briefly interrupt the flow of sustained vowels, but in some languages and singing styles voiced consonants may be sustained in the manner of a vowel.

Bel canto vocal technique

> The entire trend of Italian vocal music from the 12th century on[wards] is a fundamental principle of and characteristic of *bel canto*, that is, the search for beauty and purity of vocal tone. From this concept were derived all the consequences of the pedagogical and practical tendencies which characterize methods of *bel canto* singing and instruction from the sixteenth through the nineteenth centuries.[20]

The name of this vocal technique – *bel canto* ("beautiful singing") – aptly describes its essence. All aspects of production serve the goal of making what is culturally accepted as a pure and beautiful tone quality.

Fundamentals of *bel canto*

In *bel canto*, the ideal sound is an even, legato vocal production through all parts of the vocal range. The sound is stable, balanced, consistent, and equally resonant from the lowest to highest parts of the pitch range, and from soft to loud dynamic levels. This primacy of sustained vocal sound determines the way the vocal registers, vibrato, and text are managed.

Vocal registers

Bel canto uses the head and chest voice primarily, and training is focused on smoothing the transitions between these registers. Female vocalists sing primarily in head voice, utilizing chest or a mixed register for 36 percent to 46 percent of their range.[21] Appelman writes:

> One of the objectives of the singers of *bel canto* was the development of a vocal scale that was pure, unbroken, and uninterrupted. The transition of registers – either up or down the scale – demanded a modification in the tonal color of the topmost notes to prevent them from becoming disagreeable and harsh and to preserve the quality of the vowel sound as well as an even tonal line.[22]

It is this seamless vocal production that leads to the view among some *bel canto* voice teachers that, rather than head and chest, there is but one register. The single-register position is strengthened by the fact that the ranges of the registers overlap and that a trained singer can mix the registers by shifting gradually from one to the other – indeed, the goal of *bel canto*-trained singers. Typically, as the singer moves to higher pitches or sings at a softer dynamic level, he or she migrates toward the head register; when he or she moves toward the lower range or sings louder, the chest voice is mixed in by adding varying degrees of mass to the vocal folds.

Resonance

As noted above, the size, shape, and tension of the walls of the pharynx (throat) are major contributors to vocal resonance. In order to maximize resonance, this technique features an open throat and mouth along with a lowered larynx. Voice teachers and choral directors often refer to this as "vertical space" in the throat and mouth. Throughout the history of *bel canto* singing, "the type of vocal tone favored by many teachers was associated with a comparatively low larynx, and . . . an undesirable type of tone often was associated with a high larynx."[23]

Vibrato

In Western culture, a controlled fluctuation of pitch and intensity is called vibrato. Singing with vibrato has become a culturally accepted norm because it is perceived as adding warmth and vibrancy to the tone. Trained singers produce a relatively even vibrato at a rate of six to seven pulsations per second when singing is well-supported. A faster undulation is called a *tremolo* and a slower rate, usually a product of insufficient breath control, is called a *wobble*. While some Western choral traditions cultivate a "straight" or vibratoless tone in order to achieve pristine intonation, many Western choirs employ some vibrato.

Singing text in *bel canto*

In *bel canto* the ideal of a "beautiful tone" is served by the treatment of text, with special attention to the shape of vowels in order to maximize resonance and "singer's ring." The primary vowel is stable throughout the duration of the pitch(es) to which the word is assigned. When a diphthong such as in "ice" ([ais]) is sung, usually it is the first sound that is sustained before shifting to the second color. In short, vowels define vocal tone and are the vehicle for the musical line.

As discussed above, beginning and ending consonants frame the vowels. The skilled *bel canto* singer and choir will dispense quickly with the unvoiced consonant in order to return promptly to the resonant vowel and to use it to carry the musical line forward. Voiced consonants (such as the English pronunciation of *b, d, g, j, l, m, n, v,* and *z*) are granted enough duration to be discerned. At the beginning of a word, it is typical to place them just prior to the beat, so that the resonant vowel is sounded on the beat. When a voiced consonant occurs at the end of a word, it is sung before the end of the measured duration for that word in order to get to the next vowel on time. In sum, the goal is precise rendering of consonants so that the text is clear, but does not intrude upon the beauty of the vocal quality.

Exploring a broader musical horizon

The remainder of this chapter focuses on understanding and respectfully approximating non-*bel canto* vocal styles in choral performance. One challenge we encountered in comparing vocal techniques is the scarcity of information in written form about singing styles other than *bel canto*. In most of the world's cultures, people learn to sing through the process of enculturation, and if coaching is given, it is transmitted orally or by example. Ethnomusicologists occasionally refer to vocal techniques, but their investigations typically consider the *role* of singing in the culture, and only since the 1990s have ethnomusicologists begun to use spectrographic and x-ray technology, video, magnetic resonance imaging (MRI), and other technology to examine vocal style.[24] In addition, since there is no accepted scheme for comparing singing techniques across cultures, we draw upon our own training and experience.

Our discussion will center on these questions:

- What is *approximation*?
- In what ways do diverse vocal techniques differ from *bel canto*?
- How can *bel canto*-trained singers approximate these styles?
- What considerations should be taken when approximating vocal timbres of diverse musical traditions?

Approximating vocal timbres

By approximating vocal timbres, we mean adapting *bel canto* technique so that it resembles the target timbre as perceived by a listener. In our view, such approximation will not harm the voice, provided singers and directors follow the principles of voice conservation.[25] Classically trained singers have demonstrated that singing in other vocal styles does not have a negative impact on their vocal health.[26] They may sing jazz, gospel, or belt in a musical theater production one night and perform opera the next. Furthermore, in observing vocalists in traditions where non-*bel canto* singing is predominant, we have found they do not typically suffer from vocal disorders, even when singing from childhood well into old age.

As noted above, timbre is an essential aspect of musical expression. The acoustic differences in vocal techniques are clearly visible in spectrograms shown in figures 16.2, 16.3, and 16.4.[27] Figure 16.2 shows a phrase performed by a singer from Kyrgyzstan; Figure 16.3 shows the same phrase sung by an

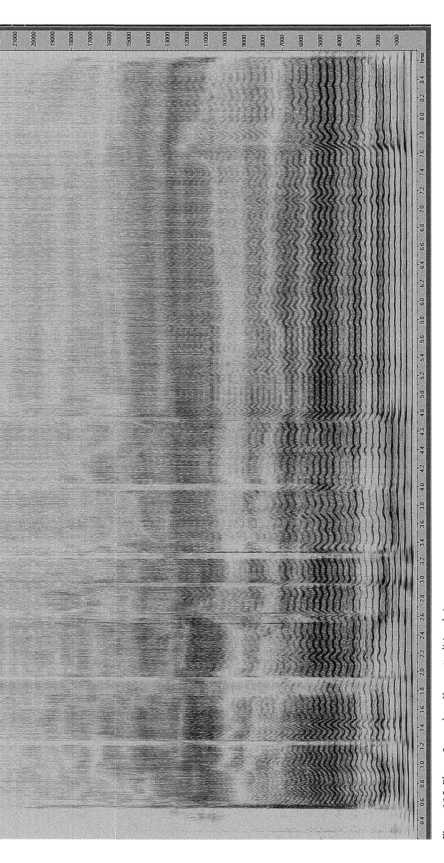

Figure 16.2 Phrase 2 sung by a Kyrgyz traditional singer

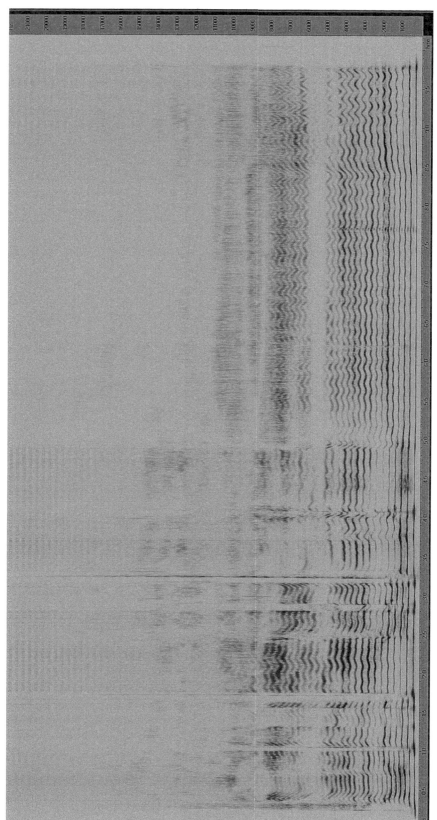

Figure 16.3 Phrase 2 sung by a *bel canto* singer

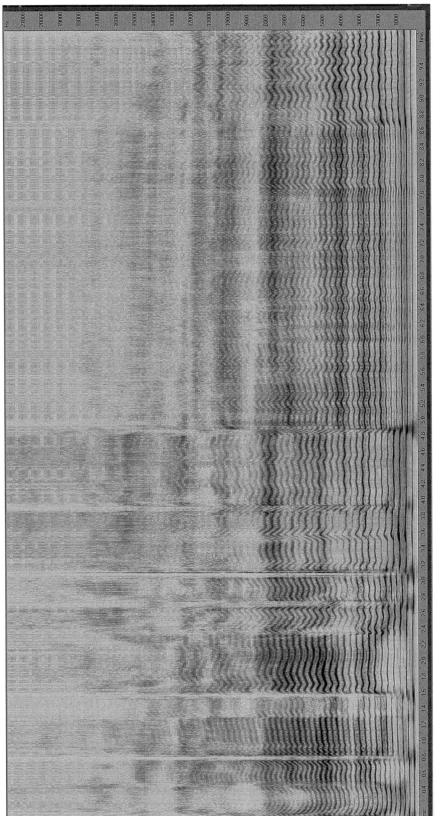

Figure 16.4 Phrase 2 sung by a *bel canto* singer approximating Kyrgyz style

American singer trained in the *bel canto* style. Figure 16.4 shows the same phrase approximated by the American singer. (She maintained minimal space in her oral cavity and raised her larynx in order to match the Kyrgyz style.) A comparison of these spectrograms yielded the following findings.

First, though the total energy in the first half of the *bel canto* version is greater than that of the Kyrgyz version, the *bel canto* singer has compressed the power of her voice into a narrow spectrum (in the region below 5kHz), while the Kyrgyz singer produces a spectrum that reaches almost 15kHz and distributes her energy more equally across the entire spectrum. Thus, while the *bel canto* version is richer in sound, the Kyrgyz version is brighter and more resonant. In the approximated version, the *bel canto* singer manages to cover a broader spectrum with nearly the same balance as the traditional Kyrgyz version.

Second, the Kyrgyz singer produces a broad *anti-formant* with center frequency at about 10kHz. (An anti-formant is an area of the spectrum with reduced energy and thus a less vibrant appearance on the spectogram. It is produced when a cavity in the vocal tract traps or absorbs a bandwidth of frequencies.) The spectrogram of the *bel canto* singer shows an anti-formant between 5 and 6kHz. These contrasting areas of anti-formants are responsible for much of the difference in sound between the two examples. By contrast, the approximated version produces an anti-formant in a frequency range that very nearly matches that of the Kyrgyz version, confirming the *bel canto* singer's closer approximation of the Kyrgyz singer's timbre.

Third, another timbral difference between the three examples is their respective articulations of consonants. In the Kyrgyz and approximation examples the consonants are soft, while in the *bel canto* example consonants are fully articulated. The result is that the vertical flow of the phrases produced by the Kyrgyz and approximating singers is smooth and unbroken, with few peaks in energy, whereas the *bel canto* singer's version shows peaks and gaps in energy corresponding to both initial and final consonants.

Exploring diverse vocal techniques

Since the purpose here is to recommend and explore approximation of diverse vocal techniques rather than to document the vocal production of indigenous singers, we describe the physical adaptations we as trained singers made in order to approach the quality to be matched. As noted above, this process does not require abandoning Western vocal training altogether. In our view, making these physical adjustments to the vocal musculature and posture expands, rather than threatens, choristers' vocal technique.

Given the vastness of this topic, we have narrowed our discussion to four aspects: Laryngeal position, Registration, Resonance, and Special techniques. In the sections entitled "Give it a try," we provide suggestions for the reader's exploration. Table 16.1 shows the adjustments we made in approximating examples from a range of cultures, illustrating that these four factors do not exist in isolation, but rather are combined in various ways to provide an infinite palette of vocal colors and effects to explore.[28]

Table 16.1 *Adjustments made in approximating various non-bel canto vocal styles*

Female singers
From Kyrgyzstan
Laryngeal position: high
Register: chest-mix
Resonance: teeth close together, vowels bright and forward in oral cavity, slight nasality
From China
Laryngeal position: high
Register: head-mix
Resonance: horizontal feel in oral cavity, wide smile; lowered soft palate to add nasal resonance
From Brazil
Laryngeal position: high
Register: chest
Resonance: relaxed position of throat and with minimal opening of oral cavity
Ornament: small scoops into most pitches
From South Africa
Laryngeal position: high (similar to belting)
Register: chest-mix
Resonance: bright vowels, feeling of height in back of mouth on low notes
Ornament: vibrato, frequent scoops and glides
From Bulgaria
Laryngeal position: high
Register: head-mix
Resonance: small oral cavity in front, wider in back
Ornament: no vibrato but with relaxed larynx
From Japan
Laryngeal position: high
Register: chest, shifting to mixed
Resonance: throat is narrow and oral cavity small; nasal resonance
Ornament: shifts of register from chest; angular ornaments and clean changes between pitches
Male singers
From Azerbaijan
Laryngeal position: medium high
Register: chest-mix in low range, head-mix in high range
Resonance: wide back of mouth; lips semi-open; bright vowels
Ornament: bleating; some bleating/pulsations used in imitation of bowed instrument
From Japan
Laryngeal position: semi-high larynx
Register: chest
Resonance: triangular opening in back of mouth; resonance felt in head and back of nasal cavity
Ornament: slides; wide, slow trill-type ornament; clean changes between pitches
Native American
Laryngeal position: high but not forced position, fairly comfortable, like a "light nasal belt"
Register: chest-mix
Resonance: highly nasal, bright vowels
Ornament: yodel-like motion, scoops, slides combined with hard-aspirate ([h]) glottal attacks
From Zimbabwe
Laryngeal position: medium/medium high
Register: chest and some chest-mix
Resonance: mostly head and pharyngeal resonance
Ornament: yodels at distance of a fourth

Laryngeal position

In contrast to the lowered larynx of *bel canto* singing, a shortened vocal tract produced by raising the larynx is common to many non-*bel canto* vocal styles. When the larynx is high, the vocal folds generate overtone patterns that result in a louder and brighter quality. This vocal posture gives a distinctive carrying power to the voice, which is important when singing occurs out of doors or in acoustically dry settings. Most researchers agree that the popular singing technique called *belting* uses the high laryngeal position.[29] Estill comments on the pervasiveness of the high laryngeal position in other traditions: "Belting is a voice quality heard in much of the ethnic music around the world: in fado of Spain, in the folk music of Eastern Europe and the Orient and in the theatre voices of the Japanese drama schools."[30]

> **Give it a try**: *A common method of finding this high position of the larynx is to speak the phrase "uh-oh," as it is said when you drop something accidentally. For bel canto singers, sustaining a pitch with the larynx in this position will feel unfamiliar. Repeat these syllables at various pitch and loudness levels, and then try sustaining either syllable on a comfortable pitch before executing a phrase.*

Registration

Use of the chest register is more prevalent in traditional singing styles around the world than in *bel canto*. Given that registers and pitch are interdependent, the *tessitura* provides a clue as to the register that is being employed.[31] For women, the tessitura of songs may extend below the range of the treble clef. It is not uncommon for the chest voice to be extended to a high range. Additionally, the range of pitches over which the head and chest registers can be mixed often begins at a higher pitch level than in *bel canto* singing. The terms *chest-mix* and *head-mix* indicate the dominant register in mixed-register production.

> **Give it a try**: *Since the bel canto male singer uses primarily chest voice, this register will be more familiar for men. A low, relaxed sigh will elicit this voice. For women who speak in the chest voice at a relatively low pitch, intoning and sustaining a spoken word is effective for beginning to explore. Both men and women should explore singing low pitches with raised and lowered larynx.*

Resonance

As noted above, the resonators of the vocal tract contribute greatly to subtle variations in vocal timbres.[32] The resonating areas in the throat, mouth, and nose can be opened, closed, combined, or shaped to produce a broad range of vocal timbres. By contrast to the vertical image used in Western singing, in some traditions the oral cavity is horizontal, with the teeth closer together and the corners of the mouth extended toward the cheeks.

In *bel canto*, the soft palate is generally raised to close off the nasal cavity, eliminating nasal resonance, while in other traditions, nasality is desirable.[33] Varying degrees of nasal resonance are possible, depending upon the size of the opening into the nasal resonators.

> **Give it a try:** *Because there is an infinite number of ways to shift and combine the various resonators, we recommend listening to a style and relying upon your natural imitative impulse to match the quality. Focusing on the vowel color can be a key to adjusting the resonators. To explore timbral variation, choose a pitch in the middle of a comfortable pitch range. Sing the following, first with a high then a low laryngeal position:*
>
> - [o] *with the vocal tract and larynx in their resting position and mouth half open.*
> - [æ] *as in "cat" with the teeth nearly together and a smile on the lips.*
> - [u] *with the soft palate low to add nasal resonance. (An easy way to tell if there is nasal resonance in your sound is to pinch your nose. If it is nasalized, the sound stops or stutters on and off.)*

Special techniques
Approaching pitches
Below are two of the many ways a tone can be approached.

Scoops and slides
A pitch may be approached from well below the target tone, scooping quickly or slowly to the target pitch, and sliding lightly or heavily over all of the pitches in between. Singers need only listen to and imitate the scooped approach.[34]

Glottal attacks
The folds can be brought together (stopped) prior to or during phonation, resulting in the abrupt onset of the sound that follows. This attack is used in *bel canto* as well as in other styles, often when a word begins with a vowel.

Releases
Notes are sometimes released with a drop in pitch, which can be subtle or pronounced. Especially when the phonation requires high subglottal pressure, a coincidental expulsion of air may be audible as the vocal folds separate more forcibly.

Ornaments
Slurs, trills, and turns
A common form of ornamentation is the movement back and forth between two pitches. This movement may be heavy, light, or even, but timing and precision vary with style. The fundamental vocal production

(laryngeal position and register) impacts the character of the ornament. For instance, singing with a high larynx may result in a trill that is more angular than the *bel canto* trill. Sometimes the trill covers an interval wider than a half or whole step with movement between pitches occurring at various speeds and durations.

Bleating

Tones may be decorated with bleating, a technique not typically included in *bel canto* training.[35] Bleating is articulated by a coordinated action of the glottis and breathing musculature, and the laryngeal position is generally high. The bleated sound wavers with minimal change of pitch. It is often used as ornamentation in traditional singing in parts of Eastern Europe and East Asia.

> **Give it a try:** *With the larynx high, sustain a pitch and sing /hihihi/ or /hehehe/ rapidly, letting the aspirant h trigger the bleating sound. Avoid changing to another pitch or stopping phonation between syllables.*

Pulsating

Pulsations are repeated accents added to a prolonged tone. Changes in both pitch and dynamic level may occur on each of the pulses. The motion is usually slower than the trill or bleat described above, and the pitch shift may be as wide as a third.

> **Give it a try:** *As you sustain a pitch, give a small intense push by contracting the abdominal muscles. The tone will become louder, and the increase in subglottal pressure may also result in a pitch change. Explore pulsations in both registers and with raised and lowered larynx.*

Yodeling

Some form of yodel is employed on nearly every continent. A yodel is an abrupt alternation between a low and high pitch, often involving a change in register accompanied by a fleeting glottal stop.

> **Give it a try:** *Sing a low pitch with good support on [o] or [e]. To facilitate the rapid shift to the head voice, change the syllable to [i] and move to a pitch at least a sixth above the lower note. In order to highlight the difference in the two registers, the chest sound needs to be full-voiced. The smooth transition between registers emphasized in bel canto makes yodeling challenging for some trained singers.*

Overtone singing

Although forms of overtone or harmonic singing can be found in a number of cultures, this unique technique has been especially cultivated by the peoples of Central Asia. In her book on Mongolian music, Carole Pegg reports that the high frequencies in overtone singing enable vocal sounds to be heard across long distances.[36] Traditionally, Mongolian and Tuvan overtone singing was performed by men, but today women also sing with this technique, known as *Khöömii* or *Xöömei*.[37] While this term encompasses several distinctly different styles, we describe a basic technique here, that of a sustained pitch whose individual overtones are highlighted. The high, whistlelike sounds are actually the amplified overtones that are present in the droned pitch, which is usually sung in chest voice. In phonating, the singer generates a static fundamental tone with a slightly high larynx. The size and shape of the oral cavity highlights individual overtones that shift when slight modifications of the tongue are made.

> **Give it a try:** *Sing a pitch in the lower third of your range in full chest voice. With the tongue near the roof of the mouth, create a small resonating space behind the front teeth as if to sing a vibrant [y] in French or German. The lips should be slightly pursed. Moving from [y] to [u], or simply making miniscule adjustments, helps to become aware of the overtones. Then sing through the spectrum of vowels in Figure 16.1 to discover the different overtones that correspond to each vowel shape. Most singers are able to produce several audible overtones, but it requires extensive practice to produce overtone melodies. Explore lowering the soft palate to add nasal resonance, widening the lips and opening the throat, and shifting the tongue to see how these changes affect the overtones.*

Table 16.1 shows the ways in which we combine these techniques when matching recorded examples from the cultures listed.[38] The adjustments recommended are based on our experience in approximating these styles and guiding others to match them, employing what Lomax dubbed "creative listening," that is, "trying to reproduce the heard quality, locating it in one's own vocal mechanism, and *then* analyzing it."[39] We suggest the following procedure in matching recorded vocal qualities, or presenting songs in any unfamiliar vocal style to the choir:

1 First, simply listen and allow the mind and body to respond by imitating the sound without extensive analysis.
2 Then make use of the suggestions as needed.
3 Sing freely as you explore, always monitoring for tension in any part of the musculature.
4 Record yourself or the group often, if possible, and listen repeatedly.
5 Take notes to help you recall the sound and how it was produced, and to help others in their attempts.

In the interest of vocal health

Vocal health is a concern for singers and choral directors alike. Excessive loud singing, especially in chest voice, may inflame the vocal folds and if prolonged can cause more serious vocal problems. When exploring unfamiliar high-demand singing styles, trauma can be minimized if the singers are conditioned to the new technique over time. In the same way that sun-sensitive individuals can tolerate sun if they spend fifteen minutes in the sun one day and twenty minutes the next, the voice can adapt to more strenuous singing if the singer is initiated gradually into the technique. This means regularly rehearsing vocally demanding songs in short rather than long segments and allowing the voice to rest afterward.

Directors should be mindful of vocal use when choosing repertory and planning rehearsals. It is important to begin each rehearsal with exercises that warm up the voice gradually, beginning with posture and breathing activities, proceeding to light singing in the mid range of the voice before exercising the extremes of the vocal range at louder dynamic levels. In general, songs that use the chest voice and high larynx should be practiced toward the end of rehearsals. Directors should encourage singers to take responsibility for resting their voices in rehearsals as needed, and relaxing when production results in muscular tension. We subscribe to the following basic practices that contribute to vocal health recommended by Thurman, Klitzke, and Hogikyan.[40]

- Maintain your body's optimum water level. Take in about six to eight glasses of water per day, each glass containing 8 ounces or 0.25 liter of water.
- Warm up the voice gradually before extensive or vigorous use, for a minimum of about seven to ten minutes. Use efficient vocal skills and move from minimal to more strenuous vocal use.
- Balance voice-use time with voice-recovery time (silence).
- Rest at the first signs of vocal fatigue or general body fatigue.
- Avoid substances that dehydrate the body and vocal cords (i.e. excess caffeine, antihistamines, alcohol, smoking, high-salt foods).
- Do not sing when the throat is inflamed from infection or extended, intense use. (Refrain from vocalizing when vocal cords are swollen, or when protective phlegm is present. This signals that the voice needs silence and the body needs rest or sleep.)

The world now offers us a wide variety of vocal music, and we advocate embracing it and performing it with musical integrity. We argue that approximating vocal timbres as described here has numerous benefits for singers, for choirs, and for building bridges between cultures.

Beyond the musical and vocal benefits, interacting with musicians from various cultures can be life-enriching and sometimes life-changing for directors and choristers alike. Through these experiences, friendships are forged – and biases and stereotypes challenged.

Music embodies aspects of the culture from which it springs, often reflecting emotions and temperaments not only through lyrics, but also through subtle aspects of melody, rhythm, harmony, and timbre. The potential for empathy and identification with unfamiliar cultures may lie in internalizing their songs and recreating all aspects of their performance to the degree possible. Such experiences provide insights into that culture that may transcend merely listening to its music, learning facts about it, viewing pictures of people, or learning about a song's context. And it is through learning about an unfamiliar culture that one better understands one's own musical culture and the wonderful and varied ways music functions in people's lives.

Select bibliography

Appelman, D. Ralph. *The Science of Vocal Pedagogy.* Bloomington: Indiana University Press, 1967.

Bunch, Meribeth. *Dynamics of the Singing Voice.* Vienna/New York: Springer-Verlag, 1997.

Estill, J. "Belting and Classic Voice Quality: Some Physiological Differences," *Medical Problems of Performing Artists* 3 (1988): 37–43.

Finchum, Hilary. "Tuvan Overtone Singing: Harmonics Out of Place." SAVAIL Working Papers. www.indiana.edu/~savail/workingpapers/tuva.html.

Furiya, Miyako. Panel session, "The Past, Present and Future of Music Education in Japan," International Society for Music Education Conference, Edmonton, Alberta, 2000.

Gerstein, Christine Wondolowski. "Early Musical Training in Bel Canto Vocal Technique: A Brief History and Philosophy." Unpublished paper, Hofstra University, Long Island, ED 393 758, 1994.

Jeon, Molly Adkins. "Bimusicality in Japanese Folksong and Italian Art Song: A Study of Vocal Timbre," in Brian A. Roberts (ed.), *Sharing the Voices: The Phenomenon of Singing: Proceedings of the International Symposium,* St. John's: Memorial University of Newfoundland, Canada, 1999.

Kantner, Claude El, and Robert West. *Phonetics.* New York: Harper & Brothers, 1960.

Kochis-Jennings, Karen Ann. "Intrinsic Laryngeal Muscle Activity and Vocal Fold Adduction Patterns in Female Vocal Registers: Chest, Chestmix, and Headmix." Doctoral dissertation, University of Iowa, 2008.

Lawrence, Van. "Laryngological Observations on 'Belting,'" *Journal of Research in Singing and Applied Vocal Pedagogy* 2, 1 (1979), 26–8.

Lomax, Alan. *Folk Song Style and Culture.* New Brunswick, NJ: American Association for the Advancement of Science, 1968.

McKinney, James C. *The Diagnosis and Correction of Vocal Faults.* Long Grove, IL: Waveland Press, Inc., 1994.

Miller, Richard. *The Structure of Singing: System and Art in Vocal Technique.* New York: Schirmer Books, 1996.

Pegg, Carole. *Mongolian Music, Dance, and Oral Narrative: Recovering Performance Traditions.* University of Washington Press, 2001.

Popeil, L. "Comparing Belt and Classical Techniques using MRI and Video-Fluoroscopy," *Journal of Singing* 56, 2 (1999), 27–29.

Schutte, H. K., and D. G. Miller, "Belting and Pop, Commercial Approaches to the Female Middle Voice: Some Preliminary Considerations," *Journal of Voice* 7, 2 (1993), 142–50.

Thurman, Leon, Carol Klitzke, and Norman Hogikyan. "Cornerstones of Voice Protection," in Leon Thurman and Graham Welch (eds.), *Bodymind and Voice: Foundations of Voice Education* (rev. edn.). Collegeville, MN: VoiceCare Network and National Center for Voice and Speech, 2000, pp. 646–55.

Titze, Ingo R. "Belting and the High Larynx Position," *Journal of Singing* 63, 5 (2007), 557–58.

Vennard, William. *Singing: The Mechanism and the Technic.* New York: Carl Fischer, 1967.

Webster Stech, Jamie. "American Woman and the Mysterious Voice: American Women Performing Gender through Singing Bulgarian Songs." 2002. depts. washington.edu/reecas/events/conf2002/regconf02.html

Zemp, Hugo et al. *Les Voix du Monde (Voices of the World).* Paris: Collection du Centre National de la Recherche Scientifique et du Musée de l'Homme, 1996. CNR-3741010/12.

17 Authentic choral music experience as "good work": the practice of engaged musicianship

DOREEN RAO

A "fresh vision" of conducting and teaching choral music

The idea of authenticity evokes many provocative thoughts. When a friend of mine said he was convinced that the notion of authenticity was highly overrated, misunderstood, and too often at odds with important elements of music making like imagination and change, I had to agree. The concept of authenticity in choral music is a frequently discussed subject connected all too often with a static definition of performance practices governed by a rigid set of rules. While the adherence to established musical traditions and historically situated performance practices is generally acknowledged as a sign of distinction, particularly within the formalized contexts of academic institutions, it is not always recognized that traditions and performance practices are necessarily dynamic, and that they offer opportunities for change and innovation.

One of the leading conductors who questions the notion of musical authenticity is Nikolaus Harnoncourt, a legend in the area of period performance, who calls for a "fresh vision" of authenticity – an examination of historical music from a diversity of perspectives. Harnoncourt criticizes the twentieth-century attempts to render historic music in its original form as the *ideal*. He questions the growing demand for "authentic" renditions of *old music as old music*. "This attitude toward historical music – the unwillingness to bring it into the present, but rather undertaking to return oneself to the past – is a symptom of the loss of a truly living contemporary music." This approach "satisfies neither the musician nor the public, both of whom reject a large portion of it."[1]

No musical tradition is frozen in time, and nor is the meaning of "authenticity." This chapter examines authenticity in conducting and teaching choral music and considers it as a dynamic and continuously evolving

This chapter is dedicated to Helmuth Rilling. My deep gratitude to Lori-Anne Dolloff whose collaborative efforts inspired the completion of this writing. Professor Dolloff introduced me to the research of Huib Schippers and she contributed her reflections on the narratives included in this chapter. I am indebted to Gordon Paine both for his insightful editing and for the conceptual challenge his questions provided me during the final stages of this writing. Professor Paine's perseverance made all the difference.

opportunity for change and innovation, a personally sensitive and socially responsive practice I call engaged musicianship. Introducing a more fluid definition of what constitutes authenticity in conducting and teaching choral music, the chapter looks beyond the formal properties of musical notation, voicing, instrumentation, and the performance setting, toward matters of cultural context and the human condition. This brief effort looks at the less tangible aspects of musical experience, including ethically driven considerations such as personal sensitivity and social responsibility.

Definitions of authenticity

The first step in this inquiry begins by examining the essence or true nature of authenticity. Even dictionary definitions vary radically, from the notion of authenticity as something made or done in the traditional or original way, fully resembling the original, to a more existential view of authenticity as an appropriate and responsible mode of human life. Most definitions relate authenticity to that which is *genuine*. Some sources define "authenticity" philosophically, as the quality of *being* genuine or true to oneself. Socrates refers to "the authenticity of self" as genuineness of thought and action.[2]

What constitutes authenticity in choral music and conducting? The answers are as diverse as they are contingent. They rely on circumstances as well as the conductor's insight, knowledge, and level of experience to determine what is appropriate or desirable in given circumstances. They also depend on the knowledge and skill level of the partners in the collaborative effort – the chorus. Ultimately, both elements relate to considerations that are closely aligned with the conductor's musical accomplishments and personal shortcomings. Whether we are ready or not to accept this notion, authenticity as we understand it in relation to our choruses and ourselves is a direct reflection of our character, personality, and spirit.

Our decisions regarding musical materials and interpretations are contingent – each and every one of them. From our choice of performance edition to how many singers are assigned to each part, we rely on both our knowledge of musical traditions and practices, and our sensitivity to the unique circumstances of the situation. Whether we use keyboard alone or a larger continuo group, perform in the original language or a singing translation, we consider both external factors, such as the information that informs our understanding, and internal factors, such as our musical intuition, empathy, and what we understand as "good work" – a topic to be explored shortly. Whether we perform with original instruments, one on a part and *senza vibrato*, or on modern instruments, with large performing forces and full-bodied singing tone, to practice authenticity is to be genuine, adaptable, cooperative, and respectful in relation to the music and the singers.

Elements of authenticity – visible and invisible

In the context of graduate studies in choral conducting, the term authentic is most often associated with the external, visible elements related to scholarly investigation, knowledge acquisition, and information gathering. We contemplate musical editions that are faithful to the composer, interpretations that are faithful to original performance practices, and professional practices that are based on accurate historical and empirical knowledge. Less often, however, do we concern ourselves with the term "authentic" in relation to the internal, invisible elements such as intuition, character, ethics, and social responsibility.

Some of the most exciting scholarship today addresses the less visible and the unseen elements associated with qualities of culturally sensitive and socially responsible choices in many professional fields, including the arts. Of particular interest is the GoodWork Project, which was undertaken in 1994 at Harvard University and led by professors Howard Gardner, Mihaly Csikszentmihalyi, and William Damon. It started by examining "good work" in journalism and genetics; over time it expanded its investigations into myriad professional fields and issued a large body of books, reports, and related documents. "Good work" in this context is defined in a dual sense: "work that is both excellent in quality and socially responsible."[3]

In the original "Good Work Project," three teams of investigators explored the ways in which leading professionals in various domains, including the arts and education, carry out "good work." Since the original project was launched, research teams throughout the United States have also looked at changes in professional practices since the September 11, 2001, attacks. They asked the question, *To what extent have our work lives changed since the terrorist attacks?* Amidst numerous cautionary tales, the report offers inspiring examples of those who carry out work that is both excellent in quality and socially responsible. They also found that consciousness of and efforts toward social responsibility have increased notably since the attacks. In taking stock of these and related findings, the present examination of authenticity is dedicated to the exploration of what constitutes "good work" in conducting and teaching choral music for the twenty-first century.

Toward engaged musicianship

How do we integrate professional practices in conducting and choral teaching that are externally defined and deemed to be of high quality with the perspectives of less visible, internal elements of personal sensitivity and social responsibility? As professionals, we are likely familiar with conducting curricula that assure the attainment of external skills and understandings related to professional skills, musical materials, and performance practices. Yet we may never have encountered curricular offerings that address the internal skills required to make culturally sensitive and socially responsible choices, invisible forms of knowing that extend beyond the conventions of urtext editions, beautiful tone, and perfect intonation. These less visible skills require ownership for both our musical work and its wider impact on the world – a form of knowing I call "engaged musicianship" – a mindfulness quality of being fully present, and engaged in community service.

Engaged musicianship as a form of twenty-first-century musicianship is embodied in the conductor's ability to practice conscious listening and concentrated musicianship supported by ethical discernment – the ability to do the right thing at the right time for the right reasons. Making culturally sensitive and socially responsible choices requires the integration of both external and internal forms of musicianship as these relate to the professional practice of conducting choirs. The external, visible skills and bodies of knowledge, including musical analysis, musicology, conducting technique, and rehearsal pedagogy, constitute the core curriculum at the majority of universities and music conservatories. But the internal, invisible skills, including reflective practices of self-awareness, concentration, and deep listening, are rarely taught. In my view, these invisible skills are in fact *core practices*, not alternative electives. They need to be included in socially conscious conducting curricula – programs that aspire to teaching conducting and choral education based on what the previously mentioned Harvard research calls "good work."

The role of reflection and contemplation

Another Harvard research team charged with the study of "good work" in education examined the role of contemplation and reflection in developing "good work" in teaching.[4] The lessons from this research suggest that contemplative forms of engagement facilitate new ideas, novel solutions, and enhanced perspectives related to "good work." While reflective practices are often associated with personal benefits such as pain reduction, stress release, or energy renewal, these same practices may also be keys to developing the essential qualities of awareness, concentration, and deep listening – qualities of attention closely associated with the musical and personal choices made by conductors and choral teachers every day.

An *authentic* choral conductor is one who embraces *engaged musicianship* practices being fully present to the music, to the chorus, and to the social conditions that benefit the quality of musical experience for artists and audiences alike. That which makes an authentic choral conductor makes an authentic person – the two are inseparable. Choral leadership based on reflective qualities of engagement that develop from the conductor's awareness, focused attention, and deep concentration on the podium differs radically from autocratic forms of leadership that fail to take into account the human beings who are our singers.

Ethically driven and socially conscious conducting curricula should embody reflective practices that include meditation and movement forms in courses designed to improve the conductor's self-awareness, listening capability, and concentration in rehearsal and performance. These internal, less visible skills requiring reverence, receptivity, and attention can be taught alongside score analysis and conducting technique.

Non-sectarian contemplative practices like mindfulness focus on developing the conductor's life skills as these relate to the power of attention and deep listening in rehearsal and performance. For example, the simple skill of "conscious breathing" or "breathing meditation" encourages the conductor's stillness, calm, and concentration. When practiced over time at the start of each conducting lesson, conscious breathing helps conductors learn to listen with their ears and with their hearts.[5] From a place of inner calm and stillness, the conductor's awareness of herself and others deepens. Yoga, tai chi, and other similar contemplative practices can be of value to both the conductor and the choir. Contemplative breathing and movement exercises can be adapted easily into rehearsal warm-ups to engage bodies and minds for a more focused and self-aware period of deep listening and musical concentration in rehearsal and performance.[6]

Summary

There are more questions than answers related to the notion of what constitutes an authentic conductor in the world today. The present investigation, however, embraces the notion of authenticity as a fluid idea rather than as something fixed or absolute. The notion that authenticity is limited to the observance of a stylized set of performance practices fails to take into account important considerations such as the relationships around us, the nature of our communities, and the social conditions of the world today.

We likely agree that part of educating the next generation of choral conductors means teaching musical analysis and musicology, style and interpretation, gesture and pedagogy; but in *relation* to what? – musical works? – the human beings who form our choirs? – the world around us? Is it possible to be musically authentic and socially insensitive? Is there a link between musical authenticity and personal integrity? Are we not morally bound to ask the important questions that ground our practices, define our curricula, and promise to impact the next generation of conductors and choral teachers?

Particularly at the advanced levels of musical study, when students presumably come to us with musical backgrounds that invite deeper levels of investigation, we may be missing an important opportunity to guide emerging conductors toward a socially responsible form of musicianship – a twenty-first-century form of musicianship that integrates the external and internal skills, linking musicality and personal sensitivity.

Working without regard to the social conditions that surround us can have serious consequences. Music making decontextualized from the realities of poverty, war, oppression, or from any moral or social engagement whatsoever misses a powerful opportunity artistically and socially to play a more active and intentional role in social inquiry and change.

We can no longer afford to teach musical performance as a form of aesthetic contemplation. A twenty-first-century musicianship must be different. What may have been considered "authentic" in nineteenth-century European society is not necessarily authentic for twenty-first-century cultures around the globe. Given the current challenges of our world, it is time for our profession to consider integrating the non-dualistic values of musical excellence and personal authenticity within our conducting education programs. This is the essence of the concept of "engaged musicianship" that I introduced earlier, an idea that will be examined again further in this chapter.

Messiah for the people

Many of us have our own stories surrounding performances of Handel's *Messiah*. Because *Messiah* is an icon of world culture, it seems fitting to use this well-known work as the basis for our examination of the meaning of *authenticity* in conducting and teaching choral music. My own experiences with one particular *Messiah* performance relate to memories of my first month as the new music director of a community-based symphonic chorus.

As I began rehearsals for a previously scheduled *Messiah* performance, it soon became clear that the large ensemble was unfamiliar with baroque-style articulations and phrasing. Through the use of dance, movement exercises, vocalizations, and lots of fun and good will, the 130-voice community chorus began enthusiastically singing new life into their beloved *Messiah*. I was confident that while our first *Messiah* together would not come close to a refined, baroque-style performance of the work, this enthusiastic and committed chorus would be able to sing an articulate, joyful, and textually informed rendition. Then came the surprise. *Oh my God, a basilica – architectural wonder, musical nightmare!*

After several weeks of rehearsals, I visited the large and looming Our Lady of Victory Basilica in Lackawanna, New York. Designated a basilica in 1926 by Pope Pius XI, the church is truly a masterpiece in the nobility of its lines, the splendor of its marble, and its massive solidity. With great pride, the chorus had chosen the basilica for its forthcoming *Messiah* concert. While this beautiful and sacred space is an architectural wonder and an ecclesiastically prominent setting for Catholics in western New York, it is an acoustical disaster for anything other than repertoire in the style of Palestrina, Duruflé, or Pärt. It was the last venue I would ever have selected for a performance of baroque music. *What now?*

From then on, things went quickly downhill. How would I reconcile this ultra-resonant cathedral acoustic with a chamber orchestra playing on modern instruments, accompanying an enormous, stylistically and vocally "developing," symphonic-size chorus? I remember thinking, Who would do this? Why would *they* schedule a *Messiah* performance in a cathedral? Pragmatist first, teacher second, and musicologist third, I thought I needed to find a technically manageable and artistically viable solution to these daunting challenges. *What would you do?*

Remembering Handel

First, I went back to Handel's life. I remembered that Handel had once performed in such an acoustic and had felt that it had been a positive, spiritual part of the music-making experience. Handel participated in about two dozen performances of *Messiah* during his lifetime and tinkered with it constantly, adding, cutting, rewriting, and transposing according to his taste and the needs of each performance. *So far, so good, I thought.*

Recalling performances of *Messiah* with the Chicago Symphony Chorus and Orchestra during the astounding Solti–Hillis era, I was reminded of the colossal staging of *Messiah* at Westminster Abbey in 1784, with hundreds of singers and instrumentalists. Though this was an extreme example, Handel's narrative account of prophecy, passion, and promise was presented in large-scale, festival-style performances well into the twentieth century.

Traditionally, musical authenticity is associated with historical correctness, manifested in performances that are conceived in relation to the "original context." But what about the lessons of Socrates, who defined authenticity as being true to oneself, being genuine in thought and action? What about *real* people singing *real* music? Somewhere between the unsustainable position of authenticity as period instruments, no vibrato and obedience to a set of rules, and the notion of authenticity as a dynamic form of sincerity, truth, innovation, and change, each one of us can and must find what constitutes a "truthful" musical experience. Regardless of how deeply we may appreciate the original context of the works we perform and the rules we have memorized, we face the realities of what world music scholars call "recontextualization": our communities and our world are different and have different needs.

Most conductors and choral teachers have found themselves in what we might call an "unsustainable position" – a situation in which they have made performance decisions based on their knowledge of period, instrumentation, ornamentation, and other traditional choices, then found to their great surprise and bewilderment that these decisions were not understood or embraced by their choruses or audiences. These cases, like the personal story that follows, illuminate a crossroads between our respect for tradition and the real-life constraints of our institutions and social circumstances.

Performance parameters

As I pondered our *Messiah* performance options (venue change was non-negotiable), I also remembered the graduate seminar I had taught the previous year. I had asked my conducting students to consider this question: "*Given your knowledge of performance practices associated with the repertoire of Bach and Handel, how would you approach the performance of this repertoire as the music director of a large community chorus?*" Some students answered that they would create an "auditioned chamber choir" from the larger choir, using only a small percentage of the membership. Others suggested that they would include the entire membership and perform a version with large forces on a nineteenth-century scale. Still others argued that they would not consider programming baroque repertoire without a chamber choir of professional singers and an orchestra of early instruments.

We continued our discussion of this problem from the various perspectives of musicology and music education. The question broadened to, "*How can conductors create stylistic, informed performances that are true to the values of diversity, inclusion, and community service while at the same time recognizing the values of historical performance practice, current research, and compositional integrity?*"

Education and experience played a significant role in the way each graduate student addressed the questions. Students who came to conducting studies from backgrounds in music education and composition answered differently from those with backgrounds in musicology and applied performance studies. Together, we examined everyone's ideas and created an elaborate epistemology of performance options based on contrasting sets of missions, values, and conditions.

The performance options comprised a mosaic of possibilities from strict adherence to historical ("informed") performance practices, to what we called modern (but "informed") performance practices. Each set of solutions was "informed" by different criteria that included cultural, social, and educational considerations that are an important part of the human experience called music making. What seemed authentic for one choir – that is, true to the values, conditions, and resources of that ensemble – was not so for other choirs. The themes of social responsibility and cultural context played a significant and recurring role in these discussions.

A case of authentocracy

The term "authentocracy" has been used to denote the negative effect that an unyielding insistence on authenticity can have on endeavors, be they musical,[7] spiritual, or material. My *Messiah* experience was to give me an object lesson in its meaning.

Confident conductor and radical optimist that I am, concerto style came to mind as a practical, "informed" solution to the performance of *Messiah* by a large, untrained symphony chorus accompanied by a small chamber orchestra in a huge cathedral. I was determined that the chorus should have what I considered to be a more "authentic" experience of Handel, one that honored this beloved oratorio with reasonable technical accuracy and stylistic integrity. Pleased with my innovative solution to the problem of style and "authenticity," I embarked on a detailed plan of singing assignments for chamber and tutti choirs.

As I began rehearsing in this manner, I saw smiles turn into frowns and enthusiasm turn into question marks. At first, I thought the challenges of learning to sing in a rhythmic, dancelike manner were beyond the technical capabilities of the chorus. So, I taught them more vocal techniques. Gradually, the atmosphere became hostile and I had absolutely no idea why the singers were so upset. In an uneasy discussion with the board president, I found out that the chorus members were upset that they were not all singing all the *Messiah* choruses, as they had done before. I thought, "They'll get over it. When they hear how brilliantly *Messiah* will sound with the benefit of clear articulations and an in-tune, well-balanced ensemble, they'll love it." *Whoops, wrong again.*

The chorus as a whole did not "love it." They told me so in many different ways, including not-so-nice written messages that suggested I was "dividing" instead of "unifying" them. This was a painful lesson indeed for someone who prides herself on high-quality musicianship and good teaching. As in all crises, however, there were important lessons to be learned.

What was the right thing to do? As the chorus grew frustrated and unhappy with their concerto-style assignments, I began to question the concept of musicianship that I had conceived: of performance as a form of *procedural knowledge.*[8] Neither the aesthetic theory of *music as knowing* nor the praxial philosophy of *music as doing* seemed sufficient for the challenges I faced.[9] And neither theoretical construct helped my choristers enjoy their *Messiah* performance experience.

Contemplating the social implications of my "failed" plan, I began to investigate the subject of music and ethics. Wayne Bowman's seminal work on this subject posits the notion that musicianship is concerned ultimately with following a moral course of action that is "right" and "just" in a given situation.[10] Closely related to the development of character and identity, this ethical way of being musical, known as "ethical discernment," requires that conductors give up attachments to generalized knowledge and do the right thing at the right time.[11] This work resonated with me and came to serve as the philosophical foundation for my concept of "engaged musicianship."

Engaged musicianship

The notion of engaged musicianship is profoundly different from the concepts of musicianship that have been addressed in the philosophical literature over the past four decades. *Engaged musicianship* extends beyond the aesthetic view, a disengaged, intellectually oriented notion of music separate from personal, social, or moral considerations.[12] It also extends beyond the more recently formulated praxial philosophy of music related to musicianship as a form of musical knowing or thinking-in-action.[13]

In the end, both the aesthetic and praxial views posited in current music education philosophy are based on standards related to rational and intellectual clarity, patriarchal assumptions that have guided our practices in choral music for too long. Historically, the starting point of our work as choral conductors in the Western tradition has been limited to *reason* – reason construed, rather narrowly, as the work of logic and intellect.[14] With few exceptions, conductors and choral teachers today perform our canon of repertoire according to the rules closely aligned with a nineteenth-century, Western European aesthetic. *Is this a problem?*

The "rules" for the performance of music from earlier times often seem to have acquired a life of their own, as if anything other than meticulous obedience renders a performance invalid. But all too often the rules we apply are separated from the social and ethical considerations situated in the reality of our own uniquely formed communities. Generalized knowledge that is separated from particular or "situated" circumstance is often dangerous. I learned this lesson the hard way through my *Messiah* experience. While it may be logically correct or technically accurate to apply a set of historically driven rules in a given situation, it may not always be *right*. The question is, *if it is not right or ethical in a given circumstance, can it be authentic?*

What is not *the right thing?* As already noted, in the personal narrative related to finding the "right way" to perform Handel's *Messiah* in a reverberant basilica acoustic with 130 untrained singers, I made my way experientially through a minefield of possible performance options. With some confidence that a concerto-style approach might work, I decided to divide the chorus in two. The small chamber chorus of more skillful singers would sing the florid, fast-moving coloratura sections, while the larger, less-skillful singers would sing the sections doubled by the tutti orchestra. While this practice is rarely followed in modern performances of *Messiah*, I thought it might be a practical solution that would help both the singers and listeners to hear structurally. At the same time, I thought it would buy me time to teach the larger chorus the vocal techniques related to baroque articulations and phrasing while assuring that the more skillful singers in the chamber chorus could successfully articulate the phrases in the reverberant performance acoustic.

With some pride at having figured out what I thought was a meaningful solution to the problem, I truly believed my decision to use a chamber/tutti approach in our *Messiah* concert was made in the best interest of my chorus. I thought the singers would grow musically to appreciate baroque style and interpretation as part of their growing musicianship. I admit that I was equally concerned that this well-known and beloved masterpiece be heard as clearly and stylistically as possible in an impossible acoustic. *Why did all hell break loose? Is what seems "right" musically, sometimes different from what is ethical socially?*

The concept of "ethical discernment," of doing the *right thing*, at the *right time* with the *right intent*, is a very difficult proposition. As Aristotle concedes, it "is not for every person, nor is it easy."[15] Many things can go wrong when one is in a situation like that I faced in performing *Messiah*, and while I thought I had made the "right" decision as a conductor and as an educator of singers, I did not take into account one particularly relevant factor: the perspectives or previous concert experiences of the singers – *their own* "historical performances" of *Messiah* in which they all stood, singing together as "one voice," for decades before I took the podium as their director.

An interview with myself

What did I forget? As a conductor, was I engaged with the music? Yes. As a teacher, did I skillfully rehearse the "rules" related to baroque performance practices and seek historically, stylistically, and pedagogically appropriate means to deal with a difficult acoustic and a chorus of unskilled singers? *Yes.* As the kind of conductor who considers herself an ethical agent in relation to music and musicians, was I sufficiently *engaged* with the singers themselves? *Probably not.* The truth is that I was so concerned with teaching in a way that I thought would empower my singers' *musicianship* that I missed the opportunity to exercise the sorely needed personal sensitivity and social responsibility incumbent on the leader of the human institution called a "chorus."

Nel Noddings's work related to the ethics of empathy would have been an ideal source of help. Had I considered Noddings's work on the "pedagogy of caring" I might have handled this situation differently:

> As we listen to our students, we gain their trust and, in an on-going relation of care and trust, it is more likely that students will accept what we try to teach. They will not see our efforts as "interference" but, rather, as cooperative work proceeding from the integrity of the relationship.[16]

Wayne Bowman suggests that as musicians interested in the education of our singers, we are *not* concerned *exclusively* with developing musicianship. We are necessarily concerned, at least in part, with people and the quality of their musical experiences.[17] While I knew the history of performance style, I didn't know the history of this particular chorus – those persons who made up this large and human body of loyal amateur singers with a long history of performing *Messiah* together. These folks loved *their Messiah – their tradition* of over seventy years. And while the chorus members understood the concept of concerto style intellectually, they rejected it emotionally.

What is the solution? Conducting *Messiah*, or any other work, with chorus is not just about the choice of musical edition, the careful crafting of rehearsals, or the employment of creative performance practices. The practice of *engaged musicianship* extends beyond these important considerations to include ethically driven and socially responsible leadership. Engaged musicians are adept at responding to changing circumstances, including those that might be unpredictable. Continuous and ongoing adjustment is a fundamental requirement.

Our work as conductors requires using skillful listening in rehearsal interactions to change and adjust musical tone, phrasing, articulation, and intonation. But do we listen deeply to our singers as people? Are we using our "listening ears" only, or are we exercising our "listening hearts" as well? Do we work in partnership with our ensemble members and in a cooperative and caring manner when problem solving is required?

Engaged musicianship embodies awareness and is a way of being fully present to a particular set of circumstances. It is thus a social endeavor, guided by concern for right action with and toward Self and Other. This form of musicianship requires openness and attributes such as receptivity, cooperation, and respect. Our work as conductors, then, is as socially situated as it is musically defined. Do we problem-solve in rehearsal and give guidance respectfully even when we have repeated ourselves relentlessly? Do we view these instructions as musical empowerment for future adaptation, or as rules to be memorized on the spot? Do we work toward long-term musicianship or are we more interested in a short-term fix?

Engaged musicianship is also a matter of caring for others that goes beyond the technical and the factual. As a form of ethical behavior, our work with choirs is a manifestation of personal authenticity that extends beyond the aesthetic realm into a form of musical performance that often transcends virtuosity or technical achievement to make a difference in people's lives.

After three years in my position in western New York, I find that some choristers still recall our concerto-style *Messiah* performance with chamber and tutti sections as a form of personal discrimination and social inequity. Although I made these choices as a "teaching opportunity," I realize that I permitted my desire for technical excellence to trump personal caring. I like to think back on this experience and the choices I made as a "nineteenth-century aesthetic hangover" – a way of thinking that lingers from my early addiction to aesthetic theories of music and music education.

Francis Sparshott writes, "Some things must be worth doing for their own sake; musical excellence is then the only proper justification for learning to do them."[18] But while musical excellence may be the "proper justification" for musical performance, excellence goes hand in hand with social responsibility and personal sensitivity – an ethically driven form of musicianship that attends to what matters most in a particular context. The essence of this theme concerns the conductor's ability to work co-operatively with her ensembles as co-creators, and in musical collaboration. Wayne Bowman articulates this succinctly:

> Excellence is at once elusive and the whole point of music, facts which necessitate that musical fluency go hand-in-hand with the development of responsibility and response-ability: a keenly intuitive "ear" for what matters in the particular musical practice at hand.[19]

Engaged musicianship then benefits "Self" and "Other" through collaborative leadership that regards the entire community of those engaged and
committed to the music. It is not only about what the conductor knows or,
for that matter, a particular set of skills. Musical success is "bound closely
to who one is, such that one's musical accomplishments and shortcomings
are inevitably and unavoidably manifestations or reflections of one's
character."[20]

What I know for sure

Remembering the haunting words of the Nigerian-born novelist Ben Okri,
who reminds us that "certainty is the enemy of creativity," this Chicago
girl reads Oprah Winfrey's monthly column "What I Know for Sure" in
The Oprah Magazine.[21] In spite of Okri's warning about certainty, I find
Oprah's journalistic initiatives affirming and entertaining. Plus, I enjoy the
easy reading that manifests feminine energy, pure and simple.

    What I know for sure is that *everything changes*. The Zen Buddhist
philosophy of "not-knowing" (known also as "beginner's mind") calls this
phenomenon "impermanence." Whatever it is called, change is a sure
thing. Years ago, gospel music was the music of my "south side" friends.
Maybe this is another Chicago "thing," but the gospel music tradition has
been an important part of my life since my schooldays singing with the
Chicago All-City High School Chorus. Gospel music, of course, has been
at the forefront of Chicago life since it first began at the Pilgrim Baptist
Church. It received its name in the 1930s from Thomas Dorsey, the blues
pianist and composer who helped to blend church spirituals with the fiery
power of rhythm and blues.

    The all-city chorus consisted of both "north side" and "south side"
students who met together on Saturday mornings – "choral keeners" as we
were called. We performed a broad spectrum of music, often with the
Chicago Symphony Orchestra in Chicago's Orchestra Hall. Our repertoire
ranged from Samuel Barber to Anton Bruckner to the blues. Gospel music
was standard fare. Despite my "whiteness," I absorbed everything about
gospel singing, and I enjoyed the assurances of my childhood friends who
told me I didn't have to be "black" to sing in the Chicago gospel tradition.
This early experience, however, did not prepare me for yet another
surprise in my first year as the new director of the large symphonic chorus
in western New York.

Messiah: a postmodern perspective

At a post-concert party following our sold-out concert of Messiah, a
member of my symphonic chorus, smiling with enthusiasm, presented

me with a CD along with a confident "you'll love it!" Being new to the
region, I had been lamenting how surprisingly "all white" the audience was
in a city where nearly sixty percent of the population was African-
American. This chorister took up my social challenge and told me I
could keep her recording over the holidays.

The CD was a gospel version of *Messiah* with a cover note written by
the recording's executive producer saying, "I'd like to thank George
[Handel] for writing such wonderful music, and God for inspiring him
(and now us)."[22] Delighted, but musically doubtful, I listened to the
recording to find with surprise that this soulful celebration of Handel's
Messiah was both moving and brilliantly crafted; it thoroughly engaged
me with its imaginative adaptations, skillful improvisations, and spiri-
tually inspired singing.

I shared this soulful *Messiah* with many fellow musicians over the
holidays, during which, in Toronto alone, more than fifteen concerts of
Handel's *Messiah* were performed. We agreed that we were fortunate to
live in a culture where a favorite musical masterpiece could be presented in
a broad spectrum of styles and interpretations. These *Messiahs* included a
plethora of versions, from strict historically conceived interpretations, to
stylistically articulated performances on modern instruments, to massive
presentations with hundreds of happy amateurs and a church organ. Add
to this an assortment of adaptations, including our postmodern gospel
arrangement, and you have what could justifiably be called a dynamic
tradition!

Summary and conclusions

In this chapter I have suggested that our profession needs a "fresh vision"
of what constitutes authenticity. On one hand, this vision must grow out
of a deep appreciation and respect for the traditions and practices of times
past. Of equal importance, as Nikolaus Harnoncourt suggested, is a
"diversity of perspectives" that must also include a deep commitment to
contemporary culture.

Authenticity in choral music involves a continuum of properties that
moves from something made in the traditional or original way, to something made of genuine thought and action. The latter concept involves
personal qualities of character and personality, suggesting that what we do
in conducting and teaching choral music is always contingent and never
separate from the invisible, internal skills and qualities of adaptability,
cooperation, receptivity, and respect.

From the Harvard University studies on the relationship between
excellence and ethics, to recent accounts of feminine wisdom in choral
music, there is a growing interest in "good work," defined in a dual sense as

work that is both excellent in quality and socially responsible. This chapter recommends the development of conducting education programs in choral music that link the teaching of visible, "external" skills and realms of knowledge such as analysis, musicology, conducting, and pedagogy, with the teaching of invisible, "internal" skills developed through reflective practices and the contemplative arts.

Engaged musicianship is a twenty-first-century extension of traditional musical excellence that includes ethically driven and socially responsible leadership, the ability of a conductor or choral teacher to make ongoing adjustments as required by the music in relation to human circumstances. The social and ethical qualities of service and caring are closely linked to this form of musicianship, in which a collaborative leadership considers the entire community of those engaged in the music. The astounding realization that both our musical accomplishments and our musical short-comings are manifestations of our personal character is strong support for the initiation of change and innovation in conductor education programs. The belief that *"we are the music we make"* is a strong invitation for curriculum renewal.

Linking the performing and contemplative arts in the education of conductors and choral teachers can prepare the next generation of dynamic music professionals to cope with the shifting grounds of our societies. Contemplative forms of engagement go beyond the benefits of stress release or energy renewal toward the facilitation of new ideas, novel solutions, and enhanced musical perspectives that are and will be required of twenty-first-century musicians and teachers.

Engaged musicianship as the study and performance of choral music in relation to the wider world diverges from the traditional Western European concept of music described earlier as "aesthetic contemplation." To conduct and teach choral music decontextualized from moral obliga-tion and social responsibility is no longer a viable option in contemporary culture. Leadership of any kind unrelated to the suffering and challenges of the world around us cannot be ignored because we are "artists."

Referencing the pioneering work of Elaine Brown, the founder of Philadelphia's Singing City, Kathy Saltzman Romey and her fellow authors suggest that our work as conductors can be a vehicle for social inquiry and change as a way "to celebrate the human voice and its power to educate, enrich, unite, and inspire."[23] Conductors and choral teachers aware of their potential to aid in the transformation of their communities and to play a more active role in twenty-first-century society are engaged in this musical form of social responsibility.

The American conductor Leonard Bernstein issued a social challenge when he wrote that our "reply to violence" should be "to make music more intensely, more beautifully, more devotedly than ever before."[24] I would describe Leonard Bernstein as a front-line "engaged musician," a peacemaker whose life as a composer and conductor was devoted to artistic, educational, and social change. The Bernstein legacy is an invitation for conductors and choral teachers in contemporary culture to do "good work" – work that is both excellent in quality and socially responsible.

Sensitive to the power of musical performance defined in relation to the social contexts of our respective communities, conductors and choral teachers may consider their musical mission as a mode of social action. This action starts in but extends beyond the rehearsal and concert halls: there are many examples of conductors and their choirs interacting with and changing the world today. From leading singing revolutions in the Baltic nations to free themselves from decades of Soviet occupation to undertaking socially innovative programs such as the Minnesota Chorale's Building Bridges, socially responsible conductors of our time are dedicated to using dynamic programming and education as vehicles for social engagement and dialogue relevant to contemporary society and social change through choral singing.[25]

As culture evolves, so too must our performance decisions and pedagogical practices renew themselves in order to meet the needs of the world today. We must be cautious not to impose a nineteenth-century, Western sense of authenticity upon a modern, twenty-first-century world view.

The bridge that connects historical traditions and practices with personal sensitivity and social responsibility, defined in this chapter as *ethical discernment* or *good work*, can be understood in the context of conducting and choral teaching as an inclusive and non-dualistic practice of *engaged musicianship* that integrates the visible and invisible skills of musical performance and teaching to benefit Self, Other, and the Divine.

Select bibliography

Bernstein, Leonard. *Findings*. New York: Simon and Schuster, 1982.
Bowman, Wayne. "Educating Musically," in Richard Colwell and Carol Richardson (eds.), *The New Handbook of Research on Music Teaching and Learning: A Project of the Music Educators National Conference*. Oxford University Press, 2002, pp. 63–84.
"Music as Ethical Encounter" (The Charles Leonhard Lecture, University of Illinois, April 17, 2000), *Bulletin of the Council for Research in Music Education* 151 (2001), 11–20.
Philosophical Perspectives on Music. New York: Oxford University Press, 1998.
Elliott, David. *Music Matters: A New Philosophy of Music Education*. New York: Oxford University Press, 1995.

Gardner, Howard, Mihaly Csikszentmihalyi, and William Damon. *Good Work: When Excellence and Ethics Meet*. New York: Basic Books, 2001.

Harnoncourt, Nikolaus. *Baroque Music Today: Music as Speech*. Portland, OR: Amadeus Press, 1995.

Leonard, Charles. "Music Education: Aesthetic Education." *Education* 74 (1953), 23–26.

Miller, Norman, Gail Hamilton and Mervyn Warren (producers) and various artists. *Handel's Messiah: A Soulful Celebration*. (CD) Word Entertainment B000002LUJ, 1992.

Rao, Doreen. *Circle of Sound Voice Education*. New York: Boosey and Hawkes, 2005.
    "Craft, Singing Craft, and Musical Experience: A Philosophical Study with Implications for Music Education as Aesthetic Education." PhD dissertation, Northwestern University, 1988.
    "Feminine Perspectives on Conducting and Teaching Choral Music," in Joan Conlon (ed.), *Wisdom, Wit, and Will: Women Choral Conductors on Their Art*. Chicago: GIA Publications, 2009.
    We Will Sing. New York: Boosey and Hawkes, 1993.

Reimer, Bennett. *A Philosophy of Music Education*. Englewood Cliffs: Prentice Hall, 1970.

Saltzman Romey, Kathy with Emilie Sweet, and Shekela M. Wanyama. "Building Bridges: Choruses Engaging Communities," in Joan Conlon (ed.), *Wisdom, Wit, and Will: Women Choral Conductors on Their Art*. Chicago: GIA Publications, 2009.

Schippers, Huib. *Facing the Music: Shaping Music Education from a Global Perspective*. New York: Oxford University Press, 2010.

Sparshott, Francis E. s.v. "Singing" (§ "Conceptual Aspects of Music Education") in Sadie Stanley (ed.), *The New Grove Dictionary of Music and Musicians*. London: Macmillan, 1980.

18 The making of a choir: individuality and consensus in choral singing

MIKE BREWER AND LIZ GARNETT

A fundamental question facing any choir is how best to respect the individuality of each of its singers while getting them all to work together for the good of the group as a whole. In this sense, a choir is a microcosm of human social life. The voice is the most personal and individual form of human expression – we can recognize people within seconds by the sound of their voice alone. Yet when people join their voices together in a choir they cannot assert that full individuality without disrupting the communal voice of the collective.

Within the Western art tradition, it is generally seen as the conductor's job to manage the negotiations between the needs of the group as a whole and those of its individual members. John Bertalot, for example, tells directors:

> At the beginning of a practice you have before you a collection of
> individuals. It's your job, within the first ten seconds of the practice, to weld
> them together into a choir – and a choir is a body of singers which feels a
> corporate sense of identity.[1]

Joseph Lewis, meanwhile, puts it this way:

> Team-work or what we call ensemble is more to be desired than
> outstanding voices, and the only possible way to obtain this "togetherness" is
> by the part being subservient to the whole; by each voice singing into the
> other voices, listening as well as singing, being content to be a strand in
> the rope, and not the whole rope, but all the while handing his or her
> contribution up to the conductor.[2]

These descriptions, however, tend to place the conductor outside the group, as a protagonist separate from the ensemble. They place the director in a role that acts on the ensemble without necessarily being part of it. This view makes sense inasmuch as the conductor's role is clearly different from that of the choristers. At the same time, the conductor is very much part of the performing ensemble, and one with an arguably disproportionate level of power over both its social dynamic and musical results. As such, conductors need to factor in their own impact on the singers as they consider how to balance the collective needs and responsibilities with the individual ones.

The choral contract

We can approach the question of how to negotiate these conflicting needs
through the ideas of the Enlightenment philosophers who grappled with
the same kinds of questions regarding the political organization of society.
The ideas of these seventeenth- and eighteenth-century philosophers,
known as the "contract theorists," have strong and illuminating parallels
with questions that modern choral practitioners are asking about such
things as the relationship between soloistic and blended approaches to
choral sound.[3]

Thomas Hobbes famously proposed in 1651 that life in the state of
nature was "solitary, poor, nasty, brutish, and short."[4] In a world without
social organization, all people would act entirely in their own interests,
and would be permanently in conflict. Thus he saw the creation of the state
as a social contract whereby individuals gave up some of their freedom in
exchange for mutual safety. Likewise, when we join a choir we are entering
into an agreement to lose something of ourselves in the interest of the
greater aim of creating a performing unity.

An alternative view of the natural state was the "noble savage," a term
associated with Rousseau's depiction of humans as inherently good unless
distorted by the stultifying conventions of society.[5] In the singing world,
this position is expressed as a mistrust of either choral or individual voice
teaching "methods" that shape individuals' voices into standardized molds
according to the expectations of particular genres.[6] The "natural" voice in
this view is seen as the means for people to achieve authentic personal
expression, to sing in a way that is true to themselves.

David Hume criticized both Hobbes' and Rousseau's interpretations of
the "state of nature."[7] He pointed out that no human being ever exists
entirely in a "natural" state, that we are born into social groups and rely on
them to survive. We can make a similar point about the "natural" voice.
People with untrained voices grow up hearing and joining in with the ways
of singing current in their social group – whether that is in church, in
football stadiums, or singing along to the radio. Just as our speaking voices
reveal the geography and class status of our upbringing, so our singing
voices carry the traces of the musical communities we have lived in.

The idea of the "state of nature" thus becomes a thought experiment
that helps us understand the structure of civil society (in the original
context) or the genre expectations and social norms of a particular choral
ensemble (in our current context). The contract theorists were trying to
make sense of changing forms of government as Europe shifted from
absolutist monarchies to more distributed, consensual forms of power.
The idea was developing that there should be a rational basis for

government, that you can rule more effectively when you have the consent of your populace than by arbitrary exercise of might.

In this sense, the choral conductor's role is that of the enlightened prince: a leader whose power is absolute in that he or she cannot be easily removed by those governed, but who rules according to rational principles.[8] On a day-to-day level there are few if any constitutional limits on how a director runs the rehearsals. But, just as monarchs will find they rule over a healthier and more prosperous country if they offer a degree of freedom and safety in return for their citizens' compliance with the law, so conductors will find greater artistry in performance if they offer individual singers room for personal development in return for compliance with their musical agenda.

Moreover, for all that the contract theorists and much of our contemporary culture are concerned with the rights of the individual, human beings remain social animals with a fundamental need for a sense of belonging. Indeed, modern evolutionary thought would reverse the chronology proposed by Hobbes and see individualism not as a primitive state that civilization needs to tame but as a more advanced development appearing only in the higher primates. Likewise, Maslow's classic studies of human needs see a sense of belonging as a more fundamental need than self-actualization.[9]

Even in individualistic cultures, that is, people join choirs to gain a communal experience. There are deep psychological pleasures in contributing to the development of something that no participant could make on their own, and there are specifically musical pleasures in singing with others. But still, of course, each member brings a personal relationship to the experience; we may all share a need for human connection, but we experience that need as individuals with our own personal histories. This is why even choirs with the most collectivistic ethos still need to attend to the needs of individual members, and why those with the most soloistic approach still need an awareness of group dynamic.

At a practical level, the negotiations between individual and group take place in both musical and social dimensions of a choir's activity. It would be easy for a conductor to think they only needed to focus on the musical dimension, since their primary task is to prepare and lead musical performances. But the social dimensions of a choir's activity can have an impact on their musical behavior, for either good or ill, particularly in amateur choirs where participation is driven by enthusiasm and personal commitment rather than professional obligation. Nonetheless, a professional singer who finds that their needs for a sense of belonging and individual growth are not being met is likely to look for work elsewhere. And, as we shall see later in the chapter, there are several facets of a choir's activity in which it is impossible to separate the two dimensions from one another.

Musical dimensions

Ensemble

The quality of consensus, of individuals cooperating to produce something that none of them could produce by themselves, is understood musically through the term "ensemble." In its ordinary, everyday usage, this may simply refer to synchronization – the extent to which the choir are performing at the same time. But the notion of "togetherness" clearly goes much deeper than this to encompass not just rhythmic precision, but a coordination of nuance or inflection, and a sense of shared understanding and common purpose.

This shared purpose is produced by the musical content the choir assembles to sing. A piece of music is experienced by listeners as a whole, not as an aggregation of parts; what individual singers might experience as separate lines, the audience hears as harmonies. The piece itself has a clear identity: it is individually recognizable, and has its characteristic themes or gestures that both declare its allegiance to a genre or tradition and mark it out as an entity in its own right. This musical "persona" generated by each piece binds the individual singers together into a unified ensemble, with its own identity independent from the identity of its constituent parts.[10]

Musical structures are thus choreographic, in that they regulate the patterns of vocal behavior of the participants, defining where all must act together, and where smaller groups strike off on more independent paths. In polyphonic music, for instance, the singing voice is as close as it can be to instrumental chamber music. Voice leading without conductor can create immediacy and accuracy, something which conductors can do well to employ in their wider armory of skills. When the conductor lets go and frees the active participation of the singers, the musical plot is all the more dramatic.

In purely mechanical terms every musical statement depends in the first instance on breathing. When string quartet players breathe together their bows are impelled by a physical unity of action. The mental process is more than metaphor; it is real. Similarly rhythm can be felt as a physical pulse which is already there before any sound is made. In choral terms that presents an argument for two upbeats, one preparatory and one for breathing. That simple act creates a bond between the performers which unites the sensations of breathing and rhythm, and is far more effective than counting beats.[11] The quality, speed, and weight of the conductor's beat also affect the emotional response in articulating the first note and the phrase that follows. If the conductor breathes with the beat, the kinesthetic response is direct and affirming.

In any choral group there will be a wide diversity of individuals, each with his or her own characteristic vowel coloration, articulation, and phonation. The question is therefore whether that individuality should be evened out in the interest of a homogeneous sound. There is no simple answer to this. In gospel music, for example, the individual improvised florid phrases are an important ingredient in the style, as is the case with Irish folk music. The operatic quartet represents a fine example of the different possibilities, and can be so individual as not to belong to a whole, or so honed that the individuality is lost, or, ideally perhaps, somewhere between the two.

Blend

Blend is an intriguing word, and we would suggest that there are two kinds, as maybe in coffee. There can be a bland blend which takes away the sharp tastes and produces what might be termed an ersatz choral sound, or a combination of tastes which together produces something more characterful than the individual ingredients, which is an exciting blend of their differences. There is a case to be made for the value of piquancy in musical taste.

Some choir directors aim for a sound so homogenized that it can be described as generic. Children's choirs tend to employ a breathy tone, which takes away the high harmonics of vowels and produces a sweet tone but which lacks the savor which might enhance the expressive quality of a particular song. Ensembles who specialise in Renaissance repertoire concentrate intensively on blending every vowel to enhance pitch matching, and at the same time work on natural tuning. The net result is an exciting physical sensation of vocal sound only available to larger forces (or to amateur singers) with specific training.

If blend is taken to mean a cohesion of sound, then in choral singing it can be divided into many musical aspects. Technical aspects of singing are discussed elsewhere in this volume, but it may be helpful to refer to just a few aspects of singing which are conducive to choral blend.

Posture and breathing

Good posture enhances the potential of a singer to make a blended sound, to sing legato, and to take advantage of possibilities of resonance. By good posture, we mean effective use of the body in allowing musculature to work freely and in balance, as encouraged by practices such as Alexander Technique or yoga. Despite being a natural and lifegiving activity, breathing is subject to a surprising number of theories and "methods." A simple definition involves the management of muscles which control the flow of air through the larynx, to enable the production of vowels to be consciously even and modulated in harmonic color at different dynamic levels. What is often called "support" can refer to the involvement of musculature down to the feet, and effective use of lower back and abdominal muscles.

Vowels

'Vowel' and 'Vocal' come from the same Latin root: Vox (voice), vocis. In Hispanic languages *vocal* serves for both. In a real sense, vowels are our voice. The production of vowels is the central strategic element in creating blend between singers. Every singer hears a vowel slightly differently, as asking the members of a choral section to sing a vowel in turn will clearly demonstrate. Since vowel production is in imitation of sounds heard internally, the vocal color produced will depend on a number of factors.

First, there are social aspects such as the local accent of the singer, which may or may not be the same as the that of the director whose vowels they copy. What is considered correct pronunciation varies between different regions of the world and between different choral genres. Establishing a choral consensus for vowel sounds will thus involve finding norms that make sense within the expectations both of the choir's singers and of its audiences. Sung accents tend to be moderated from spoken sounds, regardless of genre and location.

Second, there are questions of physiology. Vowel production depends on the balance between the position of jaw, lips, and tongue. Each singer uses the combinations in a different way. "Open" vowels where the tongue is low are often hard to blend, because there is a lack of high harmonics, and at the same time there may be tension caused by either excessively open jaw and tight throat, or clenched jaw, which limits the freedom of the sound. "Closed" vowels, where the tongue is higher in the middle, will produce a more focused tone which is easier to resonate in a group, and which can produce an immediate increase in blend. The danger here is that the tongue can be too far back, and will again close the throat.

Then there is blend through vowel modification, about which much has been written.[12] A simple rule of thumb is to think of harmonics as emanating from the lowest voice to reinforce the upper voices when singing in consonant harmony. The vowel with the most harmonics [i] when sung by a high soprano can be very piercing, so if modified (covered, in Classical styles) its upper partials will be diminished, and the overall effect will be of good blend. Similarly if the vowel [a] on the highest notes is moved to a [ə] it will blend with the underlying parts and the vowel difference will not be noticed. Words when sung with varyingly modified vowels in harmony will be deceptively clear.

Consonants

Consonants can be seen as almost contrary to blend, since they interrupt the vocal flow. Choir trainers often give emphasis to the percussive consonants to achieve clarity in communicating words. In an acoustic with considerable reverberation, the emphasis on clarity is an essential cohesive element. However, overemphasis on consonants interrupts the flow of vowels and thus the direction of a legato phrase, which is why a choir used to a resonant acoustic might sound a little lost in a dry concert hall. Good choral leaders ensure that choristers have an understanding of legato singing by rehearsing in dry acoustics.

There are a number of ways to reduce the interruption to flow which consonants may cause, and thus to enhance legato and blend. Labial consonants b and p, and linguals d and t are often subject to muscular tension and narrowing of the throat. If singers use only a light closing of the lips or a flick of the tongue, the air flow interruption will be minimal. G and k can be similarly lightened. In many cultures and singing styles there is an emphasis on the voiced labial and lingual consonants (m, n, l and ng) and on fricatives which can hold pitch (v, r, dz). These resonant consonants enable the vocalizing of sound to be continuous.

Tuning

The concept of harmony has informed aesthetic aspiration since Plato and Aristotle, in both metaphorical and physical senses. Consensus and unity in performance assume an agreed norm of harmonic structure, which arises in one sense from the musical culture and in another from the laws of physics. Musical scales, while dividing intervals according to long custom, nevertheless will eventually reach an octave, a doubled frequency. Therefore the common ground which the harmonic series dictates is a uniting factor, and a point of reference when reading the musical map.

In the twenty-first century, historical practice and the search for authenticity are well established, and a real debate is taking place about natural tuning in performance in the light of three hundred years of equal temperament. The keyboard has a lot to answer for in relation to expectation in choral intonation. The doyen of Swedish conductors, Eric Ericsson, employs the gentlest and highest sounds of the keyboard to enhance his choir's listening to upper partials – nothing could be more remote from English "note bashing" in the use of keyboard in rehearsal. In most a cappella choral music, harmonic language is simple enough to allow harmonic blend to rest on a tonal understanding of the relationship between harmonics.

Some simple examples at the heart of tuning are: the fifth from tonic to dominant is wider than on a keyboard; the semitone between leading note and tonic is wider than the keyboard (and the hopes of conductors) might suggest; the major third between tonic and mediant is lower than expected; and the major second from tonic to supertonic is wider than in equal temperament. All those examples are counter to the mindset of amateur conductors looking for a "bright" third or a high leading note, but paradoxically, once understood and heard, create real harmony in both senses. Harmonic tuning comes into its own at periods of rest, and is at the heart of every cadence.

Blending by position

The idea of improving a choir's blend by changing the position of the singers has been explored both through trial-and-error approaches and by controlled experiments in the laboratory. American choral pedagogy has a tradition of classifying and placing voices by timbre under labels such as "flute" and "reed,"[13] whilst empirical work has looked at how spacing and different approaches to vocal production interact with the placement of singers.[14] Conclusions from these studies are as yet somewhat mixed, but they are very useful for challenging assumptions about ways of doing things – which usually simply reflect the limits of experience available in our personal musical backgrounds. Different musical textures will also need different approaches. Homophonic music benefits from mixing up the singers so that each is placed next to those singing other parts, while music that dramatizes the juxtaposition of different lines or bodies of sound (polyphonic or antiphonal textures) benefits from keeping the parts spatially distinct.

Interpretation/expression

Interpretation is often seen to be the conductor's job alone. The choir is cast in the role of the conductor's "instrument," to be acted upon by the musical will of the conductor. The resulting rehearsal techniques focus on efficiency and precision, and operate at a largely concrete level. However, if we argue that the emotional dimension is central to musical expression, and at the heart of the solo performance, be it protest song, love song, war chant, tragic theatrical moment, or grand operatic aria, then to eliminate that dimension from the learning process in choral singing seems strange and arbitrary. So it can be argued that every singer in a chorus can contribute a personal emotional involvement, which bypasses learned technique, and taps into something more primal.

Expression of emotion is not necessarily a natural thing. For most singers it needs initially to be acted out. Most choristers think of themselves as a small cog in a big wheel (apart, of course, from the exhibitionists – but see below). It is a valuable tool in creating choral expression for singers to put themselves in the position of actors, putting on a character for the purpose. It is helpful to think of that character as larger than life, happier than life and to be communicating to the audience as if one to one. So an individual in a choir contributes something very specific and important to the whole.

The rehearsal techniques a director employs as a matter of course can encourage or discourage singers from engaging imaginatively with the musical content. Literal instructions and drill demand little beyond obedience, whereas approaches that ask the choir to think about the music and their response to it more reflectively produce both greater personal satisfaction and more artistic nuance.

Instead of telling the choir to sing loudly or softly, for instance, a director can ask them to work out what the dynamic level should be – whether from the composer's markings or from the shape and interaction of the vocal lines. Replacing words for expression that work in a single dimension ("loud" or "quiet") with words that require more interpretation ("triumphant" or "wistful") can help singers connect the technical act of singing with the meaning of the text. Using metaphors and imagery helps to build a shared concept of the music while giving each singer room to invest their own personal experience into it. And the more that individual singers are personally committed to the beauty and meanings of the music they sing, the more motivated they will be to fulfill the conductor's agenda.

It may seem paradoxical that a route to find artistic consensus is to invite each singer's subjective response. But what this does is promote commonality in the choir's level of engagement. Every choir contains a range of skill levels, so in a technical dimension there will always be some singers who are working at the extreme of what they can manage, while others coast along, needing less attention to achieve the same task. But the dimension of heartfelt performance works independently of technical skill, and thus can provide a means to develop a real unity of purpose and commitment that transcends technique.

The conductor's influence

Historically, the orchestral conductor started as someone who banged on the floor with a stick to keep the musicians in time. Bernstein in his *Mass* has the conductor as a traffic policeman. Much conducting teaching concentrates on this aspect of control of music; both textbooks and conducting courses, for instance, are typically structured around the systematic mastery of beat patterns.

Clarity is of course important. Indeed, if a choir has problems with synchronization, this is almost always the result of mixed messages from the conductor. If the wrist arrives at the downbeat before the fingertips, you will hear some singers coordinating the start of the bar with one, and the rest with the other. It is likewise easy for conductors to mouth the words fractionally out of time with the directions they are giving with their hands. Unanimity in rhythm thus relies on the director having both clarity of purpose in his or her concept of the music and the discipline to remove all extraneous gestures or mannerisms that might muddy the singers' view of it.

Of course, the conductor's effect on the choir goes beyond simply coordinating the performance so they sing together: the conductor communicates expressive qualities of phrasing, shaping and color at a deeply intuitive level. Many instruction manuals tell student conductors to study the score until they "become the music itself," and the reason for this is that a choir will respond to what their conductor's attention is focused upon.[15] Conductors who are worried about getting their beat patterns right will elicit a much more functional and mechanical performance than those who are deeply immersed in the flow of the music.

This kinesthetic relationship between conductor and singers can be observed when different conductors direct the same choir: the change of conductor changes their sound instantly.[16] The creation of the sound is subtle, and can be specified. Conducting with hands at face level may produce exciting high harmonics in the sound, and clear articulation and expression, but the breathing is likely to be shallow and the lower harmonics weaker. Conducting with a beat focused at waist height may well produce a rich and dark sound, and a grounded articulation and breathing, but a negative impact is likely to be the absence of gentler, more ethereal colors. Conducting with a square, clear beat is likely to produce good articulation but lack a sense of legato and of long musical lines. An exciting element is that of sculpting the sound with the hand. William Ehmann compares the act of conducting a choir with the work of a glassblower shaping and forming liquid glass, a metaphor that encompasses both the exercise of artistic intention and a careful responsiveness to the material the artist works with.[17]

It follows that conductors have it in their power to reinforce or undermine their work on blend by the way they direct. This is true both at the level of basic technique – singers will involuntarily mimic the stance and breath patterns of their conductor – and at the more refined levels of the detail of blend – if you can hone the sound by changing your hand shape, you can distort it by the same method. This is why directors should think of themselves as part of the ensemble rather than as separate from it, since the only way to solve these problems is to think of all the performers working as one organic whole. Otherwise it is depressingly easy to spend rehearsals correcting faults verbally that have arisen in response to the conducting gesture itself.[18]

Social dimensions

Amateur choral groups are a form of serious leisure in which people need to have a sense of growth or progress in order to maintain their commitment.[19] This "career" does not, however, have to be articulated through the primary musical activity in order to be valid. Individuals can contribute in many different ways, including team or committee membership, leadership of a section of the choir, music copy production, or even refreshment preparation. Those who are under-confident musically may find an organizational role that gives them scope to feel they are making a valuable and distinctive contribution.

As each individual brings their experience and needs to the choir, however, strong norms of behavior emerge within the group. John Bertalot asks:

> Do the choir put their robes away neatly? Is the vestry tidy after services, or do you, as choir director, have to tidy up when your choir have left? Once you begin to do this for them, they will let you.[20]

Choirs develop shared social habits very easily. Social validation is one of the strongest influences on people's behavior – that is, people look to see how other people are behaving to help them decide what they should do.[21] Social psychologists have named this the "chameleon effect," and shown how people join in with each other's behavior without even noticing that they are doing so.[22] This is how a choir can feel like the "same" choir over many years, even though the actual singers involved may have changed several times. This is a power that can work with either positive or negative results.

The downside of social validation is that it can be very difficult to change bad habits. If new choir members arrive at the published start time of their first rehearsal and see people continuing to arrive for the next twenty minutes, they are likely to arrive late every subsequent week. If they observe that most of the choir choose to finish their coffee before coming back after a break even when the director is ready to go on, they too will amble back into rehearsal in their own time. Telling people what the expected norms are is virtually useless if they can observe other people disregarding them – people believe what they see, not what they are told. There is a direct parallel here with the behavior of the conductor towards the choir. An instruction to sit up from a leader with poor posture is as ineffectual as a shouting instruction to sing pianissimo.

The same dynamic, though, provides the means to maintain productive habits. In the National Youth Choir of Great Britain, for example, a tradition has developed over many years of creating norms of behavior which are non-confrontational. For instance, the "five minute rule" requires singers to be in position to sing five minutes before the rehearsal or meeting time. During the five minutes, seating changes can be effected and general information disseminated, so that the rehearsal, which starts with a downbeat at the stated time, ends at the stated time with music instead of talk. The choristers are also divided into "family" groups, mixing ages and experience in the choir. "Parents" are responsible for leading teams in social activities, helping with pastoral matters, and administering tour bus arrangements within the small groups. Musical matters are in the hands of student section leaders, including note learning, rehearsal concentration, and concert deportment. All choristers sign a contract signifying their agreement to conform to modes of conduct with regard to antisocial behavior in all its forms. Consequently, the director rarely needs to assert autocratic authority, and when he does, it can be done in meetings of heads of sections and "families."

The chameleon effect is also the means by which choirs maintain many of their musical habits, from approaches to voice production to the characteristic stance and body language of their style. Musical notation, however detailed, omits a lot of information about *how* to perform the music – the inflection, the nuances, the tone colors – and this information is instead stored in the performing traditions of musical communities. People who sing together start to look more like each other, as they pick up a shared stance for singing, and shared facial expressions. They also start to sound more alike, since the shared ways of holding the body will result in shared ways of using the voice.

This shows how the factors in balance between individual and group may not be purely musical or purely social. Forceful or timid personalities can reveal themselves by the way they sing, while different musical and vocal skill sets can spill over into choir politics. We shall look at these mixed dimensions next.

Socio-musical dimensions

It is in those places where the musical and the social dimensions of choral life mesh most inextricably that the balance between individual and group is experienced at its most deeply human level. The social identities of both the choir as a whole and its constituent singers are experienced through their musical activities, while their identities as musical participants provides the shared common ground for their social interactions. This affects how people learn, how they interact together, and the values they share.

Learning styles

One important aspect in creating consensus is a recognition of a wide range of learning skills among the choir. There are a number of different educational models to describe these, some of which consider the primary sense people use to process information, others focusing more on different types of intelligence.[23] For a choral context, it may be helpful to identify them in terms of memory processes, since so much of choral rehearsal concerns how people absorb and retain music.

There is an interesting polarity between the dominant areas of different choral styles. Where a group specializes in predominantly oral traditions such as gospel, memory relies on repetition of musical phrases and a building up of harmony as appropriate to the style. This may be combined with kinesthetic, or tactile learning by integrating rhythmic movements with the musical content. At the other extreme, the professional chorister may use short-term visual recognition to perform a piece on minimal rehearsal. Indeed, even after recording sessions, professionals can experience some difficulty in remembering what they have just sung.

The learning process will always contain a number of memory skills used in a range of proportions. Visual memory can include the ability to recall whole pages of text or musical score. For most, even with limited sight-reading skills, memory serves as a reminder of sounds recalled from previous singing of a particular phrase. The learning process therefore combines visual with auditory memory, or what the Kodaly approach calls inner hearing.

Aural memory ranges from absolute pitch awareness to the phenomenon of what tends to be called tone deafness, or the inability to recall and reproduce musical pitches. At both extremes, performance will be greatly improved by practice. In rehearsal it is both helpful and fun to rehearse without instrumental help. A group of singers invited to sing a new piece will tend to find the right pitch after a few rehearsals. This achievement encapsulates an interesting partnership between aural and kinesthetic memory; it is partly our ears and partly our motor memory that enable our muscles to reproduce a sound made on a previous occasion. In helping singers with pitch retention difficulties it is important to begin with pitches that their muscles predispose them to produce. Using glissandi the musculature can be trained to change pitch incrementally. The awareness of definite pitch and intervals will follow. So the person in the choir can be helped to sing in tune by a combination of voice production and aural awareness.

Factual memory is important at many levels. It is helpful for a conductor to give background information about a piece to be sung. Some do so at the outset, giving a frame of reference, while others use a more inductive approach, involving the choristers in discussion about the emotional content or the purpose of a piece. Factual learning also embraces musical knowledge, from the basics of reading music, via interpretative instruction on the page, to an understanding of scales and chords in creating musical sentences, words rather than letters.

Learning is greatly enhanced by variation in the form of memory skills employed. Repeating a phrase in exactly the same way will show diminishing returns, while separation into its component parts will keep the brain active and aid the learning process. For example a phrase clapped, danced, chanted, and sung without words registers in different parts of the brain but will be processed simultaneously. This provides a dynamic example of individuality combining towards consensus.

Personality profiles

Different skill levels within the group will combine with personality types to have significant effects on individuals' confidence in performance and in their social interactions. One way to use these differences productively to support rather than undermine the contributions individuals make to the whole is to turn them into specific roles within the ensemble.

Disruptive or overbearing members of the group are often venting frustrations which may come from different areas of their lives, and channeling their energy can be very valuable. If given the attention they seek in the form of responsibility for others, choral poachers quickly become gamekeepers. The diva whose voice does not blend and who may express superiority through aloofness or arrogance can be given the responsibility to help less confident neighbors, and to blend with them. Confident readers of music who become bored as others catch up can be given section leading roles, and be responsible for ensuring that a small group knows the notes. Shy and reluctant members can be placed next to confident ones, and become partners in producing the music – blending by placement can be applied to personality as well as voice types. Leadership skills can be utilized in every area, whether musical or organizational. As in sport, consensus comes from teamwork and a feeling of being needed as part of a whole. A visiting conductor who may meet a choir for only one or two rehearsals is unable to make relationships with individuals, but for the regular incumbent an acquaintance with individuals is an invaluable resource.

Ethos

Some of the most successful strategies for balancing the imperatives for choral unity and individual expression are those that focus not on the group itself, but on some shared purpose or ideal to which all can contribute. The most obvious example is of faith choirs, in which the enforcement of both musical and behavioral requirements can be justified in terms not only of the good of the choir, but for the sake of the whole faith community. Secular choirs find other ideals to share: a commitment to the composer's intentions, a connection with musical style, or the desire to reach out to their audience.

The key element that determines the success of a choir ethos for gaining consensus and motivating choristers is that it should be something that is a good in its own right, and thus the choir members themselves can judge whether they are living up to it. Concrete goals such as competition success do not necessarily motivate, since it is beyond the control of the choir to achieve it – however carefully you prepare, another choir can always come along and produce a better performance. The choir ethos may work primarily in either the musical or the social dimension, although it is difficult to develop excellence in performance without placing musical commitments at the heart of the choir's identity.

Having a strong and explicit choir ethos or mission changes the dynamic of the choral contract. Instead of a compromise in which individuals are asked to curtail their own freedoms for the good of the whole, the choir's mission asks both the individuals and the collective to place themselves in the service of something more important than either. The conflict of interest implicit in the negotiation between the one and the many is subsumed within the wider mission.

Conclusion

The advantage of the choral contract over the social contract proposed by Enlightenment philosophers is that joining a choir is optional. You cannot opt out of the society you live in, but if you do not agree with the values held by the people you sing with, you can seek out a different group in which you feel what it demands of you is more in balance with what it offers.

This possibility is what ultimately delimits the power of the conductor. Singers are remarkably loyal to their choirs despite the tyranny of their directors, but they always retain the fundamental freedom to choose whether or not to participate. This is why conductors need to think of themselves as part of the group as they manage the negotiations between individuality and consensus. A conductor who refers to his or her choir as "we" or "us" has more power to effect change than one who refers to the choir as "they" or "them." After all, you cannot actually change somebody else's behavior, you can only build an environment in which they will choose to change it themselves.

There are well-established choral and pedagogical techniques available to turn a group of individuals into a choir – some of them we have discussed in this chapter, and others appear elsewhere in the book. But the success of these techniques depends on the diagnosis of the needs and characters of the actual people involved in any particular choir, as this drives the decision of which techniques to choose. The diagnosis, moreover, pertains not only to musical or vocal skills, but also to social background, personal motivations, and the cultural norms contained within different choral traditions. Every choir faces these questions, and, while there are multiple ways to answer them, both the musical success and the morale of the group rely on finding answers that will work for that ensemble.

Select bibliography

Bertalot, John. *How To Be a Successful Choir Director*. Stowmarket: Kevin Mayhew, 2002.

Brewer, Mike. *Fine-Tune Your Choir: The Indispensible Handbook for Choral Directors and Singers*. London: Faber, 2004.

Garnett, Liz. *Choral Conducting and the Construction of Meaning: Gesture, Voice, Identity*. Aldershot: Ashgate, 2009.

Lewis, Joseph. *Conducting without Fears: A Helpful Handbook for the Beginner; Part II: Choral and Orchestral Conducting*. London: Ascherberg, Hopwood and Crew, 1945.

19 A point of departure for rehearsal preparation and planning

ANN HOWARD JONES

It's what we do as conductors; it's where the composer and the performer search for one another; it's where our energy, creativity, skill, imagination, knowledge of the score, and understanding of the instrument (the chorus), all come fully into play. In my experience, I have found a rehearsal routine that varies only slightly from one situation to another. It begins with what I do before the first rehearsal.

The conductor's preparation

Score selection and study

The music I have chosen has to be intensely interesting to me so that I am eager to study it. When I study, I search for the music's essential features. Identification of these essentials is possible only through score analysis. The analytical procedure follows a hierarchy that starts with an overview (key, meter, voicing, form in the overall sense, text, etc.), goes next to the division of the large form (ABA, through-composed, etc.), the subdivision of each division into smaller sections, the breaking down of the subdivisions into groupings of measures, and, finally, the phrasing. All of these decisions are guided by a clear sense of harmonic, melodic, and rhythmic motion. Score analysis reveals the content of the music and guides me in shaping the rehearsal process.

Early in the preparation of the score, and as I discover phrase lengths, I insert marks to indicate breathing. Where possible, I assign rhythmic values to the breaths. All matters of phrasing are dependent on text, so the translation and correct pronunciation, with elision and International Phonetic Alphabet (IPA) symbols, should be inserted. Once I have made these decisions, the singers can transfer markings into their own scores.

Sometimes score study will reveal places in the music where balance problems can be anticipated. Certain sounds can be enhanced or diminished by simply adding or subtracting singers from one part to another. For instance, as a choral singer, my own scores were full of arrows

[272]   The author acknowledges the work of Christopher M. Walters in the preparation of this chapter.

indicating that I should shift up for a few notes to help cover a low soprano line, or down to help ease a high tenor part.

The planning of the actual rehearsal with the chorus is informed by my knowledge of the score. Before the rehearsals begin, I know whether a work can be sung from beginning to end or whether a piece will profit more from being broken down into sections. My inclination is to begin with a portion of a work that I think the singers can read relatively easily. Then I try to work on a more difficult passage, and finally, I try to end the rehearsal on a positive note. This might mean singing the ending and working backwards by sections to the beginning so that the chorus is always connecting back to something familiar. Knowing how a piece breaks down is essential. I have also determined in my study where the most difficult sections of a piece are and how best to approach them. Specific challenging material might be worked out as part of the vocalizing at the beginning of a rehearsal without actually looking at the score (difficult intervals, melismatic material, odd dissonances, etc.). Each conductor has a personal approach, of course, but as rehearsals go along, the process is additive. With each repetition and with continuing analysis, refinements of pitch, rhythm, phrasing, articulation, pronunciation, vocal color, intonation, and vowel unification all combine in pursuit of the composer's ideas.

The specifics of preparing a score for rehearsal must not be overlooked. This is a process in which we must be engaged if the rehearsals are to be productive and the time is to be spent effectively.

The rehearsal's beginnings

In the forty-five years that I have been rehearsing choirs, I have learned a lot about how singers learn, how they care for their instruments, and what literature is appropriate and healthy for them to sing. Wouldn't it be wonderful if singers would come to rehearsal ready to sing well, to execute the pitches, rhythms, and text, and to understand what they are singing about? Of course, that is not the way it usually is. Some preparation for healthy singing is helpful.

Readying the body

At the beginning of the rehearsal, we stretch, reach, bend, run in place, and anything else that will energize the singers, release tension, encourage proper alignment, and help everyone to concentrate on singing well. Because singing is a physical activity, it requires the same kind of stretching of the musculature, warming up, and adjustments to the alignment and breathing that is required of an athlete. This part of the rehearsal is about releasing tension, gathering and focusing mental energy, and enabling the singer to use the voice optimally.

Establishing the unison
Singers sing in octave unison quietly on [nu]. Usually the pitch I choose is an E natural. Next, they sing [nu] [o] [a], still quietly, moving up and down by half steps in the low and middle range of the voice. This encourages the singers to listen, to engage their minds and ears, to focus their attention, and to sing in the "sleeve of the sound," an expression of Robert Shaw's to suggest a core of sound within each section and within the chorus as a whole.

Manipulating the pitch
Next, again singing [nu] in octave unison, a pitch is slowly and incrementally raised by one half step. The singers interrupt the sound on each pulse over sixteen beats. Once the ability to change pitch almost imperceptibly is accomplished, singers are encouraged to monitor their own pitch routinely while singing, in full awareness of their ability to improve the pitch upward or downward by minute degrees at any given time. This exercise assists in developing skills in tuning.

Exploring dynamics
Singers are next asked to crescendo and decrescendo over a specified number of beats. This encourages the awareness of the full spectrum of dynamics available. I often ask singers to brighten the tone in crescendo and darken the tone in decrescendo, for example. The pitches sung are usually octave F-sharps and As. The altos and basses sing the lower pitch and the sopranos and tenors sing the higher one. I also ask the singers to begin the tone at *pianissimo*, *piano*, *mezzo forte*, and *forte* depending on what the music requires.

Developing range
Next, I work for evenness of tone throughout the range. Beginning again on E natural and singing [u], the singers move up a minor third, easing into [a] on the upper pitch. While keeping the lower pitch the same, the interval widens to a major third, perfect fourth, augmented fourth, and so on, until the minor seventh is reached. Then the exercise descends, this time by whole steps, until the major third is sung as the final interval. Singers are asked to sing quietly and to keep both [u] and [a] alike in quality and dynamic so that the [a] is not heard more loudly than [u]. Each pitch receives one beat in duration, with an extra beat between intervals

Example 19.1 Developing Range/Evenness of Tone

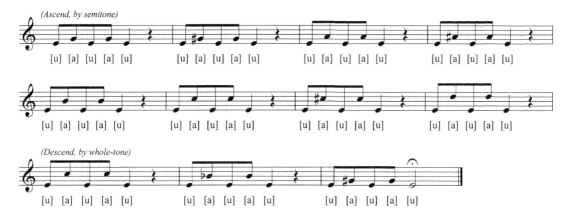

Example 19.2 Developing Range/Evenness of Tone, triple meter

for a breath and for the pianist to sound the next two pitches as appropriate. (Example 19.1)

This exercise can also be sung in triple meter, adding one full beat to the upper pitch with attention to intonation all along (Example 19.2). This allows more time for the singer to improve the intonation of the upper pitch.

Another valuable exercise is the "yawn-sigh." This exercise begins with the singer properly aligned, thinking about proper breathing, and with the oral space open, as if one is about to yawn. Then the singer sighs easily down from a high note and up from a low, while maintaining the feeling of openness. This can release tension if any has inadvertently crept in, ease the attack on a high note, and give singers the opportunity to focus on the space that the thought of a yawn creates. Throughout the sigh, the singers are able to use breath energy appropriately to explore resonance, encouraging and allowing the tone to fill the areas that the idea of a yawn opens up.

Tongue trills, lip trills and descending scales on the vowels [u] and [i] on a single pitch can also increase the singers' range and flexibility.

Defining articulations

Singers are encouraged to cultivate a beautiful, legato line as they sing vocal exercises. Therefore, I venture cautiously into the use of the same exercises to emphasize a variety of articulations. For example, while working mainly on legato singing, it is difficult for the singer to think of interrupting the tone and starting it again within a phrase. To help, I use a simple 1–3–5 arpeggio (ascending and descending, three times). I ask them to sing on [hi], quickly and staccato, with no breath between each triad. (Example 19.3)

To release the tension that can develop, I encourage bending the knees on the top note, reaching up and over the head with the arms at the top of arpeggios, or any other kind of motion to release interfering tension. A range of articulations should be explored including staccato, martellato, tenuto, and legato. If I change the 1–3–5 arpeggio to a scalar passage, remove the consonant in front of each pitch, and increase the tempo, the exercise can be useful in assisting the singer to learn to sing melismatically (Example 19.4).

Balancing the chorus

A well-planned seating arrangement with space around each singer will help facilitate good singing because the singers will be better able to monitor their own vocalism. I have found it effective to place each singer's name on a note card on each chair to indicate the seating plan for that day, that piece, or that balance. If the chorus sits SI, SII, AI, AII, TI, TII, BI and BII (from the conductor's left to right), the next-lowest or -highest voices can shift easily to the nearest part to ease balance problems. I have enjoyed rehearsing choirs in a circle. Since I am in the middle, each singer is effectively in the front row. I can therefore influence each one as might be necessary.

The majority of the conductor's work is spent studying and rehearsing. The goal is to arrive at the performance with all the work done, no loose ends left hanging, no uncertainty, and enough insight so that the composer's ideas are lifted off the page in an appropriate and compelling way. I believe this is why we rehearse.

The elements of the rehearsal

Time

Planning is essential so that the precious minutes are used effectively. Usually a few are needed for "housekeeping" (that is, announcements and instructions). Next is the all-important readying of the body and voices.

Example 19.3 Defining articulations

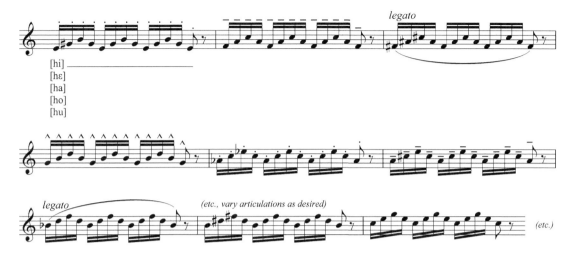

Example 19.4 Defining articulations, scalar passage

There are two useful approaches to what could happen next: the conductor can rehearse music that is new; or begin with something familiar.

More subtle considerations of time in rehearsal concern pacing. When has too much time been spent on a difficult passage, or when has all the rehearsing been at the same tempo or dynamic, or in the same style or same key? Awareness of how much time is spent on anything other than singing is also crucial. When speaking, I want to choose words carefully, modulate the pitch and tone of my voice, address problems specifically, and give positive reinforcement as much as possible. Rather than talk over the music making, it is better to stop, address the problem and then move forward.

A rehearsal that is fast-paced and challenging, with everyone occupied most of the time, is more stimulating and interesting than one that is full of gaps and wasted time. A rehearsal plan with specific amounts of time allocated for each task can be helpful.

Order

Consideration must be given to the musical quality and emotional character of a work in determining the order in which pieces are sung. A vocally taxing work needs to be followed by music that gives the singers a bit of relief. Physical or vocal exercises that release tension or reinvigorate the singers can be inserted at appropriate times.

I often overestimate the amount of music that can be covered in a single rehearsal. On the rare occasion that I need something in addition, I always have a category on my rehearsal plan called "If Time." Then if I need more material or if the plan I have made needs to be changed, I have already figured out what to do next.

Basic disciplines

Rhythm

Giving singers the responsibility for the internal subdivision is of prime importance. They are asked to divide every beat and sing these divisions on the notated pitches with text, dynamics, or articulations. The level of the division can vary. If the music moves at a fast tempo, a higher division of the beat (for instance, half notes) is often desirable. For eighth-note divisions, the singers should sing *1-and 2-and*, etcetera. Sixteenth-note divisions can be sung on *1-ee-and-uh* (1-[i]-and-[ə]), *2-ee-and-uh*, etcetera. Triple division is sung *1-and-uh, 2-and-uh, tee-and-uh*. (The syllable "tee" is substituted for the more complicated and slower "THRee"). The choice of division that will be most helpful depends on what clarifies the music the most. The counting should be delivered with a rhythmic particularity that is immediately helpful in lining up the music vertically. Robert Shaw called this "singing on the numbers" or "count singing."[1] One of Shaw's basic principles was that "the right note at the wrong time is the wrong note." The variations on the basic technique are endless. Dynamics can be overlaid and the final consonants before rests can be sounded within the counting. Almost all music can be made more precise using this technique. Music that does not lend itself to this process includes those pieces with syncopations and complicated meters, and music that is non-metric to start with. The technique should not take more time to teach than it is worth. Some reject "count singing" because it seems too mechanistic or stiff. I have rarely found this to be true. As a device for clarifying the rhythm, making it more precise, lining up the text, and rhythmicizing consonants and breathing, it is very effective.

Pitch

Music can be effectively rehearsed without pitch to emphasize the placement of syllables in complicated texts, for example. An exercise I often use is to assign the pitch E to the basses, G-sharp to the tenors, D to the altos and F-sharp to the sopranos. Each voice chants its text in rhythm, but the notated pitches are eliminated. Since pitch often falls more easily into place than rhythm, I begin with the rhythm and use it as a framework for the pitches. Singers often find themselves at the extremes of their range for an extended period of time. Because of this, singers are encouraged to employ octave transposition to protect their voices from strain. Some singers can transpose at the octave easily, while others need to be trained to sing only an occasional note of a phrase up or down an octave.

Text

The conductor must know the correct pronunciation of the words. To assist with intonation and tone quality, the vowels must be unified. Vowels are only one part of the job, however. Robert Shaw said repeatedly that we should sing every sound of every syllable. Diphthongs need audible vanishing vowels, for example, and final consonants with pitch frequently need a short and soft *schwa* [ə] for intelligibility. Subtle and sophisticated refinements are important. The ensemble's ability to rhythmically unify the text's delivery is often key to communicating clearly and to remedying issues of intonation, tone quality, and projection.

Language-specific issues that need careful attention include: double consonants and dental consonants, final consonants and their durations, the aspiration of initial consonants or glottalization of initial vowels, closed and open vowels, elision or the connection of one word to another (a famous example being the phrase "slumbers not" from "He Watching over Israel" from Mendelssohn's *Elijah*). In the end, text is the distinguishing feature of choral music. Delivering it accurately, clearly, and in an imaginative and compelling way is one of our principal charges.[2]

A problem is often encountered when shifting from count-singing to text. The pronunciation of the words can interfere with the rhythmic precision that the counting inculcated. Two principles must be constantly reinforced: the core of the vowel must be precisely on the beat, and the consonants must be fast and ahead of the beat. Singers also need to be reminded about voiced and unvoiced consonants.

Rehearsing the text without consonants can encourage a healthy singing tone and a beautiful legato line. No text can be understood, however, without carefully pronounced, projected, and rhythmically delivered consonants.

Articulation

I think of the various articulations as they relate to duration. Referring back to the exercises for the beginning of the rehearsal, I emphasize three specific kinds of articulation in addition to legato: staccato, marcato, and tenuto. It is useful to remember that all can be modified by the words *poco* or *più*. I often use *marcato e sostenuto* to suggest a strong attack followed immediately by sustained singing.

It is particularly useful for a chorus to sing in a highly rhythmic and particularized way in music that combines chorus and instruments. The singing should be more detached in general. A more refined way of thinking of it is that the singer should place the vowel on the beat and then allow it to decay slightly before the consonant or the next vowel ensues. Dotted or tied notes profit from this approach. The tone can even stop for an instant on the value of the dot or on the tie. When singing with instruments, sounds should not be as glued together as they might be when the singing is without accompaniment.

Phrasing

Score analysis gives us the basic information about phrase length and shape. Music making and interpretation are predicated upon a grasp of these structural elements. Phrasing helps with tension and release, with high and low points in the shape and, ultimately, all hinge upon the amount of breath a phrase requires. In rehearsal, cadences, key changes, repetitions, and contrasts can all be pointed out so that the ensemble sings with an informed concept of the piece's construction. Thematic and accompanimental materials can be identified and contrasted so that melodic material is in the foreground as the music is performed.

Summary

Rehearsing is not only about correct rhythm, pitch, intonation, tone quality, and diction. It is also a matter of musical rhetoric, shape, and relationships between one part and another. I can say two things with certainty: the more I know about the music, the faster and more productive the rehearsal is; and, the more I know about the music, the better teacher I am.

20 Small ensemble rehearsal techniques for choirs of all sizes

SIMON CARRINGTON

Philosophy

Can anything original really be added to the many volumes already in print containing all manner of earnest thoughts about choral rehearsal technique? Plunging into choral conducting and the teaching thereof after thirty years as a performer, I dutifully purchased various carefully selected tomes about crafting the choral rehearsal, vocal warm-ups, and the like, but soon came to the conclusion that our own ears and ideals were a more important resource.

I was fortunate to work with fine mentors and contemporaries such as Sir David Willcocks and Sir John Eliot Gardiner, and these experiences undoubtedly helped me decide my own priorities, but I am confident that there is no substitute for a steady diet of listening to the sounds and styles of choirs of all shapes and sizes while watching and evaluating their conductors. All this will help you develop your own personal palette of colors and sounds that communicate and enrich the ears, eyes, hearts, and lives of choirs, ensembles, and listeners alike.

It is an unfortunate fact that singers are generally less expert at counting and pitching than their instrumentalist colleagues. A choral conductor's duty is to instill in the singers a sense of personal responsibility and an appreciation that they can improve their ensemble skills themselves through concentration and self-discipline. Conductors should treat their singers like players, expect them to move as fast, to be as alert and fearless as a trumpet player, to count time and be as independent as a percussionist, and to pitch intervals with as good intonation as a fine string player.

I'll begin by listing my own rehearsal essentials in the hope that a few may coincide in some way with those of other conductors or help you review your own.

Essentials

Every rehearsal "technique" should contain strong elements of creative musicianship; nothing should be repeated by rote. Every twist and turn of an exercise or warm-up should be musical in some way and should add to the singers' understanding of harmony, key, phrase shape, and the power of certain lines and harmonic effects to move the spirit.

Like many of my kind I learned much of my musicianship and reading skills by being dropped into a rigorous daily routine as a small boy chorister. If I sang a wrong note, missed an entry, or came in early, I was severely admonished (a raised eyebrow from the conductor could be as devastating as a painful nudge in the ribs or a kick on the shin from my slightly older neighbor). When I arrived in the USA to begin my conducting career, I was disappointed by the levels of sight-reading and ensemble awareness, in spite of what I perceived as the efficient and pedagogically sound teaching of choral methods already received by the students. I decided to utilize the training methods of my formative years. I bought copies of the Tallis 40-part motet *Spem in alium*, and handed them out to the University of Kansas Chamber Choir. I beat a slow 4 and insisted they did all the work, counting and pitching for their lives! This remarkable piece (and any number of other polychoral pieces), rehearsed steadily with patience (but with no compromise in the form of plunking helpful notes on the piano!), remains my own choral rehearsal method book. The beautiful performance of the Tallis masterpiece under the spire of Salisbury Cathedral by those forty students from the Midwest of the USA, many of whom had never even seen the ocean before, remains the highlight of my career and proved to me that stylistic singing and musicianship can be taught by patience and determination alone and can traverse all boundaries: cultural, ethnic, and demographic.

I have continued to work around this model and always ask choir members to raise their hands to acknowledge an error as their musicianship skills develop. If I see the telltale sign I carry on without feeling the need to re-rehearse that particular passage, trusting the singers to sort out the problem themselves.

Specific techniques

It is important to imagine in your head the choral sound you wish to develop and to convey this ideal clearly and constantly to your singers.

Mine is a clear, fresh, "tall" sound with a sonic range from bright to dark, cold to warm, hard to soft. I imagine a flexible sound with a consistent intensity, and a controlled vibrato, which can range easily and swiftly from none at all to moderate – much like the vibrato of an accomplished string player.

I work consistently and persistently to develop this sound which can then become the default sound to which the choir can always return and from which we can set out afresh on each new adventure or experiment.

Beginnings

To stimulate resonance, begin rehearsals with one, two or all of the three hums ([m], [n], or [ŋ]): buzzing lips for the [m], a tingling nasal bridge for the [n], and a head full of sound with a yawning throat for the [ŋ]. Having established silence and calm breathing through the nose, give a single pitch on the keyboard or pitch-pipe (I don't believe anyone's singing voice is as pinpoint accurate or reliable as either of these instruments). Announce the name of the note and urge the singers to visualize that note on the staff as they begin. Ask for a series of specific intervals, (changing these every rehearsal), with soft glissandi between the notes to promote steady breath energy and a relaxed open throat with no bumps or clicks. Insist on plenty of flexing and stretching of the lips, chewing, gnawing, and nostril flaring throughout these exercises while expecting a perfect unison at the beginning and end of each slide.

From the hums move to the two core singing vowels [i] and [y], both of which require a focused sound, use minimum air, and need flexible lips (or "fishmouth" as this shape is often described). Think of these two vowels as the two main vowel channels – a technique I gleaned from my friend the Norwegian choral director Carl Høgset – [i ɛ e a] and [y u œ ɔ:]. With a series of melodies invented before each rehearsal containing some modest harmonic or intervallic teasers, work the singers through these two channels, ensuring that the singers maintain a fairly consistent mouth shape and just move the tongue slightly from vowel to vowel maintaining the same forward placement for all the vowels in the channel. Insist that the singers breathe in through their mouths as if through a straw or where possible through their noses, and persuade them to focus their sound as far forward as possible. At this point glissandi should be strongly discouraged, and the vocal sensation of moving from note to note should be similar to a good string player "shifting" between pitches – legato, within the same bow stroke. I also expect little or no pitch vibrato, to maintain a perfect unison and encourage consistent listening and steady breath control.

Continue to require singers to think of their sound as being centered in the sleeve of the [i] or the [y], as emerging through that sleeve or tube, and as being silver in color rather than brown. I also do not allow the vowels (and therefore the mouth) to spread sideways, and be sure to require a raised soft palate but not necessarily always a low larynx. I feel healthy vibrant singing requires a flexible larynx: sometimes low, sometimes higher, so that altos and basses can sing with brightness and elegance and don't have to sound hollow, while tenors and sopranos can sing with clean-limbed elegance at the high end of their registers without pinching and sounding thin. A male alto with a relatively high larynx can often help to bring brilliance and shimmer to a section of mezzo-sopranos.

As the voices continue to sing softly, urge ears and brains to get "louder and louder" – working harder and harder. "Big ears, small sound" is a useful mantra. Singers should be listening vertically through the harmony and horizontally towards each side of the ensemble. However much one may hope that singers do this automatically, constant but positive reminders remain essential. Insist that no one vowel be any louder or softer than its neighbor (except for sound musical reasons) to encourage the concept of line, the secret to beautiful singing. A closed [y] and a more open [a] should therefore be the same dynamic for the purpose of these exercises, which is not as straightforward as it may seem, as many singers will allow an open vowel (like [a]) to escape from the mouth louder than the so-called closed vowels surrounding it. How often does one hear small unimportant words with big vowels such as *and* emerging as the loudest event in a phrase, much like an insensitive string player allowing the use of an open string on his instrument to emerge more stridently than the fingered (or "stopped") notes surrounding it?

When the sound is established and secure, step up the aural demands, with more awkward intervals (by name not by imitation), diminished 7th arpeggios, octatonic scales, careful tuning of harmonic progressions over unison pitches, and other such devices. It is fun and invigorating to invent these exercises (perhaps based on the scores being studied) on the way to rehearsal, trying to remember the weaknesses observed previously and designing little riffs and motifs to counteract the problem patches. I would arrive in my studio, grab my rehearsal sheet for that evening and quickly notate the exercises I had conceived en route before they were forgotten.

Here are a few specimen warm-ups to demonstrate this principle: the first for consistency of tone (Example 20.1), the second for dynamic shape allied with interval security (Example 20.2), the third for tuning and enharmonics (Example 20.3). There are thousands like these of course and I urge everyone to think of their own choir's priorities, weaknesses, and needs, and to invent warm-ups specifically for each occasion. All effective warm-ups should contain a vocal technique component, an aural challenge, a dynamic shading, and an expressive quality of some kind. The IPA for the first exercise is: [i ɛ e a y u œ ɔ:].

Example 20.1 This exercise uses my two principal vowel channels the "ee" and the "ü". Encourage your singers to keep the sound forward, with a consistent color and mouth shape, and not too much jaw movement. You can certainly begin in A minor with no key signature [!], but I like to introduce key challenges whereever I can. The "aw" vowel should be the equivalent of the "o" in the word "gloria"

or anything else of a more or less challenging nature!

Example 20.2 This exercise combines a feeling for dynamic shape with a sense of key

Example 20.3 For this exercise you can choose any vowel or vowels that need work. The top line is an octatonic scale, the second teaches descending diminished 4ths and rising half steps, the third rising major 3rds and descending 5ths, and the fourth line ("bass") descending minor 6ths and ascending 4ths. The first beat of every bar is an octave unison. I suggest that all voices first sing each of the lines in unison and then put them together in harmony. The voice order below is perhaps the most practical but the parts can be exchanged at will.

Choir seating

This is very much a matter of taste but my preferred line-up formation for a chamber choir of twenty-four singers is a front row of alternating sopranos and altos and a back row of tenors and basses – also alternating. This maintains the concept of a harmonic pyramid founded on the bass line, but supports self-awareness, independence, and careful listening. I adapt this idea to choirs of all sizes and find that, even in polyphonic music, the sound is warmer, crisper, and more flexible. Even in music for one choir, dividing the choir into two, with the First Choir to the left and the Second Choir to the right of the conductor, works well. This configuration has the advantage of playing one choir against the other and thereby encouraging careful listening and evaluation by the singers themselves. However, by separating the Second Basses from the First Choir, the Firsts are deprived of the foundational harmony pitches often in the lowest bass voice. These instances may require a compromise of some kind.

The art of rhetoric – or being persuasive!

While rehearsing the essential pitches and rhythms, begin to emphasize that there should be no such thing as a "rehearsal" as such. Singers have the unique privilege of expressing text and should do so every time a phrase is sung. This leads to my top priority – rhetoric. The experience of listening to fine, disciplined choirs singing beautifully at choral conventions without ever really communicating the meaning of the text, conveying the atmosphere implied by the context, or moving listeners with the emotions being expressed has convinced me that a return to the ancient tradition of rhetoric is an essential element of the choral rehearsal process and one which I have brought to the top of my personal priority list.

In 1516 Sir Thomas More wrote in his *Utopia*:

> For all their musicke that they sing with mannes voice dothe so resemble and expresse naturall affections, the sound and tune is so applied and made agreeable to the thinge, that whether it bee a prayer, or els a dytty of gladness, of patience, of trouble, of mournynge, or of anger: the fassion of the melodye dothe so represente the meaning of the thing, that it doth wonderfullye move, stirre, pearce, and enflame the hearers myndes.[1]

The educated singers and composers of Renaissance polyphony would have enjoyed extensive study of Latin for instance and felt comfortable and confident with the stress and direction of each word and phrase. To them, what we have to study and analyze would have come naturally and without thought. They would also have studied rhetoric extensively as the main foundation of their education. The technique of using words persuasively (the best definition of the art of rhetoric, perhaps, for the non-specialist) would have been a very important part of performance practice. A sense of the expressive powers of certain intervals would also have been part of the essential training. The singers would have felt the ebb and flow of the lines naturally and understood how to communicate the changing moods implied by the texts.

With your singers:

- Study the structure of every sentence – in whatever language – in whatever period of music.
- Consider the significance of nouns and verbs beside prepositions and conjunctions.
- Consider the importance of individual adjectives and adverbs and their poetic significance.
- Have every singer mark the points of emphasis in the score.
- Consider the weight required on every syllable – some of the clumsiest word stresses often occur most in the singers' first language – familiarity breeds neglect.
- Have the singERS savOR words and names with the stresSES on the wrong sylLABles:
- Read the text aloud, questioning the stress and flow; dwell on the more powerful words and pass over the weaker.
- Don't be frightened of the diphthong where appropriate. In English, for instance, the diphthong lends much beauty to the language. Sing *light* with a gradual turn in the vowel rather than *la-eet*. On a long final chord there is nothing more touching than a choir turning a vowel naturally to round off a beautiful word – like *sound* for instance: a gradual turn to the [u] followed by a long [n] and a final [d] has audiences completely unaware of the technique but on the edge of their seats.
- Make sure that the singers understand the literal meaning of every word of a foreign text – no compromise here! Thanks to the power of the Internet, which can now provide a translation of individual words in almost any language, the all-too-familiar paraphrases provided by editors or publishers should be considered unacceptable.

Use the power of imagination to color the text

- Imagine yourself as an orator, delivering lines of text for maximum effect, appreciating the need to be as persuasive as possible.
- Consider the meaning of the emotive words and how best to depict them in sound.
- Consider how you would use the colors of your speaking voice to express frustration, anger, relief, affection, and other such variations of mood.
- Guide your singers to vary the vocal color by asking them to sing certain important pivotal chords using different tone qualities: *soft, hard*; *warm, cold*; *dark, bright*; *rich, thin* etcetera.

- Ask them to imagine their voices at different stages of their lives and to sing with an appropriate tone – to reveal quickly the palette of colors available!
- With the text as your guide and using your own judgment, suggest when they might sing with no vibrato, with a little vibrato, or with considerable vibrato!
- Likewise, guide them as to when to sing with a harder edge to the sound; with warmth; with varying degrees of air in the tone depending on the implications in the text.
  - ask for a bright focus; a medium body sound or a heavy chest tone.
  - ask for a more nasal quality; a heady quality; a reedy quality.
- Vary the "spin" of the sound to suggest the hidden meanings in the text: *calm, reflective, anticipatory, committed, intense, dramatic, melancholic, passionate, resigned.*

I like to try the technique of thinking of an opposite or a mundane concept and then releasing the proper word almost as a surprise so that nothing sounds routine to the audience. This can be carried to extremes as an exercise (*My mouth/soul doth magnify the lunch/Lord*) but the technique can be very persuasive and never fails to make the actual text more emphatic and expressive and also prevents any rehearsal becoming just a run-through! Whereas a fine orchestra can benefit from a routine rehearsal to tidy corners and settle a new or different interpretation, a choir needs to think about the interpretation of a powerful text almost every time in the manner of a fine singer of Lieder, to be sure that the singers' imagination is coloring their sound.

Rhetoric reminders

Consonants

Particularly in English and German, consonants are all different lengths.

When we speak persuasively, we taper naturally before final consonants and speak with more urgency when we repeat a phrase. We should do the same when we sing – choirs and soloists alike.

Consonants should be in the character and dynamic of the phrase. They should be clear, and neither overdone nor mannered.

The ubiquitous *s* is always audible, but softer, more liquid and voiced consonants should be relished, elongated and pitched accurately: *m, n, ng, l, ll, w, v, th, nd, mp, nt*, etc.

Vowels

Not all vowels are the same size.

Unstressed final vowels are not simply a different color, but also a different size and shape and can be given extra shading with the lips.

Place emphasis on modifying the vowel size to give a characteristic inflection to the text. There are numerous books about open and closed vowels, voice placement, and the regular use of IPA for vowel purity, but I have not yet found one that relates vowel size and word shape to give the flexibility of speech demonstrated by fine orators and actors. Listen and observe the great actor Derek Jacobi speaking the Prologue straight into the camera at the opening of Kenneth Branagh's film version of Shakespeare's *Henry V*.

Some other rehearsal disciplines

As I work so much by intuition I asked Dominick DiOrio, a member of my Yale choir and a conducting graduate, to make notes during our rehearsals. Many of the points set out in this section are the result of his invaluable help.

Text
Even when the tempo of a piece is fast, the text must still be shaped rhetorically, so the sentences make poetic sense.

Rehearsal dynamic
Rehearse passages softly to emphasize the aspect of "re-hearing" or listening. Too often singers just blast away in rehearsals without really paying attention to what's going on around them. Singing quietly enables them to notice more in the music and how their parts relate to each other.

Singing "off the voice"
Don't be afraid of this concept. Contrary to the view of certain voice teachers, singing lightly from time to time does no harm. How can the singers use their vocal mechanisms for an ever broader palette of colors? In the same way as different tones are used while speaking – for emphasis, or to express urgency, despair, delight, and any number of other emotional states – a choir makes a vast range of extra colors available by adding or subtracting the amount of air in the voice.

Spinning the tone
The idea mentioned earlier of keeping the sound "spinning" at all times is important to maintain. This is a concept which is best described with images. Encourage singers to imagine their voices spinning like frisbees or clay pigeons through the air as they sing. This helps to prevent a bland sound that lacks energy and intensity.

Problem vowels
The open [ɛ] vowel is one of the least attractive of all, particularly in the alto register. As long as space is maintained in the throat and breath is

flowing easily, advance the idea that most vowels should be considered "closed" (at least to some degree) to maintain consistency of tone. Certain voices can lose focus in different registers; conductors should listen constantly for vocal color and learn to recognize what creates a more brilliant ringing tone, encourages overtones, and helps the choral sound to carry.

Soft onsets

Phrases that begin on open vowels are a constant hazard, and techniques to avoid bumps, inaccurate pitched entries, and unwanted pop glides (coming in below pitch and gliding into place!) need constant practice. Try suggesting a deliberate [h] on the beginning of the offending word which is then gradually reduced until it is inaudible while the vocal mechanism remains the same. Vocal warm-ups of all kinds can be invented to concentrate on this issue. For soft high entries on open vowels, suggest the singers prepare on an [ŋ] with a nicely open throat (and with the appropriate vowel shape ready). They should breathe through the nose, and then drop the tongue at the last moment as the breath reverses and they sing the vowel.

Glottal stops

I use these often to express texts effectively and not only in German, where they are obligatory. A gently expressive glottal stop before the *e* of *eyes* transforms the line "Weep Oh mine eyes" – and then there's the *o* of *oh* of course!

Choices of where and where not to glottal are very personal. Try standing on stage and speaking a line to someone at the back of the hall who has never heard the text before. The more expressive the glottals, the better you'll be understood.

The expressive *w* and *y*

Work hard with your lips before *w* and with your tongue before *y*. *Weeping* and *yearning* are touching concepts and so often sound like *eeping* and *earning* in anything larger than a small, dry rehearsal room.

Crafting and articulating a phrase

The higher voices (sopranos and tenors) have to be particularly careful to maintain the integrity of phrases without always heading over-enthusiastically for the higher notes.

The danger of a plodding bass line

In the same way that a chamber orchestra is rendered distinctive by a shapely and well-articulated double bass and cello line, a choir depends on a nimble and agile vocal bass line to provide the essential energy, alacrity, and intensity. The bass line needs to phrase and shape more than any of the others.

The importance of communicative faces!
This is an area very often neglected but which makes an immeasurable contribution to whether a performance goes beyond the "passable" and becomes distinctive. Choral singers must always strive for direct facial contact – with an audience, rather than with their scores! This "open and out" communication can make a huge impact on the way the music is received. Even with highly intelligent and experienced singers, this aspect of rehearsing and performance needs to be stressed regularly.

Tempi
Rehearsal tempi should be elastic, particularly in music from the fifteenth to eighteenth centuries, where the tendency in current performance practice is to be painfully insistent.

The tactus is related to the speed and recurrence of the heartbeat, and the heartbeat can change when the music becomes excited.[2] My warm-ups contain rubato, accelerandi, and various other devices to encourage constant eye contact between singer and conductor.

Conclusion

There is a danger that choirs can suffer from *too much* rehearsal, which leaves them sounding stale beside their nimbler orchestral colleagues. I can't stress highly enough the importance of creating an atmosphere in the choral rehearsal where each choir member sings with an element of spontaneity each time a phrase is repeated. Entreat your singers to take on as much responsibility as possible. Why do you have to start a phrase three times to get it together? Why do five of the sopranos look as though they understand the context and implications behind certain key words while others plainly do not? Constantly offer your singers challenges in a positive and constructive way based on the techniques you are steadily developing with them every time you rehearse.

Never let up! The rewards for them, for the listeners, and for you are beyond measure.

Notes

1 Introduction: choral music – a dynamic global genre

1 *The Chorus Impact Study, How Children, Adults, and Communities Benefit from Choruses* (Washington, DC: Chorus America, 2009), p. 3.

2 A brief anatomy of choirs *c.*1470–1770

1 *The New Shorter Oxford English Dictionary* (Oxford University Press, 1993), "Choir."

2 At Notre Dame in Paris (1313) no one was "to receive a payment for Matins unless they have demonstrated to us that they know by heart the antiphoner and the psalter"; C. Wright, *Music and Ceremony at Notre Dame of Paris, 500–1550* (1989), p. 326.

3 Adrian Petit Coclico singles out "the Belgians, Picards and French, for whom this is almost part of their nature, so that they take the palm of victory from the rest. Thus they alone are kept in the chapels of the Pope, the Emperor, the King of France and certain other rulers"; *Compendium musices* (Nuremberg, 1552), B iv^v.

4 See F. Ll. Harrison, *Music in Medieval Britain* (1963), pp. 178, 187 etc.

5 R. C. Wegman, "From Maker to Composer: Improvisation and Musical Authorship in the Low Countries, 1450–1500," *Journal of the American Musicological Society* 49 (1996), 424.

6 Johannes Tinctoris, *Liber de arte contrapuncti* (1477), Bk. II, Ch. 20. See also P. Canguilhem, "Singing upon the Book according to Vicente Lusitano," *Early Music History* 30 (2011), 55–103.

7 Thomas Morley, *A Plaine and Easie Introduction to Practicall Musicke* (London, 1597), "Annotations Upon the Second Part" (to "*Pag.70 vers.29*").

8 Scipione Cerreto, *Della prattica musica vocale et strumentale* (Naples, 1601), p. 272.

9 Adriano Banchieri, *Cartella musicale* (Venice, 1614), p. 230.

10 Much earlier, Elias Salomo (1274) had cautioned that even for straightforward parallel organum "the number [of singers] cannot and should not be more than four, without leading to the disruption and debasement of the whole piece that is being sung"; *Scientia artis musicae*, Ch. XXX, in M. Gerbert, *Scriptores ecclesiastici* (St. Blasien, 1784), vol. III, p. 58. A late fifteenth-century theorist, however, seems to have larger numbers in mind: "with many singing *ad librum*, as they call it, the *tenorist*'s expression of the text is sufficient for all"; *Herbeni Traiectensis de natura cantus* (*c.*1496), p. 58, in E. Rice, *Music and Ritual at Charlemagne's Marienkirche in Aachen* (2009), p. 213.

11 Henri Madin, *Traité de contrepoint simple ou chant sur le livre* (Paris, 1742), pp. 1 (preface), 7. See J. Prim, "*Chant sur le livre* in French Churches in the 18th Century," *Journal of the American Musicological Society* 14 (1961), 37–49, and J.-P. C. Montagnier (ed.), *Louis-Joseph Marchand Henry Madin Traités du contrepoint simple* (2004).

12 The extent of these traditions may illuminate other matters: the significance of chant notated on tablets and walls, the importance of the *tenorista* (see Wegman, "From Maker to Composer", 445–46), the proliferation of counterpoint books, the fame achieved *as singers* by musicians we know better as "composers," and, not least, the improvisatory nature of much composed music.

13 Giacomo Razzi, 1643, in a letter to Carissimi (a potential successor to Monteverdi) outlining musical practices at St. Mark's; T. D. Culley, *Jesuits and Music* (1970), p. 332.

14 Jan Goverts, in C. J. Gonnet (ed.), "Bedevaart nach Jerusalem," in *Bijdragen voor geschiedenis van het bisdom Haarlem*, vol. XI (1882), p. 39. Cf. the practice at St. Mark's, Venice, in 1564, cited on page 19.

15 Bodleian Library, Oxford ms. Hatton 13, f. 13^{r-v}. Cf. D. Fallows, "Specific Information on the Ensembles for Composed Polyphony, 1400–1474," in S. Borman (ed.), *Studies in the Performance of Late Mediaeval Music* (1983), p. 149 (cf. p. 110).

16 Fallows, "Specific Information," p. 154 (cf. p. 114).

17 The most likely term for "composed" polyphony would have been "*chose faite.*" See Wegman, "From Maker to Composer," 441, especially n.95.

18 Nicolò Burzio, *Musices opusculum* (Bologna, 1487), Bk. ii, Ch. 6, pp. 50, 44.

19 *Submissa voce*: literally, "with a subdued voice." In the executors' account of the will *submissa voce* is rendered in French as *en fausset*, leading to the mistaken view that

falsetto singing is indicated here. Rather, it is *en fausset* that at this period means "softly," and not *submissa voce* that means "in falsetto." Cf. Fallows, "Specific Information," p. 126.

20 Undoubtedly the late setting (*a*4) of *Ave regina coelorum*, copied at Cambrai in 1464–65.

21 Fallows, "Specific Information," pp. 120–21.

22 "for three voices, mournful, sad and very exquisite," according to the chronicler of a performance in Brussels in 1501; W. F. Prizer, "Music and Ceremonial in the Low Countries: Philip the Fair and the Order of the Golden Fleece," *Early Music History* 5 (1985), 133.

23 C. Wright, "Performance Practices at the Cathedral of Cambrai 1475–1550," *Musical Quarterly* 64 (1978), 303 (cf. 296). Cf. D. Fallows, *Dufay* (1982), p. 79, inc. n.25. Under a separate foundation Dufay's Requiem was also sung annually at Cambrai from 1517 to 1521, this time by "the master of the choirboys with four or five companions chosen at his discretion"; Wright, "Performance Practices," 303.

24 The work in question is the Mass for St. Anthony of Padua (*a*3); Fallows, "Specific Information," pp. 117–20.

25 The Mass was to be sung "on the day of St. Anthony of Padua in that chapel"; Fallows, "Specific Information," p. 118. Dufay left a manuscript containing his Requiem to the cathedral's chapel of St. Stephen, where he was to be buried; R. Strohm, *The Rise of European Music 1380–1500* (1993), p. 287. *Ave regina coelorum* was evidently sung in the chapel of St. Étienne; Wright, "Performance Practices," 305.

26 Strohm, *European Music*, pp. 273 and 280–81. Under Ercole d'Este, the Ferrarese court chapel between 1471 and 1505 frequently comprised over twenty singers; L. Lockwood, *Music in Ferrara 1400–1505* (1984), p. 150.

27 D. Fallows, "The Performing Ensembles in Josquin's Sacred Music," *Tijdschrift van de Vereniging voor Nederlandse Muziekgeschiedenis* 35 (1985), 33, 56.

28 Brumel, *Missa Et ecce terrae motus est*, in B. Hudson (ed.), *Corpus Mensurabilis Musicae*, 5: *Antonii Brumel Opera Omnia*, vol. III, (1970), pp. ix–x. Lassus presumably performed the work at Munich between 1568 and 1570, when according to Michael Praetorius the court *Kapelle* boasted an unparalleled sixteen choirboys plus five or six castrati, thirteen altos, fifteen tenors and twelve basses; *Syntagma musicum*, vol. II (Wolfenbüttel, 1619), p. 17.

29 H. M. Brown, *Sixteenth-Century Instrumentation: The Music for the Florentine Intermedii* (1973), p. 129.

30 A. Seay, "The 15th-century Cappella at Santa Maria del Fiore in Florence," *Journal of the American Musicological Society* 11 (1958), 49.

31 H. J. Moser, *Paul Hofhaimer: ein Lied- und Orgelmeister des deutschen Humanismus* (1926), p. 14.

32 R. C. Wegman, *Born for the Muses: The Life and Masses of Jacob Obrecht* (1994), p. 373 (and p. 305).

33 R. C. Wegman, "The Testament of Jean de Saint Gille (†1501)," *Revue de Musicologie* 95 (2009), 18, 28.

34 In the 1470s the Sforza court requested from Venice "a boy of 14 or 15 who can sing Venetian songs, has a good voice, and some theoretical knowledge of music, who can play lute well, and sing with and without lute"; Strohm, *European Music*, p. 544.

35 Antonio de Beatis (1517), in L. Pastor, *Die Reise des Kardinals Luigi d'Aragona* (1905), p.165.

36 Wright, "Performance Practices," 306.

37 For a handful of works from the earlier part of the fifteenth century juxtaposing boys and men, see Fallows, "Specific Information," pp. 122–25.

38 Pietro Aaron, *Libri tres de institutione harmonica* (Bologna, 1516), f. 52. For works with parts specifically labeled *puer* or *pueri* ("boy/s") by Battre, Bourgois, Regis, Isaac, Obrecht, and Ockeghem, see Fallows, "Specific Information," pp. 122–23, and "The Performing Ensembles," 44–45.

39 The belief that falsetto singing was widespread long before the sixteenth century is now almost universal. Its foundations, however, are various questionable assumptions about terminology (including *falsus, fictus,* and their cognates; see n.19), about sounding pitch in relation to notation (see text, below) and about interrelated historical issues of age, maturity and status in young male singers.

40 In 1536 the chapter of Cambrai encouraged the master of the choirboys to "teach the boys of the choir to sing *submisse* or, as they say in French, in falsetto"; Wright, "Performance Practices," 309. It may be that this represents a connection, some sixty years after Dufay's death, between soft singing and falsetto in the now familiar sense (cf. n.19).

41 According to Joachim Burmeister the soprano voice was suited to boys and females, the alto to youths ("*ætati juvenili*"), tenor and bass to men; *Musica poetica* (Rostock, 1606), p. 11.

42 Wright, "Performance Practices," 309.

43 F. A. D'Accone, "The Singers of San Giovanni in Florence during the 15th Century," *Journal of the American Musicological Society* 13 (1960), 332.

44 *Ibid.*

45 J. López-Calo, *La música en la Catedral de Burgos*, vol. III (1996), p. 43.

46 G. Gerbino, "The Quest for the Soprano Voice: Castrati in Renaissance Italy," *Studi musicali* 33 (2004), 343, 320; G. M. Ongaro, "La composizione del coro e dei gruppi strumentali a San Marco dalla fine del Quattrocento al primo Seicento," in D. Howard and L. Moretti (eds.), *Architettura e musica nella Venezia del Rinascimento* (2006), p.106 etc.

47 See Gerbino, "The Quest."

48 Modern editions which fail to report a work's original clefs withhold critical information and feed the misconception that vocal scoring and choice of pitch were on the whole rather arbitrary affairs.

49 Morley, *A Plaine and Easie Introduction*, p. 166. See also Nicola Vicentino, *L'antica musica ridotta alla modern prattica* (Rome, 1555), Bk. IV, Ch. 17; trans. M. M. Maniates as *Ancient Music Adapted to Modern Practice* (1996), p. 250.

50 For an explanation of the modal background to this convention, see P. Barbieri, "*Chiavette* and Modal Transposition in Italian Practice (*c.*1500–1837)," *Recercare* 3 (1991), 17–25.

51 See Fallows, "Performing Ensembles," 52–53.

52 Pietro Cerone, *El melopeo y maestro* (Naples, 1613), p. 494. In terms of solmisation the exceptional demands of the lower two-flat notation, symbolically plumbing the depths of the gamut, simply disappear in the higher version. It has also been argued the work may originally have been clefless; P. Urquhart, "Another Impolitic Observation on *Absalon, fili mi*," *Journal of Musicology* 21 (2004), 364–68 (see also 347–48, 361, 362).

53 Gioseffo Zarlino, *Le istitutioni harmoniche* (Venice, 1558), Bk. iv, Ch. 17, p. 319. The intriguing case of Monteverdi's high-clef 1610 Magnificat *a7* is explored in A. Parrott, "Transposition in Monteverdi's Vespers of 1610," *Early Music* 12 (1984), 490–516.

54 R. Alessandrini, "Performance Practice in the *seconda prattica* Madrigal," *Early Music* 27 (1999), 636.

55 J. Armstrong, "The *Antiphonae, seu Sacrae Cantiones* (1613) of Giovanni Francesco Anerio: A Liturgical Study," *Analecta musicologica* 14 (1974), 89–150.

56 Praetorius, *Syntagma musicum*, vol. III (Wolfenbüttel, 1619), pp. 80–81. See Parrott, "Transposition," 491–94.

57 Giovanni Battista Morsolino (1582); G. Pannain, in G. Cesari (ed.), *La musica in Cremona nella seconda metà del secolo XVI* (1939), p. xvi.

58 Banchieri, *Cartella*, p. 88.

59 Parrott, "Transposition," 497.

60 See B. Haynes, *A History of Performing Pitch* (2002), pp. 369 and 142.

61 "Contratenor altus," in Stanley Sadie (ed.), *The New Grove Dictionary of Music and Musicians*, 2nd edn. (2001) (henceforth cited as *NG* 2).

62 In 1639 André Maugars noted in Rome "a great number of *castrati* for the *dessus* and for the *haut-contre*"; "Response . . .", in R. Grey (ed.), *Studies in Music* (1901), p. 226. At the papal chapel, however, Antimo Liberati still objected in 1662/63 to the suggestion of assigning castrati to alto parts; Gerbino, "The Quest," 313. (A change did eventually take place there after 1687; *NG* 2, "Chorus," p. 770.) By 1649 all the altos (and sopranos) at St. Mark's, Venice, were castrati, according to H. H. von Oeÿnhausen (see n.142).

63 See, for example, Philibert Jambe de Fer, *Épitome musical* (Lyon, 1556), pp. 51–52. The mid-eighteenth-century French *haute-contre* was still this adult male non-falsettist, quite distinct in manner from the lighter Italian tenor who now freely incorporated a falsetto or "head" voice to extend his range upwards; see A. Parrott, "Falsetto and the French: 'une toute autre marche,'" *Basler Jahrbuch für historische Musikpraxis* 26 (2002), 129–48. For a brief discussion of the English countertenor in the late seventeenth century, see A. Parrott, "Performing Purcell," in M. Burden (ed.), *The Purcell Companion* (1995), pp. 417–24.

64 An occasional lower part for a boy ("secundus puer") also occurs in, for example, the music of Obrecht and Ockeghem; Fallows, "Specific Information," pp. 44–46.

65 See A. Johnstone, "'As it was in the beginning': Organ and Choir Pitch in Early Anglican Church Music," *Early Music* 31 (2003), 506–26. Cf. D. Wulstan, *Tudor Music* (1985), pp. 200–202, where the author argues for a pitch "perhaps between a tone and a minor third" higher than today's pitch.

66 For a contrary view see Wulstan, *Tudor Music*, pp. 242–44.

67 For an argument that in England the lower boy's voice was merely "a substitute for the adult alto" (in the modern sense) for the singing of mean parts – an undocumented occurrence – see R. Bowers, "The Vocal Scoring, Choral Balance and Performing Pitch of Latin Church Polyphony in England, *c.*1390–1559," *Journal of the Royal Musical Association* 112 (1987), 67–68, and "To Chorus from Quartet: The Performing Resource for English Church Polyphony, *c.*1390–1559," in J. Morehen (ed.) *English Choral Practice, 1400–1650* (1995), pp. 38–39.

68 British Library, ms Royal 18. B. XIX (early 17th c.), f. 8ᵛ; P. Le Huray, *Music and the Reformation in England 1549–1660* (1967), p. 121.

69 Bowers, "Latin Church Polyphony," 58, 71–72.

70 B. Matthews, "Some Early Organists and Their Agreements," *The Organ* 51 (1972), 150.

71 Fallows, "Specific Information," p. 127. Instruments at this period seem generally to have been confined to the nave; Strohm, *European Music*, pp. 272–73.

72 A. Aber, *Die Pflege der Musik unter den Wettinern und wettinischen Ernestinern* (1921), p. 82.

73 G. Van Doorslaer, "La chapelle musicale de Philippe le Beau," *Revue Belge d'Archéologie et d'Histoire de l'Art* 4 (1934), 52.

74 K. Polk, "Augustein Schubinger and the Zinck: Innovation in Performance Practice," *Historic Brass Society Journal* 1 (1989), 84–87. See also Van Doorslaer, "La chapelle musicale," 50–51.

75 Jehan La Caille (1520), in Dom Bernard de Montfaucon, *Les Monumens de la Monarchie Françoise* (Paris, 1732), vol. IV, p. 178; Wright, *Notre Dame*, pp. 227, 364. These *fiffres* were most probably the cornetts mentioned in two contemporary Italian accounts; see R. Brown (ed.), *Calendar of State Papers . . . Venice*, vol. III: *1520–1526* (1869), pp. 29, 75.

76 Erasmus, "Annotations on the New Testament" (1519), *Opera omnia*, vol. VI (Leiden, 1705), col. 731.

77 K. Frey, *Der literarische Nachlass Giorgio Vasaris* (1923), pp. 40–41.

78 Vincenzo Galilei, *Dialogo della musica antica e della moderna* (Florence, 1581), p. 142.

79 Marin Mersenne, *Harmonie Universelle* (Paris, 1636), vol. III, Bk. 5, prop. xxiv. Sixteenth-century Spanish cathedrals similarly favoured the *bajón* or dulcian (Pamplona from at least 1530), presumably for its clarity and definition at the lower end of the bass range. To a 1615 memorandum proposing that from the Capilla Real "two singers of each voice, cornett, *bajón* and an organist would be enough" to attend a royal wedding in Burgos, Philip III replied that "as far as singers are concerned, four or six could go with cornett and *bajón*." The shawms and *flautas* of minstrel bands attached to certain cathedrals were distinctly less well suited to the task of supporting voices. At least initially these groups seem to have worked independently of the vocal choirs, allowing one of Seville's minstrels (1586) to double as a singer and another at Palencia (1592) to serve as both "*bajón* in polyphony" and "treble shawm in the minstrels' *capilla*." See R. Stevenson, *La música en la Catedral de Sevilla, 1478–1606* (Madrid, 1985), p. 75

(doc. 637), and K. Kreitner, "Minstrels in Spanish Churches, 1400–1600," *Early Music* 20 (1992), 536, 539, 546.

80 Matthew Locke, *The Present Practice of Musick Vindicated* (London, 1673), p. 19.

81 John Arnold, *The Compleat Psalmodist*/5 (London, 1761), p. iv (preface).

82 J. Wilson (ed.), *Roger North on Music*, (1959), p. 40.

83 At the German College, 1589; G. Dixon, "The Performance of Palestrina: Some Questions, but Fewer Answers," *Early Music* 22 (1994), 670.

84 Letter from Scipione Gonzaga to Guglielmo Gonzaga (1586); S. Niwa, "'Madama' Margaret of Parma's Patronage of Music," *Early Music* 33 (2005), 37 (and 33).

85 Stringed instruments, we are told, "ar often out of tun; (which soomtime happeneth in the mids of the Musik, when it is neither good to continue, nor to correct the fault)"; Charles Butler, *The Principles of Musik* (London, 1636), p. 103.

86 The reported "Vialls, and other sweet Instruments" at Exeter Cathedral in 1635 constitute the only exception of which I am aware. See A. Parrott, "'Grett and solompne singing': Instruments in English Church Music before the Civil War," *Early Music* 6 (1978), 186.

87 G. Kinsky, "Schriftstücke aus dem Palestrina-Kreis," in K. Weinmann (ed.), *Festschrift Peter Wagner* (1926), p. 114. In 1586 a violin had been added to the instrumental resources for *concerti* at S. Antonio, Padua; J. A. Owens, "Il Cinquecento," in S. Durante and P. Petrobelli (eds.), *Storia della musica al Santo di Padova* (1990), p. 67.

88 In 1577, according to her memoirs; R. Stevenson, *Spanish Cathedral Music in the Golden Age* (1961), p. 341.

89 In his *Spem in alium a*40, for example, Tallis uses the same five-part vocal scoring in each of eight choirs ($G_2C_2C_3C_4F_4$). Striggio's slightly earlier forty-part *Ecce beatam lucem*, however, adds to three apparently "vocal" choirs ($C_1C_3C_4F_4$) seven higher ones ($G_2C_2C_3F_3$), which may have accounted for the documented recorders, viols and trombones; see A. Parrott, "A Tale of Five Cities Revisited," *Early Music* 9 (1981), 342–43.

90 Lodovico Grossi da Viadana, *Salmi a quattro chori* (Venice, 1612), "Modo di concertare i detti salmi a quattro chori"; G. Wielakker (ed.), *Recent Researches in the Music of the Baroque Era*, vol. LXXXVI (1998), p. 2.

91 Wielakker, *Recent Researches*, p. 2.

92 A. Parrott, *The Essential Bach Choir* (2000) p. 31; see also pp. 51–57 for related questions of positioning and copy-sharing and more on the size of ripieno groups.

93 Heinrich Schütz, *Psalmen Davids* (Dresden, 1619), preface.

94 Thomas Gobert (Paris, 1646), in W. J. A. Jonckbloet and J. P. N. Land (eds.), *Musique et musiciens au XVIIe siècle* (Constantin Huygens correspondence) (1882), p. ccxvii.

95 H. Du Mont, *Cantica sacra* (Paris, 1652), "Au lecteur"; new edn., ed. J. Lionnet (1996), p. xcii.

96 According to Praetorius (1619) the term *concertando* applied "when one selects from an entire company of musicians the best and most notable among them"; *Syntagma musicum*, vol. III, pp. 4–5.

97 Praetorius, *Syntagma musicum*, vol. III, p. 196.

98 Concerted music "can be performed entirely with these parts alone, without the other vocal capellas or instruments"; Praetorius, *Syntagma musicum*, vol. III, p. 196. See Parrott, *The Essential Bach Choir*, p. 30.

99 Sébastien de Brossard on Du Mont's *grands motets*, in his *Catalogue des livres de musique* (ms, 1724), p. 140; J. R. Anthony, *French Baroque Music from Beaujoyeulx to Rameau* (1974), p. 171.

100 Harrison, *Medieval Britain*, p. 181.

101 J. Glixon, "A Musicians' Union in Sixteenth-century Venice," *Journal of the American Musicological Society* 36 (1983), 392–421.

102 Bartolomeo Bonifacio, *Rituum ecclesiasticorum ceremoniale*, f. 18^r. Cf. the reported practice of 1525, quoted on pages 8–9.

103 Viadana stipulates that the voices sing "*con gravità e schietto*" ("solemnly and plainly"); Lodovico Grossi da Viadana, "Alli virtuosi di musica," in *Lamentationes* (Venice, 1609).

104 J. Lionnet, "Performance Practice in the Papal Chapel during the 17th Century," *Early Music* 15 (1987), 9–11.

105 "Alli virtuosi di musica."

106 See Harrison, *Medieval Britain*, p. 316.

107 See N. O'Regan, "The Performance of Palestrina: Some Further Observations," *Early Music* 24 (1996), 146.

108 Emilio del Cavalieri, *Rappresentatione di Anima, et di Corpo* (Rome, 1600), "Avvertimento."

109 Hermann Finck, *Practica musica* (Wittenberg, 1556), Bk. v, f. Ss iv^v.

110 Johann Gottfried Walther, *Musicalisches Lexicon* (Leipzig, 1732), p. 139.

111 The *Missa da capella . . . fatta sopra il motetto In illo tempore del Gomberti* (a6), in Claudio Monteverdi, *Missa . . . Ac Vespere* (Venice, 1610).

112 At the church of the Annunciation (September 7, 1770); H. E. Poole (ed.), Charles Burney, *Music, Men, and Manners in France and Italy, 1770* (1969), p. 112.

113 *Ibid.*, p. 47.

114 See Parrott, *The Essential Bach Choir*, pp. 21–27.

115 Johann Adolph Scheibe, *Critischer Musicus* (Leipzig, 1745), p. 182 – reprinting an article from 1737. See also Parrott, *The Essential Bach Choir*, p. 29.

116 Johann Beer, *Musicalische Discurse* (Nuremberg, 1719), p. 11; H.-J. Schulze, "Johann Sebastian Bach's Orchestra: Some Unanswered Questions," *Early Music* 17 (1989), 13.

117 Johann Mattheson, *Der musicalische Patriot* (Hamburg, 1728), p. 64. See Parrott, *The Essential Bach Choir*, p. 118.

118 Parrott, *The Essential Bach Choir*, pp. 117–29. See also A. Parrott, "Vocal Ripienists and J. S. Bach's Mass in B Minor," *Eighteenth-Century Music* 7 (2010), 33–34, and A. Parrott, "Bach's Chorus: The Leipzig Line," *Early Music* 38 (2010), 229–31.

119 Parrott, *The Essential Bach Choir*, p. 118.

120 For questions of balance and placement, see Parrott, *The Essential Bach Choir*, pp. 131–39.

121 Martin Heinrich Fuhrmann, *Musicalischer-Trichter* (Frankfurt an der Spree, 1706). See Parrott, *The Essential Bach Choir*, pp. 29–41.

122 Parrott, *The Essential Bach Choir*, pp. 36, 68, 141–42, and Parrott, "Vocal Ripienists," 12 (also 14–15, 20, 21).

123 See Parrott, *The Essential Bach Choir*, pp. 70, 72–3, 85–92; concertists and ripienists in general are discussed at pp. 29–41 and Bach's own use of ripienists is discussed at pp. 59–92. See also Parrott, "Vocal Ripienists."

124 Bach's 1730 "Entwurff einer wohlbestallten Kirchen *Music*"; Parrott, *The Essential Bach Choir*, pp. 165, 168.

125 Parrott, *The Essential Bach Choir*, pp. 13–15.

126 Bach, "Entwurff", pp. 165, 168.

127 Heinrich Glarean, *Dodecachordon* (Basel, 1547); reprinted as *Dodecachordon*, trans. C. A. Miller, vol. I (1965), p. 209.

128 Banchieri, *Cartella*, pp. 18–19.

129 Johann Mattheson, *Der vollkommene Capellmeister* (Hamburg, 1739), p. 482.

130 Bénigne de Bacilly, *Remarques curieuses sur l'art de bien chanter* (Paris, 1668), pp. 80–81.

131 Banchieri, *Cartella*, p. 18.

132 Viadana, *Cento concerti ecclesiastici* (Venice, 1602), "A' benigni lettori."

133 Parrott, "Transposition," 492, 494.

134 Parrott, "Transposition," 507–8.

135 Ignatio Donati, *Salmi boscarecci* (Venice, 1623), "Avvertimenti."

136 Mattheson, *Critica Musica*, vol. II (Hamburg, 1725), p. 243. See M. Talbot, "Tenors and Basses at the Venetian *Ospedali*," *Acta musicologica* 66 (1994), 123–38, and "Sacred Music at the Ospedale della Pietà in Venice in the Time of Handel," *Händel-Jahrbuch* 46 (2000), 125–56. The Pietà was one of four musically active Venetian *ospedali* – not convents – and most of their *figlie di coro* were in fact women rather than girls.

137 Charles de Brosses, *Lettres familières écrites d'Italie en 1739 et 1740*, vol. II (4/1885), pp. 317–18. According to Charles Burney, "many of the girls [at the Venetian *ospedali*] sing in the counter-tenor as low as A and G, which enables them always to keep below the *soprano* and *mezzo soprano*, to which they sing the base"; P. A. Scholes (ed.), *Dr. Burney's Musical Tours in Europe*, vol. I: *An Eighteenth-Century Musical Tour in France and Italy* (1959), p. 114.

138 See J. Whittemore, *Music of the Venetian Ospedali Composers: A Thematic Catalogue* (1995).

139 Burney, in Scholes, *Dr. Burney's Musical Tours*, vol. I, p. 114.

140 Four possible approaches involve no rewriting of SATB music otherwise intended for male choirs:

SATB all parts sounding at written pitch
SSAA Tenor and Bass parts up an 8ve
SAAT Tenor part at pitch but Bass up an 8ve
SA(T) Bass part (and Tenor) omitted; or Bass part up an 8ve and both Alto and Tenor parts omitted.

141 Hauschronik II, Wiener Ursulinen, 265 (July 16, 1731); J. K. Page, "'A lovely and perfect music': Maria Anna von Raschenau and Music at the Viennese Convent of St Jakob auf der Hülben," *Early Music* 38 (2010), 411, 421.

142 Heinrich Herrmann von Oeÿnhausen (traveling in the retinue of the Landgrave of Hesse-Darmstadt); M. E. Frandsen, *Crossing Confessional Boundaries* (2006), p. 443.

143 Gottfried Ephraim Scheibel, *Zufällige Gedancken von der Kirchen-Music* (Frankfurt and Leipzig, 1721), pp. 59–61. On witnessing "two or three" women amongst the singers at St. Gudula's, Brussels, Burney commented: "If the practice were to become general, of admitting women to sing the *soprano* part in the cathedrals, it would, in Italy, be a

service to mankind, and in the rest of Europe render church music infinitely more pleasing and perfect" (1773); Scholes, *Dr. Burney's Musical Tours*, vol. II, pp. 20–21.

144 Wilson, *Roger North*, p. 271.

145 "one can only reflect on the modicum of service one would have had from them, because of their monthly indispositions, their confinements, the perpetual indolence and natural caprice of women: really there was no common sense in the idea. Thanks be to God, it has not come to pass"; L. Sawkins, "For and Against the Order of Nature: Who Sang the Soprano?" *Early Music* 15 (1987), 316.

146 This practice can perhaps be traced back to the Medici court, where from *c*.1600 ecclesiastical propriety was deemed to have been satisfied by having first Vittoria Archilei and then Francesca Caccini contribute to Holy Week services from just outside the body of the church. See, for example, S. G. Cusick, *Francesca Caccini at the Medici Court* (2009), pp. 17, 291–93.

147 *William Weston: The Autobiography of an Elizabethan*, trans. P. Caraman (1955), p. 71.

148 See P. Ranum, "A Sweet Servitude: A Musician's Life at the Court of Mlle de Guise," *Early Music* 15 (1987), 347–60.

149 S. Owens, "Professional Women Musicians in Early Eighteenth-century Württemberg," *Music & Letters* 82 (2001), 36.

150 Mattheson, *Der vollkommene Capellmeister*, p. 482.

151 *Ibid.*

152 Scheibe, *Critischer Musicus*, p. 157 (emphasis added).

153 D. Kirsch, *Lexikon Würzburger Hofmusiker* (2002), pp. 14–15.

154 S. Owens, "Professional Women Musicians in Early Eighteenth-century Württemberg," 43.

155 K. W. Niemöller, *Kirchenmusik und reichsstädtische Musikpflege im Köln des 18. Jahrhunderts* (1960), pp. 9, 198 and Passim.

156 "the musicians assembled on this occasion exceeded in abilities, as well as number, those of every band that has been collected in modern times"; Charles Burney, *An Account of the Musical Performances in Westminster Abbey and the Pantheon . . . in 1784* (London, 1785), p. vii. Burney proceeds to report half a dozen or so reported sightings of monster-scale forces – from as far back as 1515 to Jommelli's funeral in 1774, four of them reaching totals of around 300.

157 Thirteen men and around six boys, the Chapel Royal singers then "in waiting"; D. Burrows, *Handel and the English Chapel Royal* (2005), pp. 102–3.

158 The *Norwich Gazette*, reporting a public rehearsal. The numbers closely match autograph indications in the composer's score of *The King Shall Rejoice*: "C[anto] 12, H[ughes] et 6, Freem[an] et 6" and so on.

159 Handel's only other performance on this scale seems to have been of the funeral anthem for Queen Caroline at the Abbey a decade later, reportedly with "near 80 Vocal Performers" and 100 instrumentalists; *Daily Advertiser*, December 19, 1737, cited in Burrows, *Handel and the English Chapel Royal*, p. 378.

160 "the Musick is made for himself and sung by his own servants"; Sir David Dalrymple (letter), 1718, in D. Burrows, *Handel* (1994), p. 80. The local parish church of St. Lawrence, Whitchurch, served as a temporary domestic chapel.

161 [Le Cerf de la Viéville], *Comparaison de la musique italienne, et de la musique françoise*, 2nd edn. (Brussels, 1705), p. 71. At one of Handel's London opera performances in 1728, Pierre-Jacques Fougeroux noted that "the chorus consists of only four voices"; W. Dean, "A French Traveller's View of Handel's Operas," *Music & Letters* 55 (1974), 178. In 1741 the castrato Caffarelli was apparently arrested and imprisoned for "disturbing the other performers" in various ways, which included "refusing to sing in the ripieno with the others"; A. Heriot, *The Castrati in Opera* (1956), pp. 144–45.

162 Even in the 1690s more than half of Rome's twenty-five ecclesiastical choirs comprised just four or five singers, according to a list drawn up by Padre Martini; "Musici di Roma nell'anno che il Sig, Gio. Paolo Colonna si portò in Roma" (ms), in O. Mischiati, "Una statistica della musica a Roma nel 1694," *Note d'archivio* ns. i (1983), 209–27.

163 In "De torrente" a chant-like accompaniment to the duetting sopranos is supplied by a "cappella" of unison tenor and bass voices.

164 The Earl of Egmont (diary entry); W. Dean, *Handel's Dramatic Oratorios and Masques* (1959), p. 234.

165 D. Burrows, *Handel: Messiah* (1991), p. 15.

166 D. Burrows, "Lists of Musicians for Performances of Handel's *Messiah* at the Foundling Hospital, 1754–1777," *Royal Musical Association Research Chronicle* 43 (2010), 89–91.

167 D. Burrows, "Handel's Oratorio Performances," in D. Burrows (ed.), *The Cambridge Companion to Handel* (1997), p. 273.

168 Burrows, "Lists of Musicians," 97–102.

3 Choral music in the culture of the nineteenth century

1 Alfred Einstein, *Music in the Romantic Era* (New York: W. W. Norton, 1947), p. 36.

2 For an excellent synopsis of the cosmologies that drove both the eighteenth and nineteenth centuries, see Crane Brinton, *The Shaping of Modern Thought* (Englewood Cliffs, NJ: Prentice Hall Inc., 1963), chapters 4 and 5.

3 For contemporary documentation of the substance of this movement, see the "Decree on Worship of the Supreme Being, May 7, 1794 (18 Floréal, Year II)" translated from the *Gazette Nationale ou Le Moniteur Universelle*, Nonidid 19 Floréal (Jeudi, 8 May, 1794, old style) in *Church and State in the Modern Age: A Documentary History*, ed. J. F. Maclear (New York: Oxford University Press, 1995), pp. 88–90.

4 H. C. Robbins Landon, *Haydn: Chronicle and Works*, 5 vols. (Bloomington: Indiana University Press, 1976), vol. III, *Haydn in England [1791–1795]*, p. 83.

5 Don V. Moses and Robert Demaree, *The Masses of Joseph Haydn* (Frankfort, MI: Classical Heritage, 2009), p. 138.

6 Percy M. Young and James G. Smith, "Chorus (i), §4: From the mid-18th to the later 19th [centuries]," in Stanley Sadie (ed.), *The New Grove Dictionary of Music and Musicians*, 2nd edn. (London: Macmillan, 2001), vol. V, p. 780 (henceforth cited as *NG* 2).

7 A. Peter Brown, "*The Creation*: An Oratorio for all Tastes and Times," program book to Christopher Hogwood's recording of *The Creation* (L'Oiseau-Lyre CD, 430 397–2, 1990), p. 20.

8 These statistics are taken from Young and Smith, "Chorus," pp. 776–78.

9 Of course, this device had already been used by Mozart in his *Krönungsmesse*, K. 317 (1779).

10 *Andante con moto assai vivace quasi Allegretto ma non troppo* (Andante, with motion, always vivacious, sort of Allegretto, but not too much)!

11 Karin Pendle and Stephen Wilkins, "Paradise Found: The Salle le Peletier and French Grand Opera," in Mark A. Radice (ed.), *Opera in Context: Essays on Historical Staging from the Late Renaissance to the Time of Puccini* (Portland, OR: Amadeus Press, 1998), p. 173.

12 For a discussion of the English festivals and institutions, see Percy Scholes's landmark study *The Mirror of Music 1844–1944*, 2 vols. (London: Novello & Co. Ltd and Oxford University Press, 1947), specifically vol. I, pp. 149–94. For Vienna, a similarly enlightening

study is Eduard Hanslick, *Vienna's Golden Years of Music: 1850–1900*, trans. and ed. Henry Pleasants III (New York: Simon and Schuster, Inc., 1950).

13 Alice Marie Hanson, "The Social and Economic Context of Music in Vienna from 1815–1830" (PhD thesis, University of Illinois at Urbana-Champaign, 1980), pp. 149–54.

14 Hanslick, *Vienna's Golden Years*, p. 7, n.12.

15 Margaret Handford, "Birmingham," *NG 2*, vol. III, p. 615.

16 Scholes, *Mirror of Music*, vol. I, p. 8.

17 The term *Orphéon* was also used by male-chorus societies in Paris, formed at the same time in imitation of the German *Liedertafeln*; see "Orphéon," *Oxford Companion to Music*, ed. Alison Latham, *Oxford Music Online*.

18 Bernarr Rainbow, "Wilhelm, Guillaume Louis," *NG 2*, vol. XXVII, p. 387.

19 Scholes, *Mirror of Music*, vol. I, p. 11.

20 Ibid., p. 18.

21 See Catharine Melhorn's discussion of the emergence of this genre as a precedent for Mendelssohn's *Die erste Walpurgisnacht*; "Mendelssohn's *Die erste Walpurgisnacht*," DMA dissertation, University of Illinois at Urbana-Champaign, 1983, pp. 83–96.

22 Imogen Fellinger *et al.*, "Periodicals." *Grove Music Online*.

23 Mendelssohn, quoted in Julius Alf, "Komponisten in Düsseldorf. Sechs biographische Miniaturen;" in Ernst Klusen (ed.), *Studien zur Musikgeschichte des Rheinlandes* (Cologne: Arno, 1978), p. 18. Vol. 119 of Beiträge zur rheinischen Musikgeschichte. Translation by Catharine Melhorn, in her "Mendelssohn's *Die erste Walpurgisnacht*," p. 89

24 Eric Frederic Jensen, *Schumann* (Oxford University Press, 2001), p. 257.

25 Ewan West. "Liedertafel," *Grove Music Online*.

26 This development is fully explored in Mark Henderson, "The German Part-Song in the First Half of the Nineteenth Century," DMA dissertation, University of Illinois at Urbana-Champaign, 1989) and in James Smith and Percy Young, "Chorus," in *The New Grove Dictionary of Music and Musicians*, 2nd edn., vol. V (London: Macmillan, 2001), pp. 776–83.

27 Hanson, "Social and Economic Context," p. 227.

28 Originally, Schubert set Franz Grillparzer's poem (a birthday present for his daughter) for alto solo, male chorus and piano; that version of "Standchen" is now generally regarded as subordinate to the arrangement for women's voices (D. 920).

Eight male-chorus part-songs by Schubert bear the title "Trinklied"; seven (D. 75, 148, 242, 267, 356, 426/5 and 427/5) are early works (1813–16), only the "Trinklied des 16ten Jahrhunderts" (D. 847) being a product of Schubert's final years (1825).

29 John J. Silantien, "The Part Song in England, 1837–1914," DMA dissertation, University of Illinois at Urbana-Champaign, 1980, p. 150.

30 Stanley Boorman *et al*. "Music printing and Publishing, II, 3. The Age of Engraving; The Age of Offset Printing (1860–1975)." *Grove Music Online*.

31 *Ibid.*

32 Claude Palisca (edn.), *Norton Anthology of Western Music*, 4th edn. (New York: W. W. Norton, 2001). The fifth edition of this venerable collection reduces its choral component to a single excerpt from Mendelssohn's *Elijah*.

4 Choral music in the twentieth and early twenty-first centuries

1 For Bruno Walter's views on Mahler's late use of harmony and counterpoint see Constantin Floros, *Gustav Mahler: The Symphonies*, trans. Vernon and Jutta Wicker (Portland, OR: Amadeus Press, 1993), p. 242.

2 *Arnold Schoenberg Letters*, ed. Erwin Stein (London: Faber & Faber, 1987), p. 100, and *Arnold Schoenberg: Self-Portrait*, ed. Nuria Schoenberg Nono (Pacific Palisades: Belmont Music Publishers, 1988), p. 115.

3 For Arnold Schoenberg's comments see John Harbison, "The Ritual of Oedipus Rex," *Upbeat* (December 1989), 4.

4 The term "Shock of the New" was coined in 1972 by Ian Dunlop as a title for his book examining seven important exhibits of modern art. It was popularized in 1980 by art critic Robert Hughes as the title for his PBS television series and accompanying book.

5 Nick Strimple, *Choral Music in the Twentieth Century* (Portland, OR; Amadeus Press, 2002), pp. 9, 98–101.

6 Donald Francis Tovey, "Ethel Smyth: Mass in D," in his *Essays in Musical Analysis,* vol. V, *Vocal Music* (London: Oxford University Press, 1937), pp. 235–42.

7 See, for example, Elwyn Wienandt, *Choral Music of the Church* (New York: Free Press, 1965), pp. 431–35, and Elwyn Wienandt, "Jazz at the Altar?" *The Christian Century*, vol. LXXVII:12 (March 23, 1960), 346–48.

8 Martin Goldsmith, *The Inextinguishable Symphony* (New York: John Wiley & Sons, Inc., 2000), pp. 259–72.

9 United States Holocaust Museum, *Hidden History of the Kovno Ghetto* (Boston: Little, Brown and Company, 1997), pp. 149, 172–76.

10 Shirli Gilbert, *Music in the Holocaust: 1813–16, Confronting Life in the Nazi Ghettos and Camps* (Oxford University Press, 2005), pp. 21–54.

11 Stefan Hayman, "The Buchenwald Song," in *The Buchenwald Report*, trans. and ed. David A. Hackett (Oxford: Westview Press, 1995), pp. 140–42.

12 Paul Cummins, *Dachau Song: The Twentieth Century Odyssey of Herbert Zipper* (New York: Peter Lang, 1992), pp. 75–92.

13 Strimple, *Choral Music in the Twentieth Century*, p. 113.

14 Arthur Koestler, "Selection from *The Scum of the Earth*," and Denise Dufournier, "Selection from *Ravensbrück: The Women's Death Camp*," in Rebecca Rovit and Alvin Goldfarb (eds.), *Theatrical Performance during the Holocaust* (Baltimore: Johns Hopkins University Press, 1999), pp. 163–66.

15 Joža Karas, *Music in Terezín, 1941–45* (New York: Beaufort Books, 1985), pp. 139–41.

16 Henry Oertelt, *An Unbroken Chain: My Journey through the Nazi Holocaust* (Minneapolis: Levner Publishing Company, 2000), pp. 75–76.

17 William Hilsley, *When Joy and Pain Entwine: Reminiscences* (Werkhoven: Internationale School Beverweerd, 1988).

18 Personal communication between William Hilsley and the author, 26 January 1997.

19 Helen Colijn, *Song of Survival: Women Interned* (Ashland: White Cloud Press, 1995).

20 Personal communication between Jan Hanuš and the author, 19 November 2000.

5 The nature of chorus

1 We also have the less familiar *choric*, from *chorus*, to describe collective utterance and simultaneous movement.

2 See Aristotle, *On the Art of Poetry* in *Classical Literary Criticism*, trans. T. S. Dorsch (Baltimore: Penguin Classics, 1965), p. 36.

3 This has been amply discussed by Edward Cone in his *The Composer's Voice* (Berkeley: University of California Press, 1974). Cone's primary focus is on the solo voice, though he touches briefly on choral singing in his Chapter 4.

4 From the translation published by Claude Palisca in *The Florentine Camerata: Documentary Studies and Translations* (New Haven: Yale University Press, 1989), p.113. Bardi also satirizes the madrigal style thus: "while Mr. Bass, formally dressed in semibreves and minims, walks about in the ground-floor rooms of his palace, the soprano walks hurriedly with quick steps on the terrace, adorned with minims and semiminims, while Mr. Tenor and the alto go around in the rooms of the intermediate floors with still other rates of movement and dressed otherwise."

5 The element of dance is of equal importance to the musical and the verbal, but space is lacking to give it proper consideration here.

6 Attributed to Bardi; Palisca, *Florentine Camerata*, pp.144 ff.

7 *Ibid.*, p. 125.

8 Such capacious manifestations were not limited to England – see Chester L. Alwes's chapter "Choral Music in the Culture of the Nineteenth Century" in this volume.

9 For a vivid portrait of how it used to be I recommend Reginald Nettel's *Music in the Five Towns, 1840–1914* (Oxford University Press, 1944).

10 I am speaking here of course of what happens *during* services. When churches are used as concert venues the situation can become constructively ambiguous, suffusing the performance with "atmosphere," sanctified perhaps by a few words from the priest, and probably garnering applause at the end even if not always at the beginning.

11 This was described to me by the Faroese composer Sunleif Rasmussen.

12 The association of the carol with Christmas is a later development.

13 Joseph Bédier, quoted in R. L. Greene, *The Early English Carols*, 2nd edn. (Oxford: Clarendon Press, 1977), pp. xlv ff. But cf. Chapter 6, "*The Carole*," of Christopher Page, *Voices and Instruments of the Middle Ages* (London, J. M. Dent & Sons, 1987). Later in the same book Page mentions use of the word *chorus* to denote possibly a wind instrument (p. 229) or a string drum (p. 238).

14 For example in the Fayrfax Manuscript *c.*1500, and Henry VIII's Manuscript *c.*1520. These and slightly earlier polyphonic English carols are available in modern editions in *Musica Britannica*, ed. John Stevens (London: Stainer & Bell), vol. IV, *Mediaeval Carols* (1958), vol. XVIII, *Music at the Court of Henry VIII* (1973), and vol. XXXVI, *Early Tudor Songs and Carols* (1975).

15 Willa Muir was the wife of the poet Edwin Muir. The couple's translations of Kafka and Broch are highly esteemed.

16 Willa Muir, *Living with Ballads* (Oxford University Press, 1965), pp. 16, 31–2. For a broader account, see Iona and Peter Opie, *The Singing Game* (Oxford University Press, 1985), especially Chapter 1.

17 The same may also be said of quite a few carols.

18 The new context may provide the music with new kinds of significance, while also

referring back (in people's minds) to the original kind: this is a fertile area for further debate for which I lack the space here.

19 The faculty of play: see Johan Huizinga, *Homo Ludens: A Study of the Play-element in Culture*, trans. R. F. C. Hall (London: Routledge & Kegan Paul, 1949). p. 187. My references are to the English translation published in London in 1949. The original was published in 1938.

20 This paragraph directly applies Huizinga's definitions of play to the topic of music; see Huizinga, *Home Ludens*, pp. 5, 132.

21 I am using *sacred* in a sense that embraces both drama and ritual.

22 The repertoire embraced sacred music, stage works, and convivial music: madrigals, rounds, catches, and glees.

6 Choral music and tradition in Europe and Israel

1 Clytus Gottwald, "Choral Music and the Avant-Garde," in L. Reimers and B. Wallner (eds.), *Choral Music Perspectives: Dedicated to Eric Ericson* (Stockholm: Royal Swedish Academy of Music, 1993), pp. 119–34.

2 On the New Spirituality, see Richard Taruskin, *Music in the Late Twentieth Century*, vol. V of *The Oxford History of Western Music* (Oxford University Press, 2005).

3 Johann Wolfgang von Goethe, *Einfache Nachahmung der Natur, Manier, Stil*, in his *Werke*, vol. VI, *Vermischte Schrifte* (Frankfurt am Main: Insel Verlag, 1965), pp. 252–56.

7 Canada's choral landscape

1 First Nations is a legally defined term used since the 1980s to refer to Canada's indigenous peoples who are not Inuit (indigenous peoples inhabiting the Arctic regions) or Métis (of mixed indigenous and European ancestry). There are more than 630 recognized First Nation bands or governments in Canada.

2 Following the establishment of singing schools in England and the New England states (USA) whose purpose was to encourage psalm-singing and to engage more singers in this practice, the nineteenth century saw singing masters in many Canadian communities establish classes and choirs to sing psalms and hymn tunes, as well as to teach music-reading skills. Psalm- and hymn-singing were encouraged in both liturgical services and social events.

8 A multiplicity of voices: choral music in the United States

1 Executive Summary, *America's Performing Art: A Study of Choruses, Choral Singers, and Their Impact: The Chorus Impact Study* (Washington, DC: Chorus America, 2003), p. 5. A further breakdown of these numbers indicate there are approximately 270,000 choruses nationwide, with a total of approximately 12,000 professional and community choruses, at least 41,000 K-12 school choruses, and 216,000 religious choirs. These estimates do not include choirs affiliated with colleges and universities and are believed to be conservative, based on the methodology used to calculate these figures.

2 Executive Summary, *The Chorus Impact Study: How Children, Adults, and Communities Benefit from Choruses* (Washington, DC: Chorus America, 2009), p. 6.

3 So-called show choirs bring together aspects of musical theater in concerts, which feature high-energy choral singing and choreography. The first high school show choirs, called *swing choirs*, emerged in 1949 in rural Midwestern communities, inspired in part by the popular television program *The Fred Waring Show*. The influence of popular culture in the 1960s and 1970s led to more elaborate performances, featuring the addition of instrumental combos, lighting, and extensive dance routines, which have gained in popularity over the past forty years.

4 Michael Weaver, "Show Pop: History of Show Choir," www.angelfire.com.

5 Ronald McCurdy, "President's Message," *Jazz Education Journal*, 33, 3 (November 2000): 4, 101.

6 Terese M. Volk, *Music, Education and Multiculturalism: Foundations and Principles* (New York: Oxford University Press, 1998), p. 190.

7 *Ibid.*, p. 81.

8 Allen Britton, Arnold Broido, and Charles Gary, "The Tanglewood Declaration," in Robert Choate (ed.), *Documentary Report of the Tanglewood Symposium* (Washington, DC: Music Education National Conference, 1968), p. 139.

9 Mary Goetze and Carol Scott-Kassner, "The Struggle for Authenticity and Ownership: A Brief Overview of the Past and Future in Multicultural Approaches to Music Education," *The Mountain Lake Reader* (Spring 2006), 8.

10 American Boychoir, "Mission Statement." www.americanboychoir.org.

11 San Francisco Girls Chorus, "About the Chorus." www.sfgirlschorus.org.

12 Executive Summary of *America's Performing Art*, 2003, p. 5.

13 Zamir Chorale, "Music with a Mission."
www.zamir.org/about_us.html (accessed June
17, 2010).
14 The 2003 Chorus America study estimated
that approximately 20 percent of community
choral organizations support professional singers
at some level, although there is no standardized
level of payment from chorus to chorus.
15 National Endowment for the Arts,
American Masterpieces: Choral Music, ed.
Philip Brunelle (Washington, DC: NEA and
Chorus America, 2006)
16 *Ibid.*, p. 6.
17 Americans for the Arts (Organization)
Action Fund, *Congressional Arts Report Card
2008: Your Guide to Voting for the Arts in 2008*
(Washington, DC: Americans for the Arts
Action Fund PAC, 2008).
18 Foreword to *The Chorus Impact Study*.
(2009), p. 3.

9 A hundred years of choral music in Latin America 1908–2008

1 In 1511, the first two bishoprics were created
on the islands of Hispaniola and Puerto Rico.
Between 1516 and 1556, under the reign of
Charles V, twenty-two bishoprics and the
archdioceses of Lima, Santo Domingo, and
Mexico City were founded. The Spanish and
Portuguese colonial empires were theocratic
regimes and it was the monarch who directed
the emigration of clerics to the New World. In
the second half of the eighteenth century, the
political organization was characterized by the
division of the continent into viceroyalties,
known by the term "virreinato" and these, in
turn, were divided into *audiencias*
(presidencies or captaincies) as follows:
Virreinato de Nueva España (from Florida and
the west bank of the Mississippi River to Costa
Rica and the Caribbean islands); Virreinato de
Nueva Granada (Venezuela, Colombia,
Panama, and Ecuador); Virreinato del Peru
(Lima, Cuzco, and Chile); Virreinato del Rio de
La Plata (Audiencia of Charcas, which
included Bolivia and Uruguay); and the
Virreinato de Brazil.
  The following were the most outstanding
chapel masters and composers of the
virreinatos:

> Virreinato de Nueva España Cathedral of
> Mexico: Francisco Lópéz de Capillas
> (1615–73) (Spanish), Manuel de
> Zumaya (1678–1755) (Mexican), and
> Ignacio Jerusalem (1710–69) (Italian).
> Puebla Cathedral: Gaspar Fernández
> (1566–1629) (Portuguese) and Juan

> Gutiérrez de Padilla (1590–1664)
> (Spanish) – perhaps the most impor-
> tant composer of New Spain. Cathedral
> of Santiago de Cuba: Esteban Salas
> (1725–1803) (Cuban).
> Virreinato de Nueva Granada Cathedral of
> Caracas: Francisco Perez Camacho
> (1687–1725). Cathedral of Cartagena:
> Gutierre Fernandez Hidalgo (1588–
> 1620). Cathedral of Bogotá: Jose
> Cascante (1650–1702) and Juan de
> Herrera (1665–1738). Cathedral of
> Quito: Diego Lobato (1538–1610)
> (Ecuadorian, son of one of the wives
> of the Incan Atahualpa).
> Virreinato del Perú Cathedral of Lima and
> La Plata: Tomás de Torrejón y Velasco
> (1644–1728) (Spanish), Roque Cerruti
> (1683–1760) (Italian), and Juan de
> Araujo (1646–1712) (Spanish).
> Virreinato del Río de la Plata Doménico
> Zípoli (1688–1726) (Italian).
> Virreinato de Brasil Church of San
> Sebastian, Rio de Janeiro: José Maria
> Nunes García (1798–1808).

2 Fray Juan de Torquemada, *Monarquía
Indiana*. Instituto de Investigaciones
Históricas, Universidad Nacional Autónoma
de México, Bk. XVII, vol. V, p. 320.
3 F. C. Lange, *La música en Minas Gerais,
estudio preliminar* (Boletin Latinoamericano
de Música, Acervo Curt Lange Universidade de
Minas Gerais,1946).
4 Pedro Palacios y Sojo, known as Padre
Sojo, founded the Oratorio de San Felipe
Neri in 1764 and organized musical
education in Venezuela in 1783. He cultivated
coffee, and his hacienda in Chacao served as
the main center of music education and
composition during the eighteenth century.
5 From the mid eighteenth century, the
Portuguese influence generated a rococo style in
the Minas Gerais region. The most prominent
composers were Lobo de Mesquita, Inácio
Parreira Neves, and Manoel Días de Oliveira.
The German/Uruguayan musicologist Francisco
Curt Lange (1903–97), rescued most of their
works.
6 J. Orrego Salas, "Técnica y éstetica," in Isabel
Aretz (ed.), *América Latina en su música*
(UNESCO, Siglo veinte-uno editores, 1977).
7 *Gaucho* is the name given to peasants – good
horse riders – of the plains in Argentina,
Uruguay, and Rio Grande in Brazil, who
developed their own literature and folk music.
Porteño, meaning "the man born in the
port," refers to the inhabitants of Buenos Aires.
The "porteño style" is a mixture of the

European and local culture in Argentina which is evident in the music, particularly in the tango.
8 G. Béhague, *Music in Latin America* (Englewood Cliffs, NJ: Prentice Hall, 1979).
9 J. A. Calcaño, *La ciudad y su música* (Caracas: Crónica Musical de Caracas, 1956).

10 Choral music in East Asia: China, Japan, and Korea
1 On IDS, see S. Mithen, *The Singing Neanderthals: The Origins of Music, Language, Mind and Body* (London: Weidenfeld and Nicolson, 2005).
2 For East Asians, the surname normally precedes the given name; this custom is reflected in this chapter.
3 R. Bloesch and W. Weyburn, *Twentieth Century Choral Music: An Annotated Bibliography of Music Appropriate for College and University Choirs*. American Choral Directors Association Monograph No. 9 (1997).

11 New voices in ancient lands: choral music in South and Southeast Asia
1 See for example, P. Yampolsky, *Vocal Music from Central and West Flores*, Washington, DC: Smithsonian Folkways Recordings, 1995.
2 For convenience, I use "Asia/n" to refer to "South and Southeast Asia/n".
3 V. A. Coelho, "Kapsberger's Apotheosis . . . of Francis Xavier (1622) and the Conquering of India," in Richard Dellamora, and Daniel Fischlin (eds.), *The Work of Opera: Genre, Nationhood, and Sexual Difference* (New York: Columbia University Press, 1997), pp. 27–47, p. 43.

12 From chanting Quran to singing oratorio: choral music in West and Central Asia
1 Mary Boyce, *Zoroastrians: Their Religious Beliefs and Practices* (London and New York: Routledge, 2001), p. 37.
2 Adam Mez, *The Renaissance of Islam* (New York: AMS Press Inc., 1975), p. 336.
3 Habib Hassan Touma, *The Music of the Arabs* (Portland, OR: Amadeus Press, 1996), p. 158.
4 Regula Burckhardt Qureshi, "Sufi Music and the Historicity of Oral Tradition," in Stephen Blum, Philip Bohlman, and Daniel Neuman (eds.), *Ethnomusicology and Modern Music History* (University of Illinois Press, 1991), p. 109.

5 Lois Ibsen al-Faruqi, "The Mawlid," in *The World of Music*, vol. XXVIII/3 (1986), p. 85.
6 Joseph Jordania, *Who Asked the First Question: Origins of Vocal Polyphony, Human Intelligence, Language and Speech* (Tbilisi: Logos, 2006), p. 154.

13 Voices of the Pacific: the (ch)oral traditions of Oceania
1 For the purposes of this chapter, Oceania comprises Melanesia, Micronesia, Polynesia, Australia, and New Zealand. The oldest human remains from Lake Mungo, South Australia are dated almost 40,000 years ago. In New Zealand the waves of migration came from Eastern Polynesia during the period AD 800–1300. Samoa's oral history dates back to AD 1000. By the early tenth century, Tonga had the most expansive pre-European colonial empire in the Pacific. See Richard Moyle, *Tongan Music* (Auckland University Press, 1987), p. 17.
2 In Australia, Creation stories originate in the Dreaming as the ancestors sang the world into existence; in NZ the Creation story begins with the figures of Papatūānuku, the land (a powerful mother earth figure) and Ranginui, the heavens (the sky father), who have their equivalents throughout Polynesia. www.teara. govt.nz/EarthSeaAndSky/Astronomy/ RanginuiTheSky/3/en.
3 The main islands in Western Polynesia include Tonga, Niue, and Samoa and in Eastern Polynesia, the Cook Islands, Tahiti, the Marquesas, and Hawaii. Eastern Polynesians arrived first in New Zealand. The inhabitants of the Torres Strait Islands included Polynesians, Melanesians, and Aboriginals.
4 Moyle, (*Tongan Music*, p. 166)
5 *Ibid.* p. 46. Early visitors to Tonga during Cook's visit in 1777 observed the importance of rehearsal and practice before a public performance, in keeping with these expectations of excellence.
6 There were many names for chant: *waiata, haka, karanga* (New Zealand); *hula, mele, olioli* (Hawaii); *pe'e* (Cook Islands), for example.
  Detailed accounts of the songs' musical content can be found in Moyle, *Tongan Music*, and Mervyn McLean, *Weavers of Song: Polynesian Music and Dance* (Auckland University Press, 1999). Lullabies, love songs, songs of lament, war songs, paddling songs, game songs, work songs, songs of praise, taunting, and insulting songs were amongst the song types.

7 There were hunting, funeral, and gossip songs, songs of the ancestors, landscapes, animals, seasons, myths, and Dreamtime legends.

8 Caitlin Rowley (ed.), *Australia: Exploring the Musical Landscape* (Sydney: Australian Music Centre, 1998), p. 7; Bruce Chatwin, *The Songlines* (London: Cape, 1987), pp. 62 ff. In Arnhem Land, the songs were either inherited or found in dreams communicated by the spirit of a deceased singer. Thus the songs were passed on.

9 McLean (*Weavers of Song*, p. 469): *aufaipese* in Samoa, *kauhiva* in Tonga, and *waiata tira* (rows or a group of singers) in New Zealand. "Choirs" were groups of singers who sang sacred music. And the word "chorus" denoted a group of singers who sang secular music.

10 According to Christopher Marshall, a New Zealand composer who lived for a time in Samoa, the role of the conductor in Samoan performance may have some connection to the clown or *fa'aluma*. The traditional role of the clown predates choirs, and as with medieval court jesters the role was to mock the *matai* (personal communication, April 2009).

11 Moyle, (*Tongan Music*, p. 33).

12 McLean, (*Weavers of Song*, p. 403).

13 In present-day concert parties, the men perform the *haka*, the women the *poi* and together they perform modern action songs or *waiata-ringa*. In New Zealand for example, the *marae* calls or *karanga* used to welcome the guests are reserved for an older woman. http://folksong.org.nz/haere_mai/index.html gives various examples of the karanga.

14 McLean, *Weavers of Song*, p. 404.

15 Jill Stubbington, "North Australian Aboriginal Music," in J. Isaacs (ed.), *Australian Aboriginal Music* (Australia: Aboriginal Artists Agency Ltd, 1979).

16 McLean, (*Weavers of Song*, p. 396) notes that there is little evidence of formal teaching of music or dance to children in the history of Polynesia. Children learned game songs from each other but for the rest they copied the adults.

17 Dr J. E. Moulton, founder and the first principal of Tupou College, introduced this notation system in the 1860s. Richard Moyle confirms that this served a didactic purpose and was not a language of gesture (personal conversation, April 2009).

18 Personal conversation (April 2009) with Te Tuhi Robust (Director of the James Henare Centre, University of Auckland). The *waiata* are the songs and chants of the Māori, which, through their words, preserve the knowledge and the wisdom of the ancestors. There are many forms of *waiata* and a song performed is always appropriate to the occasion.

19 Margaret Orbell and Mervyn McLean, *Songs of a Kaumātua Sung by Kino Hughes* (Auckland University Press, 2002), inside cover.

20 The earliest arrival in Oceania was Willem Janszoon who made landfall at the Pennefather River on the western shore of Cape York, Australia, in the *Duyfken* (Little Dove) on February 26, 1606. Dutch explorers (Schouten and Lemaire) arrived in Tonga in 1616. Abel Janszoon Tasman's flagship, *Heemskeerck* and the *Zeehaen* sailed into Golden Bay in NZ in 1642.

21 Christopher B. Balme, in his *Pacific Performances: Theatricality and Cross-Cultural Encounter in the South Sea* (New York: Palgrave Macmillan, 2007), quotes Anne Salmond, *Two Worlds: First Meetings between Maori and Europeans 1642–1772* (Auckland: Viking, 1991) and discusses this in his Chapter 1, "Trumpets, Beaches and Women." John Mansfield Thomson, in his *Musical Images: A New Zealand Historical Journey 1840–1990* (Wellington: National Library of New Zealand, 1990), p. 11, states: "The dialogue took place between the pūkāea, a wooden trumpet, or the pūtātāra, a shell trumpet and the European Baroque trumpet, then at the height of its powers." The bay was later named Murderers' Bay after the local Māori killed four Dutch sailors; the trumpet calls were most likely interpreted as calls to war.

22 Thomson (1990), p. 12.

23 Anne Salmond, *Between Worlds: Early Exchanges between Maori and Europeans 1773–1815* (Auckland: Viking, 1997), p. 450.

24 Ibid., p. 79. "Sometimes they sing an underpart which is a third lower, except for the last 2 notes which are the same."

25 McLean, *Weavers of Song*, p. 423.

26 Ibid., p. 431.

27 In Tonga where there was a pre-European polyphony, singing in harmony was already familiar; consequently the English music proved less of a challenge. In general, Polynesian and Aboriginal tuning systems bore little resemblance to the English.

28 Richards, www.diasporas.ac.uk/assets/Richards%20small%20grants.pdf. By 1922 and during the time of Pastor Carl Strehlow from Ansbach (1871–1922), Lutheran hymns such as "Wachet auf" were being sung. By the 1930s there was a four-part choir. Today it is a women's choir. The sound is one rich in upper partials with instinctive portamento between the notes of the chorale tunes.

29 Matthew Westwood, "Religious Choirs a Constant across the Desert," *The Australian*, September 14, 2007.

30 Personal conversation with Richard Moyle (April 2009).

31 In 1814, Thomas Kendall, William Hall, and John King arrived in the Bay of Islands under the auspices of the Anglican Church Missionary Society. In 1839 Bishop Jean Baptiste François Pompallier established a French Catholic mission at Kororāreka (present-day Russell).

32 Sir George Grey laid the foundation stone in 1865.

33 Manu Boyd, "Himeni: Nurturing Spirituality through Songs of Faith," *Wai ola o OHA* 28, no. 3 (2001), 18.

34 The *Adelaider Liedertafel* dates back to 1840, recognized and officially formed in 1858.

35 The first New Zealand Eisteddfod took place in Durham Street Hall, Christchurch in 1926. The competitions included music, poetry, elocution, needlework, and cookery. The hymn tunes in the competition included *Moab, Sancteidd, and Aberdovey. In his Music Is Where You Find It: Music in the Town of Hawera, 1946: An Historical Ethnography ([Wellington]: Music Books New Zealand, 2004), p. 137, Allan Thomas also refers to recitation and singing in the context of popular music recorded in Hawera, New Zealand in 1946.*

36 The Alexander Turnbull Library in Wellington has a magnificent picture taken in 1896 of the Scandinavian Choral Singers conducted by Mr. Overley.

37 For an insightful view on Hill's life and his contribution to musical life in New Zealand and Australia, see John Mansfield Thomson, *A Distant Music: The Life and Times of Alfred Hill, 1879–1960* (Oxford University Press, 1980).

38 A poi song written and composed by Alfred Hill, dedicated to "C. F. Goldie, Esq."

39 The cantata is based on the legend of Hinemoa and Tutanekai. The Māori Opera Company performed Bennett and Flynn's opera of the same name in 1915. The legend held much attraction for European composers.

40 English-born Isaac Nathan (1790–1864), of Jewish and Polish extraction, migrated to Australia in 1841; shortly after his arrival he opened a music academy in Sydney.

41 The first to do so in New Zealand, at the recommendation of Sir John Stainer at Oxford University, was Professor William E. Thomas on October 10, 1900. He was appointed Professor of Music at the University of Auckland and director of the Auckland Choral Society.

42 A key figure in New Zealand choral music, Peter Godfrey came from King's College, Cambridge in 1958 to take up the posts of lecturer in music at the University of Auckland and Director of Music at Holy Trinity Cathedral.

43 Douglas Lilburn (1915–2001) studied with Ralph Vaughan Williams, Peter Sculthorpe (1929–) with Egon Wellesz and Edmund Rubbra, and Dorothea Franchi (1921–2003) with Herbert Howells. Later, Jenny McLeod (1941–) studied with Messiaen, Stockhausen, and Berio; David Griffiths (1950–) studied with Alexander Goehr.

44 Debra Shearer presents a similar view of the Australian composers in her "Emerging Voices in Australian Choral Music – Selected Works of Sculthorpe, Boyd, Edwards, Hopkins, Maclean, Leek, Stanhope, Grandage, Orlovich and Atherton," dissertation, Doctor of Music, Indiana University, 2003, pp.6–12.

45 Bailey (1967, p.14) *Come all ye Tonguers* is a typical example. Douglas Mews used this melody for his SATB arrangement, one of *Two NZ Folk Songs of the Sea* (1987).

46 Auckland Choral Society was established in 1855, Philharmonic Society in Sydney in 1836, and the Royal Melbourne Philharmonic Society in 1853. Simon Tipping gives an excellent view on the Orpheus Choir of Wellington in his *Orpheus: Portrait of a Choir* (Palmerston North: Dunmore Press, 2002).

47 Adrienne Simpson, *Hallelujahs and History: Auckland Choral 1855–2005* (Auckland Choral, 2005), pp. 175–223, Appendix 1: Performance Chronology of the Auckland Choral Society, now known as Auckland Choral.

48 The very famous Hawaiian *Liahona Glee Club* began in 1922; it gave concerts, sang at private functions and competed in public song contests. It was also part of the Awaiolimu Mormon Choir.

49 The Popular Methodist Māori Singers had amidst its members the famous Māori baritone Inia Te Wiata, who is remembered for his remarkable musical versatility and his skill as a master carver. *Just call me happy: Inia Te Wiata*. Atoll acd507, is a documentary of his life presented by his wife Beryl Te Wiata in 2007.

50 MGLC Melbourne (1990), Sydney Gay and Lesbian Choir (1991), GALS, NZ (1992).

51 Examples include the Sydney Street Choir, The Solidarity Choir, The Australian Byzantine Choir, Chinese Community Choirs and La Voce della Luna (Melbourne Italian Women's Choir) to name but a few.

52 www.fmhs.auckland.ac.nz/faculty/cbr/events/choir.aspx Research at the University of Auckland shows that singing may help to "rewire" the brain after brain injury.

53 In Australia, Faye Dumont's research to date identifies over two hundred Australian choral composers. As a pioneer in the teaching and training of choral conductors in Australasia, she continues to be a driving force in choral education. She directs the Melbourne Chamber Choir, the Melbourne Women's Choir, and Chorelation.

54 McLean, *Weavers of Song*, p. 381. The Tongan word *punake* (poet) is an abbreviated form of two words, *puna* to fly and *hake*, on high; the *punake* is a person whose sensibility goes up as if flying to the heights; this poet/composer/choreographer was highly regarded and was often commissioned to write for important people and events.

Queen Salote, a keen writer of love poems, dance songs and *lakalaka* (which means "to step briskly") would send for a *punake* to commission a new dance for an important occasion. A pig and a mat might well accompany the verbal request. (From a personal conversation with Richard Moyle, April 2009.)

55 From the vast number of choral works that have been composed, I have identified a select list (see page 184). They are largely works that attempt to relate to the landscape and to the many musical traditions that coexist in the Pacific.

56 Jack Body describes his *Carol to St. Stephen* as a "deconstruction/recomposition" written for 3 soloists and 12-part choir and based on a fifteenth-century carol, "Eya, martyr Stephane."

57 Shearer, "Emerging Voices," p. 70.

58 Hamilton's *Missa Pacifica* also treads between the two worlds of Asia and the Pacific.

59 See the composer's program note at http://sounz.org.nz/finder/show/works?query=Five+Lullabies&x=0&y=0.

60 Scored for women's voices, *Chaos of Delight III* is based on bird song of the New Zealand forests; the cicadas are represented by the sound of metal clickers played by each singer.

61 Shearer, "Emerging Voices," p. 56. The aboriginal melody was the first to be transcribed into Western notation and was presumed to have been collected in the nineteenth century by Perron and Freycinet.

62 Mews and McLean were colleagues on the staff of Auckland University at that time. The baritone Robert Wiremu gives a haunting performance on the New Zealand Youth Choir's disc *Winds that Whisper* (Trust Records MMT2016).

63 *Ahua* is written for kapahaka group, SATB choir, 6 soloists and symphony orchestra.

14 Choral music in Africa: history, content, and performance practice

1 J. H. K. Nketia, *African Music in Ghana: A Survey of Traditional Forms* (Accra: Longmans, 1963), p. 54.

2 A. Euba, "Nketia, J. H. K. and the African Avant-Garde," in A. Euba and C. T. Kimberlin (eds.), *Composition in Africa and the Diaspora* (Richmond, CA: MRI Press, 2008), vol. I, pp. 143–54, p. 150.

3 For Islamic influence, see the following: O. Károlyi *African Traditional and Oriental Music* (Auckland, New Zealand: Penguin Books, 1998); Mahmoud Guettat, "The State of Music in the Arab World" in R. Letts and K. Fahkouri (eds.), *The Status of Music around the World* (Paris: International Music Council, 2007), pp. 9–15.

4 J. N. Kidula, "Music Culture: African Life," in R. King (ed.), *Music in the Life of the African Church* (Waco, TX: Baylor University Press, 2008), pp. 37–57.

5 See the following recent studies. R. De Beer, "The Origins, Developments, and Current Performance Practices of African Neo-Traditional Choral Music of Southern Africa." Unpublished doctoral thesis, Nelson Mandela Metropolitan University, Port Elizabeth, 2007. M. Detterbeck, "South African Choral Music (Amakwaya): Song, Contest and the Formation of Identity." Unpublished doctoral thesis, University of Natal, Durban, 2002. G. E. Olwage, "Music and (Post) Colonialism: the Dialectics of Choral Culture on a South African Frontier." Unpublished doctoral thesis, Rhodes University, Grahamstown, 2003. One major influence in the choral tradition in Southern Africa referred to by these authors is the visit of Orpheus McAdoo and his Jubilee Singers from the United States which is the origin of the enormous choral tradition of the Cape Malayan society.

6 Examples of such choral works include *Vuka Vuka Deborah*, *No Musalaba Gogenda* and *Adanse Kronkron* by J. K. Bokwe, Arthur Kemoli, and J. H. K. Nketia respectively. See also J. N. Kidula, H. Wanjala, and W. Shitandi, "Setting Indigenous Melodies for Concert Performances: A Historical Outline on the 'Adaptation and Arrangement of African Tunes,'" paper presented during an International Music Symposium at Kenyatta University, 2002; M. Nzewi, "Challenges for African Music and Musicians in the Modern World Music Context," in C. T. Kimberlin and A. Euba (eds.), *Intercultural Music* (California: MRI Press, 1999), vol. II, pp. 201–28.

7 O. Olaniyan, "A Discourse of Yoruba Lyrics (Otherwise Known as Native Airs) as Contemporary Art Music for Christian Workship," in M. Omibiyi-Obidike (ed.), *The Art Music of Nigeria: Prospects and Problems* (Nigeria: Stirling Horden Publishers, 2001), pp. 58–69. Describing the Nigerian "native air," Herbst, Zaidel-Rudolf, and Onyeji see these compositions as a fusion of Nigerian traditional music and Western choral styles with textual setting from biblical passages or Christian stories. Anri Herbst, Jeanne Zaidel-Rudolf, and Christian Onyeji, "Written Composition," in A. Herbst, Meki Nzewi, and V. Kofi Agawu (eds.), *Musical Arts in Africa: Theory, Practice, and Education* (Pretoria: Unisa Press, 2003), pp. 144–45. These compositions are often performed by choirs in churches and are sometimes rendered as "own choice compositions for many celebrated choral competitions." Vernacular is preferred but English texts are occasionally used. Although strong polyphonic features characterize the textual style, homophonic texture may be used from time to time. "Native airs" make use of diatonic scale and European functional harmonies consisting essentially of triads and seventh chords. These are structured in an African choral technique of ostinato, call-and-response rhythm based on onomatopoeia, as well as linear harmony.

8 A. Euba, *Essays of Music in Africa*, vol. 2: *Intercultural Perspectives* (Lagos, Elekoto Music Centre Lagos, 1989).

9 *Ibid.*; O. Elly Ogalo, "Luo Afro-Classics from Kenya," unpublished MA thesis, Kenyatta University, 1995. Gabriel Musungu, "Samia-Afro-Classics: A Creative Composition," unpublished MA thesis, Kenyatta University. Herbst, et al., "Written Composition."

10 The name KUESTA is derived from two words, "kuns" (Afrikaans for "art") and "fiesta."

11 *Mashindano* and *kwaya* are Kiswahili words, which are translations of English words, "competition and choir" respectively.

12 The *isicathamiya* style of singing consists of quiet dances and soft singing that the performers utilized in order not to get caught by the police, because these festivals or concerts were sometimes used as illegal political gatherings.

13 There are only a few institutions that train choral conductors and singers, such as Kenyatta University in Kenya, the Makerere University in Kampala (Uganda) and the Nelson Mandela Metropolitan University in Port Elizabeth (South Africa). There is also only one African university where prospective musicians can study choral conducting and singing as a major or practical instrument, namely the Stellenbosch University in the Western Cape province of South Africa. It is also the only African university to host an academic choir, Schola Cantorum. This choir is utilized as laboratory for choral conductors in examinations, workshops and master classes. Both the courses offered at the two South African universities were initiated by Kåre Hanken from Norway, who had the support from the Norwegian Choral Association to establish formal choral education on the continent; Rudolf de Beer structured the curriculum at Stellenbosch University as mentioned.

14 Information provided by Angela Boetius.

15 Edzimkulu uses members of Memeza African choir (a Soweto-based choir) and a Canadian singer-songwriter Laryssa Whittaker for HIV/AIDS activism through choral performances aimed at initiating HIV/AIDs education and discussions.

16 A. A. Mensah, "Compositional Practices in African Music," in R. Stone (ed.), *The Garland Encyclopedia of World Music: Africa* (New York, Garland Publishing, 1998), pp. 208–31.

17 Some of these composers and their works have been published and/or discussed in Y. Huskisson, *The Bantu Composers of Southern Africa Supplement* (Pretoria: Human Sciences Research Council, 1983); P. Klatzow, *Composers in South Africa Today* (Cape Town: Oxford University Press, 1987); Bode Omojola, *Nigeria Art Music* (Ibadan: IFRA, 1997); M. Floyd (ed.), *Composing the Music of Africa: Composition, Interpretation and Realization* (Aldershot: Ashgate, 1999); Samha El-Kholy, "Traditional and Folk Idioms in Modern Egyptian Composition since the Fifties," in C. T. Kimberlin and Akin Euba (eds.), *Intercultural Music* (Richmond, CA: MRI Press, 1999), vol. II, pp. 33–44; O. Oluwalooye Bateye, "An Analysis of the 1st Movement of the Nigerian Folk Symphony Theatre," in Mosunmola Omibiyi-Obidike (ed), *The Art Music of Nigeria: Problems and Prospects* (Ibadan: Stirling-Horden Publishers (Nig.) Ltd., 2001), pp. 117–26; J. H. K. Nketia, *African Art Music* (Ghana: Afram Publications, 2004); J. N. Kidula, "Music Culture: African Life," the South African Music Rights Organization (SAMRO), and the Centre for Intercultural Music Arts (CIMA).

18 A. Kamel, "Egyptian Composition in the Twentieth Century," in M. Floyd (ed.),

Composing the Music of Africa: Composition, Interpretation and Realization (Aldershot: Ashgate, 1999).

19 G. F. Barz, "Tamati: Music Competition and Community Formation," in F. Gunderson and G. Barz (eds.), *Mashindano! Competitive Music Performance in East Africa* (Dar es Salaam: Nyota and Mkuki Publishers, 2000), pp. 421–28; Kidula, Wanjala, and Shitandi, "Setting Indigenous Melodies."

20 A. A. Mensah, "Compositional Practices in African Music."

21 T. Turino, *Nationalists, Cosmopolitans and Popular Music in Zimbabwe* (University of Chicago Press, 2000).

15 Globalization, multiculturalism, and the children's chorus

1 See the websites africanchildrenschoir.com and worldyouthchoir.org.

2 Igor Stravinsky, *Poetics of Music in the Form of Six Lessons* (Charles Eliot Norton Lectures, 1939–40, Harvard University Press: 1947).

3 Orpheus was founded in 1972 by cellist Julian Fifer and a group of fellow musicians who aspired to perform diverse orchestral repertoire using chamber music ensemble techniques. One of the few self-governing ensembles playing today, Orpheus continues this philosophy, performing without a conductor and rotating musical leadership roles for each work. The orchestra strives to empower its musicians by integrating them into virtually every facet of the organization, literally changing the way the world thinks about musicians, conductors, and orchestras.

16 Exploring the universal voice

1 Exceptions exist in the countries that were incorporated into the Soviet Union during the twentieth century, Turkey, and China where conservatories integrate the study of both traditional music and Western music.

2 See, for example, the Global Voices Interactive series, found at www. globalvoicesinteractive.com, or Vela Vela, available at www.molliestone.org/ PurchaseVelaVela.html.

3 Alan Lomax, *Folk Song Style and Culture* (New Brunswick, NJ: American Association for the Advancement of Science, 1968), p. 70.

4 Jamie Webster Stech, "American Women and the Mysterious Voice: American Women Performing Gender through Singing Bulgarian

Songs." 2002. http://depts.washington.edu/ reecas/events/conf2002/regconf02.html, p. 12.

5 Miyako Furiya, workshop session, International Society for Music Education, World Conference 2000, Edmonton, Canada.

6 For example, a technique called *katajjaq* is practiced by the Inuits of Canada. See Hugo Zemp et al., *Les Voix du Monde (Voices of the World)* (Paris: Collection du Centre National de la Recherche Scientifique et du Musée de l'Homme, 1996). CNR-3741010/12.

7 Richard Miller, *The Structure of Singing: System and Art in Vocal Technique* (New York: Schirmer Books, 1996).

8 D. Ralph Appelman, *The Science of Vocal Pedagogy* (Bloomington: Indiana University Press, 1967), p. 122.

9 There is some debate as to whether the phenomenon of phonation is actually a product of subglottal pressure increasing and causing the "buzz," or whether the vocal folds come together as a result of the decreased air pressure between them, a phenomenon known as the "Bernoulli effect" – or a combination of both. See William Vennard, *Singing: The Mechanism and the Technic* (New York: Carl Fisher, 1967), p. 42.

10 *Falsetto* is a *bel canto* term from the Italian, which means "false" or "falsified" voice. Western vocal pedagogy research has observed that it occurs when the front part of the vocal folds is immobilized and only a small length of the cords is used to phonate (Vennard, *Singing*, p. 71).

11 Karen Ann Kochis-Jennings, "Intrinsic Laryngeal Muscle Activity and Vocal Fold Adduction Patterns in Female Vocal Registers: Chest, Chestmix, and Headmix." Doctoral dissertation, University of Iowa, 2008, p. 98.

12 *Ibid.*

13 Miller, *The Structure of Singing*.

14 James C. McKinney, *The Diagnosis and Correction of Vocal Faults* (Long Grove, IL: Waveland Press, Inc., 1994).

15 Zemp, *Les Voix du Monde*.

16 McKinney, *Diagnosis and Correction*, p. 126.

17 *Ibid.*, p. 151.

18 Claude El Kantner and Robert West, *Phonetics* (New York: Harper & Brothers, 1960), p. 68.

19 One of the main aims of *bel canto* training is to assist in the emphasizing of a band of formants $c.2800\sim3400$ Hz, known as the singer's formant. See Meribeth Bunch, 1997. *Dynamics of the Singing Voice* (Vienna/New York: Springer-Verlag, 1997), p. 97; Miller, *The Structure of Singing*, p. 56; Vennard, *Singing*, p. 129.

20 Christine Wondolowski Gerstein, *Early Musical Training in Bel Canto Vocal*

Technique: A Brief History and Philosophy. Hofstra University, 1994. ED 393758, p. 5.

21 Kochis-Jennings, "Intrinsic Laryngeal Muscle Activity."

22 Appelman, *The Science*, p. 90. *Bel canto* pedagogy holds that in order to avoid noticeable "breaks" between the registers, singers need to maintain a laryngeal position that discourages accumulated tension, which would lead to an inability to perform the mix or transition from chest to head register (see Vennard, *Singing*, p. 58).

23 McKinney, *Diagnosis and Correction*, p. 129. Additionally, the lowered larynx position is promoted, in conjunction with a relaxed musculature at the base of the tongue and untensed jaw muscles, as a way of preventing unwanted tension from affecting the musculature (primarily the thyrohyoid, which suspends the thyroid cartilage from the hyoid bone above it) and affecting the vocal folds within (Vennard, *Singing*, pp. 108–9). The ability to dynamically shift between thicker and thinner vocal fold use and without noticeable "breaks" between registers, argues Western vocal pedagogy, would be hindered as a result of excessive tension.

24 Studies by McPherson, Mazo, Meizel, Fales, Fox, and Finchum, for instance.

25 These appear at the end of the chapter.

26 L. Popeil, "Comparing Belt and Classical Techniques using MRI and Video-fluoroscopy,"*Journal of Singing* 56, 2 (1999): 27–29; J. Estill, "Belting and Classic Voice Quality: Some Physiological Differences," *Medical Problems of Performing Artists* 3 (1988): 37–43.

27 Spectrograms depict the spectral components of sound with time running along the x axis, and frequency, measured in Hertz, along the y axis; variations in intensity, normally measured in decibels, are only roughly indicated according to the brightness scale of the colors.

28 The audio files can be downloaded at www. mjpublishing.com/ccr.

29 H. K. Schutte and D. G. Miller, "Belting and Pop, Commercial Approaches to the Female Middle Voice: Some Preliminary Considerations," *Journal of Voice* 7, 2 (1993): 142–50; Ingo R. Titze, "Belting and the High Larynx Position," *Journal of Singing* 63, 5 (2007): 557–58; Van Lawrence, "Laryngological Observations on 'Belting,'" *Journal of Research in Singing and Applied Vocal Pedagogy* 2, 1 (1979): 26–28; Estill, "Belting and Classical Voice Quality." It is not within the limits of this chapter to summarize the research and discussion of belting.

30 Estill, "Belting and Classical Voice Quality," p. 37. Fado is in fact from Portugal; belting and other styles of heavy-mechanism singing are, however, prevalent in Spain: for example flamenco's *cante jondo*, Galician and Asturian *pandeiretadas*.

31 *Tessitura*, a *bel canto* term that can mean the preferred range of a singer, is used here to mean the dominant range of notes present in a given piece.

32 Zemp, *Les Voix du Monde*.

33 With an exception to be made for European languages such as French, which frequently employ nasal consonants and their accompanying vowel colors.

34 This is not dissimilar to scoops and slides found in Western popular styles such as blues, country or rock, where they are idiomatic to the style.

35 Though it may be argued that the Baroque Italian ornament known as *gorgia* or *trillo ribattuto* comes close in effect and in manner of production.

36 Carole Pegg, *Mongolian Music, Dance, and Oral Narrative: Recovering Performance Traditions* (University of Washington Press, 2001).

37 This technique has been incorporated into Western compositions by Karlheinz Stockhausen in the 1960s, and more recently by the Australians Sarah Hopkins and Stephen Leek.

38 These examples can be heard at www. mjpublications.com/ccr.

39 Lomax, *Folk Song Style and Culture*, pp. 70–71.

40 Leon Thurman, Carol Klitzke, and Norman Hogikyan, "Cornerstones of Voice Protection," in Leon Thurman and Graham Welch (eds.), *Bodymind and Voice: Foundations of Voice Education*, rev. edn. (Collegeville MN: VoiceCare Network and National Center for Voice and Speech), pp. 646–55.

17 Authentic choral music experience as "good work": the practice of engaged musicianship

1 Nikolaus Harnoncourt, *Baroque Music Today: Music as Speech* (Portland, OR: Amadeus Press, 1995), p. 15.

2 Huib Schippers, *Facing the Music: Shaping Music Education from a Global Perspective* (New York: Oxford University Press, 2010), p. 47.

3 Howard Gardner, Mihaly Csikszentmihalyi, and William Damon, *Good Work: When Excellence and Ethics Meet* (New York: Basic Books, 2001), p. ix.

4 www.goodworkproject.org/publications/papers/?view=series Accessed April 19, 2011. Laurinda Morway, Jeff Solomon, Mimi

Michaelson, and Howard Gardner, 2001. "Contemplation and Implications for Good Work In Teaching." *GoodWork Project Report Series*, no. 6, 2001.

5 For an elaboration of this idea, see Doreen Rao, "Feminine Perspectives on Conducting and Teaching Choral Music," in Joan Conlon (ed.), *Wisdom, Wit, and Will: Women Choral Conductors on Their Art* (Chicago: GIA Publications, 2009).

6 Doreen Rao, *Circle of Sound Voice Education* (New York: Boosey & Hawkes, 2005).

7 This is true in both the realms of historical authenticity and authentic performance in world musics.

8 Doreen Rao, "Craft, Singing Craft, and Musical Experience: A Philosophical Study with Implications for Music Education as Aesthetic Education." PhD dissertation, Northwestern University, 1988.

9 "Praxial": having to do with the way in which things are done, particularly in the context of the traditions and standards of a particular discipline, such as conducting, teaching, or medicine, for example.

10 Wayne Bowman, "Educating Musically," in Richard Colwell and Carol Richardson (eds.), *The New Handbook of Research on Music Teaching and Learning: A Project of the Music Educators National Conference* (Oxford University Press, 2002), pp. 63–84.

11 Wayne Bowman, "Music as Ethical Encounter" (The Charles Leonhard Lecture, University of Illinois, April 17, 2000), *Bulletin of the Council for Research in Music Education* 151 (2001), 11–20.

12 The aesthetic philosophy of music education was first introduced by University of Illinois Professor Charles Leonard, a student of Suzanne Langer at Columbia University, in his article "Music Education: Aesthetic Education." (*Education* 74 (1953), 23–26). The notion of music education as aesthetic education was further developed and refined by Bennett Reimer in his book *A Philosophy of Music Education* (Englewood Cliffs: Prentice Hall, 1970), which became an influential text.

13 The concept of non-verbal forms of musical knowing as procedural knowledge was first articulated by this author in her dissertation "Craft, Singing Craft, and Musical Experience." Described by David Elliott as "a praxial philosophy of music education" in his *Music Matters: A New Philosophy of Music Education* (New York: Oxford University Press, 1995), musical thinking-in-action has been closely associated with music education for the past ten years.

14 Bowman, "Music as Ethical Encounter."

15 *Ibid.*

16 Nel Noddings, "Caring In Education," *The Encyclopedia of Informal Education*, 2005. www.infed.org/biblio/noddings_caring_in_education.htm. Accessed September 16, 2010.

17 Bowman, "Music as Ethical Encounter."

18 Francis E. Sparshott, s.v. "Singing." (Section, "Conceptual Aspects of Music Education") in Stanley Sadie (ed.), *The New Grove Dictionary of Music and Musicians* (London: Macmillan, 1980).

19 Bowman, "Music as Ethical Encounter," p. 11.

20 *Ibid.*, p. 12.

21 www.goodreads.com/author/quotes/31425.Ben_Okri. Accessed April 19, 2011.

22 Norman Miller, Gail Hamilton, and Mervyn Warren (producers) and various artists 1992. *Handel's Messiah: A Soulful Celebration*. World Entertainment B000002LUJ. *Handel's Messiah: A Soulful Celebration* is a reinterpretation of Handel's *Messiah*, widely praised for its use of multiple genres of African-American music, including spirituals, blues, ragtime, big band, jazz fusion, R&B, and hip hop. The album received the 1992 Grammy Award for Best Contemporary Soul Gospel Album.

23 Kathy Saltzman Romey with Emilie Sweet and Shekela M. Wanyama, "Building Bridges: Choruses Engaging Communities," in Joan Conlon (ed.), *Wisdom, Wit, and Will: Women Choral Conductors on Their Art* (Chicago: GIA Publications, 2009), p. 77.

24 www.wosu.org/archive/jfk/remembrance.php, accessed April 19, 2011. Quoted from Leonard Bernstein, *Findings* (New York: Simon & Schuster, 1982).

25 This and many other examples of "community engagement" programs are described in Saltzman Romey et al., "Building Bridges," pp. 73–101.

18 The making of a choir: individuality and consensus in choral singing

1 John Bertalot, *How to Be a Successful Choir Director* (Stowmarket: Kevin Mayhew, 2002), p. 28.

2 Joseph Lewis, *Conducting without Fears: A Helpful Handbook for the Beginner*, Part II: *Choral and Orchestral Conducting* (London: Ascherberg, Hopwood and Crew, 1945), p. 10.

3 Elizabeth Ekholm reviews the debate between soloistic and blended approaches to choral tone in "The Effect of Singing Mode and Seating Arrangement on Choral Blend and Overall Choral Sound," *Journal of Research in Music Education* 48 (2000), 123–35.

4 Thomas Hobbes, *Leviathan*, ed.
J. A. C. Gaskin (Oxford University Press,
2008), p. 84. For general introductions to
contract theory philosophers see Christopher
W. Morris (ed.), *The Social Contract Theorists:
Critical Essays on Hobbes, Locke and Rousseau*
(New York: Rowman and Littlefield, 1999).
5 Jean-Jacques Rousseau, *The Social Contract*
(Ware: Wordsworth Editions, 1998)
(originally published 1762). In fact, the term
"noble savage" comes from a play by Dryden,
but it has come to be used as a shorthand for
Rousseau's ideas.
6 For instance, the Natural Voice
Practitioners Network in the UK promotes an
ideal of singing "without worrying about
having a good voice or getting it right'" (see
www.naturalvoice.net).
7 David Hume, *A Treatise of Human Nature:
Being an Attempt to Introduce the
Experimental Method of Reasoning into Moral
Subjects* (London: Penguin, 2004) (originally
published 1739).
8 The constitutional relationship between
choir and conductor is interesting here. In
some amateur choirs the director actually is
elected by the membership, although this is
less common than being appointed by a
management committee. In professional
choirs the body that appoints the director is
usually separate from the singers, who are
appointed in turn by the director. The
structure of a choir's governance will only
usually have a significant impact on the choir's
working relationships at times of crisis,
although it will be broadly consistent with the
ethos and aims of the group.
9 See Abraham H. Maslow, *Toward a
Psychology of Being*, 3rd edn. (Hoboken, NJ:
John Wiley and Sons, 1998).
10 Edward T. Cone presents the original idea
of "musical personae" in *The Composer's Voice*
(Berkeley: California University Press, 1974).
Peter Johnson develops the idea in a discussion
of how the performer's voice interacts with the
identity of the work: "The Legacy of
Recordings," in John Rink (ed.), *Musical
Performance: A Guide to Study and Practice*
(Cambridge University Press, 2002).
11 See Mike Brewer, *Fine-Tune Your Choir:
The Indispensable Handbook for Choral
Directors and Singers* (London: Faber, 2004),
p. 25.
12 See, for example, Johan Sundberg, *The
Science of the Singing Voice* (DeKalb: Northern
Illinois University Press, 1987).
13 See, for example, Brian R. Busch, *The Complete
Choral Conductor: Gesture and Method* (New York:
Schirmer, 1984), p. 240.

14 See, for example, Ekholm, "Singing
Mode and Seating Arrangement;" and
James Daugherty, "Choir Spacing and
Formation: Choral Sound Preferences in
Random, Synergistic, and Gender-Specific
Chamber Choir Placements," *International
Journal of Research in Choral Singing* 1
(2003), 48–59.
15 See, for example, Donald Neuen, *Choral
Concepts: A Text for Conductors* (Belmont:
Schirmer/Thomas Learning, 2002).
16 For a discussion of the neurological and
psychological mechanisms that underlie this
practical phenomenon, see Liz Garnett, *Choral
Conducting and the Construction of Meaning:
Gesture, Voice, Identity* (Aldershot: Ashgate,
2009), particularly Part IV.
17 William Ehmann, *Choral Directing*,
trans. G. Wiebe (Minneapolis: Augsburg,
1968), p. 116.
18 See James Jordan, *Evoking Sound:
Fundamentals of Choral Conducting and
Rehearsing* (Chicago: GIA Publications, 1996),
pp. 288–97, for a well-developed
troubleshooting guide for these kinds of
problems.
19 Robert A. Stebbins, *Serious Leisure: A
Perspective for Our Time* (New Brunswick, NJ:
Aldine Transaction, 2007).
20 Bertalot, *How to Be a Successful Choir
Director*, p. 122.
21 Robert B. Cialdini, *Influence: Science and
Practice*, 4th edn. (Boston: Allyn and Bacon,
2001).
22 Tanya L. Chartrand and John A. Bargh,
"The Chameleon Effect: The Perception–
Behavior Link and Social Interaction," *Journal
of Personality and Social Psychology* 76 (1999),
893–910.
23 Useful introductions to this area can be
found in Richard Riding and Stephen Rayner,
*Cognitive Styles and Learning Strategies:
Understanding Style Differences in Learning
and Behaviour* (London: David Fulton, 1998)
and Howard Gardner, *Multiple Intelligences:
New Horizons in Theory and Practice*, 2nd edn.
(New York: Basic Books, 2006). See also Keith
Swanwick, *Music, Mind and Education*
(London: Routledge, 1988).

**19 A point of departure for rehearsal
preparation and planning**
1 Robert Shaw (1916–99), American
conductor. Shaw's career began in in the 1940s
New York, where he prepared choruses for
Arturo Toscanini and Bruno Walter. In 1949,
he formed the Robert Shaw Chorale, which
quickly established itself as America's

premiere touring choral ensemble – over thirty performance tours abroad were subsequently organized by the US State Department. Shaw's conducting posts included brief assignments with the San Diego and Cleveland symphonies, prior to his most significant appointment as Music Director of the Atlanta Symphony in 1967. In 1988, Shaw became Music Director Emeritus and Conductor Laureate of the Atlanta Symphony, after having raised both the Atlanta Symphony and the Atlanta Symphony choruses to international stature. A long-standing relationship with Telarc enabled Shaw to record almost every major choral and choral–orchestral work over the course of his career – his catalogue of recordings may be his most important legacy. The recipient of numerous awards, honors, and fellowships – including fourteen Grammys and Kennedy Center Honors – he has been dubbed the "dean of American choral conductors." See the biography by Keith C. Burris, *Deep River: The Life and Music of Robert Shaw* (Athens, GA: Hill Street Press, 2011).

2 A few diction resources warrant mention here, such as: John Moriarty, *Diction: Italian, Latin, French, German ... the Sounds and 81 Exercises for Singing Them* (Boston: E.C. Schirmer Music Co., 1975); Madeleine Marshall, *The Singer's Manual of English Diction* (New York: Schirmer Books, 1953); and Joan Wall et al., *Diction for Singers: A Concise Reference for English, Italian, Latin, German, French, and Spanish Pronunciation* (Dallas: Pst, 1990)

20 Small ensemble rehearsal techniques for choirs of all sizes

1 Judy Tarling, *The Weapons of Rhetoric: A Guide for Musicians and Audiences* (St. Albans: Corda Music, 2005).

2 *Tactus* is the fifteenth- and sixteenth-century term for "beat."

Select bibliography

Abasova, Elmira. *Uzeir Gadzhibekov: Put' Zhizni i Tvorchestva* [Uzeyir Hajibeyov: His Life and Music]. Baku: Elm, 1985.

Abbott, P., and J. Hawn (eds.) *Recommended Canadian Choral Repertoire*, vol. 3: *The Folk Song*. Montreal, QC: Association of Canadian Choral Conductors, 2006.

Recommended Canadian Choral Repertoire, vol. 4: *Sacred, Secular and Christmas*. Montreal, QC: Association of Canadian Choral Conductors, 2008.

Abdullaev, Rustambek. *Obriad i Muzyka v Kontekste Kul'tury Uzbekistana i Tsentral'noi Azii* [Ritual and Music in the Context of the Culture of Uzbekistan and Central Asia]. Tashkent: Swiss Agency for Development and Cooperation, 2006.

Ammar, Faruk Khasan. "Rannee Mnogogolosie na Vostoke" [Early Polyphony in the East], *Sovetskaia Muzyka* 7 (1975), 112–16.

Appelman, D. Ralph. *The Science of Vocal Pedagogy*. Bloomington: Indiana University Press, 1967.

Aretz, I. (ed.) *America Latina en su música*. Mexico: Siglo XXI Editores, SA, 1977.

Asuaje de Rugels, A., M. Guinand, and B. Bottome *Historia del Movimiento Coral y de las Orquestas Juveniles en Venezuela*. Caracas: Departamento de Relaciones Públicas de Lagoven, 1986.

Bailey, Rona and Herbert Roth, (eds.) with musical arrangements by Neil Colquhoun. *Shanties by the Way: A Selection of New Zealand Popular Songs and Ballads*. Christchurch: Whitcombe and Tombs Ltd, 1967.

Balme, Christopher B. *Pacific Performances: Theatricality and Cross-Cultural Encounter in the South Sea*. New York: Palgrave Macmillan, 2007.

Barz, G. F. *Performing Religion: Negotiating Past and Present in Kwaya Music of Tanzania*. Amsterdam: Rodopi, 2003.

"Politics of Remembering: Performing History(-ies) in Youth Choir Competitions in Dar es Salaam, Tanzania," in F. Gunderson and G. Barz (eds.), *Mashindano! Competitive Music Performance in East Africa*. Dar es Salaam: Nyota and Mkuki Publishers, 2000, pp. 379–406.

"*Tamati*: Music Competition and Community Formation," in F. Gunderson and G. Barz (eds.), *Mashindano! Competitive Music Performance in East Africa*. Dar es Salaam: Nyota and Mkuki Publishers, 2000, pp. 421–28.

Basler, P. *Missa Kenya: For SATB Chorus and Tenor Solo with Horn, Percussion and Piano Accompaniment*. Lauderdale: Plymouth Music Company, 1996.

Bastian, H. G. *Kinder optimal fördern – mit Musik*. Mainz: Atlantis-Schott, 2001.

Musik(erziehung) und ihre Wirkung. Eine Langzeitstudie an Berliner Grundschulen. Mainz: Schott, 2000.

Béhague, G. *Music in Latin America: An Introduction*. Englewood Cliffs, NJ: Prentice Hall, 1979.

Beliaev, Viktor. *Central Asian Music: Essays in the History of the Music of the Peoples of the USSR*. Middletown, CT: Wesleyan University Press, 1975.

Bernstein, Leonard. *Findings*. New York: Simon & Schuster, 1982.

Bloesch, R., W. Wasson, and G. Paine. *Twentieth Century Choral Music: An Annotated Bibliography of Music Appropriate for College and University Choirs*. American Choral Directors Association Monograph, No. 9. Lawton, OK: ACDA, 1997.

Bokwe, J. K. "Vuka Debora," in J. S. M. Khumalo (ed.), *South Africa Sings*, 2 vols. Vol. 1. Braamfontein: SAMRO, 1998.

Bowman, Wayne. "Educating Musically," in Richard Colwell and Carol Richardson (eds.), *The New Handbook of Research on Music Teaching and Learning: A Project of the Music Educators National Conference*. Oxford University Press, 2002, 63–84.

"Music as Ethical Encounter" The Charles Leonhard Lecture, University of Illinois, April 17, 2000, *Bulletin of the Council for Research in Music Education* 151 (2001), 11–20.

Philosophical Perspectives on Music. New York: Oxford University Press, 1998.

Boyce, Mary. *Zoroastrians: Their Religious Beliefs and Practices*. New York: Routledge, 2001.

Boyd, Manu. "Himeni: Nurturing Spirituality through Songs of Faith," *Wai ola o OHA* 28, no. 3 (2001), 18.

Bunch, Meribeth. *Dynamics of the Singing Voice*. Vienna/New York: Springer-Verlag, 1997.

Burris, Keith. *Deep River: The Life and Music of Robert Shaw*. Chicago: GIA, 2012.

Calcaño, J. A. *La ciudad y su música*. Caracas: Crónica Musical de Caracas, 1956.

Chase G., Pan American Union, and Library of Congress. *A Guide to the Music of Latin America: A Joint Publication of the Pan American Union and the Library of Congress*. New York: AMS Press, 1972.

Chatwin, Bruce. *The Songlines*, London: Cape, 1987.

Chelkowski, Peter (ed.) *Ta'zieh: Ritual and Drama in Iran*. New York University Press, 1979.

Choral Works by Canadian Composers: A Selective Guidelist of Published Choral Compositions by British Columbia Composers. Vancouver, BC: British Columbia Choral Federation, 2004.

Coelho V. A. "Kapsberger's Apotheosis . . . of Francis Xavier (1622) and the Conquering of India," in R. Dellamora and D. Fischlin (eds.), *The Work of Opera: Genre, Nationhood, and Sexual Difference*. New York: Columbia University Press, 1997, pp. 27–47.

Conlon, Joan, (ed.) *Wisdom, Wit, and Will: Women Choral Conductors on Their Art*. Chicago, IL: GIA Publications, 2009.

de Beer, R. "The Origins, Developments, and Current Performance Practices of African Neo-Traditional Choral Music of Southern Africa". Doctoral dissertation, Nelson Mandela Metropolitan University, Port Elizabeth, 2007.

L. Mbuyamba, et al. "Dossier Africa," in J. Tagger (ed.), *International Choral Bulletin*. Louvigny: IFCM International Office, 2006, pp. 5–17.

de Quadros, A. "Choral Life in India," *International Choral Bulletin*, vol. 12, 2 (1993), 33–37.

"From old ragas to new voices: experiencing contemporary Indian choral music."
The Phenomenon of Singing International Symposium – *Sharing the Voices*, St.
John's, Newfoundland, 1998, pp. 178–83.

Decker, Harold A., and Julius Herford (eds.). *Choral Conducting: A Symposium*,
2nd edn. Englewoods Cliffs, NJ: Prentice Hall, 1988.

Deslandres, G. *Choral Life in France*. Barcelona, November 11, 2006. www.xtec.es/
entitats/rmcc/mediterrania/Choral_Life_in_France.pdf.

Detterbeck, M. "South African Choral Music (Amakwaya): Song, Contest and the
Formation of Identity." Doctoral dissertation. University of Natal, Durban, 2002.

DeVenney, David P. *American Choral Music since 1985*. New York: General Music
Publishing Co., 1999.

Source Readings in American Choral Music. Monographs and Bibliographies in
American Music, vol. 15. Missoula, MT: College Music Society, 1995.

During, Jean. "What is Sufi Music?" in Leonard, Lewisohn (ed.), *The Legacy of
Mediaeval Persian Sufism*. London: Khaniqahi Nimatullahi Publications, 1992,
pp. 277–87.

Ekwueme, L. E. N. "Composing Contemporary African Choral Music: Problems
and Prospects," in C. T. Kimberlin and A. Euba (eds.), *Intercultural Music*.
Richmond, CA: MRI Press, 1999. vol. II, pp. 77–88.

Elliott, David. *Music Matters: A New Philosophy of Music Education*. New York:
Oxford University Press, 1995.

Estill, J. "Belting and Classic Voice Quality: Some Physiological Differences," *Medical
Problems of Performing Artists* 3 (1988), 37–43.

Euba, A. *Essays of Music in Africa*, vol. 2: *Intercultural Perspectives*. Lagos: Elekoto
Music Centre Lagos, 1989.

"Nketia, J. H. K. and the African Avant-Garde," in A. Euba and C. T. Kimberlin
(eds.), *Composition in Africa and the Diaspora*. Richmond, CA: MRI Press,
2008, vol. I, pp. 143–54.

Al-Faruqi, Lois Ibsen. "The Mawlid," *World of Music* 28, 3 (1986), 79–87.

Feldman, Walter. "Musical Genres and Zikr of the Sunni Tarikats of Istanbul,"
in Raymond Lifchez (ed.), *The Dervish Lodge: Architecture, Art, and
Sufism in Ottoman Turkey*. Berkeley: University of California Press, 1992,
pp. 187–202.

Finchum, Hilary. "Tuvan Overtone Singing: Harmonics Out of Place." SAVAIL
Working Papers. www.indiana.edu/~savail/workingpapers/tuva.html.

Fischer, E. (ed.) *Chorgesang als Medium von Interkulturalität: Formen, Kanäle,
Diskurse*. Stuttgart: Steiner, 2007.

Furiya, Miyako. Workshop session, International Society for Music Education, World
Conference, Edmonton, Alberta, Canada, 2000.

Gardner, Howard, Mihaly Csikszentmihalyi, and William Damon. *Good Work: When
Excellence and Ethics Meet*. New York: Basic Books, 2001.

Geisler, U. and K. Johansson (eds.) *Choir in Focus 2010*. Göteborg: Bo Ejeby Förlag,
2010.

Gerstein, Christine Wondolowski. "Early Musical Training in Bel Canto Vocal
Technique: A Brief History and Philosophy." Unpublished paper, Hofstra
University, Long Island, ED 393 758, 1994.

Glenn, Carole (ed.) *In Quest of Answers: Interviews with American Choral Conductors.* Chapel Hill, NC: Hinshaw Music, 1991.

Godfrey, Peter. "Choral Music in New Zealand: The Problem of a Country without a Tradition," Unpublished speech, 1975.

Goethe, Johann Wolfgang von. *Einfache Nachahmung der Natur, Manier, Stil* [1789]. In Goethe *Werke*, ed. E. Seiger, vol. VI: Vermischte Schriften (pp. 252–56). Frankfurt am Main: Insel Verlag, 1965.

Gottwald, Clytus. "Choral Music and the Avant-Garde," in L. Reimers and B. Wallner (eds.), *Choral Music Perspectives: Dedicated to Eric Ericson.* Stockholm: Royal Swedish Academy of Music, 1993, pp. 119–34.

Grau, A. *Choral Conducting: The Forging of the Conductor.* Caracas: GGM Editores, 2009.

Guettat, M. "The State of Music in the Arab World," in R. Letts and K. Fahkouri (eds.), *The State of Music around the World.* Paris: International Music Council, 2007.

Harnoncourt, Nikolaus. *Baroque Music Today: Music as Speech.* Portland, OR: Amadeus Press, 1995.

Hawn, J. and C. Murray (eds.) *Recommended Canadian Choral Repertoire*, vol. 5: *Seasonal Favourites*, Halifax, NS: Association of Canadian Choral Conductors, 2010.

Hedell, K. *Svenska körer sjunger svenskt?* Uppsala: Institutionen för musikvetenskap, 2007. www.korcentrum.uu.se/filedownload.php?id=6

Herbst, A., A. Zaedel, J. Rudolph, and C. Onyeji. "Written Composition," in A. Herbst, Meki Nzewi, and V. Kofi Agawu (eds.), *Musical Arts in Africa: Theory, Practice and Education.* Pretoria: Unisa, 2003.

Hitchcock, H. Wiley and Stanley Sadie (eds.) *The New Grove Dictionary of American Music.* London and New York: Macmillan Press, 1986.

Huskisson, Y. *The Bantu Composers of Southern Africa Supplement.* Pretoria: Human Sciences Research Council, 1983.

ICCM (International Center for Choral Music). General Report 2005–2008. www.ifcm.net/public/doc/476.pdf

Irving, David. "The Pacific in the Minds and Music of Enlightenment Europe," in *Eighteenth-Century Music* 2, 2 (2005), pp. 205–29.

Jeon, Molly Adkins. "Bimusicality in Japanese Folksong and Italian Art Song: A Study of Vocal Timbre," in Brian A. Roberts (ed.), *Sharing the Voices: The Phenomenon of Singing.* St. John's: Faculty of Education, Memorial University of Newfoundland, Canada, 1999.

Jonas, Holly Higgins. *In Their Own Words: Canadian Choral Conductors.* Toronto: Dundurn Press, 2001.

Jordania, Joseph. *Who Asked the First Question: Origins of Vocal Polyphony, Human Intelligence, Language and Speech.* Tbilisi: Logos, 2006.

Kallman, Helmut, Gilles Potvin, and Kenneth Winters (eds.) *Encyclopedia of Music in Canada.* University of Toronto Press, 1981, 1992.

Kantner, Claude El, and Robert West. *Phonetics.* New York: Harper & Brothers, 1960.

El-Kholy, S. "Traditional Folk Idioms in Modern Egyptian Composition since the Fifties," in C. T. Kimberlin and E. Euba (eds.), *Intercultural Music.* Richmond, CA: MRI Press, 1999, vol. II, pp. 33–44.

Kidula, J. N. "Making and Managing Music in African Christian Life," in R. King (ed.), *Music in the Life of the African Church*. Waco, TX: Baylor University Press, 2008, pp. 101–16.

"Music Culture: African Life," in R. King (ed.), *Music in the Life of the African Church*. Waco, TX: Baylor University Press, 2008, pp. 37–56.

"The Choral Arrangements and Performance Practice of Arthur Kemoli," in A. Euba and C. T. Kimberlin (eds.), *Composition in Africa and the Diaspora*. Richmond, CA: MRI Press, 2008, vol. I, pp. 109–30.

King, R. "Beginnings: Music in the African Church," in R. King (ed.), *Music in the Life of the African Church*. Waco, TX: Baylor University Press, 2008, pp. 1–16.

"Music Culture: Euro-American Christianity," in R. King (ed.), *Music in the Life of the African Church*. Waco, TX: Baylor University Press, 2008, pp. 17–36.

Kioka Eizaburo (ed.) *One Thousand Years of Church Music*. Tokyo: Kyokai Ongaku Shuppan Kanko Kai, 1939.

Kishibe, S. and K. B. Shinkokai. *The Traditional Music of Japan*. Tokyo: Kokusai Bunka Shinkokai, 1969.

Klatzow, P. *Composers in South Africa Today*. Cape Town: Oxford University Press, 1987.

Kochis-Jennings, Karen Ann. "Intrinsic Laryngeal Muscle Activity and Vocal Fold Adduction Patterns in Female Vocal Registers: Chest, Chestmix, and Headmix." Doctoral dissertation, University of Iowa, 2008.

Kultur in bewegung. Das Programm "Kultur" 2007–2013. European Union 2009. ec. europa.eu/culture/pub.

Kunst, Kultur und interkulturelle Dialog. Vienna: EDUCULT – Institut für die Vermittlung von Kunst und Wissenschaft, 2008.

Kunstfactor. *Monitor amateurkunst in Nederland 2009*. Utrecht: Kunstfactor, 2009.

Lawrence, Van. "Laryngological Observations on 'Belting,'" *Journal of Research in Singing and Applied Vocal Pedagogy* 2, 1 (1979): 26–8.

Leonard, Charles. "Music Education: Aesthetic Education," *Education* 74 (1953): 23–6.

Levin, Theodore. *The Hundred Thousand Fools of God: Musical Travels in Central Asia (and Queen's, New York)*. Bloomington: Indiana University Press, 1996.

Lindholm, S.. 2004. "Children's Choir – a Serious Medium." www.listento.no/mic.nsf/ doc/art2004011611272498600595.

Little, Jenny. "Report of a Preliminary Survey of the Music of Nga Pu Toru No. 80," from *Working Papers in Anthropology, Archaeology, Linguistics and Maori Studies*. Department of Anthropology, University of Auckland, 1989.

Liu, Ching-chih and Mason, C. *A Critical History of New Music in China*. Hong Kong: Chinese University Press, 2010.

Lomax, Alan. *Folk Song Style and Culture*. New Brunswick, NJ: American Association for the Advancement of Science, 1968.

Mamedova, Leyla. *Khorovaia Muzyka Azerbaidzhana* [Choral Music of Azerbaijan]. Baku: Adiloglu, 2010.

McGee, Timothy J. *The Music of Canada*. New York: W.W. Norton & Company, 1985.

McKinney, James C. *The Diagnosis and Correction of Vocal Faults*. Long Grove, IL: Waveland Press, Inc., 1994.

McLean, Mervyn. *Weavers of Song: Polynesian Music and Dance*. Auckland University Press, 1999.

Mensah, A. A. "Compositional Practices in African Music," in R. Stone (ed.), *The Garland Encyclopedia of World Music: Africa*. New York: Garland Publishing, 1998, pp. 208–31.
  "Music of the South Sahara," in E. May (ed.), *Musics of Many Cultures*. Berkeley: University of California Press, 1980, pp. 172–94.

Meredith, V., P. Abbott, and B. Clark (eds.) *Recommended Canadian Choral Repertoire*. Montreal, QC: Association of Canadian Choral Conductors, 2002.
  Recommended Canadian Choral Repertoire, vol. 2: *Sacred*. Montreal, QC: Association of Canadian Choral Conductors, 2004.

Mez, Adam. *The Renaissance of Islam*. New York: AMS Press Inc., 1975.

Milanca Guzmán, M. *La música venezolana: de la Colonia a la República*. Caracas: Monte Avila Editores Latinoamericana, 1994.

Miller, Norman, Gail Hamilton, and Mervyn Warren (producers) and various artists. *Handel's Messiah: A Soulful Celebration* (CD). Word Entertainment B000002LUJ, 1992.

Miller, Richard. *The Structure of Singing: System and Art in Vocal Technique*. New York: Schirmer Books, 1996.

Mithen, S. *The Singing Neanderthals: The Origins of Music, Language, Mind and Body*. London: Weidenfeld and Nicolson, 2005.

Mittler, B. *Dangerous Tunes: The Politics of Chinese Music in Hong Kong, Taiwan, and the People's Republic of China since 1949*. Wiesbaden: Harrasowitz Verlag, 1997.

Moyle, Richard *Tongan Music*. Auckland University Press, 1987.

Mulyadi, M., M. Satiadarma, and A. Soemantri. "Choral Life in Indonesia," *International Choral Bulletin*, vol. 30, 2 (2011), 9–13.

Mussulman, Joseph. *Dear People . . . Robert Shaw: A Biography*. Bloomington: Indiana University Press, 1979.

Navarro, J. "Music in the Philippines Protestant Church: 1960–2000," in Brian Roberts (ed.), *Chapters in Philippine Church History*. Manila: Memorial University of New foundland Faculty of Education, 2001, pp. 451–62.

Nizomov, Asliddin. *Sufizm v Kontekste Muzykal'noi Kul'tury Narodov Tsentral'noi Azii*. [Sufism in the Context of the Musical Culture of the Peoples of Central Asia]. Dushanbe: Irfon, 2000.

Njoora, T. "Music Composition and Its Awesome Responsibilities: Some Hard Issues that Frame Creativity and Output," *Journal of East African Musical Arts Education* 2 (2005), 62–72.

Nketia, J. H. K. *African Art Music*. Ghana: Afram Publications, 2004.
  African Music in Ghana: A Survey of Traditional Forms. Accra: Longmans, 1963.
  The Music of Africa. London: Gollancz, 1974.

Nzewi, M. "African Music Creativity and Performance: The Science of the Sound Voices: A World Forum of Music Therapy," 2006. From www.voices.no/mainissues/mi40006000199.html

"Challenges for African Music and Musicians in the Modern World Music Context," in C. T. Kimberlin and A. Euba (eds.), *Intercultural Music.* Richmond, CA: MRI Press, 1999, vol. II, pp. 201–28.

Musical Practice and Creativity: An African Traditional Perspective. Germany: Iwalewa-Haus, University of Bayreuth, 1991.

Okafor, R. "Types of Music in Nigeria," in R. C. Okafor and L. N. Emeka (eds.), *Nigerian Peoples and Culture for Higher Education.* Enugu: New Generations Ventures, 1994, pp. 140–66.

Olaniyan, O. "A Discourse of Yoruba Lyrics (Otherwise Known as Native Airs) as Contemporary Art Music for Christian Worship," in M. A. Omibiyi-Obidike (ed.), *The Art Music of Nigeria: Prospects and Problems.* Ibadan: Stirling-Horden Publishers, 2001, pp. 58–69.

Olwage, G. E. "Music and (Post) Colonialism: The Dialectics of Choral Culture on a South African Frontier." Unpublished doctoral thesis. Rhodes University, 2003.

Orbell, Margaret and Mervyn McLean. *Songs of a Kaumātua Sung by Kino Hughes,* Auckland University Press, 2002.

Paine, Gordon (ed.) *Five Centuries of Choral Music: Essays in Honor of Howard Swan.* Stuyvesant, NY: Pendragon Press, 1988.

Palmer, A. *Contemporary Japanese Choral Music.* Clarence, NY: Mark Custom, 1992.

Parrott, Andrew. *The Essential Bach Choir.* New York: Boydell Press, 2000.

Pegg, Carole. *Mongolian Music, Dance, and Oral Narrative: Recovering Performance Traditions.* University of Washington Press, 2001.

Pitman, Walter. *Elmer Iseler: Choral Visionary.* Toronto: Dundurn Press, 2008.

Plaza, J. B., and de Plaza, N. *La música en nuestra vida: escritos 1925–1965.* Caracas: Fundación Vicente Emilio Sojo, Fundación Juan Bautista Plaza, Ministerio de Educación, Cultura y Deportes, Consejo Nacional de la Cultura, 2000.

Popeil, L. "Comparing Belt and Classical Techniques using MRI and Video-fluoroscopy," *Journal of Singing* 56, 2 (1999): 27–29.

Qureshi, Regula Burckhardt. "Sounding the Word: Music in the Life of Islam," in Lawrence Eugene Sullivan (ed.), *Enchanting Powers: Music in the World's Religions.* Cambridge, MA, 1997, pp. 263–98.

"Sufi Music and the Historicity of Oral Tradition," in Stephen Blum, Philip Bohlman, and Daniel Neuman (eds.), *Ethnomusicology and Modern Music History.* Urbana and Chicago: University of Illinois Press, 1991, pp. 103–20.

Ramón y Rivera, L. F. *La Música Colonial Profana.* Caracas: Instituto Nacional de Cultura y Bellas Artes, 1966.

Rao, Doreen. *Circle of Sound Voice Education.* New York: Boosey and Hawkes, 2005.

"Craft, Singing Craft, and Musical Experience: A Philosophical Study with Implications for Music Education as Aesthetic Education." Doctoral dissertation, Northwestern University, 1988.

"Feminine Perspectives on Conducting and Teaching Choral Music," in Joan Conlon (ed.), *Wisdom, Wit, and Will: Women Choral Conductors on Their Art.* Chicago: GIA Publications, 2009.

We Will Sing. New York: Boosey and Hawkes, 1993.

Reimer, Bennett. *A Philosophy of Music Education.* Englewood Cliffs: Prentice Hall, 1970.

Reimers, L. and B. Wallner, (eds.) *Choral Music Perspectives: Dedicated to Eric Ericson*. Stockholm: Royal Swedish Academy of Music, 1993.

Richards, Fiona (ed.) *The Soundscapes of Australia: Music, Place and Spirituality*. Burlington, VT: Ashgate, 2006.

Rieth, D. E., Jr. *A Study of Choral Music in Kenya: The Contribution of Its Composers and the Influences of Traditional and Western European Musical Style*. Michigan: UMI Dissertation Services, 1998.

Rowley, Caitlin (ed.) *Australia: Exploring the Musical Landscape*. Sydney: Australian Music Centre, 1998.

Sakata, Hiromi Lorraine. *Music in the Mind: The Concepts of Music and Musician in Afghanistan*. Washington, DC: Smithsonian Institution Press, 2002.

Salmond, Anne. *Between Worlds: Early Exchanges between Maori and Europeans 1773–1815*. Auckland: Viking, 1997.

 Two Worlds: First Meetings between Maori and Europeans 1642–1772. Auckland: Viking, 1991.

Saltzman Romey, Kathy with Emilie Sweet and Shekela M. Wanyama. "Building Bridges: Choruses Engaging Communities," in Joan Conlon (ed.), *Wisdom, Wit, and Will: Women Choral Conductors on Their Art*. Chicago: GIA Publications, 2009.

Saw, S. "An Overview of Choral Activities in Malaysia," *International Choral Bulletin* 30 (2011), 5–7.

Say, Ahmet. *The Music Makers in Turkey*. Ankara: Music Encyclopedia Publications, 1995.

Schippers, Huib. *Facing the Music: Shaping Music Education from a Global Perspective*. New York: Oxford University Press, 2010.

Schutte, H. K., and D. G. Miller "Belting and Pop, Commercial Approaches to the Female Middle Voice: Some Preliminary Considerations," *Journal of voice*, 7, 2 (1993): 142–50.

Seyidova, Saadat. *Gadim Azerbaijan Merasim Musigisi* [The Music of Ancient Azerbaijani Rituals]. Baku: Mars-Print, 2005.

Shearer, Debra. "Emerging Voices in Australian Choral Music – Selected Works of Sculthorpe, Boyd, Edwards, Hopkins, Maclean, Leek, Stanhope, Grandage, Orlovich and Atherton." D. Mus. dissertation, Indiana University, 2003.

Sheng, T. "A Choral Miracle on Our Tiny Island: Singapore Choirs," *International Choral Bulletin*, 30, 2 (2011), pp. 14–17.

Shiloah, Amnon. *Music in the World of Islam: A Socio-Cultural Study*. Detroit: Wayne State University Press, 1995.

Shzr Ee, T. "Story of Choirs in Singapore." www.nac.gov.sg/choraldirectroy/story_choirs/history1.html (accessed May 3, 2011).

Simpson, Adrienne. *Hallelujahs and History: Auckland Choral 1855–2005*. Auckland Choral, 2005.

Skyllstad, K. "Creating a Culture of Peace: The Performing Arts in Interethnic Negotiations," *Intercultural Communication* 4 (November 2000).

Sparshott, Francis E. s.v. "Singing" (section "Conceptual Aspects of Music Education"), in Stanley Sadie (ed.), *The New Grove Dictionary of Music and Musicians*. London: Macmillan, 1980.

Statistics published by, among others, the Deutscher Musikrat, the British Arts Council, the Irish Arts Council, the Italian State Department for Culture, and diverse music information centers.

Strimple, N. *Choral Music in the Twentieth Century*. Milwaukee, WI: Amadeus Press, 2002.

Stubbington, Jill. "North Australian Aboriginal Music," in J. Isaacs (ed.), *Australian Aboriginal Music*. Australia: Aboriginal Artists Agency Ltd., 1979.

Tadzhikova, Zoia. "Svadebnye Pesni Tadzhikov" [Wedding Songs of the Tajiks], in *Istoriia i Sovremennost': Problemy Muzykal'noi Kul'tury Narodov Uzbekistana, Turkmenii i Tadzhikistana* [History and Modernity: The Problems of the Musical Cultures of Uzbekistan, Turkmenistan and Tajikistan]. Moscow: Muzyka, 1972, pp. 249–66.

Tarling, Judy. *The Weapons of Rhetoric: A Guide for Musicians and Audience*. St. Albans: Corda Music, 2005.

Taruskin, Richard. *Music in the Late Twentieth Century*, *The Oxford History of Western Music*, vol. 5, Oxford University Press, 2005.

Thomas, Allan. *Music Is Where You Find It: Music in the Town of Hawera, 1946: An Historical Ethnography*. Wellington: Music Books New Zealand, 2004.

Thomson, John Mansfield. *A Distant Music: The Life and Times of Alfred Hill, 1870–1960*. Oxford University Press, 1980.

  Musical Images: A New Zealand Historical Journey 1840–1990. Wellington: National Library of New Zealand, 1990.

Thurman, Leon, Carol Klitzke, and Norman Hogikyan. "Cornerstones of Voice Protection," in Leon, Thurman, and Graham Welch (eds.), *Bodymind and Voice: Foundations of Voice Education* (rev. edn.). Collegeville, MN: VoiceCare Network and National Center for Voice and Speech, 2000, pp. 646–55.

Tiemstra, S. S. *The Choral Music of Latin America: A Guide to Composition and Research*. New York: Greenwood Press, 1992.

Tipping, Simon. *Choir of the World*. Palmerston North, New Zealand: Dunmore Press, 2002.

  Orpheus: Portrait of a Choir. Palmerston North, New Zealand: Dunmore Press, 2002.

Titze, Ingo R. "Belting and the High Larynx Position," *Journal of Singing* 63, 5 (2007), 557–58

Touma, Habib Hassan. "The Fidjri, a Major Vocal Form of the Bahrain Pearl-Divers," *World of Music* 19, 3–4 (1977): 121–33.

  The Music of the Arabs. Portland, OR: Amadeus Press, 1996.

Tsutsumi, M. "A History of the Japan Choral Association." Dissertation, Florida State University, 2007.

Turino, T. *Nationalists, Cosmopolitans and Popular Music in Zimbabwe*. University of Chicago Press, 2000.

Veneracion, A. "Choral Music in the Philippines," *International Choral Bulletin* 20, 3 (2001), 4–5.

Vennard, William. *Singing: The Mechanism and the Technic*. New York: Carl Fischer, 1967.

Walker, R. *Music Education, Cultural Values, Social Change and Innovation*. Springfield, IL: Charles Thomas, 2007.

Webster Stech, Jamie. "American Woman and the Mysterious Voice: American Women Performing Gender through Singing Bulgarian Songs." 2002. depts. washington.edu/reecas/events/conf2002/regconf02.html

Westwood, Matthew. "Religious Choirs a Constant across the Desert," *The Australian*, September 14, 2007.

Whiteoak, John and Aline Scott-Maxwell (eds.) *The Currency Companion to Music and Dance in Australia.* Sydney: Currency Press, 2003.

Yampolsky, Philip. *Vocal Music from Central and West Flores.* Washington, DC: Smithsonian/Music of Indonesia, 9. Folkways Recordings, 1995.

Yanov-Yanovskaya, Natalia. *Mutal' Burkhanov: Vremia, Zhizn', Tvorchestvo.* [Mutal Burkhanov: Epoch, Life, Works]. Tashkent: Media Land, 1999.

Zemp, Hugo et al. *Les Voix du Monde (Voices of the World).* Paris: Collection du Centre National de la Recherche Scientifique et du Musée de l'Homme, CNR-3741010/, 1996

Index

Cambridge Companions to Music